Rich Christians in an Age of Hunger

Rich Christians in an Age of Hunger

Moving from Affluence to Generosity

By Ronald J. Sider

WORD PUBLISHING

Dallas·London·Vancouver·Melbourne

Permission to quote from the following sources is gratefully acknowledged:

The Great Ascent by Robert L. Heilbroner. Copyright © 1963
by Robert L. Heilbroner, Harper & Row Publishers.

What Do You Say to a Hungry World? By Stanley Mooneyham.
Copyright © 1975 by Stanley Mooneyham.

How to Make the World a Better Place by Jeffrey Hollender.
Copyright © 1990 by Jeffrey Hollender, William Morrow & Co., Publishers.

Table 6 on page 25 from *Poverty and the Environment* by Alan B. Burning.
Copyright © 1989, Worldwatch Institute.

Table 15, page page 151, World Bank, *World Development Report, 1992*
(New York: Oxford University Press, 1992).

Table 18, page 177 from UNDP, *Human Development Report*, 1994
(New York: Oxford University Press, 1994).

Table 19, page 179 from UNDP, *The World's Women*, 1995
(United Nations Development Programme, 1995).

Table 21, Page 205, from John and Sylvia Ronsvalle, *The State of Church Giving through 1994*
(Champaign: Empty Tomb, Inc., 1997).

Table 22, page 251 from *State of the World 1990* by Lester Brown. Copyright © 1990,
Worldwatch Institute.

Library of Congress Cataloging-in-Publication Data
Sider, Ronald J.
Rich Christians in an age of hunger : moving from affluence to generosity / by Ronald J.
Sider. – [4th ed.]
p. cm.
Includes bibliographical references.
ISBN 0-8499-1671-2
1. Hunger—Religious aspects—Christianity. 2. Wealth—Religious aspects—Christianity.
3. Economics—Religious aspects—Christianity. 4. Food supply—Religious aspects—
Christianity. 5. Simplicity—Religious aspects—Christianity. 6. Economics in the Bible.
I. Title.

BR115.H86S53   1997   97-13279
261.8'5 DC21   CIP

Printed in the United States of America

00 01 02 03 04 QPV 5 4 3 2 1

For Ted, Michael, and Sonya

Contents

❧

Foreword
Rich Christians in an Age of Hunger

Matthew 9:36 focuses on the compassion of Jesus for the crowds of people that he encountered. Two thousand years later, the compassion of Christ is needed more than ever. "Rich Christians in an Age of Hunger" details the enormous needs, articulates the biblical principals relating to poverty, and suggests strategies for Christians to seek justice for those in need.

In moving readers toward a deeper understanding of God's view of poverty, Dr. Sider clearly explains the biblical imperative for Christians to oppose great extremes of wealth and poverty. One of his illustrations is a modern parable about a twisting mountain road. A visitor observes that there are numerous terrible wrecks and asks why the townspeople don't build a tunnel through the mountain. Their reply focuses on the important role of the trained and efficient ambulance drivers and the economic investment in businesses along the road. Dr. Sider advocates that Christians become tunnel builders rather than ambulance drivers--seek solutions rather than simply respond to recurring crises.

Ellen White recognized that responding to basic human needs is ministering as Christ did. "The followers of Christ are to labor as He did. We are to feed the hungry, clothe the naked, and comfort the suffering and afflicted. We are to minister to the despairing and inspire hope in the hopeless . . . When we love the world as He has loved it, then for us His mission is accomplished." (*Desire of Ages*, p 350, 641)

Time is short as we prepare for the soon return of our Lord, yet we cannot ignore the millions of poverty-stricken people who populate this earth. Malnourishment, fear, and despair block the words of the gospel and short-circuit understanding of the Redeemer's gift of salvation. The Blessed Hope does not flourish when the ability to survive until tomorrow or next week is in question.

The first edition of this book appeared within a few years of my experience as the last American Adventist worker to evacuate Saigon as that city's defenses crumbled. I will never forget the hard decisions regarding who would leave and who would stay to face persecution and possible death. Lives were at stake. The consequences of leadership decisions were gut-wrenching--the sense of personal accountability, staggering. With sincere prayers for God's guidance we did what we could.

Times have changed, and Dr. Sider has updated this call to action. While I still break into a sweat when remembering that harrowing evacuation, now I am struck with an even greater sense that leadership decisions affect millions of lives. It is time to prepare for the evacuation from this earth, but first we must reach the people.

As you read this book, do so with prayer and openness to God. It is a message that will affect your attitudes and will make a positive impact on your Christian experience.

Ralph S. Watts, Jr.
President
Adventist Development and Relief Agency (ADRA)

Preface to the Twentieth Anniversary Edition

The world has changed, and so have I. In the twenty years since I wrote *Rich Christians in an Age of Hunger*, amazing changes have occurred in the world.

Communism has collapsed. Expanding market economies and new technologies have reduced poverty. "Democratic capitalism" has won the major economic/political debate of the twentieth century. Communism's state ownership and central planning have proven not to work; they are inefficient and totalitarian. Market economies, on the other hand, have produced enormous wealth. And not only in Western nations. Many Asian countries have adopted market economies. The result has been a dramatic drop in poverty in the world's most populous continent. In 1970, chronic undernourishment plagued 35 percent of the people in the entire developing world. Twenty-one years later—in spite of rapid population growth—only 20 percent were chronically undernourished.

My thinking has also changed. I've learned more about economics. And I have continued to study the Scriptures.

When the choice is communism or democratic capitalism, I support democratic government and market economies. That does not mean, however, that the Bible prescribes either democracy or markets. Nor does it mean ignoring the problems and injustices of today's market-oriented economies.

The collapse of communism is not the only dramatic change since I originally wrote this book. Tragically, many of the other changes are bad rather than good. Environmental decay—especially in the developing world—has grown dangerously. Materialism and consumerism, the collapse of biblical ethical standards, and the breakdown of the family have increased at a galloping pace. Daily headlines about corporate mergers underline the fact that global economic power has become much more centralized. Anyone who honestly evaluates the way today's market economies function cannot ignore these growing dangers. Nor dare we forget that in most nations, there is a large minority (sometimes a majority) who have virtually no capital, and therefore, almost no ability to enjoy the benefits of today's market economies. I believe that a market-oriented economy is clearly better than any alternative framework we now know. I also believe that private property is so good that everybody ought to have some. Precisely if we think that market economies offer a good framework, we should be eager to correct their weaknesses.

My biblical analysis has also changed at one substantial point. I have thought a lot about what the Bible tells us about equality and equity. I never thought that biblical revelation demanded absolute equality of income and wealth. But I used to be more concerned than I am today with the proportion of income and wealth that different groups possess.

I feel absolutely confident, however, that the biblical understanding of "economic equality," or equity, demands at least this: *God wants every person, or family, to have equality of economic opportunity at least to the point of having access to the necessary resources (land, money, education) to be able to earn a decent living and participate as dignified members of their community.* This kind of equality of economic opportunity is, as revised chapter 4 argues, a clear, powerful biblical demand—which, if implemented in our world, would help correct a terrible evil that still persists after twenty years of change.

We still live with over a billion desperately poor neighbors. Another two billion struggle in near poverty with very little hope for a decent life. Nor has God's special concern for the poor changed. Hundreds of biblical texts tell us that God still measures our societies by what we do to the poorest. Jesus' words still remind those with abundance that, if they do not feed the hungry and clothe the naked, they go to hell.

What has changed is our knowledge of how to empower the poor. Many Asian countries have successfully combined substantial government programs designed to lift the poorest with a basic market framework. The result? Hundreds of millions have escaped poverty.

One of the greatest success stories of the last twenty years is the explosion of micro-loans. Millions of desperately poor people have received tiny loans of $75, $200, or $500 so they could start small businesses and thus provide a better living for their families. We now know that micro-loans produce stunning transformation in poor communities.

I'll never forget Mrs. Kumar's joyous, confident smile. She lives in a tiny one-room house in a poor village in South India near Bangalore. A couple of years ago the Bridge Foundation (a Christian micro-loan organization founded by Indian evangelical leaders Vinay and Colleen Samuel) gave her and her husband, Vijay, a small loan of $219. They purchased a small, inexpensive sound system and a bicycle. With this equipment, the Kumars are able to provide the sound system for weddings, funerals, and other celebrations for poor villages in several surrounding communities. They now own three sound systems and hire a couple of employees.

Mrs. Kumar proudly showed me the new lighting equipment, and the bicycle loaded down with their third sound system. Their little one-room cement house with a thatched roof has no indoor plumbing, but I could see many improvements. Family income had grown significantly. Most importantly, the Kumars had new dignity, hope, and confidence.

Most of the poor want to earn their own way. They have enormous social capital: intact families, a desire to work, pride, and integrity. But they need some help.

That is exactly what more and more organizations providing micro-loans are doing. The one I know best is Opportunity International. My friend David Bussau is one of its key leaders.[1] David was a wealthy Australian businessman when God called him and his wife, Carol, to move their family to one of the poorest villages of Indonesia. Slowly they learned how to make tiny loans to very poor people. In the last five years, Opportunity International has loaned over $46 million and provided more than 275,000 jobs. In the next five years, from 1997 to 2001, Opportunity plans to help one million families. On the average, each loan costs about $500, which includes everything, even training, and is repaid at interest. These loans improve a family of five's standard of living by about 50 percent within one year.

Scores of Christian and other organizations are now empowering millions of desperately poor people through micro-loans.

Sometimes we are tempted to despair or cynicism, thinking that things are hopeless and that nothing we do makes any difference. But it does. Only a few of us, like Vinay and Colleen Samuel, and David and Carol Bussau, need to live among the poor. But almost all of us can afford $500 to help a poor family improve their standard of living by 50 percent in a year.

Could that really change the big picture of massive global poverty? Christians today have a total annual income of over 10 trillion dollars. On the average, a loan to help a family of five costs $500. Let's suppose the Christians of the world gave just 1 percent of their income for micro-loans. (And let's suppose the efficiency ratio remained what it is now in Opportunity International.) Do you know how long it would take to improve the lot of the poorest one billion by 50 percent—using just 1 percent of global Christian income? *Just one year!*

By themselves, of course, small loans cannot end all poverty. As chapter 7 demonstrates, some people are poor because of misguided personal choices and others because of unfair systems. Coming to a living, personal faith in Christ reduces poverty. So does wise political activity that creates more just legal and economic structures.

We have the money. And we know what to do. Are we generous enough to do it? In 1960, the world's richest 20 percent had 30 times more than the poorest 20 percent. Thirty years later, the richest had 60 times as much. But the percentage of their giving had dropped dramatically.

Tragically so many rich Christians are missing Jesus' path to joy and self-fulfillment. We are neglecting the fact that genuine joy and enduring happiness flow from practicing Jesus' paradoxical teaching that it is better to give than to receive.

Millions of North Americans and Western Europeans are in despair as they seek in vain for happiness through ever greater material abundance. The idolatrous materialism of the economic rat race creates alcoholics, ruined marriages, and heart attacks.

Jesus, on the other hand, offers true joy—not through getting, but through giving. We cannot gain happiness by seeking it directly. It comes as a by-product as we give ourselves to others. I can personally witness to this truth. Many suppose that the lifestyle I have written about and sought to live is hard and painful. In truth, my life overflows with joy and fulfillment. This book is truly a guide to joy and self-fulfillment.

I do not mean to hide the fact that I report heart-wrenching facts and call for costly living. Millions of people die unnecessarily every year because rich folk like you and me have ignored the Bible's clear teaching that God measures the integrity of our faith by how we respond to the poor. So I report the tragic facts of hunger and starvation (Part One), explain the biblical teaching about God's special compassion for the poor and weak (Part Two), and show what causes poverty (Part Three).

But the book also shares exciting news (Part Four) about how you and I can assist the poor to help themselves—and in the process, also help ourselves. Joy and happiness do come from giving. By spending less on ourselves, we can transform the lives of neighbors who will die unless we care.

We live in an age of both enormous wealth and widespread poverty. We know what to do to empower the poor. Will we do it? Will rich Christians (which includes virtually all readers of this book) also be generous? Will we share the capital that the poor need to earn a decent living? Rich, generous Christians could, in the next twenty years, dramatically reduce poverty in our world if we would become partners with God's poor. This twentieth anniversary edition invites us to that exhilarating, transforming journey.

*All royalties from this book are being donated to Christian charitable organizations.

Acknowledgments

I have benefited from the critical comments of many good friends who read parts of the first draft: Judy and John F. Alexander, Arthur Simon, Edgar Stoesz, Richard Taylor, Carol and Merold Westphal. Since I am not an economist, I particularly appreciate the extensive help of two friends who are: Carl Gambs and John Mason. I stubbornly rejected their advice on occasion. Hence they cannot be faulted for the results. But their help and friendship are deeply appreciated.

To Debbie Reumann and Titus Peachy I give special thanks for long hours spent at the typewriter. To Mrs. Anne Allen who typed some of the early chapters, I want to express deep appreciation for her superb secretarial and administrative assistance over several years.

Finally, I want to thank *HIS* magazine for publishing an early version of chapter 7, and Ashland Theological Seminary and Emmanuel School of Religion for the opportunity to present parts of this material as public lectures.

Perhaps all books must be lived before they are written. That is certainly true of books like this one. I make no claim to be living out the full implications of this book. But I have begun the pilgrimage. The most important reason I am even a little way down the path is my wife, Arbutus Lichti Sider. Always enthusiastic about a simpler living standard, spontaneously generous, and eager to experiment, she has slowly tugged me along. For her critical reading of the manuscript, for our life together without which this book would never have been possible, and for her love, I express my deepest appreciation.

Note to the second edition:
In revising chapters 1, 2, 6, and 9, I benefited greatly from the extensive assistance of Roland Hoksbergen, now assistant professor of economics at

Calvin College. His help and patience are deeply appreciated. In addition, a number of friends who are economists provided critical reaction either to the first edition or to a preliminary draft of the second: Robert Chase, Carl Gambs, Donald Hay, Carl Kreider, John Mason, Henry Rempel, and John P. Tiemstra. None of them, I am sure, will be fully satisfied with all my final decisions. Their much appreciated counsel, however, has significantly improved the text.

Helping on this revised edition, Robin Songer was her usual efficient, precise self as she worked with my short deadlines.

Note to the third edition:

I am grateful to many people who provided critical suggestions and data for the third edition: John Mason, Nancy Alexander, Stephen L. S. Smith, Tom Sine, Calvin DeWitt, Roland Hoksbergen, Linwood Geiger, Joe Sheldon, Michael Trueblood, Larry Hollar, Bill Ray, Don Reeves, Gil Heebner, Grant Power, and Philip Shea helped with research. My colleague, Tom McDaniel, provided invaluable help to enable different computers to communicate. Ketly Pierre worked overtime at the typewriter. My administrative secretary, Naomi Miller, helped with the manuscript in addition to providing her usual superb support as a partner in my diverse ministries. And Mary Beekley-Peacock did a fantastic job supervising the total revision, doing much of the necessary updating and retyping several chapters. To all these friends, I say thanks.

Note to the fourth edition:

I owe special thanks to a number of people who contributed to this twentieth anniversary edition. Ron Sage provided superb help as my primary research assistant, and economists Linwood Geiger and George Monsma devoted many hours of precious time to offer detailed suggestions. David Moberg at Word demonstrated unusual commitment to this project as he made time in his hectic schedule to oversee the numerous, critical aspects of publishing a book. Julie Link at Blue Water Ink became a friend as she carefully edited the manuscript. Many friends offered important suggestions and/or found time for a critical reading of parts of the manuscript: Vinay Samuel, Chris Sugden, David Beckman, Marc Cohen, Dick Hoehn, Don Reeves, Andrew Steer, Tim Dearborn, Jim Wallis, Norman Ewert, Rob Van Drimmelen, Arthur Simon, Robert Hadley, Wesley Balda, Janis Balda,

Barbara Bouder, Patricia Boyland, Carol Cool, Catherine Kroeger, Arthur Scotchmer, Sheila Scotchmer, Richard Wright, and Daniel Schwartz. Graduate assistants David Kuguru and Chris and Joan Hoppe-Spink tracked down materials, and many of my colleagues at Evangelicals for Social Action—Cliff Benzel, Fred Clark, Dwight Ozard, Heidi Rolland-Unruh, Terry Cooper, Keith Pavlischek, Fred Krueger, and Stan LeQuire—offered valued insight. My gifted administrative assistant, Naomi Miller, handled numerous, diverse tasks with her usual grace and skill. To our three children, who continue to make us proud, I express special appreciation for carrying the burdens that go with having this kind of book dedicated to them. To my wife, Arbutus, who has lived this book with me for thirty-six years of marriage, I feel a depth of gratitude that words can hardly begin to communicate.

Part One

Poor Lazarus and Rich Christians

We usually compare our budgets and lifestyles with those of our affluent neighbors. Part One invites you to compare yourself with the poorest one-half of the world's people.

1

A Billion Hungry Neighbors

Sometimes I think, "If I die, I won't have to see my children suffering as they are." Sometimes I even think of killing myself. So often I see them crying, hungry; and there I am, without a cent to buy them some bread. I think, "My God, I can't face it! I'll end my life. I don't want to look any more!"[1]

—*Iracema da Silva*
resident of a slum in Brazil

Cᴀɴ ᴏᴠᴇʀꜰᴇᴅ, comfortably clothed, and luxuriously housed persons understand poverty? Can we truly feel what it is like to be a nine-year-old boy playing outside a village school he cannot attend because his father is unable to afford the books? (Which, incidentally, would cost less than my wife and I spent on entertainment one evening during the writing of this book.) Can we comprehend what it means for poverty-stricken parents to watch with helpless grief as their baby daughter dies of a common childhood disease because they, like at least one-quarter of our global neighbors today, lack access to elementary health services? Can we grasp the awful truth that thirty-four thousand children die every day of hunger and preventable diseases?

To help us imagine what poverty means, a prominent economist itemized the "luxuries" we would have to abandon if we were to adopt the lifestyle of our 1.3 billion neighbors who live in desperate poverty.

We begin by invading the house of our imaginary American family to strip it of its furniture. Everything goes: beds, chairs, tables, television set, lamps. We will leave the family with a few old blankets, a kitchen table, a wooden chair. Along with the bureaus go the clothes. Each member of the family may keep in his "wardrobe" his oldest suit or dress, a shirt or blouse. We will permit a pair of shoes for the head of the family, but none for the wife or children.

We move to the kitchen. The appliances have already been taken out, so we turn to the cupboards. . . . The box of matches may stay, a small bag of flour, some sugar, and salt. A few moldy potatoes, already in the garbage can, must be hastily rescued, for they will provide much of tonight's meal. We will leave a handful of onions, and a dish of dried beans. All the rest we take away: the meat, the fresh vegetables, the canned goods, the crackers, the candy.

Now we have stripped the house: the bathroom has been dismantled, the running water shut off, the electric wires taken out. Next we take away the house. The family can move to the toolshed. . . .

Communications must go next. No more newspapers, magazines, books—not that they are missed, since we must take away our family's literacy as well. Instead, in our shantytown we will allow one radio. . . .

Now government services must go. No more postman, no more firemen. There is a school, but it is three miles away and consists of two classrooms. . . . There are, of course, no hospitals or doctors nearby. The nearest clinic is ten miles away and is tended by a midwife. It can be reached by bicycle, provided that the family has a bicycle, which is unlikely. . . .

Finally, money. We will allow our family a cash hoard of $5.00. This will prevent our breadwinner from experiencing the tragedy of an Iranian peasant who went blind because he could not raise the $3.94, which he mistakenly thought he needed to receive admission to a hospital where he could have been cured.[2]

It is difficult to obtain precise statistics, but the best estimate is that 1.3 billion people live in that kind of grinding poverty.[3] According to a World Bank study released in 1996, they live on less than one dollar a day.[4] In addition to these 1.3 billion who live in almost absolute poverty, another two billion are very poor. In fact, a majority of people today—three billion—live on less than two dollars a day.[5]

Hunger and starvation stalk our world. Famine and disease are alive and well on planet earth. Thirty-four thousand children die every day of hunger and preventable diseases.[6] Seventeen million people die every year from infectious and parasitic diseases we know how to prevent.[7]

The news, however, is not all bad. We have made great progress in some developing countries over the past few decades. Since 1970, both the number and percentage of hungry people—i.e., those who regularly lack enough calories for an active healthy life—have fallen significantly in the developing countries. In 1970, 918 million people, or 35 percent of the developing world, were chronically undernourished. By 1991, those figures had fallen to 841 million people, which was 20 percent of the people in the developing countries.[8]

The main reason for this improvement has been the dramatic growth of many of the economies in Asia, where much of the world's poor lives. The number of chronically undernourished in Asia declined from 785 million (36 percent of the region's population) in 1975 to 540 million (20 percent of the population) in 1990.[9] Indonesia is one of the success stories. It has experienced healthy economic growth (4.2 percent GNP per capita each year from 1980–1993)[10] and was able, during the 1970s and 1980s, to use that wealth to reduce poverty from almost 60 percent to less than 20 percent of the population.[11]

Unfortunately, the picture is not so bright in Africa and Latin America. The number of hungry people in Latin America has risen slightly, from 53 million in 1970 to 58 million in 1990. In Sub-Saharan Africa, both the number and percentage of hungry people have increased. In 1970, the figure was 103 million (38 percent of the region's population). By 1991 it rose to 215 million (43 percent of the population).[12]

We cannot know the exact number of people lacking minimally adequate diets, clothing, and shelter. And it varies depending on harvests, war, and natural disasters. Even though we have seen some significant improvement, the overall picture is still tragic. Over a billion desperate neighbors live in wrenching poverty—and another two billion are poor.

New Economic Divisions in the World

Almost all of the 1.3 billion desperately poor people live in what used to be called the Third World. For many years, all countries that were not a part of the developed world (whether capitalist or communist) were lumped together as "Third World" nations. But changes in the last twenty years, especially since the four-fold increase of oil prices in 1973–1974, have necessitated a new division. The World Bank's *World Development Report 1995* divides countries into four categories: low income, lower-middle income, upper-middle income, and high income.[13]

Low-income countries (3.1 billion people). India, China, Bangladesh, Pakistan, and many African countries, including Ethiopia, Burundi, Chad, Tanzania, Nigeria, and some of the former Soviet bloc countries, such as Georgia and Armenia, belong to the low-income countries. The per capita GNP in low-income countries ranges from $90 to $660 per year.[14] The *World Development Report 1995* states that infant mortality rates are nine times higher in the low-income countries than in the developed world (i.e., the high-income countries), and population growth rates are higher (see Tables 2 and 5).[15] Typically, only 59 percent of people in low-income countries are literate, though in Burkina Faso literacy is 18 percent and in Armenia it is 99 percent.[16]

There have been significant improvements in a number of these low-income countries, including dramatic change in China. We know what to do to reduce the agony even more. Yet hundreds of millions still live unnecessarily in appalling conditions.

Lower-middle-income countries (1.1 billion people). This category includes many Latin American countries, such as Bolivia ($760), a few of the richest African nations like Cameroon ($820), many of the former Soviet bloc, such as Ukraine ($820) and Russia ($2,340), and some Asian nations like the Philippines ($850) at the bottom of the scale and Thailand ($2,110) at the top. The annual per capita GNP in these countries range from $696 to $3005. These countries have a somewhat brighter future although they still have large numbers of very poor people.

Upper-middle-income countries (501 million people). Included in this category are the richest Latin American nations (e.g., Argentina and Mexico) and rapidly developing nations like South Korea. Per capita GNP ranges from Venezuela's $2,840 to Portugal's $9,130.

High-income countries (812 million people). Per capita GNP in these developed countries ranges from New Zealand's $12,600 to Switzerland's $35,760. For the U.S., it is $24,740, the UK, $18,060, and Japan, $31,490.[17]

Uneven Distribution

Over the past few decades, economic growth in the developing countries has differed by region (see Table 1). We see healthy growth in most areas during 1965–73. However, beginning in the 1970s, the regions begin to diverge. The annual growth of the Gross Domestic Product (GDP) in Sub-Saharan Africa was actually 1 percent during the 80s. But the population was growing so fast that the *per capita* GDP actually declined an average of 0.8 percent each year from 1980 to 1993.[18] Latin America's per capita growth slowed in the late 70s and then declined slightly during the 80s and early 90s. This is in stark contrast to the situation in East and South Asia. East Asia, including China, South Korea, and Taiwan, experienced annual per capita growth of 6.4 percent from 1980 to 1993. South Asia, including India and Pakistan, experienced an annual 3 percent per capita growth during the same period.[19]

Table 1—Annual GDP per capita growth by region 1965–93

Region	1965–73	1973–80	1980–93
Sub-Saharan Africa	3.2%	0.1%	−0.8%
East Asia	5.1%	4.7%	6.4%
South Asia	1.2%	1.7%	3.0%
Mid East, N. Africa	5.5%	2.1%	−2.4%
Latin America and Caribbean	3.7%	2.6%	−0.1%
Source: World Bank[20]			

Economic growth by itself, however, is not enough. Everyone in a country, especially the poorest, should benefit. Too often, however, overall economic growth primarily benefits the richest. In Brazil a military dictatorship strongly supported by the United States fostered real economic growth at the rate of 10 percent per year from 1968 to 1974. Growth of about 9 percent per year continued through 1980,[21] and then slowed to 0.3 percent from 1980 through 1993.[22]

Who profited? Even Brazil's own minister of finance admitted in 1972 that only 5 percent of the people had benefitted from the fantastic growth of the Brazilian economy. The Brazilian government did not challenge a 1974 study showing that the real purchasing power of the poorest two-thirds of the people had declined by more than one-half in the preceding ten years. In 1989, two-thirds of Brazilian families tried to survive on less than $500 a month.[23] In 1980, 40 percent of the total population suffered from malnutrition.[24] In 1980–93, 16 percent of all children under age five suffered from moderate or severe stunting due to malnutrition.[25]

Today 60 million Brazilians live in extreme poverty. Thirty-two million go hungry every day.[26] In 1989 (the most recent figures available), the richest 10 percent of the population received 51.3 percent of the country's income, while the poorest sixty percent received 15.9 percent.[27] Tragically, Brazil's rapid economic growth has done far too little to help the people who need it most.

In contrast, Indonesia, a large, populated country with vast natural resources like Brazil, experienced annual economic growth of 3.5 percent from 1960 to 1970 and 7.8 percent from 1970 to 1981. The poor fared much better over this period. In 1976, the poorest 40 percent in Indonesia received 14.4 percent of the national income. By 1987, their share increased to 21.2 percent. In Brazil, in 1972, the poorest 40 percent received 7.0 percent—and only 8.1 percent in 1983.[28]

The Alarins are a poor Philippino family. Mr. Alarin makes 70 cents on good days as an ice vendor. Several nights a month Mrs. Alarin stays up all night to make a coconut sweet which she sells on the street. Total income for her midnight toil is 40 cents. Cooking utensils are their only furniture. The family had not tasted meat for a month when the president of World Vision visited them and wrote this account:

> Tears washed her dark, sunken eye-sockets as she spoke: "I feel so sad when my children cry at night because they have no food. I know my life will never change. What can I do to solve my problems? I am so worried about the future of my children. I want them to go to school, but how can we afford it? I am sick most of the time, but I can't go to the doctor because each visit costs two pesos [28 cents] and the medicine is extra. What can I do?" She broke down into quiet sobbing. I admit without shame that I wept with her.[29]

The tears and agony of the world's poor are captured in the words of Mrs. Alarin. World poverty is a hundred million mothers like Mrs. Alarin, weeping because they cannot feed their children.

Famine Redefined

The rich today can ignore famine because it manifests itself differently than in the past.

> In earlier historical periods, . . . whole nations . . . experienced widespread starvation and death. Today the advancement in both national and international distribution systems has concentrated the effects of food scarcity among the world's poor, wherever they are.[30]

People with money can always buy food; famine affects only the poor. When food scarcity triples the price of grain imports, as it did from 1972 to 1974, middle- and upper-income persons in developing countries continue to eat. But people already devoting 60 to 80 percent of their income to food simply eat less and die sooner. Death usually results from diseases that underfed bodies cannot resist.

Children are the first victims. In low-income countries, the infant mortality rate is nine times higher than in high-income countries. Malnutrition contributes to the death of many children. In 1994, UNICEF reported that 190 million children under five were chronically malnourished. The same report named malnourishment as a factor in one-third of the 13 million deaths of children under five each year.

There is hope, however. In three years, Tanzania's nutrition program more than halved the rate of severe malnutrition. The cost of Tanzania's nationwide program today is $2.50 per child.[31] We could drastically reduce the high child mortality rates in developing countries, which are about nine times higher than those in established market economies. According to the World Bank, "if death rates in poor countries were reduced to those prevailing in rich countries, 11 million less children would die each year."[32]

Are rich Christians generous enough to save these lives?

Carolina Maria de Jesus helps us feel the terror and anguish endured by the poor in a land where they could have enough food. This uneducated but brilliant woman struggling to survive in the slums of Brazil's second largest city, Sao Paulo, kept a daily record of her feelings on scraps of paper. Later they were published in a gripping diary called *Child of the Dark*.

Today I'm sad. I'm nervous. I don't know if I should start crying or start running until I fall unconscious. At dawn it was raining. I couldn't go out to get any money [she gathered junk each day to earn money for food]. . . . I have a few tin cans and a little scrap that I'm going to sell to Senhor Manuel. When Joao came home from school, I sent him to sell the scrap. He got 13 cruzeiros. He bought a glass of mineral water: two cruzeiros. I was furious with him. . . .

The children eat a lot of bread. They like soft bread but when they don't have it, they eat hard bread. . . .

Oh Sao Paulo! A queen that vainly shows her skyscrapers that are her crown of gold. All dressed up in velvet and silk but with cheap stockings underneath—the favela [the slum].

The money didn't stretch far enough to buy meat, so I cooked macaroni with a carrot. I didn't have any grease, it was horrible. Vera was the only one who complained yet asked for more.

"Mama, sell me to Dona Julita, because she has delicious food."[33]

A former president of World Vision visited the home of Sebastian and Maria Nascimento, a poor Brazilian couple whose home was a one-room, thatched lean-to with a sand floor. Inside, one stool, a charcoal hibachi, and four cots covered with sacks partly filled with straw were the only furniture. He wrote this heart-rending account about his visit:

My emotions could scarcely take in what I saw and heard. The three-year-old twins, lying naked and unmoving on a small cot, were in the last act of their personal drama. Mercifully, the curtain was coming down on their brief appearance. Malnutrition was the villain. The two-year-old played a silent role, his brain already vegetating from marasmus, a severe form of malnutrition.

The father is without work. Both he and Maria are anguished over their existence, but they are too proud to beg. He tries to shine shoes. Maria cannot talk about their condition. She tries, but the words just will not come. Her mother's love is deep and tender, and the daily deterioration of her children is more than she can bear. Tears must be the vocabulary of the anguished soul.[34]

Carolina's little girl need not have begged to be sold to a rich neighbor. And while Sebastian and Maria's twins lay dying, there was an abundance of food in the world. But it was not divided fairly. The well-to-do in Brazil had plenty to eat. Over two hundred million U.S. citizens were consuming enough food (partly because of high consumption of grain-fed livestock) to feed over one billion people in the poor countries. Oxford economist Donald Hay has pointed out that a mere 2 percent of the world's grain harvest would be enough, if shared, to erase the problem of hunger and malnutrition around the world![35]

This is how famine has been redefined, or rather, redistributed! It no longer inconveniences the rich and powerful. It strikes only the poor and powerless. Since the poor usually die quietly in relative obscurity, the rich of all nations comfortably ignore this kind of famine. But famine—redefined and redistributed—is alive and well. Even in good times, millions and millions of persons go to bed hungry, and children's brains vegetate and their bodies succumb prematurely to disease.

Poverty's Children

Poverty means illiteracy, inadequate medical care, disease, and brain damage.

Illiteracy

Only 48 percent of India's 866.5 million people could read in 1990.[36] For Pakistan's 116 million, the number is 36 percent. In 1960 only 40 percent of the developing world was literate, but that increased to 64 percent by 1990. However, the number of people who cannot read also has grown, and the increase in literacy has not kept pace with population growth. Consequently, the number of illiterates has increased by nearly 120 million since 1960—to 940 million in 1990. Nor has literacy spread evenly. In Africa, 50 percent are literate. The figure is 60 percent in Asia and 84 percent in Latin America.[37]

Inadequate Medical Care and Disease

People in the industrialized North have enjoyed the security of modern medicine for so long that we assume it is now available for all. Indeed, things have gotten better. The World Bank reports that health conditions across the world have improved more in the past 40 years than in all preceding human history.[38] In 1950, life expectancy in the developing countries was 40 years. In 1990, it was 63 years. Child mortality (under age 5) was 280 out of 1,000 in 1950, but had declined to 101 out of 1,000 by 1994.

Table 2—Infant Mortality Per 1000 Live Births, 1993
Finland —4
Japan ———5
Germany ———6
Australia ———7
U.K. ———7
Cuba ———9
U.S.———9
Chile ———15
Ukraine———21
Russia ———28
China ———35
Egypt ———46
Guatemala ———53
Malawi ———141
Mozambique ———164
Sierra Leone ———164
Angola ———170
Niger———194
Source: UNICEF [44]

In spite of these improvements, the United Nations reports that 1.45 billion people still have no access to health services; 1.33 billion do not have access to safe water; and 2.25 billion do not have access to sanitation.[39] This is significant because in houses with clean water and sanitation, children are 60 percent less likely to die than in houses without those services.[40] In addition, 17 million people die each year from infectious and parasitic diseases such as diarrhea, malaria, and tuberculosis.[41]

Lacking both food and medicine, poor nations have a much higher infant mortality rate than the developed world.

The cost of cleaner water and better sanitation is relatively small. The

World Health Organization has reported that an annual increase in preventive care of 75 cents per person in the Third World could save 5 million lives every year. That would take less than $3 billion. Surely the people of the wealthier nations can find $3 billion to save 5 million people. The National Center for Health Statistics reports that people in the United States spend between $30 and $50 billion each year on diets and related expenditures to reduce their calorie intake.[43]

Brain Damage

No one knows how many poor children have suffered irreversible brain damage due to insufficient protein during childhood. But in 1994 there were 190 million malnourished children under the age of five.[44]

> Marli, a happy six-year-old girl from Rio de Janeiro is just one of these. Marli looks normal in every way. Healthy. Happy. There is just one thing wrong with her. She can't learn. At first the teachers thought perhaps her difficulty was psychological, the result of neglect in a family of eleven children. Her younger sister had the same problem. But after careful observation and testing, it became evident that Marli, a child of Brazil's poor and wretched favelas [slums], was unable to learn because as an infant her malnourished body could not produce a healthy brain.[45]

Permanent brain damage caused by protein deficiency is one of the most devastating aspects of world poverty. Eighty percent of total brain development takes place between conception and age two. Adequate protein intake—precisely what over one-third of all children under five in developing countries do not have—is necessary for proper brain development.[46] A study in the early 1980s in Mexico found that a group of severely malnourished children under five had an IQ thirteen points lower than a scientifically selected, adequately fed control group.[47] Medical science has demonstrated that severe malnutrition produces irreversible brain damage.

When a poor family runs out of food, the children suffer most. For people eking out a day-to-day existence, an inactive child is not as serious a problem as an inactive wage earner. But malnutrition produces millions of retarded children that become a serious problem in the future.

Hunger, illiteracy, disease, brain damage, death. That's what grinding poverty means. About one billion impoverished people of the world experience this anguish regularly. A little more help from rich nations would save many lives.

Developing nations must also change their priorities. The United Nations reports that 12 percent of the $125 billion developing countries spend on the military each year could provide health care for all their citizens, including immunization of all children, elimination of severe malnutrition, reduction of moderate malnutrition by half, and provision of safe drinking water for all.[48] According to UNICEF, developing country governments spend a total of approximately $440 billion per year. But just over 10 percent of that (about $50 billion) goes to nutrition, basic health care, primary education, family planning, clean water, and safe sanitation. If that proportion were increased to 20 percent, approximately $30 billion more per year would be available. In most countries, that would be enough to construct basic social safety nets.[49]

Making Progress

The results of modest efforts can be dramatic. During the 1980s and 1990s, a few inexpensive actions saved the lives of millions of children. During that time, the immunization levels in the developing world rose from 20 percent to about 80 percent today.[50] Not more than a decade ago, about 75 million children contracted measles each year and more than 2.5 million died. Today, thanks to improvements in health care and immunization, only 25 million children get measles each year—and only 1 million die.[51] Vaccines now save the lives of at least 1.5 million children annually. And the vaccines cost an average of only $1.50 per child.[52]

Immunization levels have soared. The World Health Organization's immunization program in developing countries has helped to raise the number of children immunized against the six major diseases from 15 percent ten years ago to 80 percent today. The program saves more than 3 million lives per year yet costs a mere $15 per child ($1.4 billion per year). Every $1 spent on childhood immunization saves $10 in future medical costs.[53]

The success story on river blindness shows how much can be done at a modest cost. A cooperative effort among the Food and Agriculture Organization (FAO), the United Nations Development Programme (UNDP), the World Bank, and the World Health Organization (WHO) set out in 1974 to combat river blindness in eleven African countries. Spread by a parasitic worm, this disease causes intense itching, debilitation, and eventually blindness. The initial effort involved spraying biodegradable insecticides (which are harmless to the environment) and using drugs developed and donated by Merck & Co. The program has been a wonderful success. Each year it protects more than 30 million people from the disease, at an annual cost of less than $1 per person. More than 1.5 million people who were once seriously infected have totally recovered. The total cost of the project, from 1974 to its anticipated conclusion around 2002, will be about $570 million. In addition to protecting millions of people, the project allows farmers to return to more than 60 million acres of previously abandoned cropland.[54]

Iodine deficiency is another terrible problem that could be easily solved. Goitre, the swelling of the thyroid gland due to iodine deficiency, results in mental impairment and affects 655 million people. Of these, 26 million suffer brain damage and 5.7 million will become cretins (people with stunted, deformed bodies and brains). The solution? Iodize each country's salt supply, which costs only 5 cents per person per year.[55] The total cost of such a program would be around $100 million—less than two modern fighter planes.[56]

Oral rehydration therapy (ORT) is an inexpensive health procedure that prevents children from dehydrating from diarrhea. In 1980, 10,000 children died every day from diarrheal dehydration. By 1993, that was down to 5,000. But that is still about two million every year that could be saved.[57] Bags of oral rehydration salts cost about 10 cents each. They can be used by parents themselves.[58] With a little more help, millions more would live.

In the 1990 World Summit for Children, held by UNICEF, more than 100 developing countries set ten goals for immunization and health care for 1995 and ten more for 2000. One goal for 1995 was the immunization of at least 80 percent of the children against the six major vaccine-preventable childhood diseases. Many of the countries have reached that goal. A goal for the year 2000 is the elimination of polio around the world. Specialists disagree as to whether or not total eradication can happen by 2000. But we have—thanks to a cooperative effort of Rotary International, the United Nations, and the World Health Organization—already made enormous progress. By 1991, we had successfully eliminated polio in the Western Hemisphere.[59] By 1996, that success had spread to 145 countries.[60]

We are making progress. Modest expenditures have reduced malnutrition and greatly increased immunization levels. Approximately 2.5 million fewer children will die in 1996 than in 1990.[61] UNICEF estimates that the total cost of providing basic social services in the developing countries, including health, education, family planning, and clean water, would cost $30 to $40 billion per year.[62] The rich of this world spend more than this on golf each year.[63]

Progress in reducing poverty, of course, does not flow only from improved health care for the poor. Expanding market economies have significantly reduced poverty in Asia (see chapter 8). And there are a wide range of changes—both personal and structural—that you and I can make to reduce the agony of poor people (see chapters 9–11).

Population

The population explosion is another fundamental problem. Not until 1830 did the world have one billion people. It took only one hundred years more to add another billion. Within a mere thirty years another billion human beings appeared. The fourth billion arrived in only fifteen years, by 1975. And by mid-1995, the earth held more than 5.7 billion people.[64] *The Population Bulletin* predicts that world population will reach 6 billion before the turn of the century (see Table 3).[65] Experts predict that we will reach 7 billion by the year 2010.[66] The median prediction for the year 2050 is 10 billion.[67]

There is good news here, too, however. Fertility rates (the average number of children each woman will bear) have declined from 6.1 births per woman in the early 1960s to 3.6 in 1994. The population, though, is far from stable. The reason? So many young people are entering their reproductive years. Even if most couples today have fewer children than previous generations (which they are doing), the number of children born still will be higher than in past decades.[68]

Table 3—Years Required to Add One Billion People		
	Years required	Year reached
First billion	10,000 plus	1830
Second billion	100	1930
Third billion	30	1960
Fourth billion	15	1975
Fifth billion	12	1987
Sixth billion	12	1999

Source: Lester Brown, The Twenty-Ninth Day (New York: Norton, 1978, p. 74. (slightly updated)[69]

A population of 100 million people growing at 1.5 percent per year expands to 145 million in 25 years, and 443 million in 100 years. And a population of 100 million growing at 3 percent (which is the rate for Sub-Saharan Africa, which has 586 million people[70] expands to 438 million in 50 years and 1,922 million in 100 years.

Table 4—Population Increase over 25, 50, and 100 Years			
Population growth rate per cent per year	Ratio of projected population to current population		
	25 years	50 years	100 years
0.5	1.13	1.28	1.65
1.0	1.28	1.65	2.70
1.5	1.45	2.11	4.43
2.0	1.64	2.69	7.24
2.5	1.85	3.44	11.81
3.0	2.09	4.38	19.22
3.5	2.36	5.58	31.19

The population explosion prompts some people to apocalyptic hysteria. One group ran an advertisement in 1976 in many newspapers, including the *New York Times* and the *Wall Street Journal*. Drafted by William Paddock and Garrett Hardin, among others, the statement declared, "The world as we know it will likely be ruined before the year 2000. . . . The momentum toward tragedy is at this moment so great that there is probably no way of halting it."[71]

Such views are alarmist, pessimistic, and flatly untrue, as Harvard professor Amartya Sen pointed out in a careful assessment in 1994.[72] Population trends in the last twenty years offer some hope. Whereas the overall population growth rate in the world was about 2 percent in 1960, the Population Reference Bureau's *1995 World Population Data Sheet* indicates that it has dropped to 1.5 percent. We can be grateful for the improvement. But the present rate of population growth is still dangerously high. At this rate, the population will double in forty-five years, to over 11 billion people.[73] We are already damaging the environment to feed today's 5.7 billion—and not all of those receive sufficient food.

Table 5—Population Growth Rate Per Year for Selected Countries (mid 1995)					
	Growth rate	Population mid 1995 (in millions)		Growth rate	Population mid 1995 (in millions)
Russia	-0.6%	147.5	India	1.9%	930.6
Germany	−0.1%	81.7	Philippines	2.1%	68.4
U.K.	0.2%	58.6	Mexico	2.2%	93.7
Japan	0.3%	125.2	Mozambique	2.7%	17.4
U.S.	0.7%	263.2	Pakistan	2.9%	129.7
Canada	0.7%	29.6	Nigeria	3.1%	101.2
Australia	0.8%	18.0	Zaire	3.2%	44.1
China	1.1%	1,218.8	Iraq	3.7%	20.6
Brazil	1.7%	157.8	Zaire	3.2%	44.1
			World	1.5%	5,700.0

Source: Population Reference Bureau, 1995 World Population Data Sheets.

In considering the issue of population growth, it is important to remember that although Northern developed nations now have much lower population growth rates than developing nations (see Table 5), the number of children per family in Western Europe and North America was much higher in the latter half of the last century than the two children per family common now. Infant mortality rates of course were also higher. Despite this, however, family size and population growth in the industrializing nations at that time were quite close to the size and growth rates in many developing countries since World War II. Affluence and decline in population growth seem to go together, in the long term anyway.

Fortunately, empowering the poor is a quick way to reduce the population explosion (see chapters 2 and 11). When poor people receive adequate food, health care, and education (especially women), population growth drops dramatically.

Limits to Growth?

Along with widespread poverty and the population explosion, a third set of complex, interrelated issues makes our dilemma even more difficult. How long can the earth sustain the present rate of industrialization? What will be the effect of the resulting pollution?

In 1992, the U.S. National Academy of Sciences and the Royal Society of London issued a joint report that began, "If current predictions of population growth prove accurate and patterns of human activity on the planet remain unchanged, science and technology may not be able to prevent either irreversible degradation of the environment or continued poverty for much of the world."[74] In 1993, 58 national science academies from around the world issued a similar warning.[75]

During the 1980s, per capita levels of arable land fell by 1.9 percent annually.[76] UNICEF reports that every year 42 million acres (the size of Oklahoma) of tropical forests are destroyed and about 15 million acres (the size of West Virginia) of dry lands turn into deserts.[77] Approximately 67 million acres of soil (the size of Colorado) lose virtually all their productivity each year. In addition, an area the size of India and China combined (about 1.2 billion acres) has been significantly downgraded for agricultural production.[78] Scientists warn that carbon dioxide and other "greenhouse gases" are slowly warming the world to a point where catastrophic changes in climate are possible in the next century.

The Future and Our Response

Widespread hunger, the population explosion, environmental decay, and the possible necessity of slowing industrialization (at least in the affluent nations) compound the difficulties of trying to share the world's resources more justly. Not surprisingly, predictions of doomsday are legion. What are our prospects?

Senator Mark Hatfield (a prominent evangelical leader and four-term Republican Senator) warned, "The greatest threat to this nation [the United States] and the stability of the entire world is hunger. It's more explosive than all the atomic weaponry possessed by the big powers. Desperate people do desperate things, and remember that nuclear fission is now in the hands of even the developing nations."[79]

A U.S. Presidential Commission on World Hunger (composed of Democrats and Republicans, conservatives and liberals) repeated this warning:

> The most potentially explosive force in the world today is the frustrated desire of poor people to attain a decent standard of living. . . . The Commission believes that promoting economic development in general, and overcoming hunger in particular, are tasks far more critical to U.S. national security than most policy makers acknowledge or even believe. Since the advent of nuclear weapons, most Americans have been conditioned to equate national security with the strength of strategic military forces. The Commission considers this prevailing belief to be a simplistic illusion.[80]

In a 1992 address, U.N. Secretary General Boutros Boutros-Ghali stated that the deepest causes of conflict are "economic despair, social injustice, and political oppression. Only a society of democratically protected human rights can offer the stability that can sustain development over time."[81] Global cooperation to reduce hunger and injustice is essential for enduring peace.

What will Christians do in this time of swelling affluence and persistent poverty? Will we dare to remember that the God we worship tells us that "whoever is kind to the poor lends to the Lord" (Proverbs 19:17)? Will Christians have the courage to seek justice for the poor, even if that means disapproval by affluent neighbors?

Where will you and I stand? With the starving or the overfed? With poor Lazarus or the rich man? Most of the rich countries are at least nominally Christian. What an ironic tragedy that an affluent, "Christian" minority in the world continues to hoard its wealth while hundreds of millions of people hover on the edge of starvation!

One popular fundamentalist newsletter (with a circulation of over

60,000) has called on Christians to stockpile new dried foods. In a most ingenious combination of apocalyptic piety and slick salesmanship, the newsletter quoted several "Bible scholars" to prove that some Christians will live through the tribulation. And the conclusion? Since we cannot be absolutely certain where we will be during the tribulation, we ought to purchase a seven-year supply of reserve foods for a couple of thousand dollars![82]

In an age of affluence and poverty most Christians, regardless of theological labels, are tempted to succumb to the heresy of following society's materialistic values rather than biblical truth. Advertisements offer demonically convincing justifications for enjoying our affluence and neglecting three billion poor neighbors.

Imagine what one quarter of the world's Christians could do if they became truly generous. A few of us could move, as David and Carol Bussau did, to desperately poor areas. The rest of us could defy surrounding materialism. We could refuse to let our affluent world squeeze us into its consumeristic mold. Instead, we could become generous non-conformists who love Jesus more than wealth. In obedience to our Lord, we could empower the poor through small loans, community development, and better societal systems. And in the process, we would learn again his paradoxical truth that true happiness flows from generosity.

Study Questions

1. What are your strongest feelings as you read this chapter?
2. What facts were most surprising to you? Most disturbing?
3. How has famine been redefined?
4. What concretely does poverty mean in day-to-day life?
5. How do you think most Christians you know would respond if they truly understood the problem of world hunger?

2

The Affluent Minority

*I used to think when I was a child, that Christ might have been exag-
gerating when he warned about the dangers of wealth. Today I know
better. I know how very hard it is to be rich and still keep the milk of
human kindness. Money has a dangerous way of putting scales on one's
eyes, a dangerous way of freezing people's hands, eyes, lips and hearts.[1]*
—Dom Helder Camara

"CREATE MORE DESIRE" shrieked an inch-high headline for an unusually
honest ad in the *New York Times*. It continued: "Now, as always, profit and
growth stem directly from the ability of salesmanship to create more desire."[2]

Costly, manipulative advertising bombards us at every turn, and its primary purpose is not to inform; it is to create desire. Luxurious houses in
Better Homes and Gardens make our perfectly adequate houses shrink by comparison into dilapidated, tiny cottages in need of immediate renovation. The
advertisements for the new fall fashions make our almost new dresses and suits
from previous years look shabby and old-fashioned.

We in the U.S. spend more money on advertising than on all our public
institutions of higher education.[3] In 1994 we spent $149 billion,[4] and in 1996
the figure climbed to $174 billion.[5] In 1995, worldwide expenditures for
advertising were $385 billion,[6] much of which was used "to convince us that
Jesus was wrong about the abundance of possessions."[7]

One of the most astounding things about the affluent minority is that we
honestly think we barely have enough to survive in modest comfort.
Constant, seductive advertising helps to create this destructive delusion.
Advertisers regularly deceive us into thinking that we genuinely need one
luxury after another. We are convinced that we are in competition with our

neighbors. So we buy another dress, sports jacket, or sports car, and thereby force up the standard of living.

The ever more affluent standard of living is the god of twentieth-century North America, and the adman is its prophet.

Advertising reclassifies luxuries as necessities. Our postman once delivered an elegant brochure complete with glossy photographs of exceedingly expensive homes. The brochure announced the seductive lie that *Architectural Digest* would help quench "man's passionate *need* for beauty and *luxury*" (my emphasis). How much luxury do we *need*?

The average American child watches three and one-half hours of television per day. The average adult watches five hours a day, which means 21,000 commercials a year. This means that over a period of seventy years, the average person will watch about one and one-half million commercials, which will devour about one and one-half years of the person's life.[8]

Sometimes advertising overkill is hilarious. An evangelical book discount house once created this promotional gem: "Your mouth is going to water, and your soul is going to glow, when you feast your eyes on the bargains which have been providentially provided for your benefit this month." (I promptly ordered books worth twenty-four dollars.)

Promises, Promises

Perhaps the most demonic part of advertising is that it attempts to persuade us that material possessions will bring joy and fulfillment. "That happiness is to be attained through limitless material acquisition is denied by every religion and philosophy known to man, but is preached incessantly by every American television set."[9]

Advertisers promise that their products will satisfy our deepest needs and inner longings for love, acceptance, security, and sexual fulfillment. The right deodorant will bring acceptance and friendship. The newest toothpaste or shampoo will make us irresistible. A comment by New York jewelry designer Barry Kieselstein shows how people search for meaning and friendship in things: "A nice piece of *jewelry you can relate to is like having a friend* who's always there" (emphasis mine).

A bank in Washington, D.C., advertised for new savings accounts with the question, "Who's gonna love you when you're old and grey?"

For a decade, my own savings bank used a particularly enticing ad: "Put a little love away. Everybody needs a penny for a rainy day. Put a little love away." Responsible saving is good stewardship. But promising that a bank account guarantees love is unbiblical, heretical, and demonic. This ad teaches the Big Lie of our secular, materialistic society. But the words and music were so seductive that they danced through my head hundreds of times.

If no one paid any attention to these lies, they would be harmless. But advertising has a powerful effect on all of us, and it shapes the values of our children.

In a sense we pay too little attention to advertisements. Most of us think we ignore them, but in fact they seep into our subconsciousness. We experience them instead of analyze them. John V. Taylor suggested that Christian families ought to adopt the slogan "Who are you kidding?" and shout it in unison every time a commercial appears on the television screen.[11]

Where Did It All Begin?

Theologian Patrick Kerans has argued that commitment to unlimited growth and an ever-increasing materialistic "standard of living" is really a sell-out to the Enlightenment. During the eighteenth century, many Western thinkers decided that science was the only way to find knowledge. This thinking elevated all things quantitative and devalued all things non-quantitative. Thus intangible values such as community, trust, friendship, and the beauty of creation became less important. It is hard to measure the value of friendship, unspoiled nature, and justice. But Gross National Product (GNP) is easy to measure. The result is our competitive growth economy where economic success and material things are all-important to many people.[12]

If Christianity is true and Kerans is correct, our society will eventually collapse. A social structure built on the heretical ideas that the scientific method is the only way to reach truth and value and that material things are all-important will eventually self-destruct.

Much (but not all) advertising contains a fundamental inner contradiction.[13] Advertisers know that we all long for the qualities of life that will satisfy our deepest needs; we long for significance, love, and joy. Marketing recognizes these needs and hooks into them. But then, in order to sell us more gadgets, it promotes the big lie. It says that love and fulfillment come from more and more material abundance.

Christians, of course, know that affluence does not guarantee love, beauty, acceptance, and joy. Our deepest joy comes from right relationships—with God, neighbor, and the earth. But our inherent bent toward idolatry gives advertisers the power to convince us that more gadgets and bigger bank accounts are an easy way to meet our needs. As a result, people persist in the fruitless effort to quench their thirst for meaning and fulfillment with an ever-rising river of possessions.

The personal result is agonizing distress and undefined dissatisfaction. The social result is environmental pollution and neglected poor people. Affluence fails to satisfy our restless hearts. It also keeps us from sharing food and assistance with our more than one billion hungry neighbors. Will we affluent Christians have the generosity and faithfulness to refuse to conform to society's seductive advertising?

How Affluent Are We?

By any objective criterion, the five percent of the world's people who live in the United States are an incredibly rich aristocracy living on the same little planet with over a billion desperately poor neighbors. Combined with the rest of North America, Europe, and Japan, we comprise an affluent northern aristocracy. Our standard of living, compared with that of over a billion very poor neighbors, is at least as luxurious as was the lifestyle of the medieval aristocracy compared with their serfs.

With a few exceptions, the rich countries are in the northern hemisphere. The poor countries are more to the south. The north-south division is one of the most dangerous fault lines in the world today.

And the chasm widens every year. In 1960, the income of the richest 20 percent of countries in the world was 30 times the income of the poorest 20 percent. In 1991, according to the United Nations Development Programme, that figure had risen to 61 to 1.[14] This figure counts everyone inside a given country in the same way. But in every country, of course, some are much richer than others. The gap is vastly greater when you compare the richest twenty percent no matter where they live. The United Nations estimates that the richest 20 percent of the world's persons are at least 150 times richer than the poorest 20 percent.[15] The net worth of the 358 billionaires on the planet listed by *Forbes* in 1994 was equal to the combined income of the bottom 45 percent of the world's population (2.35 billion people).[16]

The GNP provides one standard of comparison between rich and poor.

Table 6—Growing Inequality, 1950–1990

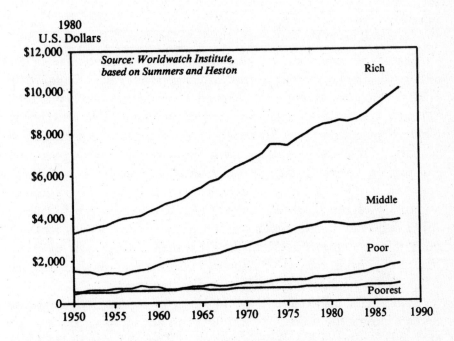

A country's GNP is the sum of all goods and services produced in a year.[17] By dividing a country's GNP by its population, you arrive at a per capita GNP.[18] As Table 7 shows, the per capita GNP in the United States was $24,470 in 1993. In India it was $300.[19]

Table 7—Per Capita GNP in 1993 (U.S. Dollars)

Switzerland	35,790
Japan	31,490
United States	24,470
United Kingdom	18,060
Mexico	3,610
Egypt	660
India	300
Kenya	270
Bangladesh	220
Ethiopia	100

Source: World Bank, World Development Report 1995 (New York: Oxford University Press, 1995), pp. 162–163.

Virtually all authorities agree that the chasm will widen still more in the next decade. In 1995, the World Bank made several projections for growth in GNP per capita for various regions around the world through the year 2010. Using the optimistic projections, for every $1 increase in GNP per capita in the developing countries, a $13 increase is projected for the industrialized countries.[20] From 1980 to 1993, the low-income countries actually grew faster per year (3.7 percent) than the high-income countries (2.2 percent). However, with China and India excluded from that group of low-income countries, the figure is only 0.1 percent. Over the same period, Sub-Saharan Africa declined 0.8 percent each year. The picture is even bleaker for those thirty-three countries the World Bank has defined as severely indebted. Instead of growing, their GNP declined 1.1 percent each year. So, with the exception of a few countries, the gap is still widening.[21]

Even when a poor country has a higher percentage rate of growth, the absolute income still widens! An increase of 3.7 percent to a poor country's per capita income of $300 means that on average each person has $11.10 more. But an increase of 2.2 percent to a rich country's per capita income of $15,000, adds $330 more per person! This is the reason that the ratio of income of the richest one-fifth of countries to the poorest one-fifth increased from 30:1 in 1960 to 61:1 in 1991.

Merely comparing per capita GNP, however, is misleading.[22] Haircuts cost $25.00 in New York and only 65 cents in Bangladesh, but the New York haircut is not worth 38 times more![23] Development specialists have tried to improve on the GNP comparisons.

One new measure is called Purchasing Power Parity (PPP). To understand how it is better, you need to understand how the GNP is figured. GNP per capita is usually expressed in terms of U.S. dollars. Economists calculate a country's GNP per capita and then convert it to U.S. dollars using the market rate for foreign exchange. For example, the GNP per capita in Bangladesh is 8,333 taka (the local currency), which will buy U.S. $220. But 8,333 taka will purchase far more in Bangladesh than $220 will purchase in the United States, mostly because wages are lower.

The PPP eliminates this distortion. A similar bundle of goods in both countries is priced to see how much each currency can actually purchase. Then GNP per capita is adjusted into PPP dollars that are equal and comparable among countries. Table 8 shows that Bangladesh's GNP per capita in PPP dollars is actually $1,290. This means that the Bangladeshi, with 8,333 taka, can only get $220 U.S. dollars in the foreign currency market, but can purchase goods in Bangladesh that would cost $1,290 to purchase in the United States. Poor countries do not appear to be as poor when measured in PPP dollars.[24]

Does that mean that people in poor countries are really not so poor after all? Yes, but only slightly. They are still very poor. Table 8 on the following page shows that the average person in India and Bangladesh (where 1 billion people live) has a PPP of between $1220 and $1290. That would be like trying to live in the U.S. on less than $110 a month! Imagine a family of four trying to survive in the U.S. or Canada on $440. If they rent an apartment for $400 a month, they have $40 left for food, transportation, clothing, medicine—and everything else.

Another measure of countries' well being is the Human Development Index (HDI). Created in 1990 by the United Nations Development Programme, it attempts to measure well being more broadly than simply by how much money people have. It uses three measures—life expectancy, education (adult literacy and mean years of schooling combined), and income (purchasing power parity dollars per capita). Each of the three are weighted equally to produce the HDI. The HDI is rated from zero to one—higher numbers mean the country is better off in those three areas. The HDI measures how effectively a country is using its wealth for education and health care. A country's standing changes when the availability of education and health care, not just purchasing power, are taken into account.

Table 8—Comparison of Different Measures of Wealth

Country	GNP/Capita (1993)	PPP/Capita (1993)	HDI (1992)	PPP per capita minus HDI (1992)
U.S.	$24,750	$24,750	.937	−1
Switzerland	$35,760	$23,660	.925	−11
Japan	$31,490	$20,850	.937	+5
U.K.	$18,060	$17,210	.916	+5
Canada	$19,970	$20,230	.950	+5
Saudi Arabia	$7,510	$11,170	.762	−43
Ecuador	$1,200	$4,240	.613	−23
Pakistan	$430	$2,170	.483	−28
India	$300	$1,220	.425	+7
Kenya	$270	$1,290	.481	+7
Bangladesh	$220	$1,290	.364	−5

Sources: World Bank and United Nations[25]

When evaluating countries based on GNP per capita and the HDI index, the biggest differences occur in the oil-exporting countries. The earnings from oil exports provide healthy incomes, so those nations are high on the world's GNP per capita list. But the money has been used to enrich a few rather than to educate and provide health care for the general population. (See Table 8.) Saudi Arabia was thirty-third in the world in GNP per capita in 1992, but was seventy-sixth in the world in the HDI index. This means that Saudi Arabia has a high income per capita, but is not educating nor providing health care for its population as well as other countries at a similar income level.

A comparison of energy usage underscores our affluence. Because of a lengthening list of luxuries—numerous electrical gadgets and toys, large air-conditioned cars, skyscrapers, and so on—North Americans consume more than twice as much energy per person as their counterparts in industrialized countries like Japan and Switzerland.[26] And we use 25 times as much as the average Brazilian, 60 times the average Indian, 191 times the average Nigerian, and 351 times the average Ethiopian.[27]

The percentage of income spent on food in different countries provides another stark comparison (see Table 9). In the United States it is a mere 10 percent. In the United Kingdom, it is 12 percent. In the Philipines it is 53 percent.[28]

Agony and anguish are concealed in the simple statistics of Table 9. For persons spending 10 percent of their disposable income on food, a 50-percent increase in food costs is a minor irritation. But for the one already spending 50 percent of income on food, a 50-percent increase means hunger, malnutrition, and perhaps starvation.

Table 9—Expenditures for Food—1987 (as percent of disposable personal income)	
United States	10%
Canada	11%
United Kingdom	12%
Australia	15%
France	16%
Italy	19%
Thailand	27%
Colombia	28%
Sri Lanka	50%
Philippines	53%

Source: USDA, Economic Research Service[29]

Calorie consumption tells the same story. People in many poor nations consume fewer than the daily minimal calorie requirements while people in North America and Western Europe have more than they need. While lack of food destroys millions in poor lands, too much food is devastating millions in affluent countries. According to a survey carried out from 1988 to 1991 by the National Center for Health Statistics, the number of overweight adults in the United States has increased from 26 to 34 percent over the last decade.[30]

The U.S. will add about 50 million people to its population over the next forty years, and those 50 million will have approximately the same global impact in terms of resource consumption as 2 billion more people in India. Due to over-consumption, small numbers of affluent people strain the earth's limited resources far more than much larger numbers of poor people.[31]

The different scales and comparisons all tell the same story. The rich one-fifth are incredibly wealthy and the poorest one-fifth are desperately poor. Those of us in developed countries make up only one-fifth of the world's population. But we "control 85 percent of its income and consume 70 percent of its energy, 75 percent of its metals, and 85 percent of its wood. [We also] produce two-thirds of all greenhouse gases."[33]

Table 10—Calorie Supply Per Capita as Percentage of Requirements, 1988–1990

Ireland	157
France	143
United States	138
Japan	125
Canada	122
Brazil	114
China	112
Guatemala	103
Pakistan	99
Ghana	93
Bangladesh	88
Zambia	87
Ethiopia	73
Chad	73
Afghanistan	72

Source: UNICEF[32]

The facts are clear. North Americans, Europeans, and Japanese devour an incredibly unequal share of the world's available resources. Whether measured in terms of GNP, PPP, or energy and food consumption, we are many, many times more affluent than the poor majority of our sisters and brothers. And the chasm widens every year.

Poverty at $40,000 a Year?

It was late 1974. Millions were dying from starvation. But that was not the concern of Judd Arnett, a syndicated columnist with Knight Newspapers. In a column read (and probably believed) by millions of North Americans, Arnett lamented the fact that people earning $40,000 a year (in 1994 dollars) were on the edge of poverty.

> One of the great mysteries of life to me is how a family in the $40,000 bracket, before taxes, or even $50,000 can meet all its obligations and still educate its children.[34]

A few years later *Newsweek* did a story entitled "The Middle Class Poor," calmly reporting that U.S. citizens earning $33,000, $40,000, or even

$55,000 a year felt they were at the edge of poverty.[35] One resident of New York City grumbled that "you just can't live in this city on a hundred thousand dollars a year."[36] In the fall of 1995, a U.S. congressman announced that his salary of $163,000 per year put him in the lower middle class.[37]

To the vast majority of the world's people, such statements would be unintelligible—or dishonest. To be sure, we do need $30,000, $50,000 or even more each year if we insist on having two cars, an expensively furnished, sprawling suburban home, a $300,000 life insurance policy, new clothes every time fashions change, the most recent "labor-saving devices" for home and garden, an annual three-week vacation, and so on. Many North Americans have come to expect precisely that. But that is hardly life at the edge of poverty.

How Generous Are We?

The United States is one of the richest nations in the world. But the U.S. government ranks dead last (in percentage of GNP) among major Western donors of foreign aid. The United Kingdom ranks only slightly higher— seventh from the bottom.

Table 11—Estimated Official Development Assistance from Industrialized Countries as Percentage of GNP (1993)			
Denmark	1.03	Australia	.35
Norway	1.01	Switzerland	.33
Sweden	.98	U.K.	.31
Netherlands	.82	Italy	.31
France	.63	Austria	.30
Finland	.46	Japan	.26
Canada	.45	New Zealand	.25
Belgium	.39	Ireland	.20
Germany	.37	United States	.15

Source: World Bank[32]

Popular opinion does not reflect this reality. One survey discovered that more than two-thirds (69 percent) of Americans thought that the United States is more generous in foreign aid than other developed nations.[39] Perhaps our illusion of generosity is a protective device. To justify our affluence, we foster an image of a generous nation dispensing foreign aid on a grand scale.

The United States did display national generosity at the end of World War II. At the height of the Marshall Plan (begun in 1947 to rebuild war-torn Europe) we annually gave 2.79 percent of our total GNP.[40] But by 1960 the figure for foreign aid had dropped to .53 percent of GNP, and by 1993 it had plummeted to a mere .15 percent (see Table 11). That amounts to a mere $37.70 per person.[41] The richer we have become, the less we share with others.

The same pattern holds for most rich nations. In 1961 and 1962, rich countries as a whole gave .52 percent of their total GNP in foreign aid. By 1965, it had decreased to .48. By 1970 it had declined to .34 percent. By 1993 the figure had fallen to a mere .30 percent. Ironically, between 1965 and 1980 the economies of rich countries grew at an annual rate of 3.6 and between 1980 and 1993 at an annual rate of 2.2 percent.[42] Although vastly richer, we shared a smaller percentage.

A comparison of Western expenditures on foreign aid and the military is startling. In 1991, all major aid donors spent 3.55 percent of their GNP on military expenditures but gave only 0.34 percent of their GNP for economic aid. In 1992, world military spending was $815 billion, which was the combined income of 49 percent of the world's people.[43] The level of military spending today is still four times the combined annual incomes of the poorest 25 percent of the developing world's population, the more than one billion poorest people.[44]

As the author of the widely respected annual *World Military and Social Expenditures* points out, "the developed countries still spend over ten times more on the military . . . than on aid for the economic development of the poorer countries."[45]

Is that the way we want to use our abundance?

Fortunately, we live in a day when military expenditures are being reduced. The breathtaking changes in Eastern Europe and the former Soviet Union have led most politicians to support substantial reductions. Between 1987 and 1994, global military spending declined at an estimated annual rate of 3.6 percent. That yielded a cumulative peace dividend of $935 billion—$810 billion in industrialized countries and $125 billion in developing countries.[46] Tragically, we were not willing to spend the peace dividend on increasing foreign aid for the poor.

Table 12—Developed Country Government Expenditures on Military and Foreign Aid, 1960 - 1991 (in billions of 1987 U.S. dollars)

	1960	1980	1991
Military	$295	447	534
As % of GNP	5.92%	3.95%	3.55%
Foreign Aid	$19.1	42.3	50.5
As % of GNP	0.38%	0.37%	0.34%

Source: Sivard, World Military and Social Expenditures 1993, p. 42

Rationalizing Our Affluence

It would be impossible for us as a rich minority to live with ourselves if we did not invent plausible justifications. These rationalizations take many forms. Analyzing a few of the most common may help us spot each year's new models.

Lifeboat Ethics

Garrett Hardin, a distinguished biologist at the University of California at Santa Barbara, popularized the term *lifeboat ethics*. He provoked impassioned, widespread debate with his provocative articles on the subject.[47] He argued that we should not help the poor with food or aid. According to his theory, each rich country is a lifeboat that will survive only if it refuses to waste its limited resources on the hungry masses swimming in the water around it. If we eat together today, we will all starve together tomorrow. Furthermore, since poor countries "irresponsibly" permit unrestrained population growth, starvation is the only way to check the ever-growing number of hungry mouths. The poor will always reproduce like rabbits until starvation reduces their number. Hence, increased aid merely postpones the day of reckoning. Aid simply preserves more persons for ultimate starvation. Therefore it is ethically correct to help them learn the hard way—by letting them starve now.

Hardin ignores data which show that poor countries can (and have) cut population growth fairly rapidly when they concentrate on improving the lot of the poor. If the poor have a secure food supply, access to some (relatively inexpensive) health services, and modest educational opportunities population growth tends to decline quickly. Lester Brown summarizes these findings:

> There is striking evidence that in an increasing number of poor countries . . . birth rates have dropped sharply despite relatively low per capita income. . . . Examination of societies as different as China, Barbados, Sri Lanka, Uruguay, Taiwan, The Indian Punjab, Cuba and South Korea suggests a common factor. In all these countries, a large portion of the population has gained access to modern social and economic services—such as education, employment, and credit systems. . . . There is increasing evidence that the very strategies which cause the greatest improvement in the welfare of the entire population also have the greatest effect on reducing population growth.[48]

Harvard economist Amartya Sen makes the same point in his important 1994 essay on population.[49]

Education for women is especially important. Bread for the World reports that "education, especially of girls, is . . . strongly correlated with lower birthrates. . . . In Bangladesh, a midday meal program designed to increase the enrollment of girls in school resulted in a 25 percent decline in birthrates over six years."[50] Education delays the time when women marry and begin having children. It gives them more self-confidence in making reproductive decisions with their husband.

The right kind of aid—focused especially on empowering the poorest and educating women—will help check population growth.[51] Hardin suggests doing nothing at a time when the right kind of action could produce dramatic improvement.

Another omission in Hardin's thesis is even more astonishing. He totally ignores the fact that the ever-increasing affluence among the rich minority is one of the fundamental causes of the crisis. It is false to suggest that there is not enough food to feed everyone. There is enough—if it is fairly distributed. The United Nations Development Programme reports that there is enough food available to offer everyone on the planet 2,500 calories per day (200 more than the minimum necessary).[52] The boat in which the rich sail is not an austerely equipped lifeboat. It is a lavishly stocked luxury liner.

Hardin's proposal, of course, is also unrealistic. Hungry nations left to starve would not disappear in submissive silence. India is one of the nations sometimes nominated for this dubious honor. A nation with nuclear weapons would certainly not tolerate such a decision.[53]

To Evangelize the Rich

A second rationalization has a pious ring to it. Some evangelical Christians argue that they must live in affluence to evangelize the wealthy. Rationalization is dreadfully easy. Garden Grove Community Church in California has a lavish, multi-million-dollar plant complete with a series of water fountains that begin spraying when the minister touches a button in the pulpit. The pastor, Robert Schuller, defends his luxurious facilities:

> We are trying to make a big, beautiful impression upon the affluent non-religious American who is riding by on this busy freeway. It's obvious that we are not trying to impress the Christians! . . . Nor are we trying to impress the social workers in the County Welfare Department. They would tell us that we ought to be content to remain in the Orange Drive-In Theater and give the money to feed the poor. But suppose we *had* given this money to feed the poor? What would we have today? We would still have hungry, poor people and God would not have this tremendous base of operations which He is using to inspire people to become more successful, more affluent, more generous, more genuinely unselfish in their giving of themselves.[54]

Beautiful church construction is sometimes appropriate. But how many more glass cathedrals would we build if we first examined the needs of the billion plus people who live on one dollar a day?

Trickle Down Wealth

A lively conversation that I had some years ago with a wealthy friend illustrates a third widespread rationalization. This prominent business leader insisted that the best thing he could do for the poor was to buy more things for himself. If he purchased more Jaguars, he argued, then the economy would grow and the poor would have more jobs. This is a dangerous half-truth. Fortunately, some of the benefits of a growing economy do trickle down to the poor—at least to a degree. My response to my friend, however, was that if he spent $100,000 less on Jaguars and used that $100,000 for direct economic empowerment of the poor (via David Bussau's micro-loans, for example), the poor would benefit far more quickly and substantially. That way, the $100,000 would offer the same stimulus to the economy and immediately reduce poverty. My friend insisted that buying Jaguars would work just as well.

Where does valid justification end and rationalization begin?

We must, of course, avoid simplistic legalism. Christians certainly ought to live in the suburbs as well as the inner city. But those who defend an affluent lifestyle on the basis of their call to witness to the rich must ask themselves hard questions:

- How much of my affluent lifestyle is directly related to my witnessing to rich neighbors?

- How much of it could I abandon for the sake of Christ's poor and still be able to witness effectively?

- Indeed how much of it *must* I abandon in order to faithfully proclaim the biblical Christ who taught that failure to feed the poor leads to eternal damnation (Mt 25:45-46)?

In the coming decades rationalizations for affluence will abound. They will be popular and persuasive. "Truly, I say to you, it will be hard for a rich person to enter the kingdom of heaven" (Mt 19:23). But all things are possible with God—if we will hear and obey his Word. We can move toward a more hopeful future for our world and more genuine joy and fulfillment in our personal lives if we affluent Christians will dare to allow the Bible to shape our relationship to a billion sons and daughters of poor Lazarus. Will rich Christians also be generous?

Study Questions

1. How is the gap between rich and poor different than you had thought?
2. What are some of the best measures of that gap?
3. How does advertising contribute to our problem? What are some of the theological questions raised by advertising?
4. How does solving poverty help reduce overpopulation?
5. What rationalizations of affluence are most convincing? For yourself? Your friends?
6. Is there any sense in which this book is about joy and self-fulfillment? How?

Part Two

A Biblical Perspective on the Poor and Possessions

"If you preach the gospel in all aspects with the exception of the issues which deal specifically with your time you are not preaching the gospel at all."[1]

Social scientists who examined the factors that shape American attitudes on matters related to the development of the poorest nations discovered that religion plays no significant role at all! Those with deep religious beliefs are no more concerned about assistance and development for the poor than are persons with little or no religious commitment.[2]

Most wealthy Christians have failed to seek God's perspective on the plight of our billion hungry neighbors—surely one of the most pressing issues of our time.

Bur I refuse to believe that this failure must inevitably continue. I believe there are millions of affluent Christians who care more about Jesus than anything else in the world. There are millions of Christians who will take any risk, make any sacrifice, forsake any treasure, if they see clearly that God's Word demands it. That is why Part Two—A Biblical Perspective on the Poor and Possessions—is the most important section of this book.

Part Two is full of Scripture. But even so it is only a small selection of the vast volume of biblical material. My book *For They Shall Be Fed* contains almost two hundred pages of biblical texts that relate directly to the four chapters in this section.[3]

3

God and the Poor

He who is kind to the poor lends to the Lord (Proverbs 9:17).

I know that the Lord maintains the cause of the afflicted, and executes justice for the needy (Psalm 140:12).

Is GOD BIASED in favor of the poor? Is he on their side in a way that he is not on the side of the rich? Some theologians say yes.[1] But until we clarify the meaning of the question, we cannot answer it correctly. Does it mean that God desires the salvation of poor people more than that of the rich? Does it mean that God and his people treat the poor so much differently from the way the ungodly treat them that God seems to have a special concern for the poor and oppressed? Furthermore, just who are "the poor" in the Bible?

The Hebrew words for the poor are *ani, anaw, ebyon, dal,* and *ras. Ani* (and *anaw,* which originally had approximately the same meaning) denotes one who is "wrongfully impoverished or dispossessed."[2] *Ebyon* refers to a beggar imploring charity. *Dal* connotes a thin, weakly person such as an impoverished, deprived peasant.[3] Unlike the others, *ras* is an essentially neutral term. In their persistent polemic against the oppression of the poor, the prophets used the terms *ebyon, ani,* and *dal.* In the New Testament, the primary word for the poor is *ptochos,* which refers to someone, like a beggar, who is completely destitute and must seek help from others. It is the Greek equivalent of *ani* and *dal.*[4] Thus the primary connotation of "the poor" in Scripture has to do with low economic status usually due to calamity or some form of oppression.

The Scriptures also teach that some folk are poor because they are lazy and slothful (e.g., Proverbs 6:6–11; 19:15; 20:13; 21:25; 24:30–34). And, of course, the Bible speaks of voluntary poverty for the sake of the kingdom.

The most common biblical connotation of "the poor," however, relates to those who are economically impoverished due to calamity or exploitation.[5] This chapter deals with this last category.

We can answer the questions about God's alleged bias toward the poor only after finding biblical answers to five related questions: (1) What concern for the poor did God disclose at pivotal points in history when he revealed himself (especially the Exodus, the destruction of Israel and Judah, and the Incarnation)? (2) In what sense does God identify with the poor? (3) Of what significance is the fact that God frequently chooses to work through the poor and oppressed? (4) What does the Bible mean by the recurring teaching that God frequently destroys the rich and exalts the poor? (5) Does God command his people to have a special concern for the poor?

Pivotal Points of Revelation History

The Bible clearly and repeatedly teaches a fundamental point that we often overlook. At the crucial moments when God displayed his mighty acts to reveal his nature and will, God also intervened to liberate the poor and oppressed.

The Exodus

God displayed his power at the Exodus in part to free oppressed slaves. When he called Moses at the burning bush, part of God's intent was to end suffering and injustice: "I have seen the affliction of my people who are in Egypt, and have heard their cry because of their taskmasters; I know their sufferings, and I have come down to deliver them out of the hand of the Egyptians" (Exodus 3:7–8).

This text does not reflect an isolated perspective on the great event of the Exodus. Each year at the harvest festival the Israelites repeated a liturgical confession celebrating the way God had acted to free their poor, oppressed nation.

A wandering Aramean was my father; and he went down into Egypt and sojourned there. . . . And the Egyptians treated us harshly, and afflicted us, and laid upon us hard bondage. Then we cried to the Lord the God of our fathers, and the Lord heard our voice, and saw our affliction, our toil, and our oppression; and the Lord brought us out of Egypt with a mighty hand. (Deuteronomy 26:5–8)

The God of the Bible cares when people enslave and oppress others. At the Exodus, God acted to end economic oppression and bring freedom to slaves.

The liberation of slaves was not, of course, God's only purpose in the Exodus. He also acted because of his covenant with Abraham, Isaac, and Jacob. In addition, God wanted to create a special people to whom he could reveal himself.[6] Both of these concerns were central to God's activity at the Exodus. The liberation of a poor, oppressed people, however, was also at the heart of God's design. The following passage discloses God's multifaceted purpose in the Exodus:

Moreover I have heard the groaning of the people of Israel whom the Egyptians hold in bondage and I have remembered my covenant [with Abraham, Isaac, and Jacob]. . . . I will bring you out from under the burdens of the Egyptians, and I will deliver you from their bondage, and I will redeem you with an outstretched arm and with great acts of judgment, and I will take you for my people, and I will be your God; and you shall know that I am the Lord your God, who has brought you out from under the burdens of the Egyptians. (Exodus 6:5–7)

Yahweh wanted his people to know him as the One who freed them from slavery and oppression.

The preamble to the Ten Commandments, probably the most important portion of the entire law for Israel, begins with this same revolutionary truth. Before he gives the two tables of the law, Yahweh identifies himself: "I am the Lord your God, who brought you out of the land of Egypt, out of the house of bondage" (Deuteronomy 5:6; Exodus 20:2). Yahweh is the one who frees from bondage. The God of the Bible wants to be known as the liberator of the oppressed.

The Exodus was the decisive event in the creation of the chosen people. We distort the biblical interpretation of this momentous occasion if we fail to see that the Lord of the universe was at work correcting oppression and liberating the poor.

Destruction and Captivity

Soon after the Israelites settled in the Promised Land, they discovered that Yahweh's passion for justice was a two-edged sword. When they were oppressed, it led to their freedom. But when they became the oppressors, it led to their destruction.

When God called Israel out of Egypt and made his covenant with them, God gave them his law so that they could live together in peace and justice. But Israel failed to obey the law of the covenant. As a result, God destroyed Israel and sent his chosen people back into captivity.

Why?

The explosive message of the prophets is that God destroyed Israel because of their mistreatment of the poor. Idolatry was an equally prominent reason, but too often we remember only Israel's "spiritual" problem of idolatry and overlook the startling biblical teaching that economic exploitation also sent the chosen people into captivity.

The middle of the eighth century B.C. was a time of political success and economic prosperity unknown since the days of Solomon.[7] But it was precisely at this moment that God sent his prophet Amos to announce the unwelcome news that the northern kingdom of Israel would be destroyed. Behind the facade of prosperity and fantastic economic growth, Amos saw oppression of the poor. He saw the rich "trample the head of the poor into the dust of the earth" (2:7). He saw that the lifestyle of the rich was built on oppression of the poor (6:1–7). He denounced the rich women (*cows* was his word!) "who oppress the poor, who crush the needy, who say to their husbands, 'Bring, that we may drink!'" (4:1). Even in the courts the poor had no hope because the rich bribed the judges (5:10–15).

Archaeologists have confirmed Amos's picture of shocking extremes of wealth and poverty.[8] In the early days of settlement in Canaan, the land was distributed more or less equally among the families and tribes. Most Israelites enjoyed a similar standard of living. In fact, archaeologists have found that houses as late as the tenth century B.C. were all approximately the same size. But by Amos's day, two centuries later, everything had changed. Bigger, better built houses were found in one area and poorer houses were huddled together in another section.[9] No wonder Amos warned the rich, "You have built houses of hewn stone, but you shall not dwell in them" (5:11)!

God's word through Amos was that the northern kingdom would be destroyed and the people taken into exile (7:11, 17).

> Woe to those who lie upon beds of ivory, and stretch themselves upon their couches, and eat lambs from the flock, and calves from the midst of the stall. . . . Therefore they shall now be the first of those to go into exile, and the revelry of those who stretch themselves shall pass away. (6:4, 7)

A few years after Amos spoke it happened just as God had said. The Assyrians conquered the northern kingdom and took thousands into captivity. Because of their mistreatment of the poor, God destroyed the northern kingdom—forever.

As in the case of the Exodus, we dare not ignore another important factor. The nation's idolatry was also a central cause of their destruction. Because they had forsaken Yahweh for idols, the nation was destroyed (Hosea 8:1–6; 9:1–3).[10] According to the prophets, then, the northern kingdom fell because of both idolatry and economic exploitation of the poor.

God sent other prophets to announce the same fate for the southern kingdom of Judah. Isaiah warned that destruction from afar would befall Judah because of its mistreatment of the poor:

> Woe to those who decree iniquitous decrees. . . . to turn aside the needy from justice and to rob the poor of my people of their right. . . . What will you do on the day of punishment, in the storm which will come from afar? (Isaiah 10:1–3)

Micah denounced those in Judah who "covet fields, and seize them; and houses, and take them away; they oppress a man and his house, a man and his inheritance" (2:2). As a result, he warned, Jerusalem would one day become "a heap of ruins" (3:12).

45

Fortunately, Judah was more open to the prophetic word, and the nation was spared for a time. But oppression of the poor continued. A hundred years after Isaiah, the prophet Jeremiah again condemned the wealthy who had amassed riches by oppressing the poor:

> "Wicked men are found among my people; they lurk like fowlers lying in wait. They set a trap; they catch men. Like a basket full of birds, their houses are full of treachery; therefore, they have become great and rich, they have grown fat and sleek. They know no bounds in deeds of wickedness; they judge not with justice the cause of the fatherless, to make it prosper, and they do not defend the rights of the needy. Shall I not punish them for these things?" says the Lord, "and shall I not avenge myself on a nation such as this?" (Jeremiah 5:26–29)

Even at that late date Jeremiah offered hope if the people would forsake both injustice and idolatry. "If you truly execute justice one with another, if you do not oppress the alien, the fatherless or the widow . . . and if you do not go after other gods to your own hurt, then I will let you dwell in this place, in the land that I gave of old to your fathers for ever" (Jeremiah 7:5–7).

But they continued to oppress the poor and helpless (Jeremiah 34:3–17). As a result, Jeremiah persisted in warning that God would use the Babylonians to destroy Judah. In 587 B.C. Jerusalem fell, and the Babylonian captivity began.

The destruction of Israel and Judah was not mere punishment. God used the Assyrians and Babylonians to purge his people of oppression and injustice. In a remarkable passage, Isaiah showed how God would attack his foes and enemies (that is, his chosen people!) in order to purify them and restore justice.

> How the faithful city [Jerusalem] has become a harlot, she that was full of justice! Righteousness lodged in her, but now murderers. Your silver has become dross, your wine mixed with water. . . . Every one loves a bribe and runs after gifts. They do not defend the fatherless, and the widow's cause does not come to them. Therefore the Lord says, the Lord of hosts, the Mighty One of Israel: "Ah, I will vent my wrath on my enemies, and avenge myself on my foes. I will turn my hand against you and will smelt away your dross as with lye and remove all your alloy.

And I will restore your judges as at the first, and your counselors as at the beginning. Afterward you shall be called the city of righteousness, the faithful city. (Isaiah 1:21–26)

The catastrophe of national destruction and captivity reveals the God of the Exodus still at work correcting the oppression of the poor.

The Incarnation

Christians believe that God revealed himself most completely in Jesus of Nazareth, so to understand God's work in the world it is important to understand how the Incarnate One defined his mission.

Jesus' words in the synagogue at Nazareth, spoken near the beginning of his public ministry, throb with hope for the poor. He read from the prophet Isaiah:

The Spirit of the Lord is upon me, because he has anointed me to preach good news to the poor. He has sent me to proclaim release to the captives and recovering of sight to the blind, to set at liberty those who are oppressed, to proclaim the acceptable year of the Lord. (Luke 4:18–19)

After reading these words, Jesus informed his audience that this Scripture was now fulfilled in himself. The mission of the Incarnate One included freeing the oppressed and healing the blind. (It was also to preach the gospel, which is equally important, but the focus of this book precludes further discussion of it.)[11] The poor are the only group specifically singled out as recipients of Jesus' gospel. Certainly the gospel he proclaimed was for all, but he was particularly concerned that the poor realize that his good news was for them.

Some try to avoid the clear meaning of Jesus' statement by spiritualizing his words. Certainly, as other texts show, he came to open our blinded hearts, to die for our sins, and to free us from the oppression of guilt. But that is not what he means here. The words about releasing captives and liberating the oppressed are from Isaiah. In their original Old Testament setting they unquestionably referred to physical oppression and captivity. In Luke 7:18–23, which contains a list similar to the one in Luke 4:18–19, it is clear that Jesus is referring to material, physical problems.[12]

Jesus' actual ministry corresponded precisely to the words of Luke 4. He spent considerable time ministering to lepers, despised women, and other marginalized folk. He healed the sick and blind. He fed the hungry. And he warned his followers in the strongest possible words that those who do not feed the hungry, clothe the naked, and visit the prisoners will experience eternal damnation (Matthew 25:31–46).

At the supreme moment of history, when God took on human flesh, the God of Israel was still liberating the poor and oppressed and summoning his people to do the same. That is the central reason for Christian concern for the poor.

It is not just at the Exodus, captivity, and Incarnation, however, that we learn of God's concern for the poor, the weak, and the oppressed. The Bible is full of passages that speak of this. Two illustrations from the Psalms are typical of a host of other texts.

Psalm 10 begins with despair. God seems to have hidden himself far away while the wicked prosper by oppressing the poor (vv. 2, 9). But the psalmist concludes with hope:

> The hapless commits himself to thee; thou hast been the helper of the fatherless. . . . O Lord, thou wilt hear the desire of the meek . . . thou wilt incline thy ear to do justice to the fatherless and the oppressed. (vv. 14, 17–18)

Psalm 146 is a ringing declaration that to care for the poor is central to the very nature of God. The psalmist exults in the God of Jacob because he is both the creator of the universe and the defender of the oppressed.

> Praise the Lord! Praise the Lord, O my soul . . . Happy is he whose help is the God of Jacob, whose hope is in the Lord his God, who made heaven and earth, the sea, and all that is in them; who keeps faith for ever; who executes justice for the oppressed; who gives food to the hungry. The Lord sets the prisoners free; the Lord opens the eyes of the blind. The Lord lifts up those who are bowed down; the Lord loves the righteous. The Lord watches over the sojourners, he upholds the widow and the fatherless; but the way of the wicked he brings to ruin. (vv. 1, 5–9)

According to Scripture, defending the weak, the stranger, and the oppressed is as much an expression of God's essence as creating the universe. Because of who he is, Yahweh lifts up the mistreated.[13] The foundation of Christian concern for the hungry and oppressed is that God cares especially for them.

God Identifies with the Poor

God not only acts in history to liberate the poor, but in a mysterious way that we can only partly fathom, the Sovereign of the universe identifies with the weak and destitute. Two proverbs state this beautiful truth. Proverbs 14:31 puts it negatively: "Those who oppress the poor insult their Maker" (NRSV). Even more moving is the positive formulation: "He who is kind to the poor lends to the Lord" (19:17). What a statement! Assisting a poor person is like helping the Creator of all things with a loan.

Only in the Incarnation can we begin to perceive what God's identification with the weak, oppressed, and poor really means. "Though he was rich," Paul says of our Lord Jesus, "yet for your sake he became poor" (2 Corinthians 8:9).

Jesus was born in a small, insignificant province of the Roman Empire. His first visitors, the shepherds, were viewed by Jewish society as thieves. His parents were too poor to bring the normal offering for purification. Instead of a lamb, they brought two pigeons to the Temple (Luke 2:24; compare Leviticus 12:6–8). Jesus was a refugee (Matthew 2:13–15). Since Jewish rabbis received no fees for their teaching, Jesus had no regular income during his public ministry.[14] (Scholars belonged to the poorer classes in Judaism.) Nor did he have a home of his own. Jesus warned an eager follower who promised to follow him everywhere, "Foxes have holes, and birds of the air have nests; but the Son of man has nowhere to lay his head" (Matthew 8:20). He sent out disciples with very little to sustain them (Luke 9:3; 10:4).

God did not become flesh as a wealthy aristocrat. However, it is also true that Jesus' family probably was not from the poorest class. At Jesus' birth, Joseph and Mary must have been fairly poor—as their sacrifice shows. And as refugees in Egypt they probably had very little. But Jesus lived much of his life in a carpenter's family in Nazareth, and Galilean carpenters in Jesus' day normally earned a reasonable income. So we should not think of the family in which Jesus grew up as living in poverty.[15]

Jesus, however, identified with the poor in important ways. He insisted that his preaching to the poor was a sign that he was the Messiah. When John the Baptist sent messengers to ask him if he were the long expected Messiah, Jesus simply pointed to his deeds: he was healing the sick and preaching to the poor (Matthew 11:2–6). Jesus also preached to the rich. But apparently it was his particular concern to preach to the poor that validated his claim to messiahship. His extensive engagement with the poor and disadvantaged contrasted sharply with the style of his contemporaries. Was that part of the reason he added a final word to take back to John: "Blessed is he who takes no offense at me" (Matthew 11:6)?

The clearest statement about Jesus' identification with the poor is in Matthew 25: "I was hungry and you gave me food, I was thirsty and you gave me something to drink. . . . I was naked and you gave me clothing. . . . Truly, I tell you, just as you did it to one of the least of these who are members of my family, you did it to me" (Matthew 25:35–36, 40; NRSV).

What does it mean to feed and clothe the Creator of all things? We cannot know. We can only look on the poor and oppressed with new eyes and resolve to heal their hurts and help end their oppression.

If Jesus' teaching in Matthew 25:40 is startling, its parallel is terrifying: "Truly, I say to you, as you did it not to one of the least of these, you did it not to me" (v. 45). What does that mean in a world where millions die each year while rich Christians live in affluence?

What does it mean to see the Lord of the universe lying by the roadside starving and walk by on the other side? We cannot know. We can only pledge, in fear and trembling, not to kill him again.

God's Special Instruments

When God selected a chosen people, he picked poor slaves in Egypt. When God called the early church, many of the members were poor. When God became flesh, he chose, for our sakes, to become poor (2 Corinthians 8:9). Are these facts isolated phenomena or part of an important pattern?

God could have selected a rich, powerful nation as his chosen people. Instead he chose oppressed slaves. God called out an impoverished, enslaved people to be his special instrument of revelation and salvation for all people. (See also the story of Gideon in Judges 6:15–16; 7:2.)

In the early church, many members were poor. In a book sketching the social history of early Christianity, Martin Hengel points out that the early Gentile Christian communities "were predominantly poor."[16] The apostle Paul marveled at the kind of people God called into the church:

> Not many of you were wise according to worldly standards, not many were powerful, not many were of noble birth; but God chose what is foolish in the world to shame the wise, God chose what is weak in the world to shame the strong, God chose what is low and despised in the world, even things that are not, to bring to nothing things that are, so that no human being might boast in the presence of God.
> (1 Corinthians 1:26–29)

Likewise James:

> My brothers and sisters, do you with your acts of favoritism really believe in our glorious Lord Jesus Christ? For if a person with gold rings and in fine clothes comes into your assembly, and if a poor person in dirty clothes also comes in, and if you take notice of the one wearing the fine clothes and say, "Have a seat here, please," while to the one who is poor you say, "Stand there," or, "Sit at my feet," have you not made distinctions among yourselves, and become judges with evil thoughts? Listen, my beloved brothers and sisters. *Has not God chosen the poor in the world to be rich in faith and to be heirs of the kingdom that he has promised to those who love him?* But you have dishonored the poor. Is it not the rich who oppress you? Is it not they who drag you into court? Is it not they who blaspheme the excellent name that was invoked over you?
> (James 2:1–7 NRSV, italics added)

The rhetorical question in verse 5 (in italics) indicates that the Jerusalem church was far from rich. But the passage illustrates how the church so often forsakes God's way and opts instead for the way of the world. At both the Exodus and the emergence of the early church, God chose poor folk as his special instruments.

We must, however, beware of overstating the case. Abraham seems to have been well off. Moses lived at Pharaoh's court for forty years. Not all the early Christians were poor. Paul and Luke were educated and at least reasonably well-to-do. God does not work exclusively through impoverished, oppressed people. There is, nonetheless, a sharp contrast between God's procedure and ours. When we want to effect change, we almost always contact people with influence, prestige, and power. When God wants to save the world, he often selects slaves, prostitutes, and sundry other disadvantaged folk.

Again, the Incarnation is important. God might have entered history as a powerful Roman emperor living in luxurious power at the center of the greatest empire of the time. Or he could have appeared at least as an influential Sadducee with a prominent place in the Sanhedrin in the holy city of Jerusalem. Instead he came and lived as a carpenter in the small town of Nazareth—a place too insignificant to be mentioned either in the Old Testament or the writings of Josephus, the first-century Jewish historian.[17] Yet this is how God chose to effect our salvation.

I am not suggesting that God never uses rich, powerful people as his chosen instruments. He has and does. But we almost always choose such people. God, on the other hand, frequently selects the poor to carry out his most important tasks. He sees potential that we do not. And when the task is done, the poor and weak are less likely to boast that they deserve the credit. God's frequent selection of the lowly to be his special messengers of salvation to the world is striking evidence of his special concern for them. And his incarnation as a carpenter rather than an emperor shows that our natural way of thinking—that only the rich and powerful can change history—is contrary to God's way of thinking.

Why Does God Cast Down the Rich?

Jesus' story of the rich man and Lazarus illustrates a fourth teaching prominent throughout Scripture. God actually works in history to cast down some rich, powerful people. Does that sound too strong? Listen to the biblical texts.

Mary's Magnificat puts it simply and bluntly:

> My soul magnifies the Lord. . . . He has put down the mighty from their thrones, and exalted those of low degree; he has filled the hungry with good things, and the rich he has sent empty away. (Luke 1:46, 52–53)

Centuries earlier, Hannah's song proclaimed the same truth:

> There is none holy like the Lord, there is none besides thee. . . . Talk no
> more so very proudly, let not arrogance come from your mouth. . . . The
> bows of the mighty are broken, but the feeble gird on strength. Those
> who were full have hired themselves out for bread, but those who were
> hungry have ceased to hunger. . . . The Lord makes poor and makes
> rich. . . . He raises up the poor from the dust; he lifts the needy from the
> ash heap. (1 Samuel 2:2–8)

Jesus pronounced a blessing on the poor and a curse on the rich:

> Blessed are you poor, for yours is the kingdom of God. Blessed are you
> that hunger now, for you shall be satisfied. . . . Woe to you that are rich,
> for you have received your consolation. Woe to you that are full now, for
> you shall hunger. (Luke 6:20–25)[18]

"Come now, you rich, weep and howl for the miseries that are coming
upon you" (James 5:1) is a frequent theme of biblical revelation.

Why does Scripture declare that God sometimes reverses the good for-
tunes of the rich? Is it because creating wealth is bad? No. The Bible says
exactly the opposite. Is God engaged in class warfare? Not at all. Scripture
never says that God loves the poor more than the rich. But it does regularly
assert that God lifts up the poor and disadvantaged. And it frequently
teaches that God casts down the wealthy and powerful in two specific situations: (1) when they become wealthy by oppressing the poor; or (2) when
they fail to share with the needy.

Casting Down Rich Oppressors

Why did James warn some rich folk he knew to weep and howl because of
impending misery? Because they had cheated their workers:

> You have laid up treasure for the last days. Behold, the wages of the
> laborers who mowed your fields, which you kept back by fraud, cry out;
> and the cries of the harvesters have reached the ears of the Lord of

hosts. You have lived on the earth in luxury and in pleasure; you have fattened your hearts in a day of slaughter. (James 5:3–5)

God does not have class enemies. But he hates and punishes both oppression and neglect of the poor. And the rich, if we accept the repeated warnings of Scripture, are frequently guilty of one or both.[19]

Long before the days of James, the psalmist knew that the rich were often rich because of oppression. He took comfort in the assurance that God would punish such evildoers:

In arrogance the wicked hotly pursue the poor. . . . His ways prosper at all times. . . . He thinks in his heart, "I shall not be moved; throughout all generations I shall not meet adversity." . . . He lurks in secret like a lion in his covert; he lurks that he may seize the poor, he seizes the poor when he draws him into his net. . . . Arise, O Lord; O God, lift up thy hand; forget not the afflicted. . . . Break thou the arm of the wicked and evildoer. . . . O Lord, thou wilt hear the desire of the meek; thou wilt strengthen their heart, thou wilt incline thy ear to do justice to the fatherless and the oppressed. (Psalm 10)

God announced the same message through the prophet Jeremiah:

Wicked men are found among my people; they lurk like fowlers lying in wait. They set a trap; they catch human beings. Like a basket full of birds their houses are full of treachery; therefore they have become great and rich, they have grown fat and sleek. They know no bounds in deeds of wickedness; they judge not with justice the cause of the fatherless, to make it prosper, and they do not defend the rights of the needy. Shall I not punish them for these things? says the Lord. (Jeremiah 5:26–29)

Nor was the faith of Jeremiah and the psalmist mere wishful thinking. Through the prophets, God announced devastation and destruction for both rich individuals and rich nations who oppressed the poor. And it happened as they predicted.

Jeremiah pronounced one of the most biting, satirical diatribes in all of Scripture against the unjust King Jehoiakim of Judah:

"Woe to him who builds his house by unrighteousness, and his upper rooms by injustice; who makes his neighbor serve him for nothing, and does not give him his wages; who says, "I will build myself a great house with spacious upper rooms," and cuts out windows for it, paneling it with cedar, and painting it with vermilion. Do you think you are a king because you compete in cedar? Did not your father eat and drink and do justice and righteousness? Then it was well with him. He judged the cause of the poor and needy; then it was well. Is not this to know me?" says the Lord. But you have eyes and heart only for your dishonest gain, for shedding innocent blood, and for practicing oppression and violence. Therefore thus says the Lord concerning Jehoiakim: "With the burial of an ass he shall be buried, dragged and cast forth beyond the gates of Jerusalem." (Jeremiah 22:13–19)

Jehoiakim, historians think, was assassinated.[20]

God destroys whole nations as well as rich individuals because of their oppression of the poor. We have already examined a few of the pertinent texts.[21] One more is important. Through Isaiah, God declared that the rulers of Judah were rich because they had cheated the poor. Surfeited with affluence, the wealthy women had indulged in self-centered wantonness, oblivious to the suffering of the oppressed. The result, God said, would be destruction.

The Lord enters into judgment with the elders and princes of his people: "It is you who have devoured the vineyard, the spoil of the poor is in your houses. What do you mean by crushing my people, by grinding the face of the poor?" says the Lord God of hosts. The Lord said: Because the daughters of Zion are haughty and walk with outstretched necks, glancing wantonly with their eyes, mincing along as they go, tinkling with their feet; the Lord will smite with a scab the heads of the daughters of Zion. . . . In that day the Lord will take away the finery of the anklets, the headbands, and the crescents. . . . Instead of perfume there will be rottenness; and instead of a girdle, a rope; and instead of well-set hair, baldness; and instead of a rich robe, a girding of sackcloth; instead of beauty, shame. Your men shall fall by the sword and your mighty men in battle. (Isaiah 3:14–25)

When the rich oppress the poor and weak, the Lord of history is at work pulling down their houses and kingdoms.

Neglecting the Poor

Sometimes Scripture simply accuses the rich of failure to share with the needy and does not suggest that the wealth was acquired in unjust ways. But the result is the same.

In the story of the rich man and Lazarus, Jesus does not say that the rich man exploited Lazarus (Luke 16). He merely shows his lack of concern for the sick beggar lying outside his gate. "Clothed in purple and fine linen [the rich man] feasted sumptuously every day" (Luke 16:19). Lazarus, on the other hand, "desired to be fed with what fell from the rich man's table" (Luke 16:21). Did the rich man deny hungry Lazarus even the scraps? Perhaps not. But obviously he had no real concern for him.

Such sinful neglect of the needy infuriates the God of the poor. When Lazarus died, God comforted him in Abraham's bosom. When the rich man died, torment confronted him.[22] The meaning of the name Lazarus, "one whom God has helped," underlines the basic point.[23] God aids the poor, but the rich who neglect poor neighbors go to hell.

Clark Pinnock is surely correct when he notes that the story of the rich man and Lazarus "ought to explode in our hands when we read it sitting at our well-covered tables while the third world stands outside."[24] It is not merely the Law and the Prophets but also Jesus our Lord who declares the terrifying word that God destroys the rich when they fail to assist the poor.

The biblical explanation of Sodom's destruction provides another illustration of this fearsome truth. If asked why Sodom was destroyed, most Christians would point to the city's sexual perversity. But that is a one-sided view of what Scripture teaches. Ezekiel says that one important reason God destroyed Sodom was that it stubbornly refused to share with the poor!

> Behold, this was the guilt of your sister Sodom: she and her daughters had pride, surfeit of food, and prosperous ease, but did not aid the poor and needy. They were haughty, and did abominable things before me; therefore I removed them, when I saw it. (Ezekiel 16:49–50; see also Isaiah 1:10–17)

The text does not say that they oppressed the poor, although they may have. It simply accuses them of failing to assist the needy.

Affluent Christians remember Sodom's sexual misconduct and forget its sinful unconcern for the poor. Is it because the former is less upsetting? Have we allowed our economic self-interest to distort our interpretation of Scripture? Undoubtedly we have. But to the extent of our belief in scriptural authority, we will permit painful texts to correct our thinking. As we do, we will acknowledge in fear and trembling that the God of the Bible wreaks horrendous havoc on some kinds of rich people—not because he does not love those who are rich (God loves everyone equally), but because the rich sometimes oppress the poor or neglect the needy.

God's Concern and Ours

Since God cares so much for the poor, it is hardly surprising that God wants his people to do the same.

Equal justice for the poor in court is a constant concern of Scripture. The law commanded it (Exodus 23:6). The psalmist invoked divine assistance for the king so that he could provide it (Psalm 72:1–4). And the prophets announced destruction because the rulers stubbornly subverted it (Amos 5:10–15).

Widows, orphans, and strangers also receive frequent attention.

> You shall not wrong a stranger or oppress him, for you were strangers in the land of Egypt. You shall not afflict any widow or orphan. If you do afflict them, and they cry out to me, I will surely hear their cry; and my wrath will burn, and I will kill you with the sword, and your wives shall become widows and your children fatherless. (Exodus 22:21–24)

"The fatherless, widows, and foreigners," John F. Alexander has observed, "each have about forty verses that command justice for them. God wants to make it very clear that in a special sense he is the protector of these weak ones. Strangers are to be treated nearly the same as Jews, and woe to people who take advantage of orphans or widows."[25]

Rare indeed are Christians who pay any attention to Jesus' command to show bias toward the poor in their dinner invitations.

> When you give a dinner or a banquet, do not invite your friends or your brothers or your kinsmen or rich neighbors. . . . But when you give a feast, invite the poor, the maimed, the lame, the blind, and you will be blessed, because they cannot repay you. (Luke 14:12–14; see also Hebrews 13:1–3)

Jesus was using hyperbole, a typical technique of Hebrew literature to emphasize his point. He did not mean to forbid parties with friends and relatives. But he did mean that we ought to entertain the poor and disadvantaged (who cannot reciprocate) at least as often—and perhaps a lot more often—than we entertain friends, relatives, and "successful" folk. Have you ever known a Christian who took Jesus that seriously?

The Bible specifically commands believers to imitate God's special concern for the poor and oppressed. In the Old Testament, Yahweh frequently reminded the Israelites of their former oppression in Egypt when he commanded them to care for the poor. God's unmerited concern for the Hebrew slaves in Egyptian bondage is the model to imitate (Exodus 22:21–24; Deuteronomy 15:13–15).

Jesus taught his followers to imitate God's mercy in their lending as well.

> If you do good to those who do good to you, what credit is that to you? . . . If you lend to those from whom you hope to receive, what credit is that to you? . . . Lend, expecting nothing in return. Your reward will be great, and you will be children of the Most High; for he is kind to the ungrateful and the wicked. Be merciful, just as your Father is merciful. (Luke 6:33–36 NRSV)

Why lend without expecting return? Because that is the way our Father acts. Jesus' followers are to reverse normal human patterns precisely because they are sons and daughters of God and want to reflect his nature.

When Paul took up the collection for the poor in Jerusalem, he pointedly reminded the Corinthians that the Lord Jesus became poor so that they might become rich (2 Corinthians 8:9). When John called on Christians to share with the needy, he first mentioned the example of Christ: "We know love by this, that he laid down his life for us—and we ought to lay down our lives for one another" (1 John 3:16 NRSV). Then, in the very next verse, he urged Christians to give generously to the needy. It is the amazing self-sacrifice of Christ that Christians are to imitate as they relate to the poor and oppressed.

We have seen that God's Word commands believers to care for the poor. In fact the Bible underlines the command by teaching that when God's people care for the poor, they imitate God himself. But that is not all.

God's Word teaches a very hard, disturbing truth. *Those who neglect the poor and oppressed are really not God's people at all*—no matter how frequently they practice their religious rituals nor how orthodox are their creeds and confessions.

God thundered again and again through the prophets that worship in the context of mistreatment of the poor and disadvantaged is an outrage. Isaiah denounced Israel (he called it Sodom and Gomorrah!) because it tried to worship Yahweh and oppress the weak at the same time:

> Hear the word of the Lord, you rulers of Sodom! Give ear to the teaching of our God, you people of Gomorrah! "What to me is the multitude of your sacrifices? . . . Bring no more vain offerings; incense is an abomination to me. New moon and sabbath and the calling of assemblies—I cannot endure iniquity and solemn assembly. Your new moons and your appointed feasts my soul hates; . . . even though you make many prayers, I will not listen; your hands are full of blood." (Isaiah 1:10–15)

What does God want? The very next verses tell us. "Cease to do evil, learn to do good; seek justice, correct oppression; defend the fatherless, plead for the widow" (Isaiah 1:16–17).

Equally powerful are Isaiah's words against mixing fasting and injustice:

> Why have we fasted, and thou seest it not? Why have we humbled ourselves, and thou takest no knowledge of it?" Behold, in the day of your fast you seek your own pleasure, and oppress all your workers. . . . Is not this the fast that I choose: to loose the bonds of wickedness, to undo the thongs of the yoke, to let the oppressed go free, and to break every yoke? Is it not to share your bread with the hungry, and bring the homeless poor into your house? (Isaiah 58:3–7)

God's words through the prophet Amos are also harsh:

I hate, I despise your feasts, and I take no delight in your solemn assemblies. Even though you offer me your burnt offerings and cereal offerings, I will not accept them. . . . But let justice roll down like waters, and righteousness like an ever-flowing stream. (Amos 5:21–24)[26]

Earlier, the prophet had condemned the rich and powerful for oppressing the poor. They even bribed judges to prevent redress in the courts. Their worship was a mockery and an abomination to the God of the poor, who wants justice, not mere religious rituals.[27]

God has not changed. Jesus repeated the same theme. He warned the people about the scribes "who devour widows' houses and for a pretense make long prayers" (Mark 12:40). Their pious-looking garments and frequent visits to the synagogue were a sham. Jesus was a Hebrew prophet in the tradition of Amos and Isaiah. Like them he announced God's outrage against those who try to mix pious practices and mistreatment of the poor.

The prophetic word against religious hypocrites raises a difficult question. Are the people who call themselves by Christ's name truly God's people if they neglect the poor? Is the church really the church if it does not work to free the oppressed?

We have seen how God declared that the people of Israel were really Sodom and Gomorrah rather than the people of God (Isaiah 1:10). God could not tolerate their exploitation of the poor and disadvantaged any longer. Hosea solemnly announced that, because of their sins, Israel was no longer God's people and he was no longer their God (Hosea 1:8–9). In fact, God destroyed them.

Jesus expressed it even more pointedly. To those who do not feed the hungry, clothe the naked, and visit the prisoners, he will speak a terrifying word at the final judgment: "Depart from me, you cursed, into the eternal fire prepared for the devil and his angels" (Matthew 25:41). The meaning is clear. Jesus intends that his disciples imitate his own concern for the poor and needy. Those who disobey will experience eternal damnation.

But perhaps we have misinterpreted Matthew 25. Some people think that "the least of these" (v. 45) and "the least of these who are members of my family" (v. 40 NRSV) refer only to Christians. This exegesis is not certain. But even if the primary reference of these words is to poor believers, other aspects of Jesus' teaching not only permit but require us to extend the meaning of

Matthew 25 to both believers and unbelievers who are poor and oppressed. The story of the good Samaritan teaches that anybody in need is our neighbor (Luke 10:29–37). Matthew 5:43–45 (NRSV) is even more explicit:

> You have heard that it was said, "You shall love your neighbor and hate your enemy." But I say to you, Love your enemies and pray for those who persecute you, so that you may be children of your Father in heaven; for he makes his sun rise on the evil and on the good, and sends rain on the righteous and on the unrighteous.

The ideal in the Qumran community (known to us as the place where the Dead Sea Scrolls were found) was indeed to "love all the sons of light" and "hate all the sons of darkness" (1 QS 1:9–10, the Essenes' Community Rule). Even in the Old Testament, Israelites were commanded to love the neighbor who was the child of their own people and ordered not to seek the prosperity of Ammonites and Moabites (Leviticus 19:17–18; Deuteronomy 23:36). But Jesus forbids his followers to limit their concern to the neighbors who are members of their own ethnic or religious group. On the other hand, he commands his followers to imitate God, who does good for all people everywhere.

As George Ladd said, "Jesus redefines the meaning of love for neighbor; it means love for any man in need."[28] In light of the parable of the good Samaritan and the clear teaching of Matthew 5:43–48, one is compelled to say that part of the full teaching of Matthew 25 is that those who fail to aid the poor and oppressed (whether they are believers or not) are simply not the people of God.

We find the same message in 1 John 3:17–18 (NRSV): "How does God's love abide in anyone who has the world's goods and sees a brother or sister in need and yet refuses help? Little children, let us love, not in word or speech, but in truth and action." (See also James 2:14–17.)

Again the words are plain. What do they mean for rich Christians who demand increasing affluence while poor Christians in developing nations suffer from malnutrition, deformed bodies and brains, even starvation? The text says that if we fail to aid the needy, we do not have God's love—no matter what we may say. It is deeds that count, not pious phrases and saintly speeches. Regardless of what we do or say at 11:00 A.M. on Sunday morning, rich Christians who neglect the poor are not the people of God.

But still the question persists. Does continuing sin mean that professing believers are really not Christians? Obviously not. The Christian knows that sinful selfishness continues to plague even the most saintly. Salvation is by grace alone, not works of righteousness. We are members of the people of God not because of our own righteousness but solely because of Christ's death for us.

That response is true—but inadequate by itself. Matthew 25 and 1 John 3 surely mean more than that the people of God are disobedient (but still justified all the same) when they persistently neglect the poor. These verses pointedly assert that some people so disobey God that they are not his people at all in spite of their pious profession. Neglect of the poor is one of the oft repeated biblical signs of such disobedience. Certainly none of us would claim that we fulfill Matthew 25 perfectly. And we cling to the hope of forgiveness. But there comes a point (and, thank God, he alone knows where!) when neglect of the poor is not forgiven. It is punished. Eternally.

Is it not possible that many rich "Christians" have reached that point? North Americans and Europeans earn sixty-one times as much as the people in poor countries, but we give only a tiny fraction of our affluence to the church. Most churches spend much of that pittance on themselves. Can we claim we are obeying the biblical command to have a special concern for the poor? Can we honestly say we are imitating God's concern for the poor and oppressed? If the Bible is true, can we seriously hope to experience eternal love rather than eternal separation from the God of the poor?

The biblical teaching that Yahweh has a special concern for the poor and oppressed is without ambiguity. But that does not mean, as some assert today, that God is biased in favor of the poor. In fact, Scripture explicitly forbids partiality. "You shall do no injustice in judgment; you shall not be partial to the poor or defer to the great, but in righteousness shall you judge your neighbor" (Leviticus 19:15; also Deuteronomy 1:11). Exodus 23:3 contains the same injunction: "Nor shall you be partial to a poor man in his suit."

The most crucial point for us, however, is not God's impartiality, but rather the result of his freedom from bias. The text declares Yahweh's impartiality and then immediately portrays God's tender care for the weak and disadvantaged. "For the Lord your God is God of gods and Lord of Lords, the great, the mighty, and the terrible God, who is not partial and takes no bribe. He executes justice for the fatherless and the widow, and loves the sojourner, giving him food and clothing" (Deuteronomy 10:17–18).

God is not partial. He has the same loving concern for each person he has created.[29] Precisely for that reason he cares as much for the weak and disadvantaged as he does for the strong and fortunate. By contrast with the way you and I, as well as the comfortable and powerful of every age and society, normally act toward the poor, God seems to have an overwhelming bias in favor of the poor. But he is biased only in contrast with our sinful unconcern. It is only when we take our sinful preoccupation with the successful and wealthy as natural and normative that God's equal concern for all looks like a bias for the poor.

Is God on the Side of the Poor?

Before we can answer whether or not God is on the side of the poor, we need to remember some things God is not. First, as mentioned above, God is not biased. Second, material poverty is not a biblical ideal. Third, being poor and oppressed does not make people members of the church. (The poor disobey God just as much as the rich and middle class; they too need to repent and be saved by God's justifying grace.) Fourth, God does not care more about the salvation of the poor than of the rich. Fifth, we dare not start with some ideologically interpreted context of oppression (for example, Marxist analysis) and then reinterpret Scripture from that ideological bias. Sixth, God does not overlook the sin of those who are poor due to sloth or alcoholism. God punishes such sinners.[30]

God, however, is not neutral. His freedom from bias does not mean that he maintains neutrality in the struggle for justice. The Bible clearly and repeatedly teaches that God is at work in history exalting the poor and casting down the rich who got that way by oppressing or neglecting the poor. In that sense, God is on the side of the poor. He has a special concern for them because of their vulnerability.

God demands that all people have the opportunity to earn a reasonable living. For that reason, he works to empower the poor. The God of the Bible is, in the sense just indicated, on the side of the poor precisely because he is not biased, precisely because he is a God of impartial justice who cares equally about everyone.

The rich often neglect or oppose justice because it demands that they end their oppression and share with the poor. God actively opposes that kind of rich person and rich society, but that does not mean God loves the rich any less than the poor. God longs for the salvation of the rich and the poor. God desires fulfillment, joy, and happiness for all his creatures, and he knows that neither those who are oppressed nor those who do the oppressing find those things.

God's equal concern for everyone, however, does not mean that God is neutral in contexts of neglect and oppression. Genuine biblical repentance and conversion lead people to turn away from all sin—including economic oppression.[31] Salvation for the rich includes freedom from the sin of being unjust. Thus God's desire for the salvation and fulfillment of the rich is in complete harmony with the scriptural teaching that God is on the side of the poor in the specific sense that God actively seeks justice for those who are oppressed and neglected. In fact, by pulling down oppressors and lifting up the oppressed, God does what is good for both groups.

Our problem is not primarily one of ethics. It is not that we have failed to live what our teachers have taught. It is that our theology itself has been unbiblical. By largely ignoring the central biblical teaching of God's special concern for the poor, our theology has been profoundly unorthodox. The Bible has just as much to say about this doctrine as it does about Jesus' resurrection. And yet we insist on the resurrection as a criterion of orthodoxy and largely ignore the equally prominent biblical teaching that God actively demands justice for the poor and the oppressed.

Please do not misunderstand my point. I am not saying that the resurrection is unimportant. The bodily resurrection of Jesus of Nazareth is absolutely central to Christian faith and anyone who denies it has fallen into heresy.[32] But if centrality in Scripture is any criterion of doctrinal importance, the biblical teaching about God's concern for the poor ought to be an important doctrine for Christians.

Those who consider themselves most orthodox have fallen into theological liberalism on this issue. We usually think of liberalism in terms of classical nineteenth-century liberals who denied the deity, the atonement, and the bodily resurrection of Jesus our Lord. And that is correct. People who abandon those central biblical doctrines have indeed fallen into terrible heresy. But notice what the essence of theological liberalism is—it is allowing our thinking and living to be shaped by society's views and values rather than by biblical revelation. Liberal theologians thought that belief in the deity of Christ and his bodily resurrection was incompatible with modern science, and they followed supposedly scientific thinking rather than Scripture.

Theologically conservative Christians rightly called attention to this heresy—and then tragically made exactly the same move in another area. We have allowed the economic values of our affluent, materialistic society to shape our thinking and acting toward the poor.

In evangelical circles today it is much easier to insist on an orthodox Christology than to insist that God has a special concern for the poor. We have allowed our theology to be shaped by the economic preferences of our materialistic contemporaries rather than by Scripture. And that is to fall into theological liberalism. We are not nearly as orthodox as we claim to be.

Past failure, however, is no reason for despair. I think we mean it when we sing, "I'd rather have Jesus than houses or lands." I think we mean it when we write and affirm doctrinal statements that boldly declare our willingness to believe and live whatever Scripture teaches.

But if we do mean it, if we do believe the biblical doctrine that God and his people have a special concern for the poor and oppressed, we must teach it and live it in a world of injustice and starvation. Unless we drastically reshape both our theology and our church life so that God's concern for the poor and oppressed is as central in our theology and programs as it is in Scripture, we will demonstrate to the world that our verbal commitment to *sola scriptura* is a dishonest ideological support for an unjust, materialistic status quo.

According to the Bible, it is central to the very nature of God to demand justice for the poor and oppressed. In light of this biblical teaching, how biblical is our theology? I think we must confess that rich Christians are largely on the side of the rich rather than the poor. But imagine what would happen if all our church institutions—our youth organizations, our publications, our colleges and seminaries, our congregations and denominational headquarters—would all dare to undertake a comprehensive two-year examination of their programs and activities to answer this question: Is there the same balance and emphasis on justice for the poor and oppressed in our programs as there is in Scripture? If we were to do this with an unconditional readiness to change whatever did not correspond with the scriptural revelation of God's special concern for the poor and oppressed, I predict that we would unleash a new movement of biblical social concern that would transform the world.

I hope and believe that in the next decades millions of Christians will allow this important biblical truth to fundamentally reshape our culturally conditioned theology and our unbiblically one-sided programs and institutions. If that happens, we will forge a new, truly biblical theology of liberation that will change the course of modern history.

Study Questions

1. Review the five major foundations for the thesis that God has a special concern for the poor. Which do you find most convincing? Least convincing? Why?
2. Why does it seem that God is biased toward the poor? In what ways is he always unbiased?
3. Does the preaching and teaching you hear place as much emphasis on the welfare of the poor as does the Bible? If not, how do you explain the difference?
4. If we ignore the poor, what are we saying about our belief in God?
5. What does Matthew 25:31–46 really mean?

4

Economic Fellowship and Economic Justice

I do not mean that others should be eased and you burdened, but that as a matter of equality your abundance at the present time should supply their want, so that their abundance may supply your want, that there may be equality. As it is written, "He who gathered much had nothing over, and he who gathered little had no lack." (2 Corinthians 8:13–15)

GOD REQUIRES radically transformed economic relationships among his people because sin has alienated us from God and from each other. The result is personal selfishness, structural injustice, and economic oppression. Among the people of God, however, the power of sin is broken. The community of the redeemed is to display a dramatically new set of personal, social, and economic relationships. The quality of life among the people of God is to be a sign of the coming perfection and justice that will be revealed when the kingdoms of this world finally and completely become the kingdom of our Lord at his Second Coming.

God wants structures where those who can work have the productive resouces to earn their own way, and those who cannot work are adequately cared for. Economic relationships that are redeemed within the body of Christ will point convincingly to the coming kingdom. And—as if that were not enough—the loving oneness among Christians is to become so visible that it convinces the world that Jesus came from the Father (John 17:20–23).

Does this mean this chapter applies only to the church? Not at all.

There is, of course, a difference between theocratic Israel or a voluntary community of Christian believers on the one hand and a modern, secular, pluralistic society on the other. I believe that the first application of the biblical teaching on economic relations is to the church, and I expect the church to be well ahead of the rest of society in implementing God's will. But I also believe there is a secondary application of the biblical social vision to secular society. God's revelation to Israel about how to structure society for the sake of wholeness and justice was not arbitrary. Rather, it is the Creator's communication about how people live together in social harmony. To the extent that a modern society approximates the biblical ideal in any area (say, economic justice), to that extent it will experience wholeness. This chapter therefore also provides important clues about a biblical perspective on economic justice for the whole society.

Central to the discussion is the biblical material on Israel and the land.[1]

Capital in an Agricultural Society

The contrast between early Israel and surrounding societies was striking.[2] In Egypt, most of the land belonged to Pharaoh or the temples. In most other near-Eastern contexts a feudal system of landholding prevailed. The king granted large tracts of land, worked by landless laborers, to a small number of elite royal vassals. Only at the theological level did this feudal system exist in early Israel. Yahweh the King owned all the land and made important demands on those to whom he gave it to use. Under Yahweh, however, each family had their own land. Israel's ideal was decentralized, and family "ownership" understood as stewardship under Yahweh's absolute ownership. In the period of the Judges, the pattern in Israel was, according to one scholar, "free peasants on small land holdings of equal size and apportioned by the clans."[3]

Land was the basic capital in early Israel's agricultural economy, and the land seems to have been divided in such a way that each extended family had the resources to produce the things needed for a decent life.

Joshua 18 and Numbers 26 contain accounts of the division of the land. They represent Israel's social ideal with regard to the land. In Joshua 18:1-10, the people came before God in an act of worship and then proceeded to measure the land and share it (by casting lots) among the various tribes. Numbers 26:52-56 states that the land was allocated according to the size of each tribe. Some approximation of equality of land ownership is implied. Albrecht Alt, a prominent Old Testament scholar, goes so far as to say that the prophets understood Yahweh's ancient regulation on property to be "one man-one house-one allotment of land."[4] Decentralized land ownership by extended families was the economic base for a relatively egalitarian society of small landowners and vinedressers in the time of the Judges.[5]

The story of Naboth's vineyard (1 Kings 21) demonstrates the importance of each family's ancestral land. Frequent Old Testament references about not moving ancient boundary markers (e.g., Deuteronomy 19:14; 27:17; Job 24:2; Proverbs 22:28; Hosea 5:10) support the concept that Israel's social ideal called for each family to have available to them the land needed to supply life's necessities.

"Necessities" is not be to understood as the minimum necessary to keep from starving. In the nonhierarchical, relatively egalitarian society of small farmers depicted above, families possessed resources to earn a living that would have been considered reasonable and acceptable, not embarrassingly minimal. That is not to suggest that every family had exactly the same income. It does mean, however, that every family had an equality of economic opportunity up to the point that they had the resources to earn a living that would enable them not only to meet minimal needs of food, clothing, and housing but also to be respected participants in the community. Possessing their own land enabled each extended family to acquire the necessities for a decent life through responsible work.

The Year of Jubilee

Two astonishing biblical texts—Leviticus 25 and Deuteronomy 15—show how important this basic equality of opportunity was to God. The jubilee text in Leviticus demanded that the land return to the original owners every fifty years. And Deuteronomy 15 called for the release of debts every seven years.

Leviticus 25 is one of the most radical texts in all of Scripture,[6] at least it seems that way to people committed either to communism or to unrestricted capitalism. Every fifty years, God said, the land was to return to the original owners! Physical handicaps, death of a breadwinner, or lack of natural ability may lead some families to become poorer than others. But God does not want such disadvantages to lead to ever-increasing extremes of wealth and poverty with the result that the poor eventually lack the basic resources to earn a decent livelihood. God therefore gave his people a law to guarantee that no family would permanently lose its land. Every fifty years, the land returned to the original owners so that every family had enough productive resources to function as dignified, participating members of the community (Leviticus 25:10–24).

In an agricultural society, land is capital, so land was the basic means of producing wealth in Israel. At the beginning, as we have seen, the land was divided more or less equally among the tribes and families.[7] Apparently God wanted that basic equality of economic opportunity to continue. Hence his command to return all land to the original owners every fifty years. Private property was not abolished. Regularly, however, the means of producing wealth was to be equalized—up to the point of every family having the resources to earn a decent living.

What is the theological basis for this startling command? Yahweh's ownership of everything is the presupposition. The land cannot be sold permanently because Yahweh owns it: "The land shall not be sold in perpetuity, for the land is mine; for you are strangers and sojourners with me" (Leviticus 25:23).

God, the landowner, permits his people to sojourn on his good earth, cultivate it, eat its produce, and enjoy its beauty. But we are only stewards. Stewardship is one of the central theological categories of any biblical understanding of our relationship to the land and economic resources.[8]

Before and after the year of jubilee, land could be "bought" or "sold." Actually, the buyer purchased a specific number of harvests, not the land itself (Leviticus 25:16). And woe to the person who tried to get more than a just price for the intervening harvests from the date of purchase to the next jubilee!

> If the years are many you shall increase the price, and if the years are few you shall diminish the price, for it is the number of the crops that he is selling to you. You shall not wrong one another, but you shall fear your God; for I am the Lord your God. (Leviticus 25:16–17)

Yahweh is Lord of all, even of economics. There is no hint here of a sacred law of supply and demand that operates independently of biblical ethics and the Lordship of Yahweh. The people of God should submit to God, and God demands economic justice among his people.

The assumption in this text that people must suffer the consequences of wrong choices is also striking. A whole generation or more could suffer the loss of ancestral land, but every fifty years the basic source of wealth would be returned so that each family had the opportunity to provide for its basic needs.

Verses 25–28 imply that this equality of opportunity is a higher value than that of absolute property rights. If a person became poor and sold his land to a more prosperous neighbor but then recovered enough to buy back his land before the jubilee, the new owner was obligated to return it. The original owner's right to have his ancestral land to earn his own way is a higher right than that of the second owner to maximize profits.

This passage prescribes justice in a way that haphazard handouts by wealthy philanthropists never will. The year of jubilee was an institutionalized structure that affected all Israelites automatically. It was the poor family's right to recover their inherited land at the jubilee. Returning the land was not a charitable courtesy that the wealthy might extend if they pleased.[9]

Interestingly, the principles of jubilee challenge both unrestricted capitalism and communism in a fundamental way. Only God is an absolute owner. And the right of each family to have the means to earn a living takes priority over a purchaser's "property rights" or a totally free market economy. At the same time, jubilee affirms not only the right but the importance of private property managed by families who understand that they are stewards responsible to God. This text does *not* point us in the direction of the communist model where the state owns all the land. God wants each family to have the resources to produce its own livelihood. Why? To strengthen the family (This is a very important "pro-family" text!). To give people the freedom to participate in shaping history. And to prevent the centralization of power and totalitarianism, which almost always accompanies centralized ownership of land or capital by either the state or small elites.

One final aspect of Leviticus 25 is striking. I believe it is more than coincidental that the trumpet blast announcing the jubilee sounded on the Day of Atonement (Leviticus 25:9). Reconciliation with God is the precondition for reconciliation with brothers and sisters.[10] Conversely, genuine reconciliation with God leads inevitably to a transformation of all other relationships. Reconciled with God by the sacrifice on the Day of Atonement, the more prosperous Israelites were summoned to liberate the poor by freeing Hebrew slaves and by returning all land to the original owners.[11]

Unfortunately, we do not know whether the people of Israel ever practiced the year of jubilee. The absence of references to it in the historical books suggests that it may never have been implemented.[12] Regardless of its antiquity or possible lack of implementation, however, Leviticus 25 remains a part of God's authoritative Word.

The teaching of the prophets about the land underlines the principles of Leviticus 25.

In the tenth to the eighth centuries B.C., a major centralization of landholding occurred. Poorer farmers lost their land, becoming landless laborers or slaves. The prophets regularly denounced the bribery, political assassination, and economic oppression that destroyed the earlier decentralized economy described above. Elijah condemned Ahab's seizure of Naboth's vineyard (1 Kings 21). Isaiah attacked rich landowners for adding field to field until they dwelt alone in the countryside, because the smaller farmers had been destroyed (Isaiah 15:5–8).

The prophets, however, did not merely condemn. They also expressed a powerful eschatological hope for a future day of justice when all would have their own land again. In the "latter days," the future day of justice and wholeness, "they shall all sit under their own vines and under their own fig trees" (Micah 4:4; cf. also Zechariah 3:10). No longer will the leaders oppress the people; instead they will guarantee that all people again enjoy their ancestral land (Ezekiel 45:1–9, especially vv. 8–9).

In the giving of the land, the denunciation of oppressors who seized the land of the poor, and the vision of a new day when once again all will delight in the fruits of their own land and labor, we see a social ideal being depicted in which families are to have the economic means to earn their own way. A basic equality of economic opportunity up to the point that all can at least provide for their own basic needs through responsible work is the norm. Failure to act responsibly has economic consequences, so there is no assumption of equality. Hints of economic incentive for extra effort also are present. Central, however, is the demand that each family have the necessary capital (land) so that responsible stewardship will result in an economically decent life.[13]

The Sabbatical Year

God's law also provides for liberation of soil, slaves, and debtors every seven years. Again the concern is justice for the poor and disadvantaged as well as the well-being of the land.

Every seven years the land is to lie fallow (Exodus 23:10–11; Leviticus 25:2–7).[14] The purpose, apparently, is both ecological and humanitarian. Not planting any crops every seventh year helps preserve the fertility of the soil. It also was God's way of showing his concern for the poor: "For six years you shall sow your land and gather in its yield; but the seventh year you shall let it rest and lie fallow, that the poor of your people may eat" (Exodus 23:10–11). In the seventh year the poor were free to gather for themselves whatever grew spontaneously in the fields and vineyards.

Hebrew slaves also received their freedom in the sabbatical year (Deuteronomy 15:12–18). Poverty sometimes forced Israelites to sell themselves as slaves to more prosperous neighbors (Leviticus 25:39–40).[15] But this inequality and lack of property, God decrees, is not to be permanent. At the end of six years Hebrew slaves are to be set free. And masters are to share the proceeds of their joint labors with departing male slaves:

> And when you let him go free from you, you shall not let him go empty handed; you shall furnish him liberally out of your flock, out of your threshing floor, and out of your wine press; as the Lord your God has blessed you, you shall give to him. (Deuteronomy 15:13–14; see also Exodus 21:2–6).

The freed slave would thereby have the means to earn his own way.[16]

The sabbatical provision on loans is even more surprising (Deuteronomy 15:1–6) if, as some scholars think, the text calls for cancellation of debts every seventh year.[17] Yahweh even adds a footnote for those with a sharp eye for loopholes: It is sinful to refuse a loan to a poor man just because it is the sixth year and financial loss might occur in twelve months.

> Be careful that you do not entertain a mean thought, thinking, "The seventh year, the year of remission, is near," and therefore view your needy neighbor with hostility and give nothing; your neighbor might cry to the Lord against you, and you would incur guilt. Give liberally and be ungrudging when you do so, for on this account the Lord your God will bless you in all your work and in all that you undertake. (vv. 9–10)

As in the case of the year of jubilee, this passage involves structured justice rather than mere charity. The sabbatical release of debts was an institutionalized mechanism to prevent the kind of economic divisions where a few people would possess all the capital while others had no productive resources.

Deuteronomy 15 is both an idealistic statement of God's demand and also a realistic reference to Israel's sinful performance. Verse 4 promises that there will be no poor in Israel—*if* they obey all of God's commands! But God knew they would not attain that standard. Hence the recognition that poor people will always exist (v. 11). The conclusion, however, is not permission to ignore the needy because hordes of paupers will always exceed available resources. God commands precisely the opposite: "Since there will never cease to be some in need on the earth, I therefore command you, 'Open your hand to the poor and needy neighbor, in your land'" (v. 11).

Jesus knew, and Deuteronomy implies, that sinful persons and societies will always produce poor people (Matthew 26:11). Rather than justifying neglect, however, God intends that this knowledge will be used by his people as a reminder to show concern and to create structural mechanisms that promote justice.

The sabbatical year, unfortunately, was practiced only sporadically. Some texts suggest that failure to obey this law was one reason for the Babylonian exile (2 Chronicles 36:20–21; Leviticus 26:34–36).[18] Disobedience, however, does not negate God's demand. Institutionalized structures to reduce poverty are central to God's will for his people.

Laws on Tithing and Gleaning

Israel's laws on tithing and gleaning are part of God's provision for those who temporarily lack productive capital. The law calls for one tenth of all farm produce to be set aside as a tithe.

> At the end of every three years you shall bring forth all the tithe of your produce in the same year; . . . and the Levite . . . and the sojourner, the fatherless, and the widow, who are within your towns, shall come and eat and be filled; that the Lord your God may bless you. (Deuteronomy 14:28–29; see also Leviticus 27:30–32; Deuteronomy 26:12–15; Numbers 18:21–32)[19]

The poor widow Ruth was able to survive because of this law. When she and Naomi returned to Bethlehem penniless, Ruth, the grandmother of the future King David, went into the fields at harvest time and gathered the stalks of grain dropped by the gleaners (Ruth 2). God's law that farmers should leave for the poor some of the harvest, including the corners of grain fields, made it possible for Ruth to do this. Grapes that had been dropped accidentally also were to be left. "You shall leave them for the poor and for the sojourner: I am the Lord your God" (Leviticus 19:10).

The memory of their own poverty and oppression in Egypt was to prompt them to leave generous gleanings for the poor, the sojourner, the widow, and the fatherless. "You shall remember that you were a slave in the land of Egypt; therefore I command you to do this" (Deuteronomy 24:22).

The laws on gleaning did not guarantee handouts; Ruth had to work hard for the grain she received. But they did guarantee poor people the opportunity to acquire basic necessities.[20]

Models to Follow and Avoid

How do we apply biblical revelation concerning the year of jubilee, the sabbatical year, tithes, and gleaning to today's situation? Should we try to incorporate these mechanisms into modern society? Are these laws, or the basic principles behind them, applicable to the church at all?

God gave Israel the law so that they would know how to live together in peace and justice. The church is now the new people of God (Galatians 3:6–9; 6:16; 1 Peter 2:9–10). As Paul and other New Testament writers indicate, parts of the Mosaic law (the ceremonial law, for instance) do not apply to New Testament believers (i.e., the church). But there is no indication that God's moral law has ceased to apply (Matthew 5:17–20, Romans 8:4).[21] And embedded in the civil law of the Old Testament are principles that both guide the church and also inform our understanding of economic justice for society.

How then do we apply the laws we have discussed? Should we try to revive the ones in Leviticus 25 and Deuteronomy 15?

Certainly not. The specific provisions of the year of jubilee are not binding today. Modern technological society is vastly different from rural Palestine. If Kansas farmers left grain standing in the corners of their fields, it would not help the hungry in inner-city New York or rural India. We need methods appropriate to our own civilization. It is the principles, not the details, that are important today.

The history of the prohibition against charging interest illustrates this. The annual rate of interest in the ancient Near East was incredibly high—often 25 percent or more.[22] It is not hard, therefore, to understand the reason for a law that prohibits charging interest to fellow Israelites (Exodus 22:25; Deuteronomy 23:19–20; Leviticus 25:35–38).[23] According to *The International Critical Commentary*, this legislation reflects a time when most loans were not commercial but charitable. Commercial loans to establish or extend a business were not common. Most loans were needed by a poor person or by someone in an emergency.[24] The texts on interest make it clear that the well-being of the poor is a central concern: "If you lend money to my people, to the poor among you, you shall not deal with them as a creditor; you shall not exact interest from them" (Exodus 22:25). The legislation on interest is part of an extensive set of laws designed to protect the poor and to prevent the creation of a class of desperately poor folk with no productive resources.

Failing to understand this, the Christian church attempted to apply these texts in a legalistic way. Several church councils wrestled with the question. Eventually, in 1179 at the Third Lateran Council, all interest on loans was prohibited. But the results were tragic. Medieval monarchs invited Jews, who were not bound by the church's teaching, to be money lenders. This practice resulted in intense anti-Semitism and in casuistic schemes developed by theologians to circumvent the prohibition.[25]

This misguided preoccupation with the letter of the law and the resulting adoption of an unworkable, legalistic application helped discredit, or at least obscure, the important biblical teaching that the God of the poor is Lord of economics—Lord even of interest rates. It also contributed to the modern mentality that views loans and banking—indeed the whole field of economics—as independent and autonomous. From the standpoint of revealed faith, of course, such a view is heretical. It stems from modern secularism, not from the Bible.[26]

This history warns us against wooden application of God's living Word. But we dare not let past mistakes end in timid silence. These biblical texts demand that Christian lenders count the borrower's need more important than their own maximization of profit.

In applying the biblical teachings on the year of jubilee, the sabbatical year, gleaning, and tithing, then, we must discover the underlying principles. Then we can search for contemporary strategies to give flesh to these basic principles.

The texts we have examined show that God wills justice, not mere charity. Therefore, Christians should work to eliminate poverty among believers. At the same time, Christians informed by the biblical understanding of economic justice will search for effective structures in the larger society that enable every family to have the basic capital needed to earn a living. There is an implication here that private property is so good that God wants everybody to have some!

Jesus' New Community

First-century Christians reaffirmed the Old Testament teaching. Jesus walked the roads of Galilee announcing the startling news that the kingdom of peace and righteousness was at hand. Economic relationships in the new community of his followers were a powerful sign confirming this awesome announcement.

The Hebrew prophets had not only predicted that Israel would be destroyed because of her idolatry and oppression of the poor; they had also proclaimed a message of hope—the hope of a future messianic kingdom. The days are coming, they promised, when God will raise up a righteous branch from the Davidic line. Peace, righteousness, and justice will then abound in a new, redeemed society. When the shoot comes from the stump of Jesse, Isaiah predicted, the poor and meek will finally receive their due: "With righteousness he shall judge the poor, and decide with equity for the meek of the earth" (Isaiah 11:4; see also Isaiah 9:6–7; 61:1; Jeremiah 23:5; Hosea 2:18–20).

The essence of the good news that Jesus proclaimed was that the expected messianic kingdom had come.[27] Certainly the kingdom Jesus announced disappointed popular Jewish expectations. He did not recruit an army to drive out the Romans. He did not establish a free Jewish state. But neither did he remain alone as an isolated, individualistic prophet. He called and trained disciples. He established a visible community of disciples joined together by their submission to him as Lord.

His new community began to live the values of the promised kingdom. As a result, all relationships, even economic ones, were transformed in the community of Jesus' followers.

They shared a common purse (John 12:6).[28] Judas administered the common fund, buying provisions or giving to the poor at Jesus' direction (John 13:29). The new community of sharing extended beyond Jesus and the Twelve. It included a number of women whom Jesus had healed. The women traveled with Jesus and the disciples, sharing their financial resources with them (Luke 8:1–3; see also Mark 15:40–41).[29]

Starting with this understanding, some of Jesus' words gain new meaning and power. Consider his advice to the rich young man.

When Jesus asked the rich young man to sell his goods and give to the poor, he did not say, "Become destitute and friendless." Rather, he said, "Come, follow me" (Matthew 19:21). In other words, he invited him to join a community of sharing and love, where his security would not be based on individual property holdings, but on openness to the Spirit and on the loving care of new-found brothers and sisters.[30]

Jesus invited the rich young man to share the joyful common life of his new kingdom.

Jesus' words in Mark 10:29–30 used to puzzle me:

> Truly, I say to you, there is no one who has left house or brothers or sisters or mother or father or children or lands, for my sake and for the gospel, who will not receive a hundredfold now in this time, houses and brothers and sisters and mothers and children and lands, with persecutions, and in the age to come eternal life.

Why, I used to wonder, did he end his advice with a promise that seems too good to be true: "But seek first his kingdom and his righteousness, and all these things [i.e., food, clothing, and so on] shall be yours as well." I didn't know how to make sense out of this seemingly naive statement.

But the words came alive with meaning when I read them in the context of what was happening among his followers. Jesus had begun a new community, a new social order, a new kingdom of faithful followers who were experiencing redeemed economic relationships.

The common purse of Jesus' disciples symbolized their amazing availability to each other. In that kind of community, there *would* be genuine economic security. Each person would indeed have many more loving brothers and sisters than before. The economic resources available in difficult times would in fact be compounded a hundredfold and more. The resources of the entire community of obedient disciples would be available to anyone in need. Such unprecedented unselfishness would certainly challenge surrounding society so pointedly that many would want to join while others, out of jealousy, would want to destroy through persecution. But even in the most desperate days, the promise would not be empty. Even if persecution led to death, children of martyred parents would receive new mothers and fathers in the community of believers.

In the community of the redeemed, all relationships are being transformed. Jesus and his first followers vividly demonstrated that the old covenant's pattern of economic relationships among God's people is not only to be continued but also deepened.

The Jerusalem Model

The massive economic sharing of the earliest Christian church is indisputable. "Now the company of those who believed were of one heart and soul, and no one said that any of the things which he possessed was his own, but they had everything in common" (Acts 4:32).

The evidence in the early chapters of Acts is abundant and unambiguous (Acts 2:43–47; 4:32–37; 5:1–11; 6:1–7). The early church continued the pattern of economic sharing practiced by Jesus. Immediately after reporting the three thousand conversions at Pentecost, Acts notes that "all who believed were together and had all things in common" (2:44). Whenever anyone was in need, they shared. Giving surplus to needy brothers and sisters was not enough. They regularly dipped into capital reserves and sold property to aid the needy. Barnabas sold a field he owned (4:36–37). Ananias and Sapphira sold property, but then lied about the price (5:3–4).

Long ago, God promised Israel that obedience would eliminate poverty among his people (Deuteronomy 15:4). That promise came true in the earliest church. "There was not a needy person among them, for as many as were possessors of lands or houses sold them; . . . and distribution was made to each as any had need" (Acts 4:34–35).

Two millennia later the texts still throb with the joy and excitement of the first community. They ate meals together "with glad and generous hearts" (Acts 2:46). They experienced an exciting unity as all sensed they "were of one heart and soul" (4:32). They were not isolated individuals, struggling alone to follow Jesus. A new community, in which all areas of life (including economics) were being transformed, became a joyful reality.

The evangelistic impact of their demonstration of oneness is striking. The texts repeatedly relate the transformed economic relationships in the Jerusalem church to their phenomenal evangelistic outreach:

> And day by day, attending the temple together and breaking bread in their homes, they partook of food with glad and generous hearts, praising God and having favor with all the people. And the Lord added to their number day by day. (Acts 2:46–47)

The joy and love expressed in their common life was contagious.

Acts 4 underlines the evangelistic impact of their transformed economic relationships. Verse 32 describes their sweeping economic sharing, and the very next verse adds, "And with great power the apostles gave their testimony to the resurrection of the Lord Jesus" (v. 33). Jesus' prayer that the loving unity of his followers would be so striking that it would convince the world that he had come from the Father has been answered—at least once! It happened in the Jerusalem church. The unusual quality of their economic life together gave power to the apostolic preaching.

Acts 6 gives a striking example of how the new system worked. Apparently the Jerusalem church included a significant minority of Hellenists (Greek-speaking Jews, perhaps even Greeks that had converted to Judaism). Somehow, the Jewish-speaking majority had overlooked the needs of the Hellenist widows. When the injustice was pointed out, the church's response was startling. The seven men chosen to look after the matter were all from the minority group! Every one of their names is Greek.[31] The church turned over its funds for needy widows to the minority group that had been discriminated against. What was the result of this new kind of financial fellowship? "And the word of God increased; and the number of disciples multiplied greatly in Jerusalem" (Acts 6:7).

Redeemed economic relationships in the early church resulted in the spread of the Word of God. What a sobering thought! Could the same thing happen today? Would similar economic changes produce a dramatic increase of believers? Probably. Are those who talk about the importance of evangelism prepared to pay the price?

The earliest church did not insist on absolute economic equality. Nor did they abolish private property. Peter reminded Ananias that he had been under no obligation either to sell his property or to donate the proceeds to the church (Acts 5:4). Sharing was voluntary, not compulsory.[32] But love for brothers and sisters was so overwhelming that many freely abandoned legitimate claims to private possessions. "No one said that any of the things which he possessed was his own" (4:32). That does not mean that everyone donated everything. Later in Acts we read that John Mark's mother, Mary, still owned her own house (12:12). Additional passages indicate that others retained some private property.

The tense of the Greek words confirms this interpretation. In both Acts 2:45 and 4:34, the verbs denote continued, repeated action over an extended period of time. Thus the meaning is, "they often sold possessions," or, "they were in the habit of regularly bringing the proceeds of what was being sold."[33] The text does not suggest that the community abolished all private property or that everyone immediately sold everything. It suggests instead that over a period of time, whenever there was need, believers sold lands and houses to aid the needy.

What then was the essence of the transformed economic relationships in the Jerusalem church? The best way to describe their practice is to speak of sweeping liability for and availability to each other. Their sharing was not superficial or occasional. Regularly and repeatedly, "they sold their possessions and goods and distributed them to all, as any had need" (2:45). If the need was greater than current cash reserves, they sold property. They simply gave until the needs were met. The needs of the sister and brother, not legal property rights or future financial security, were the deciding factors. For the earliest Christians, oneness in Christ meant sweeping liability for and availability to the other members of Christ's body.

Unfortunately most Christians ignore the example of the Jerusalem church. Perhaps it is because of the economic self-interest of affluent Christians. We have developed convenient rationales for relegating the pattern of the Jerusalem church to the archivists' attic of irrelevant historical trivia. Why did Paul have to take a collection for the Jerusalem church a few decades later? A modern book offers the familiar response:

> The trouble in Jerusalem was that they turned their capital into income, and had no cushion for hard times, and the Gentile Christians had to come to their rescue. It is possible not to live for bread alone, not to be overcome by materialist values, and at the same time to act responsibly; and this is why the Church may be grateful for the protest of the commune movement, but still consider that it has no answer.[34]

But were the Jerusalem Christians really irresponsible, naive communal-types whom we should respect but certainly not imitate? It is essential to insist that the Jerusalem principle of sweeping financial availability does not require communal living. It did not in Jerusalem. The Christian commune is only one of many faithful models. We dare not let the communal hobgoblin distort our discussion of the Jerusalem model.

But why did the Jerusalem church run into financial difficulty? It is unlikely that economic sharing was to blame. More likely the need was due to a unique set of historical circumstances. Jerusalem attracted an unusually large number of poor people. Since Jews considered alms given in Jerusalem to be particularly meritorious, the many pilgrims to the city were especially generous. As a result, crowds of impoverished beggars flocked to the city. In addition, a disproportionately large number of the elderly gravitated to the Holy City to die or wait for the Messiah (see Luke 2:25, 36). Also, because Jerusalem was the center of Jewish faith, it attracted a large number of rabbis, who depended on charity because they were not paid for teaching. Their students likewise often were poor. Hence the large number of religious scholars in Jerusalem swelled the ranks of the destitute.[35]

And that was not all. Natural disasters struck at mid-century. The Roman historians Suetonius and Tacitus report recurring food shortages and famines during the reign of the Emperor Claudius (A.D. 41–54). Josephus dates such shortages in Palestine around A.D. 44 to 48.[36] At one point, famine was so severe that the Antioch church quickly sent assistance (Acts 11:27–30).

Special circumstances within the first church also caused unusual poverty. Jesus' particular concern for the poor and oppressed probably attracted a disproportionately large number of impoverished persons. Acts records considerable persecution (8:1–3; 9:29; 12:1–5; 23:12–15), so Christians probably experienced discrimination in employment which wreaked havoc with their normal income.[37] Finally, the original Twelve seem to have given up their means of livelihood when they moved from Galilee to Jerusalem, so their need for support would have increased the demand on the church's resources.

These are some of the many reasons why the first community of Christians faced financial difficulty at mid-century. Misguided generosity was not likely a significant factor. In fact, the unusually large number of poor in their midst is probably what made dramatic sharing such an obvious necessity. That the rich among them gave with overflowing generosity to meet a desperate need indicates unconditional discipleship, not naive idealism.

The costly generosity of the first church stands as a challenge to Christians of all ages. They gave visible expression to the oneness of believers. In the new messianic community of Jesus' first followers, God was redeeming all relationships.

Was the beauty of this example a vision that quickly faded? Many believe it was. But the actual practice of the early church proves the contrary.

Economic Koinonia

Paul broadened the vision of economic sharing in a dramatic way by devoting a great deal of time to raising money for Jewish Christians in Jerusalem among Gentile congregations in Greece. In the process he developed intrachurch assistance (within one local church) into interchurch sharing among the scattered congregations of believers. Since Jerusalem is in Asia and Greece belongs to Europe, Paul pioneered intercontinental economic sharing in the church.

From the time of the Exodus, God had taught his chosen people to exhibit transformed economic relations among themselves. With Peter and Paul, however, biblical religion moved beyond one ethnic group and became a universal, multiethnic faith. Paul's collection demonstrated that the oneness of believers entails economic sharing across ethnic and geographic lines.

Paul's concern for economic sharing in the body of Christ began early. Famine struck Palestine in A.D. 46. In response, the believers at Antioch gave *"every one according to his ability,* to send relief to the brethren who lived in

Judea" (Acts 11:29, italics mine). Paul helped Barnabas take this economic assistance from Antioch to Jerusalem.[38]

That trip was just the beginning of Paul's concern for economic sharing. For several years he devoted much time and energy to his great collection. He discusses his concern in several letters. In Galatians he expresses eagerness to assist the poor Jerusalem Christians (Galatians 2:10). He mentions it also in the letter to Rome (Romans 15:22–28) and notes it briefly in 1 Corinthians 16:1–4. The collection is a major preoccupation in 2 Corinthians 8–9. He also arranged for the collection in the churches of Macedonia, Galatia, Corinth, Ephesus, and probably elsewhere.[39]

Knowing he faced certain danger and possible death from angry Jews in Jerusalem, Paul nevertheless insisted on accompanying the offering. While delivering this financial assistance he was arrested for the last time. His letter to the Romans shows that he was not blind to the danger (Romans 15:31). Friends and prophets repeatedly warned Paul as he and the representatives of the contributing churches journeyed toward Jerusalem (Acts 21:4, 10–14). But Paul had a deep conviction that this financial symbol of Christian unity mattered far more even than his own life. "What are you doing, weeping and breaking my heart?" he chided friends imploring him not to accompany the others to Jerusalem. "For I am ready not only to be imprisoned but even to die at Jerusalem for the name of the Lord Jesus" (Acts 21:13). So he continued the journey. His passionate commitment to economic sharing with brothers and sisters led to his final arrest and martyrdom (see Acts 24:17). This is not to suggest that some economic ideal had replaced Paul's central commitment to Christ. But it does mean that Paul understood that embracing Christ means embracing Christ's body and that living out the oneness of Christ's body demands economic sharing.

Why was Paul so concerned with the financial problems of the Jerusalem church? Because of his understanding of Christian fellowship. The word *koinonia* plays an important role in Paul's theology, and it is central in his discussion of the collection.

Koinonia means fellowship with someone or participation in some thing. Believers enjoy fellowship with the Lord Jesus (1 Corinthians 19).[40] Experiencing the *koinonia* of Jesus means having his righteousness imputed to us. It also entails sharing in the self-sacrificing, cross-bearing life he lived (Philippians 3:8–10). Nowhere is the Christian's fellowship with Christ experienced more powerfully than in the Eucharist. Sharing in the Lord's Supper draws the believer into a participation (*koinonia*) in the mystery of the cross: "The cup of blessing which we bless, is it not a participation [*koinonia*] in the blood of Christ? The bread which we break, is it not a participation [*koinonia*] in the body of Christ?" (1 Corinthians 10:16).

Paul's inference is that *koinonia* with Christ involves *koinonia* with all the members of the body of Christ. "Because there is one bread, we who are many are one body, for we all partake of the one bread" (1 Corinthians 10:17; see also 1 John 1:3–4).

As Ephesians 2 teaches, Christ's death for Jew and Gentile, male and female, has broken down all ethnic, gender, and cultural dividing walls. In Christ there is one new person, one new body of believers. When the brothers and sisters share the one bread and the common cup in the Lord's Supper, they symbolize their participation in the one body of Christ.

That is why the class divisions at Corinth so horrified Paul. Apparently wealthy Christians were feasting at the Eucharistic celebration while poor believers were going hungry. Paul angrily denied that they were eating the Lord's Supper at all (1 Corinthians 11:20–22). In fact, they were profaning the Lord's body and blood because they did not discern his body (1 Corinthians 11:27–29). "All who eat and drink without discerning the body, eat and drink judgment against themselves" (v. 29).

But what did Paul mean when he charged that they did not discern the Lord's body? To discern the Lord's body is to understand and live the truth that fellowship with Christ is inseparable from membership in his body, where our oneness in Christ far transcends differences of race or class. Discernment of that one body of believers leads to sweeping availability to and responsibility for the other sisters and brothers. Discernment of that one body prompts us to weep with those who weep and rejoice with those who rejoice. Discernment of that one body is totally incompatible with feasting without sharing in costly ways with other members of the body who are hungry. Those who live a practical denial of their unity and fellowship in Christ, Paul insists, drink judgment on themselves when they go to the Lord's table. In fact, they do not really partake of the Lord's Supper at all.

Once we understand the implication of Paul's teaching on discerning the body in the Lord's Supper, we dare not rest until the scandal of starving Christians is removed. As long as any Christian anywhere in the world is hungry, the Eucharistic celebration of all Christians everywhere in the world is imperfect.

For Paul, intimate fellowship in the body of Christ has economic implications, for he uses the same word, *koinonia*, to designate financial sharing among believers. Early in Paul's ministry, after a dramatic debate, the Jerusalem leaders endorsed his mission to the Gentiles. When they extended the "right hand of fellowship" (*koinonia*), they stipulated a single tangible expression of that fellowship, and Paul promised financial assistance for his fellow Christians in Jerusalem (Galatians 2:9–10).[41]

Paul frequently used the word *koinonia* as a synonym for "collection." He speaks of the "liberality of the fellowship" (*koinonia*) that the Corinthians' generous offering would demonstrate (2 Corinthians 9:13, my translation; see also 8:4).[42] He used the same language to report the Macedonian Christians' offering for Jerusalem. It seemed good to the Macedonians "to make fellowship [*koinonia*] with the poor among the saints at Jerusalem (Romans 15:25, my translation). Indeed, this financial sharing was just one part of a total fellowship. The Gentile Christians had come to share in (he uses the verb form of *koinonia*) the spiritual blessings of the Jews. Therefore it was fitting for the Gentiles to share their material resources. Economic sharing was an obvious and crucial part of Christian fellowship for Paul.[43]

Paul's first guideline for sharing was general: Give all you can. Each person should give "as he may prosper" (1 Corinthians 16:2). But that does not mean a small donation that costs nothing. Paul praised the Macedonians who "gave according to their means . . . and beyond their means" (2 Corinthians 8:3). The Macedonians were extremely poor. Apparently they faced particularly severe financial difficulties at the time when Paul asked for a generous offering (2 Corinthians 8:2). But still they were generous. No hint here of a mechanical ten percent for pauper and millionaire. Giving as much as you can is the Pauline pattern.

Second, giving was voluntary (2 Corinthians 8:3). Paul specifically noted that he was not issuing a command to the Corinthians (2 Corinthians 8:8). Legalism is not the answer.

Paul's third guideline is the most startling. In advising the Corinthians how to share, Paul used the word *equality*.

"I do not mean that others should be eased and you burdened, but that as a matter of equality your abundance at the present time should supply their want, so that their abundance may supply your want, that there may be equality." To support his principle, Paul alludes to the biblical story of the manna. "As it is written, 'He who gathered much had nothing over, and he who gathered little had no lack'" (2 Corinthians 8:13–15).

According to the Exodus account, Moses commanded the people to gather only as much manna as they needed for one day (Exodus 16:13–21). One omer (about four pints) per person would be enough, Moses said. Some greedy souls, however, apparently tried to gather more than they could use. But when they measured what they had, they had just one omer per person. "He that gathered much had nothing over, and he that gathered little had no lack" (16:18).

Paul quotes from the biblical account of the manna to support his guideline for economic sharing. In the wilderness, God provided equal portions of manna for all his people. Now the Corinthians were to give "that there may be equality" in the body of Christ.

Does this mean that God's standard for economic relations—whether in the church or society—is absolute equality of economic resources and consumption? I doubt it. Other biblical texts presuppose different economic outcomes based on individuals' choices.[44]

At a minimum, however, it summons us to share economically so that those who cannot provide for their own basic necessities are cared for. The text at least demands an equality of outcome up to the point that those who cannot provide for their own basic necessities receive a generous supply from others.

It is exciting to see how the biblical teaching on transformed economic relationships among God's people created in the early church a concern for the poor that was unique. Writing about A.D. 125, the Christian philosopher Aristides painted the following picture of economic sharing in the church:

> They walk in all humility and kindness, and falsehood is not found among them, and they love one another. They despise not the widow, and grieve not the orphan. He that hath, distributeth liberally to him that hath not. If they see a stranger, they bring him under their roof, and rejoice over him, as it were their own brother: for they call themselves brethren, not after the flesh, but after the spirit and

in God; but when one of their poor passes away from the world, and any of them see him, then he provides for his burial according to his ability; and if they hear that any of their number is imprisoned or oppressed for the name of their Messiah, all of them provide for his needs, and if it is possible that he may be delivered, they deliver him. And if there is among them a man that is poor and needy, and they have not an abundance of necessaries, they fast two or three days that they may supply the needy with their necessary food.[45]

By A.D. 250 the church at Rome supported fifteen hundred needy persons. According to the German scholar Martin Hengel, this kind of economic sharing was unique in the late Roman Empire.[46]

That this transformed lifestyle made a powerful impression on outsiders is clear from a grudging comment by a pagan emperor. During his short reign (A.D. 361–63), Julian the Apostate tried to stamp out Christianity. But he was forced to admit to a fellow pagan "that the godless Galileans [Christians] feed not only their poor but ours also." With chagrin he acknowledged that the pagan cult which he had tried to revive had failed miserably in the task of aiding the poor.[47]

Over and over God commanded his people to live together in community in such a way that all families would have the resources to earn a decent livelihood and that those who could not care for themselves would be generously taken care of. This principle is at the heart of the Old Testament legislation on the jubilee, the sabbatical year, tithing, gleaning, and loans. Again and again, Jesus instructed his followers to share with those in need. When some Christians became so poor that they lacked basic necessities, others generously shared.

The powerful evangelistic impact of economic sharing indicates that God approved and blessed the practice of the Jerusalem church. When in some places Scripture commands transformed economic relationships among God's people and in other places describes God's blessing on his people as they implement these commands, we can be sure that we have discovered a normative pattern for the church today.

The continuity of biblical teaching and practice on this point is striking. The Bible repeatedly and pointedly reveals that God wills transformed economic relationships among his people. Paul's collection was a simple application of this principle. Paul's method was different from that of Leviticus 25 (the people of God in Paul's time were a multiethnic body living in different lands), but the principle was the same. Since the Greeks at Corinth were now part of the people of God, they were to share with the poor Jewish Christians at Jerusalem—that there might be redeemed economic relationships among God's people.

How Then Shall We Live?

Certainly the church today need not slavishly imitate every detail of the life of the early church depicted in Acts. It is scriptural teaching, not the action of the Jerusalem church, that is normative. But that does not mean that we can dismiss the economic principles described in Acts and the Pauline letters.

Scripture offers two crucial clues about the nature of economic justice that God demands. First, God wants all people to have the productive resources to be able to earn a decent living and be dignified members of their community. We should work to structure society so that all people who can work have access to the resources to earn a decent living in today's global economy. Second, God wants the rest of us to provide a generous share of the necessities of life to those who cannot work.

The first application of the biblical teaching is to the church. Present economic relationships in the worldwide body of Christ are unbiblical and sinful; they hinder evangelism and desecrate the body and blood of Jesus Christ. The dollar value of the food North Americans throw in the garbage each year equals about one-fifth of the total annual income of all the Christians in Africa.[48] It is a sinful abomination for one part of the world's Christians to grow richer year by year while our brothers and sisters ache and suffer for lack of minimal health care, minimal education, and even—in some cases—enough food to escape starvation.

Like the rich Corinthian Christians who feasted without sharing with the hungry members of the church (1 Corinthians 11:20–29), we have failed to comprehend the concept that the church worldwide is one body. The tragic consequence is that we profane the body and blood of the Lord Jesus we worship. Christians in the United States spent $15.7 billion on new church construction alone in the six years between 1984 and 1989.[49] Would we go on building lavishly furnished expensive church buildings if members of our own congregations were starving? Do we not flatly contradict Paul if we live as if African or Latin American Christians are not also part of Christ's one body along with those in our home congregation?[50]

The division between the *haves* and *have nots* in the Body of Christ is a major hindrance to world evangelism. Hungry people in the Third World have difficulty accepting a Christ preached by people who symbolize (and often defend the materialism of) the richest societies on earth.

Lost opportunities and past and present sin, however, must not blind us to potential progress. We live in a world dangerously divided between rich and poor. If a mere fraction of rich Christians would begin to apply biblical principles of economic sharing, the world would be astounded. Few other steps would have such a powerful evangelistic impact today. The mutual love and unity within Christ's body would convince many that Jesus indeed came from the Father (John 17:20–23).

The church is the most universal body in the world today. It has the opportunity to live a new model of sharing at a crucial moment in world history. Because of its concern for the poor, the church in the past pioneered the development of schools and hospitals. Later, secular governments institutionalized the new models. In the late twentieth century, a dangerously divided world awaits a new model of economic sharing. Will there be enough rich Christians who are also generous?

Study Questions

1. Do most Christians you know think that their faith in Christ has anything to do with their economic relationships with others in the worldwide body of Christ? How does the Bible challenge their assumptions?

2. What are the basic implications of the jubilee and the sabbatical release of debts for today?

3. What would be the best words to describe the economic sharing occurring in the earliest church at Jerusalem?

4. What are the implications of Paul's intercontinental offering for the global church today?

5. What does the Bible tell us about economic justice in society?

5

Thinking Biblically about Property and Possessions

In the house of the righteous there is much treasure. (Proverbs 15:6)

Do not wear yourself out to get rich; have the wisdom to show restraint. (Proverbs 23:4)

"TELL ME WHAT YOU THINK ABOUT MONEY," Billy Graham says, "and I can tell you what you think about God."[1] What is our attitude about money telling the world about our belief in God? Are we in agreement with God on the subject? Do we even know what God says about it? What does God say about real estate? The poor? The rich? Does money matter to God?

Private Property

The Ten Commandments sanction private property implicitly and explicitly.[2] God forbids stealing, indeed even coveting the house, land, or animals of one's neighbors (Exodus 20:15, 17; Deuteronomy 5:19, 21; see also Deuteronomy 27:17; Proverbs 22:28). Jesus commanded his followers to give to the poor and to loan money even when there was no reasonable hope of repayment (Matthew 6:2–4; 5:42; Luke 6:34–35). The ability to make loans depends on the possession of property and money, so Jesus must have assumed such were legitimate. His disciple Simon Peter owned a house that Jesus visited frequently (Mark 1:29); in fact, those who owned houses had an opportunity to provide hospitality to God's servants (Luke 10:5–7).

Not even the dramatic economic sharing in the first Jerusalem church led to a rejection of private ownership (see chapter 4). Throughout biblical revelation the legitimacy of private property is constantly affirmed.[3]

Absolute Rights

But the right of private property is not absolute. From the perspective of biblical revelation, property owners are not free to seek their own profit without regard for the needs of their neighbors.

Some modern folk disagree. They think that the right of private ownership is absolute, and they argue that Adam Smith proves them right.

Smith published a book in 1776 that has profoundly shaped Western society in the past two centuries.[4] Smith argued that an invisible hand would guarantee the good of all if each person would pursue his or her own economic self-interest in the context of a competitive society. Supply and demand for goods and services were to be the sole, or at least primary, determinants of prices and wages. If the law of supply and demand reigns, and if all seek their own advantage within a competitive, nonmonopolistic economy, the good of society will be served. Adam Smith might not agree fully, but modern advocates of pure laissez-faire economics conclude that owners of land and capital therefore have not only the right but also the obligation to seek as much profit as possible, and they reject virtually all government intervention in the economy as a violation of the absolute right of private property.

Such a viewpoint may be attractive to the economically successful. Indeed, laissez-faire economics has been espoused by some as the Christian economics.[5] In reality, however, it is, to a substantial degree, a product of the Enlightenment.[6] It reflects a modern, secularized perspective rather than the biblical truth that God is Lord even of economics. That is not to say that socialist economies are better than market economies. A basic market framework plus the right kind of private and governmental activity to empower the poor is the best alternative known today (see chapters 8 and 11). But that is very different from a pure laissez-faire or libertarian approach that rejects almost all government intervention in the economy.

The pure laissez-faire and the pagan Roman attitude toward private property parallel each other. Carl F. H. Henry, former editor of *Christianity Today*, contrasts the biblical and Roman understandings:

> The Roman or Justinian view derives ownership from natural right; it defines ownership as the individual's unconditional and exclusive power over property. It implies an owner's right to use property as he pleases . . . irrespective of the will of others.

Henry admits that this pagan view "still remains the silent presupposition of much of the free world's common practice today."[7]

Absolute Owner

According to biblical faith, Yahweh is Lord of all things. He is the sovereign Lord of history. Economics is not a neutral, secular sphere independent of his Lordship. Economic activity, like every other area of life, is to be subject to God's will and revelation.

How does the biblical view that Yahweh is Lord of all of life require a modification of the common belief that the right of private property is absolute and inviolable? The Bible insists that God alone has an absolute right to property. Furthermore, it teaches that this Absolute Owner places significant limitations on how his people are to acquire and use his property.

The psalmist summarized the biblical view of Yahweh's absolute ownership: "The earth is the Lord's and the fullness thereof, the world and those who dwell therein" (Psalm 24:1). "Whatever is under the whole heaven is mine," God informed Job (Job 41:11; see also Psalm 50:12; Deuteronomy 26:10; Exodus 19:5). It is precisely because absolute ownership of the land rested with Yahweh rather than the Israelite farmers that God could command the return of the land every fiftieth year: "The land shall not be sold in perpetuity, for the land is mine; for you are strangers and sojourners with me" (Leviticus 25:23).

People Principle

As absolute owner, God places limitations on the acquisition and use of property. According to the Old Testament, "the right to property was in principle subordinated to the obligation to care for the weaker members of society."[8] That is the clear implication of the legislation on the jubilee, the sabbatical year, gleaning, and interest (as discussed in chapter 4). Property owners did not have the right to harvest everything in their fields. They were to leave some for the poor. When an Israelite farmer purchased land, he really only bought the use of the land until the year of jubilee (Leviticus 25:15–17). Indeed, even the right to use the land for the intervening years was not absolute. If a relative of the seller appeared, the purchaser had to sell the land back promptly. Or if the seller recovered financial solvency, he had the right to buy back his land immediately (Leviticus 25:25–28). The purchaser's right of ownership was subordinate to the original owner's right to possess his ancestral land.

God wants all people to have access to the productive resources to be able to earn a living. Justice for everyone, particularly the disadvantaged, takes precedence over the rights of the person able to pay the market price for land. Thus, the rights of the poor and disadvantaged to possess the means to earn a decent living take precedence over the rights of the more prosperous to make a profit.

At the same time, biblical principles by no means support a communist economic system. Biblical principles point in the direction of decentralized private ownership that allows families to control their economic destinies. As stewards of the land and other economic resources that belong ultimately to God, they have the responsibility and privilege of earning their own way and sharing generously with others. This kind of decentralized economic system empowers all people to be coworkers with God. It also protects everyone against centralized economic power that might threaten freedom and promote totalitarianism (as when the state owns the means of production or when small groups of elites control huge multinational corporations).

The Old Testament attitude toward property stems from the high view of persons held in Israel. Old Testament scholars have pointed out that Israel, unlike other ancient civilizations such as Babylon, Assyria, and Egypt, considered all citizens equal before the law. In other societies, social status (royal official, poor man, priest) determined how a person's offense was judged and punished. In Israel all citizens were equal before the law. This high view of persons made property less important.

Whereas in neighboring states property offenses such as theft or robbery were frequently punished with death, this was not the case under God's law. The life of even the most degraded person is worth more than the most valuable possession.[9]

The case of slaves illustrates the respect for persons. All other ancient civilizations viewed slaves as mere property. Owners were free to treat slaves according to their whims. But in Israel the slave was a person, not a piece of property. Specific laws guaranteed certain rights to slaves (Exodus 21:20, 26–28; Deuteronomy 23:15–16).

> The fact that, in accordance with God's order, the life of every individual, even of the poorest, is of greater value than all material things—this fact represents an insurmountable stumbling block to all economic developments which make profits for the few out of human misery.[10]

The Danger of Riches

An abundance of possessions can easily lead us to forget that God is the source of all good. We trust in ourselves and our wealth rather than in the Almighty. When we focus on ourselves, we forget not only God but also the people he created. In our self-absorption, we are fooled by the pleasure of possessing.

Most Christians in the Northern Hemisphere simply do not believe Jesus' teaching about the deadly danger of possessions. Jesus warned that possessions are highly dangerous—so dangerous, in fact, that it is extremely difficult for a rich person to be a Christian at all. "It is easier for a camel to go through the eye of a needle than for someone who is rich to enter the kingdom of God" (Luke 18:25). Christians in the United States live in one of the richest societies in the history of the world, surrounded by a billion desperately needy neighbors and another two billion who are poor. We are far more interested in whether the economy grows than in whether the lot of the poor improves. We insist on more and more, and reason that if Jesus was so unAmerican that he considered riches dangerous, then we must ignore or reinterpret his message.

Forgetting God

But he said it all the same. Matthew, Mark, and Luke all record the terrible warning: "How hard it is for those who have riches to enter the kingdom of God!" (Luke 18:24; Matthew 19:23; Mark 10:23). The context of this saying shows why possessions are dangerous. Jesus spoke these troubling words to his disciples immediately after the rich young man had decided to cling to his wealth rather than follow Jesus (Luke 18:18–23). Riches are dangerous because their seductive power frequently persuades us to reject Jesus and his kingdom.

The sixth chapter of 1 Timothy reinforces Jesus' teaching. Christians should be content with the necessities of food and clothing (v. 8). Why?

> Those who want to be rich fall into temptation, and are trapped by many senseless and hurtful desires that plunge people into ruin and destruction. For the love of money is a root of all kinds of evils; and in their eagerness to be rich some have wandered away from the faith and pierced themselves with many pains. (1 Timothy 6:9–10)

A desire for riches prompts some people to do almost anything for the sake of economic success. The result, Scripture warns, is anguish now and damnation later.

That economic success tempts people to forget God was already a biblical theme in the Old Testament. Before the Israelites entered the Promised Land, God warned them about the danger of riches.

> Take heed lest you forget the Lord your God . . . lest, when you have eaten and are full, and have built goodly houses and live in them, and when your herds and flocks multiply, and your silver and gold is multiplied, and all that you have is multiplied, then your heart be lifted up, and you forget the Lord your God. . . . Beware lest you say in your heart, "My power and the might of my hand have gotten me this wealth" (Deuteronomy 8:11–14, 17).

Fighting Wars

Not only do possessions tempt us to forsake God, but the pursuit of wealth often results in war and neglect of the poor. "What causes wars, and what causes fightings among you?. . . You desire and do not have; so you kill. And you covet and cannot obtain; so you fight and wage war" (James 4:1–2). A quick glance through world history confirms this tragic truth.

Forgetting the Poor

Instead of fostering more compassion toward the poor, riches often harden the hearts of the wealthy. Scripture is full of instances in which rich persons are unconcerned about the poor at their doorstep (Isaiah 5:8–10; Amos 6:4–7; Luke 16:19–31; James 5:1–5). Dom Helder Camara, a Brazilian archbishop who devoted his life to seeking justice for the poor, makes the point forcefully:

> I used to think, when I was a child, that Christ might have been exaggerating when he warned about the dangers of wealth. Today I know better. I know how very hard it is to be rich and still keep the milk of human kindness. Money has a dangerous way of putting scales on one's eyes, a dangerous way of freezing people's hands, eyes, lips, and hearts.[11]

Possessions are positively dangerous because they often encourage unconcern for the poor, because they lead to strife and war, and because they seduce people into forsaking God. Even more, they put people in the never ending loop of covetousness.

Coveting without End

The use of the word *covetousness* (which occurs nineteen times in the New Testament) reflects the biblical understanding of the dangers of riches. The Greek word *pleonexia* (translated "covetousness" or "greed") means "striving for material possessions."[12]

Jesus' Parable of the Rich Fool vividly portrays the nature of covetousness. When a man came running to Jesus for help in obtaining his share of a family inheritance, Jesus refused to consider the case. Perceiving the real problem, Jesus instead warned of the danger of covetousness. "Take care! Be on your guard against all kinds of greed [*pleonexia*]; for one's life does not consist in the abundance of possessions" (Luke 12:15). Knowing that the man was obsessed with material things, Jesus told him a story about a rich fool.

> The land of a rich man produced abundantly. And he thought to himself, "What should I do, for I have no place to store my crops?" Then he

said, "I will do this: I will pull down my barns and build larger ones, and there I will store all my grain and my goods. And I will say to my soul, 'Soul, you have ample goods laid up for many years; relax, eat, drink, be merry.'" But God said to him, "You fool! This very night your life is being demanded of you. And the things you have prepared, whose will they be?" So it is with those who store up treasures for themselves but are not rich toward God (Luke 12:16–21 NRSV).

The rich fool is the epitome of the covetous person. He has a greedy compulsion to acquire more and more possessions, even though he does not need them. And his phenomenal success at piling up more and more property and wealth leads to the blasphemous conclusion that material possessions can satisfy all his needs. From the divine perspective, this attitude is sheer madness. He is a raving fool.

One cannot read the Parable of the Rich Fool without thinking of our own society. We madly multiply sophisticated gadgets, bigger houses, fancier cars, and fashionable clothes—not because such things truly enrich our lives but because we are driven by an obsession for more and more. Covetousness, a striving for more and more material possessions, has become a cardinal vice of modern civilization.

The New Testament has a great deal to say about covetousness. In its essence, it is idolatry. Scripture teaches that greedy persons must be expelled from the church. Certainly no covetous person will inherit the kingdom. Giving people over to their covetousness is divine punishment for sin. In Romans 1 Paul indicates that God sometimes punishes sin by letting sinners experience the ever more destructive consequences of their continuing rebellion against God. "And since they did not see fit to acknowledge God, God gave them up to a base mind and to improper conduct. They were filled with all manner of wickedness, evil, covetousness, . . . murder, strife, deceit" (Romans 1:28–29). Covetousness is one of the sins with which God punishes our rebellion. The Parable of the Rich Fool suggests how the punishment works. Since we are made for communion with the Creator, we cannot obtain genuine fulfillment when we seek it primarily in material possessions. Hence we seek ever more frantically and desperately for more houses and bigger barns. Eventually we worship our possessions. As Paul indicates, covetousness becomes idolatry (Ephesians 5:5; Colossians 3:5).

Christians today are not at all surprised that Paul urged the Corinthians to excommunicate a church member living with his father's wife (1 Corinthians 5:1–5). But we quietly overlook the fact that Paul, in the same paragraph, also urged them not to associate or even eat meals with those who claim to be Christians but are guilty of greed.

Are we not guilty of greed when we demand an ever-higher standard of living while neglecting millions of children who are starving to death each year? Is it not time for the church to begin applying church discipline to those guilty of this sin?[13] Would it not be more biblical to apply church discipline to people whose greedy acquisitiveness has led to "financial success" than to elect them to the board of elders?

Such action may be the last means we have of communicating the biblical warning that greedy persons will not inherit the kingdom.

> Do you not know that the wicked will not inherit the kingdom of God? Do not be deceived; neither the sexually immoral, nor idolators, nor adulterers, nor male prostitutes, nor homosexual offenders, nor thieves, nor the greedy [the covetous], nor drunkards, nor slanderers, nor swindlers will inherit the kingdom of God. (1 Corinthians 6:9–10 NIV)

Covetousness is just as sinful as idolatry and adultery.

Another unambiguous statement about covetousness, or greed, appears in Ephesians: "Be sure of this, that no fornicator or impure person, or one who is greedy (that is, an idolater), has any inheritance in the kingdom of Christ" (5:5). These biblical passages should drive us all to our knees. I am afraid that I have been repeatedly and sinfully covetous. The same is true of the vast majority of the Christians who read this book.

Possessions are dangerous. They lead to a multitude of sins, including idolatry. Christians today desperately need to turn away from their covetous civilization's grasping materialism.

The Ring and the Beloved

Yes, possessions are dangerous. But they are not innately evil.[14] Biblical revelation begins with creation. And created things, God said, are good (Genesis 1).

Biblical faith knows nothing of the ascetic notion that forsaking food, possessions, or sex is inherently virtuous. To be sure, these created goods are, as St. Augustine said, only rings from our Beloved. They are not the Beloved himself. Sometimes particular circumstances—such as an urgent mission or the needs of the poor—may require their renunciation. But these things are part of God's good creation. Like the ring given by the beloved, they are signs of God's love. If we treasure them as good tokens of his affection, instead of mistaking them for the Beloved himself, they are marvelous gifts that enrich our lives.

God's provision for Israel's use of the tithe symbolizes the scriptural perspective (Deuteronomy 14:22–27). Every third year the tithe was given to the poor. In the other years, however, the people were to go to the place of worship and have a fantastic feast. They were to have a great big, joyful celebration! "Before the Lord your God, in the place which he will choose, to make his name dwell there, you shall eat the tithe of your grain, of your wine, and of your oil, and the firstlings of your herd and flock" (Deuteronomy 14:23). Those who lived far from the place of worship could sell the tithe of their produce and take the money with them. Listen to God's directions for the party: "Spend the money for whatever you desire, oxen, or sheep, or wine or strong drink, whatever your appetite craves; and you shall eat there before the Lord your God and rejoice" (Deuteronomy 14:26). God wants his people to celebrate the glorious goodness of creation.

Jesus' example fits in perfectly with the Old Testament view. Certainly he said a great deal about the danger of possessions. But he was not an ascetic. He was happy to join in marriage celebrations and even contribute the beverage (John 2:1–11). He dined with the prosperous. Apparently he was sufficiently fond of feasts and celebrations that his enemies could spread the false rumor that he was a glutton and a drunkard (Matthew 11:19). Christian asceticism has a long history, but Jesus' life undermines its basic assumptions.

A short passage in 1 Timothy succinctly summarizes the biblical view: "In the latter days people will forbid marriage and advocate abstinence from foods. But this is misguided, "for everything created by God is good, and nothing is to be rejected if it is received with thanksgiving" (1 Timothy 4:4).

The biblical teaching on the goodness of creation does not contradict the other biblical themes. Possessions are dangerous, and God's people must practice self-denial to aid the poor and share the gospel. But we must maintain a biblical balance. It is not because food, clothes, wealth, and property are inherently evil that Christians today must lower their standard of living. It is because others are starving. Creation is good. But the one who gave us this gorgeous token of affection has asked us to share it with our sisters and brothers.

Righteousness and Riches

If we respect God and people, understand the dangers of riches, and delight in the goodness of creation, will prosperity follow? Does our obedience guarantee it? Is it true that "in the house of the righteous there is much treasure" (Proverbs 15:6)? Is the reverse also true? Are riches a sure sign of righteousness?

Biblical Balance

The Bible certainly does not romanticize poverty. It is a curse (2 Samuel 3:29; Psalm 109:8–11). Sometimes it is the result of sin, but not always. A fundamental point of the book of Job is that poverty and suffering are not always due to disobedience. In fact, they can be redemptive (Isaiah 53). Even so, poverty and suffering are not inherently good. They are tragic distortions of God's good creation.

Prosperity and wealth, on the other hand, are good and desirable. God repeatedly promised his people Israel that obedience would bring abundant prosperity in a land flowing with milk and honey (Deuteronomy 6:1–3). "All these blessings shall come upon you . . . if you obey the voice of the Lord your God. . . . And the Lord will make you abound in prosperity, in the fruit of your body, and in the fruit of your cattle, and in the fruit of your ground" (Deuteronomy 28:2, 11; see also 7:12–15). That God frequently rewards obedience with material abundance is a clear teaching of Scripture.

But the threat of a curse always accompanied the promise of blessing (Deuteronomy 6:14–15; 8:11–20; 28:15–68). One of God's most frequent commands to his people was to feed the hungry and to seek justice for the poor (see chapters 3–4). For repeatedly ignoring this command, Israel experienced God's curse. Many rich people in the days of Amos and Isaiah were rich, not because of divine blessing, but because of sinful oppression of the poor. God consequently destroyed the nation.

More biblical texts warn of God's punishment of those who neglect or oppress the poor than tell us that material abundance results from obedience.[15] The two statements, however, are not contradictory. Both are true. It is the biblical balance that we need.

The Bible does teach that God rewards obedience with prosperity. But it denies the converse. It is a heresy, particularly common in rich nations, to think that wealth and prosperity are always a sure sign of righteousness. They may be the result of sin and oppression, as in the case of Israel (see chapter 3). The crucial test is whether the prosperous are obeying God's command to bring justice to the oppressed.[16] If they are not, they are living in damnable disobedience to God. On biblical grounds, therefore, one can be sure that prosperity in the context of injustice results from oppression rather than obedience and that it is not a sign of righteousness.

The connection between righteousness, prosperity, and concern for the poor is explicitly taught in Scripture. The picture of the good wife in Proverbs 31 provides one beautiful illustration. This woman is a diligent businessperson who buys fields and engages in trade (vv. 14, 16, 18). She is a righteous woman who fears the Lord (v. 30). Her obedience and diligence clearly bring prosperity. But material possessions do not harden her heart against the poor: "She opens her hand to the poor, and reaches out her hands to the needy" (v. 20). Psalm 112 is equally explicit:

> Happy are those who fear the Lord who greatly delight in his commandments. . . . Wealth and riches are in their houses, . . . they are gracious, merciful, and righteous. It is well with those who deal generously and lend, who conduct their affairs with justice. . . . They have distributed freely, they have given to the poor (vv. 1, 3–5, 9 NRSV).

The righteous person shares generously with the poor. She works to establish justice for the oppressed. That kind of life is a sign that one's prosperity results from obedience rather than oppression.

God wills prosperity with justice. As John V. Taylor has pointed out so beautifully, the biblical norm for material possessions is "sufficiency."[17] Proverbs 30:8–9 is a marvelous summary:

> Give me neither poverty nor riches; feed me with the food that is need-
> ful for me, lest I be full, and deny thee, and say, "Who is the Lord?" or
> lest I be poor, and steal, and profane the name of my God.

Rich Christians must be careful not to distort the biblical teaching that
God sometimes rewards obedience with material abundance. Wealthy persons who make Christmas baskets and give them to relief agencies have not
satisfied God's demand. God wills justice for the poor, not occasional charity. And justice means things like the jubilee and the sabbatical remission of
debts. It means economic structures that guarantee all people access to the
productive resources needed to earn a decent living. Prosperity without that
kind of biblical concern for justice unambiguously signifies disobedience.

Pious Poor

The Old Testament teaches that material possessions sometimes result from
divine blessing. But is this view compatible with Jesus' saying: "Blessed are
you poor, for yours is the kingdom of God" (Luke 6:20)? Does Jesus consider
poverty itself a virtue? Furthermore, how can one reconcile the Lucan version of this beatitude with Matthew's version: "Blessed are the poor in spirit"
(Matt. 5:3)?

The development of the idea of the "pious poor" in the centuries just
prior to Christ helps answer these questions. Already in the Psalms the poor
were often identified as the special objects of God's favor and protection precisely because they were oppressed by the wicked rich (see Psalm 9:18;
10:1–2).[18] When Greece and then Rome conquered Palestine, they forced
Hellenistic culture and values on the Jews. Those who remained faithful to
Yahweh often suffered financially. Thus the term *poor* came to be used to
describe faithful Jews.

> It was virtually equivalent to pious, God fearing and godly, and reflects
> a situation where the rich were mainly those who had sold out to the
> incoming culture and had allowed their religious devotion to become
> corrupted by the new ways. If the poor were the pious, the faithful and
> largely oppressed, the rich were the powerful, ungodly, worldly, even
> apostate.[19]

In such a setting the righteous are often poor and hungry, not just "in spirit" but materially. Matthew has not "spiritualized" Jesus' words. He has simply captured another aspect of Jesus' original meaning. Jesus was talking about those faithful persons who so hungered for righteousness that they sacrificed even their material prosperity when that became necessary. Jesus did not mean that poverty and hunger are desirable in themselves. But in a sinful world where, frequently, success and prosperity are possible only if one transgresses God's law, poverty and hunger are indeed a blessing. The kingdom is for precisely such people.

Jesus' comment in Mark 10:29–30 adds further clarification. He promised that those who forsake all for the kingdom will receive a hundredfold even in this life. He even included houses and lands, part of the good creation intended for our enjoyment. In the same sentence, however, he also promised persecution. Sometimes—perhaps most of the time—the wicked, powerful, and rich will persecute those who dare to follow Jesus' teaching without compromise. Hunger and poverty sometimes result. In such a time poor and hungry disciples are indeed blessed.

In our day some who have dared to preach and live what the Bible teaches about the poor and possessions have experienced terrible persecution. Christians in Latin America have experienced torture, some even death, because they identified with the poor.

Carefree Living

Most of us, however, face far more subtle pressures. Society's prevailing materialism mocks those who try to follow Jesus' carefree attitude toward possessions. Imagine the social disapproval that would descend upon anyone who suggested that Jesus' words should guide the advertising business or even church construction.

> Therefore I tell you, do not worry about your life, what you will eat, or about your body, what you will wear. For life is more than food, and the body more than clothing. Consider the ravens: they neither sow nor reap, they have neither storehouse nor barn, and yet God feeds them. Of how much more value are you than the birds! And can any of you by worrying add a single hour to your span of life? If then you are not able

to do so small a thing as that, why do you worry about the rest? Consider the lilies, how they grow: they neither toil nor spin; yet I tell you, even Solomon in all his glory was not clothed like one of these. But if God so clothes the grass of the field, which is alive today and tomorrow is thrown into the oven, how much more will he clothe you—you of little faith! And do not keep striving for what you are to eat and what you are to drink, and do not keep worrying. For it is the nations of the world that strive after all these things and your Father knows that you need them. Instead, strive for his kingdom, and these things will be given to you as well (Luke 12:22–31 NRSV; see also 2 Corinthians 9:8–11).

Jesus' words are anathema both to Marxists and to certain kinds of capitalists: to Marxists because they worship mammon by claiming that economic forces are the ultimate causal factors in history; to some capitalists because they worship mammon by idolizing economic efficiency and success as the highest goods.[20] Indeed, at another level, Jesus' words are anathema to the ordinary, comfortable Christian. In fact, I must confess that I cannot read them without an underlying sense of uneasiness. The beauty and appeal of Luke 12:22–31 always overwhelm me. But the passage also reminds me that I have not, in spite of continuing struggle and effort, attained the kind of carefree attitude Jesus depicts.

The Secret

What is the secret of such carefree living? First, many people cling to their possessions instead of sharing them because they are worried about the future. But is not such an attitude finally unbelief? If we really believe that God is who Jesus said he is, then we can begin to live without anxiety for the future. Jesus taught us that God is our loving Father. That is why we can call him *abba*, a tender, intimate word like papa (Mark 14:36). If we really believe that the almighty Creator and Sustainer of the cosmos is our loving papa, then we can begin to cast aside anxiety about earthly possessions.

Second, such carefree living presupposes an unconditional commitment to Jesus as Lord. We must genuinely want to seek first the kingdom of heaven. Jesus was blunt. We cannot serve God and possessions. "No one can serve two masters; for either he will hate the one and love the other, or he will be devoted to the one and despise the other. You cannot serve God and mammon" (Matt. 6:24). Mammon is not some mysterious pagan God. The word *mammon* is simply the Aramaic word for wealth or property.[21] Like the rich young ruler and Zacchaeus, we must decide between Jesus and riches. Like the merchant in Jesus' parable, we must decide between the kingdom of heaven and our affluent life: "The kingdom of heaven is like a merchant in search of fine pearls, who, on finding one pearl of great value, went and sold all that he had and bought it" (Matthew 13:45–46; see also v. 44). Either Jesus and his kingdom matter so much that we are ready to sacrifice everything else, including our possessions, or we are not serious about Jesus.

Its Sacrifice

If Jesus is truly Lord and if we trust in a loving heavenly Father, then we can courageously live without anxiety about possessions. That kind of carefree unconcern for possessions, however, is not merely an inner spiritual attitude. It involves action. Immediately following the moving statement about the carefree life of the ravens and lilies, Jesus says, "Sell your possessions, and give alms; provide yourselves with purses that do not grow old, with a treasure in the heavens that does not fail. . . . For where your treasure is, there will your heart be also" (Luke 12:33–34).

If there are poor people who need assistance, Jesus' carefree disciple will help—even if that means selling possessions. People are vastly more important than property. The "laying up [of] treasure in heaven" is accomplished by helping others. "In Jewish literature, the good deeds of a religious person are often described as treasures stored up in heaven."[22] One stores up treasure in heaven by doing righteousness on earth. And aiding the poor is one of the most basic acts of righteousness. Jesus does not mean that we earn salvation by assisting the needy. But he does mean to urge his followers—out of gratitude for God's forgiving grace—to be so unconcerned with property that they gladly sell it to aid the poor and oppressed. Such activity is an integral part of living a life of joyful unconcern for possessions.

But a difficult question remains. Did Jesus mean that we should sell *all* our possessions? How literally should we understand what he said in Luke

6:30: "Give to every one who begs from you; and of him who takes away your goods do not ask them again"?

Jesus sometimes engaged in typical Jewish hyperbole to make a point. He hardly meant in Luke 14:26 that one must actively hate father and mother in order to be his disciple. But we have become so familiar with Jesus' words, so accustomed to compromising their call to radical discipleship and unconditional commitment, that we weaken his real intent. What 99 percent of North Americans need to hear 99 percent of the time is this: "Give to everyone who begs from you," and "sell your possessions." It is certainly true that Jesus' followers continued to own some private property. But Jesus clearly taught that the kind of substantial sharing he desired would involve selling possessions. His first followers at Jerusalem took him seriously. If rich Christians today want to experience Jesus' carefree outlook on property and possessions, they will need to do the same.

Other parts of the New Testament continue the same theme. Bishops must not be lovers of money (1 Timothy 3:3; Titus 1:7). Deacons likewise dare not be "greedy for gain" (1 Timothy 3:8). In many churches today, "success" in business is one of the chief criteria for selection to the church board. Is that not a blatant reversal of biblical teaching on the importance of possessions? Even those who are rich should be careful not to set their hope in "certain riches." Instead, they should trust in God and share generously (1 Timothy 6:17–18). "Keep your life free from love of money, and be content with what you have; for he has said, 'I will never fail you nor forsake you'" (Hebrews 13:5). Our future is secure not because of our possessions but because it rests in the hands of a loving, omnipotent Father. If we truly trust in him and are unconditionally submitted to his Lordship, we can confidently imitate Jesus' carefree unconcern for property and possessions.

In a consumer society that increasingly measures a person's worth and importance by the amount of his or her material possessions, biblical Christians will reject materialism without falling into asceticism. They will delight in the splendor of the material world but not forget that things cannot ultimately satisfy. They will enjoy the good earth and celebrate its abundance without neglecting sacrificial sharing with the needy. They will distinguish between necessities and luxuries. They will enjoy possessions while recognizing their seductive danger. When forced to choose between Jesus and possessions, they will gladly forsake the ring for the Beloved.

Study Questions

1. How does the biblical perspective on private property challenge modern ideas?

2. What are the dangers of possessions? Why is this part of biblical truth especially difficult for modern folk to grasp?

3. What is the biblical connection between righteousness and riches? How is this truth perverted today?

4. How would you change your life if you were truly to implement Jesus' teaching about carefree living?

5. How does St. Augustine's image of the ring and the Beloved summarize the proper attitude toward possessions?

6

Social Evil: Sin Embedded in Societal Systems

You yourself were not anti-Semitic. . . . You had your Jewish neighbors in to dinner. . . . But if you did not protest against [Hitler's] public policy which made them wear armbands, defrauded them of property, and shipped them off to death, your little kindnesses were of no importance whatever.[1]

—*Richard G. Watts*

NORTHEAST HIGH SCHOOL in Philadelphia was famous for its superb academic standards and its brilliant, long-standing athletic triumphs. The second oldest school in the city, Northeast had excellent teachers and a great tradition. And it was almost entirely white. Then in the mid-fifties, the neighborhood began to change. Black people moved in. Whites began to flee to the Greater Northeast, a new, all-white section of Philadelphia. A new high school soon became a necessity in this developing, overwhelmingly white area.

When the excellent new school was completed in 1957, it took the name of the old one, and with the name went the memories and traditions as well as the school's history of academic excellence and athletic triumph. The new school also took all the academic and athletic trophies and awards, school colors, songs, as well as the powerful alumni and their treasury. Worst of all, the teachers were given the option of transferring to the new Northeast High. Two-thirds of them did.[2]

The inner-city school was renamed Edison High, and the black students attending it had nothing but an old, rapidly deteriorating building, frequent substitute teachers, and no traditions. The subsequent years have not brought better teachers nor adequate teaching materials. The academic record since 1957 has been terrible. But Edison High has one national record. More students from Edison died in the U.S. Army in Vietnam than from any other high school in the United States.

Who was responsible for this terrible evil? Local, state, and federal politicians who for decades had promoted de facto housing segregation? The school board? Parents who had, at best, only a partial picture of what was going on? Christian community leaders? White students at the new Northeast High whose excellent education and job prospects have been possible, in part, because of the poor facilities and bad teachers left behind for the black students at Edison?

Many would deny any personal responsibility. "That's just the way things are!" And they would be quite right. Long-standing patterns in jobs and housing created a system that automatically produced Edison High. But that hardly silences the query about responsibility. Do we sin when we participate in evil social systems and societal structures that unfairly benefit some and harm others?

Neglect of the biblical teaching on structural injustice or institutionalized evil is one of the most deadly omissions in many parts of the church today. Christians frequently restrict ethics to a narrow class of "personal" sins. In a study of over fifteen hundred ministers, researchers discovered that theologically conservative pastors spoke out on sins such as drug abuse and sexual misconduct,[3] but failed to preach about the sins of institutionalized racism and unjust economic structures that destroy just as many people.

There is an important difference between consciously willed, individual acts (like lying to a friend or committing an act of adultery) and participation in evil social structures. Slavery is an example of the latter. So is the Victorian factory system that had ten-year-old children working twelve to sixteen hours a day. Both slavery and child labor were legal, but they destroyed people by the millions. They were institutionalized, or structural, evils.

In the twentieth century, evangelicals have become imbalanced in their stand against sin, expressing concern and moral outrage about individual sinful acts while ignoring, perhaps even participating in, evil social structures. But the Bible condemns both.

The Old Testament

Speaking through his prophet Amos, the Lord declared,

> For three transgressions of Israel, and for four, I will not revoke the pun-
> ishment; because they sell the righteous for silver, and the needy for a
> pair of shoes—they that trample the head of the poor into the dust of the
> earth, and turn aside the way of the afflicted; a man and his father go in
> to the same maiden, so that my holy name is profaned (Amos 2:6–7).

Biblical scholars have shown that some kind of legal fiction or technicality
underlies the phrase "selling the needy for a pair of shoes."[4] This mistreatment of the poor was *legal!* In one breath God condemned two detestable
practices: sexual misconduct *and* the legalized oppression of the poor. Sexual
sins and economic injustice are equally displeasing to God.

The prophet Isaiah also condemned both personal and social sin:

> Woe to those who join house to house, who add field to field, until there
> is no more room, and you are made to dwell alone in the midst of the
> land. The Lord of hosts has sworn in my hearing: "Surely many houses
> shall be desolate, large and beautiful houses, without inhabitant. . . .
> Woe to those who rise early in the morning, that they may run after
> strong drink, who tarry late into the evening till wine inflames them!"
> (Isaiah 5:8–9, 11)

Equally powerful is the succinct, satirical summary in verses 22 and 23 of
the same chapter:

> Woe to those who are heroes at drinking wine, and valiant men in
> mixing strong drink, who acquit the guilty for a bribe, and deprive the
> innocent of his right!

Here, in one brief denunciation, God condemns both those who amass large
landholdings at the expense of the poor and those who are drunkards.
Economic injustice is just as abominable to our God as drunkenness.

Some young activists suppose that as long as they fight for the rights of minorities and oppose militarism they are morally righteous, regardless of how often they shack up for the night with a man or woman involved with them in the fight for social morality.

Some of their elders, on the other hand, suppose that because they do not sleep around they are morally upright even though they live in segregated communities and own stock in companies that exploit the poor. From a biblical perspective, however, robbing your workers of a fair wage and robbing a bank are both sinful. Voting for a racist because he is a racist and sleeping with your neighbor's wife are both sinful. Silent participation in a company that carelessly pollutes the environment and thus imposes heavy costs on others and destroying your own lungs with tobacco are both sinful.

In the first edition of this book, I said that social evil hurts more people than personal evil. That may be true in the developing world, but I no longer believe that it is true in North America and Western Europe. Within the industrialized nations, the agony caused by broken homes, sexual promiscuity, marital breakdown, domestic violence, and divorce probably equals the pain caused by structural injustice. That is not to deny or deemphasize the latter. It is merely to underline the fact that both kinds of evil devastate societies today.

God clearly reveals his displeasure at evil *institutions* through the prophet Amos. (To understand the meaning of this passage, keep in mind that Israel's court sessions were held at the city gate.)

> They hate him who reproves in the gate. . . . I know how many are your transgressions, and how great are your sins—you who . . . take a bribe, and turn aside the needy in the gate. . . . Hate evil, and love good, and establish justice in the gate." (Amos 5:10–15)

"Let justice roll down like waters . . ." (Amos 5:24) is not abstract verbalization. The prophet is calling for justice in the legal system. He means, get rid of the corrupt legal system that allows the wealthy to buy their way out of trouble but gives the poor long prison terms.

The dishonest and corrupt individuals in the legal system are not the only ones who stand condemned. Laws themselves are sometimes an abomination to God:

> Can wicked rulers be allied with thee, who frame mischief by statute? They band together against the life of the righteous, and condemn the innocent to death. But the Lord has become my stronghold, and my God the rock of my refuge. He will bring back on them their iniquity and wipe them out for their wickedness; the Lord our God will wipe them out. (Psalm 94:20–23)

The Jerusalem Bible has an excellent rendition of verse 20: "You never consent to that corrupt tribunal that imposes disorder as law." God wants his people to know that wicked governments "frame mischief by statute." Or, as the New English Bible puts it, they contrive evil "under cover of law."

God proclaims the same word through the prophet Isaiah:

> Woe to those who decree iniquitous decrees, and the writers who keep writing oppression, to turn aside the needy from justice and to rob the poor of my people of their right. . . . What will you do on the day of punishment, in the storm which will come from afar? To whom will you flee for help, and where will you leave your wealth? Nothing remains but to crouch among the prisoners or fall among the slain. For all this [God's] anger is not turned away and his hand is stretched out still. (Isaiah 10:1–4)

It is possible to make oppression legal. Now, as then, legislators devise unjust laws, and bureaucrats implement the injustice. But God shouts a divine woe against rulers who use their official position to write unjust laws and unfair legal decisions. Legalized oppression is an abomination to our God. Therefore, God calls his people to oppose political structures that frame mischief by statute.

God hates evil economic structures and unjust legal systems because they destroy people by the hundreds and thousands and millions. We can be sure that the just Lord of the universe will destroy wicked rulers and unjust social institutions (see 1 Kings 21).

Another side to institutionalized evil makes it especially pernicious. Structural evil is so subtle that we become ensnared without fully realizing it. God inspired his prophet Amos to utter some of the harshest words in Scripture against the cultured upper-class women of his day:

> Hear this word, you cows of Bashan . . . who oppress the poor, who crush the needy, who say to [your] husbands, "Bring, that we may drink!" The Lord God has sworn by his holiness that, behold, the days are coming upon you, when they shall take you away with hooks, even the last of you with fishhooks. (Amos 4:1–2)

The women involved may have had little direct contact with the impoverished peasants. They may never have fully realized that their gorgeous clothes and spirited parties were possible partly because of the sweat and tears of the poor. In fact, they may even have been kind on occasion to individual peasants. (Perhaps they gave them "Christmas baskets" once a year.) But God called these privileged women "cows" because they participated in social evil. Before God they were personally and individually guilty.[5]

If we are members of a privileged group that profits from structural evil, and if we have at least some understanding of the evil yet fail to do what God wants us to do to change things, we stand guilty before God. Social evil is just as displeasing to God as personal evil. And it is more subtle.

Some people disagree. John Schneider has sharply criticized my views on social sin. First, he says that I argue that structural evil is "morally indistinguishable from personal evil."[6] Actually, however, I do not say or believe that. Structures do not have minds and wills in the way individuals do. Evil systems cannot repent of their sins, receive forgiveness through Christ's atonement, receive baptism, and be on their way to eternal life, the way sinful persons can. Responsibility is not the same thing as guilt. Every individual in a society has some responsibility to correct the evil around them, whether the evil is individual or corporate, but that does not mean each person is guilty of every sin in their society.

Years ago, I rejected the notion that "a person is guilty in the same sense and to the same degree as his grandfather or fellow citizen for a wrong done by the grandfather or fellow citizen."[7] There are clear biblical examples of persons confessing the sins of their ancestors and relatives (Daniel 9:4-20;

Nehemiah 1:4-5; Isaiah 6:1-5). But Ezekiel 18:1-20 explicitly teaches that the individual who sins, not relatives or neighbors, is the one God considers guilty.

But do we sin personally when we participate in an evil system? That depends on our knowledge and our response. If we have absolutely no understanding of the evil, then our participating does not involve personal sin. If we do understand something of the evil and do all God wants us to do to correct the injustice, then again, we do not sin. Persons sin by participating in evil systems when they understand, at least to some degree, that the system displeases God but fail to act responsibly to change things.

Schneider, however, argues secondly that we often do not know about our involvement in sinful social structures. "Usually, we have no way to know about them."[8] Therefore we are not guilty even though we participate in them. Schneider is partly right here. If we know absolutely nothing about the evil of some system we participate in, then, as I just argued, we do not personally sin by our participation.

Three additional points, however, are crucial. First, the fact that I have no knowledge of a system's evil and am not personally guilty before God for participating in that system does not change the fact that the system is nonetheless wicked and evil and stands under God's condemnation. God always hates structural evils and works to end their injustice. Whether or not I have any understanding of a system's oppression does not change the objective fact that it is an abomination to our holy God.

Furthermore, most of the time, people living in and benefiting from unjust structures know something—albeit not everything—about their evil. In fact, very often we know enough to choose not to learn more lest we feel guilty. Mafia wives know enough about their husband's activity to decide not to ask many questions. Rich Christians know enough about the ravages of poverty that we turn off the TV special on poverty in the Third World or inner city. We rush past the bookstore's section on economic justice. Why? Because we know that knowing more will make us morally obligated to change. Are we not guilty, to some extent, for choosing not to know about evils that benefit us and injure others? "All who do evil hate the light and do not come to the light, so that their deeds may not be exposed" (John 3:20).

Finally, different levels of understanding and conscious choice also correspond to different levels of responsibility and guilt. The mafia wife who tries not to know very much is not guilty in the same way as the mafia leader who personally orders executions. But surely she has some understanding, some guilt, and some responsibility.

Schneider has a third, fascinating argument. Jesus lived and worked as a carpenter in an empire full of all kinds of structural injustices. Therefore "it was simply impossible that he not profit from very great structural evils. And so far as we know he did nothing directly to change them."[9] In short, either Jesus was a sinner or my understanding of social sin is mistaken.

Not really. I have never said any one person must do everything to correct an evil system. Each person should do all God wants him or her to do. God's call on each individual's life varies. We sin as participants in evil social structures only if we understand something of their wickedness and then fail to do what God wants us to do to correct the evil. It is simply not true that Jesus did nothing to correct unjust structures. He spoke against economic oppressors. He condemned wicked rulers.[10] He formed a new community that began to live a new transformed lifestyle precisely in the area of economic sharing and neglect of the marginalized. And he rose from the dead and sent the Holy Spirit so his disciples would have the divine power to challenge evil in every form it takes.

It is also important to remember that Jesus lived under an imperialistic Roman dictatorship. He did not have the political opportunities of citizens living in a democracy. Furthermore, as the Jewish Messiah, he was called to live and minister among the Jews of Palestine, not to engage in direct action either to preach the Gospel in Rome or to correct Roman injustice.[11] Since Jesus was sinless, we can assume that he did all God wanted him to do to correct the injustice of his day.

Unfair systems and oppressive structures are an abomination to God, and "social sin" is the correct phrase to categorize them. Furthermore, as we understand their evil, we have a moral obligation to do all God wants us to do to change them. If we do not, we sin. That is the clear implication of Amos' harsh attack on the wealthy women of his day. It is also the clear implication of James 4:17: "Whoever knows what is right to do and fails to do it, for him it is sin."

The New Testament

In the New Testament,[12] the word *cosmos* (world) often conveys the idea of structural evil.[13] In Greek thought, the word *cosmos* referred to the structures of civilized life, especially the patterns of the Greek city state that were viewed as essentially good.[14] But the biblical writers knew that sin had invaded and distorted the structures and values of society.

Frequently, therefore, the New Testament uses the word *cosmos* to refer, in C. H. Dodd's words, "to human society in so far as it is organized on wrong principles."[15] "When Paul spoke of 'the world' in a moral sense, he was thinking of the totality of people, social systems, values, and traditions in terms of its opposition to God and his redemptive purposes."[16]

Before conversion, Christians follow the values and patterns of a fallen social order: "You were dead in your transgressions and sins, in which you used to live when you followed the ways of the world" (Ephesians 2:1–2). Paul, in his letter to the Romans (12:1–2), and John, in his gospel, urge Christians not to conform to this world's pattern of evil systems and ideas.

> Do not love the world or the things in the world. The love of the Father is not in those who love the world; for all that is in the world—the desire of the flesh, the desire of the eyes, the pride in riches—comes not from the Father but from the world. And the world and its desires are passing away, but those who do the will of God live forever. (1 John 2:15–17 NRSV)

Behind the distorted social structures of our world, Paul says, are fallen supernatural powers under the control of Satan himself. After Paul said that the Ephesians, before their conversion, had "followed the ways of this world," he added: "and of the ruler of the kingdom of the air, the spirit who is now at work in those who are disobedient" (Ephesians 2:2). Paul warns that "our struggle is not against flesh and blood, but against the rulers, against the authorities, against the powers of this dark world and against the spiritual forces of evil in the heavenly realms" (Ephesians 6:12).

Both Jews and Greeks in Paul's day believed that good and evil supernatural beings were behind the scenes influencing social and political structures.[17]

To modern secular folk, that view of the supernatural belongs to George Lucas and Stephen King. But when I look at the demonic evil of social systems like Naziism, apartheid, and communism, or even the complex mixture of racism, unemployment, sexual promiscuity, substance abuse, and police brutality in American inner cities, I have no trouble believing that Satan and his gang are hard at work fostering oppressive structures and thus doing their best to destroy God's good creation.

These fallen supernatural powers twist and distort the social systems that we social beings require for wholeness. By seducing us into wrong choices that create evil systems, by working against attempts to overcome oppressive structures, and sometimes by enticing politicians and other leaders to use the occult, these demonic powers shape our world. Evil is far more complex than the wrong choices of individuals. It also lies outside us in oppressive social systems and in demonic powers that delight in defying God by corrupting the social systems that his human image-bearers need.

Pope John Paul II has rightly insisted that evil social structures are "rooted in personal sin." Social evil results from our rebellion against God and our consequent selfishness toward our neighbors. But the accumulation and concentration of many personal sins create "structures of sin" that are both oppressive and "difficult to remove."[18] When we choose to participate in and benefit from evil social systems, we sin against God and our neighbors.

God's Response

The prophets bluntly warned people about the way the God of justice responds to oppressive social structures. God cares so much about the poor that he works to destroy social systems that tolerate and foster poverty. Repeatedly God declared that he would destroy the nation of Israel because of two things: its idolatry and its mistreatment of the poor (see, for example, Jeremiah 7:1–15).

Attention to both of these is crucial. We dare not become so preoccupied with horizontal issues of social injustice that we neglect vertical evils such as idolatry. Modern Christians seem to have an irrepressible urge to fall into one extreme or the other. But the Bible corrects our one-sidedness[19] by making it clear that both lead to destruction. God destroyed Israel and Judah because of both their idolatry and their social injustice.

Here, however, our focus is on the fact that God destroys oppressive social structures. Amos' words, which could be duplicated from many other places in Scripture, make this divine response clear:

> Because you trample upon the poor and take from him exactions of wheat, you have built houses of hewn stone, but you shall not dwell in them. (5:11)

> "Woe to those who lie upon beds of ivory, and stretch themselves upon their couches, and eat lambs from the flock, . . . but [who] are not grieved over the ruin of Joseph! Therefore they shall now be the first of those to go into exile . . ." (6:4, 6–7)

> Hear this, you who trample upon the needy, and bring the poor of the land to an end, saying, "When will the new moon be over, that we may sell grain? And the sabbath, that we may offer wheat for sale . . . and deal deceitfully with false balances, that we may buy the poor for silver and the needy for a pair of sandals . . . ?" (8:4–6)

> "Behold, the eyes of the Lord God are upon the sinful kingdom, and I will destroy it from the surface of the ground. . . ." (9:8)

Within a generation after Amos, the northern kingdom of Israel was completely wiped out.

Probably the most powerful statement of God's work to destroy evil social structures is in the New Testament—in Mary's Magnificat. Mary glorified the Lord who "has put down the mighty from their thrones, and exalted those of low degree; [who] has filled the hungry with good things, and the rich he has sent empty away" (Luke 1:52–53).

The Lord of history is working just as hard today to bring down sinful societies where wealthy classes live by the sweat, toil, and grief of the poor.

An Indian bishop once told me a story that underlines the importance of understanding social sin. A mental institution in his country had a fascinating way of deciding whether patients were well enough to go home. They would take a person over to a water tap, place a large water bucket under the tap, and fill the bucket with water. Then, leaving the tap on, they would give the person a spoon and say, "Please empty the bucket." If the person started dipping the water out one spoonful at a time and never turned the tap off, they knew he or she was still crazy!

Too often Christians, like the Indian mental patients, work at social problems one spoonful at a time. While working feverishly to correct symptoms, they fail to do anything to turn off the tap (e.g., change legal systems and economic policies that hurt people). And they remain confused and frustrated by how little progress they are making.

Understanding the biblical concept of social sin is essential to understanding the seriousness of unfair systems. At the same time, honest discussion should not leave people wallowing in guilt or feeling burdened to correct every global evil.

The proper response to sin is repentance. And genuine repentance leads to unconditional, divine forgiveness. Whenever we become aware of conscious participation in unjust systems, we should ask God's forgiveness. God does not want us to feel or be guilty; he wants us to be forgiven. He wants us to rejoice in grace—and, in the power of the Spirit, to live differently.

However, living differently—doing all God wants us to do to change structural injustice—by no means involves trying to do everything. We each have our own unique gifts and calling. God wants many of us to fast and pray about social sin. Most should study, and many should write and speak out. Some should join and support organizations promoting social justice. Others should run for political office. All of us should ask how changes in our personal lifestyle could help model a better world. But God does not want anyone to feel guilty for not doing everything—or for taking time off for relaxation and recreation. Everyone should prayerfully ask God what limited, specific things God wants him or her to concentrate on. It was God, after all, who made us finite with only twenty-four hours each day. Being called to do all God wants us to do to correct social sin is not a heavy burden. It is an invitation to joy and meaning in life, an occasion for blessing our neighbors, and a wondrous opportunity to be a co-worker with the Lord of history.

Study Questions

1. What was wrong about the situation at Edison High? Who was responsible?
2. How do Amos and Isaiah condemn both personal and social sin? If they were alive today, what might they say?
3. What happens when individuals or churches become preoccupied only with personal sin, or only with social sin? How balanced is your church?

Part Three

What Causes Poverty?

CONSERVATIVES BLAME the poor for their misery. Liberals reject that view as hard-hearted and wrong-headed. Rather than blaming the victims, liberals argue, we should condemn the structures that create poverty. Conservatives scoff at such bleeding-heart liberals who cannot see or will not admit how sinful choices about sex, drugs, alcohol, and work contribute significantly to poverty.

Who is right? And wrong? Both. There is no single cause of poverty. Personal sinful choices and complex social structures cause poverty. So do misguided cultural ideas, natural and human disasters, and lack of appropriate technology. Whether one examines long-term poverty in U.S. cities or rural poverty in the Third World, the causes are complex.[1] Chapters 7 and 8 probe this complexity.

As we explore these many, interrelated, complex causes, a basic reminder is essential. No finite person knows enough to reach complete understanding. I do not pretend that these chapters contain the final word. They simply represent my best effort to listen as objectively as I can to careful, responsible scholars. Wherever I have failed to do that, I hope others will correct me.

It is essential that disagreement about the specific analysis in parts three and four not be confused with disagreement over parts one and two. I claim considerably more certainty about my conclusions in the first two parts of this book than in the following parts. Of course, even the biblical analysis in part two is less than perfect. But disagreement over complex economic issues is fundamentally different from disagreement about biblical principles.

7

Poverty's Complex Causes

*Lazy people should learn a lesson from the way ants live. . . .
Drunkards and gluttons will be reduced to poverty. (Proverbs 6:6;
23:21 Today's English Version)*

*Woe to those who make unjust laws . . . to deprive the poor of their
rights. (Isaiah 10:1–2 NIV)*

T O REDUCE the suffering of the poor, it is essential to know what causes
poverty. If we think most poverty results from laziness when, in fact,
inadequate tools and unfair systems are major factors, our best efforts will
fail. If we think unjust structures are the only cause of poverty when, in fact,
personal choices play a role, we also will fail. To be successful, we have to
start with truth.

Sinful Personal Choices

A few people are poor due to their own laziness, and some people are poor
due to their own wrong choices. Choosing to misuse drugs, alcohol, and sex
contributes significantly to poverty. To state that bluntly is not to join some
callous conservative plot to ignore poor people or "blame the victim." It is
simply to admit the truth. The Bible clearly teaches it (Proverbs 6:6–11; 14:23;
23:21; 24:30–34), and reality regularly provides examples of drug addicts, alcoholics, and sexually promiscuous persons whose tragically wrong choices
have landed them in wrenching poverty.

    Never, of course, do we make our choices in a vacuum. Lack of a good
education, unemployment, racism, neglect in childhood—these and many

other complex factors flow together to provide a setting in which sinful choices are easy and good choices are hard.

But to deny that persons make individual choices which help create poverty denies reality. It also obscures the fact that evangelism and divine transformation of rebellious sinners is central to the solution of some forms of poverty. When sinful personal choices contribute significantly to a person's poverty, no solution will work that does not include spiritual transformation.

Unbiblical Worldviews

Misguided cultural values and non-Christian worldviews also create poverty.

Hinduism's complex theology and practice of the caste system is a major cause of poverty in India, where approximately 150 million "untouchables" live in agonizing poverty while the upper castes feel little obligation to change things. Why? Because the Hindu worldview teaches that people in the higher castes are there due to good choices in previous incarnations and those in the lowest castes are there because of evil choices in earlier incarnations. If the untouchables submit to their lot, the reigning theology explains, they will do better in the next incarnation. This worldview nurtures fatalism among the poor and complacency among the powerful.

What India needs is a worldview that rightly names the gaping disparity as sinful and unjust and proclaims the equal worth and dignity of all people. In short, India's untouchables need the Gospel. They need to hear the biblical truth that all persons are created in the image of God—that the God of history sides with the oppressed and invites them to be co-workers in shaping a just society for all.

Cultural values play a central role both in fostering poverty and in creating wealth. Those who think, as animists do, that the rivers and trees are living spirits, will not dam rivers to create hydroelectric power nor cut forests to manufacture paper. Those who think, as some Eastern monists do, that the material world is an illusion to be escaped, will not waste much time creating material abundance. And those who think, as modern materialists do, that nothing exists except the material world, will search ever more frantically for meaning and joy in ever-increasing material possessions—even if the result is environmental destruction and neglect of the poor.

What we need is a biblical worldview—a genuinely biblical view of persons, history, and the material world. Then we will treasure material possessions without worshipping them. We will seek justice for all because every person bears the divine image. And we will respect God's creation as we exercise our God-given stewardship, using the rivers and trees to create sustainable civilizations of wholesome abundance.

Cultural values and underlying worldviews make a difference. Massachusetts Institute of Technology (MIT) economist Lester Thurow points out that China had the technology to create the industrial revolution and conquer the globe centuries before Europe did.

> At least eight hundred years before they were to occur in Europe, China had invented blast furnaces and piston bellows for making steel; gunpowder and the cannon for military conquest; the compass and rudder for world exploration; paper, movable type, and the printing press for disseminating knowledge; suspension bridges; porcelain; the wheeled metal plow, the horse collar, a rotary threshing machine and a mechanical seeder for improving agricultural yields; a drill that enabled them to get energy from natural gas; and the decimal system, negative numbers, and the concept of zero to analyze what they were doing. Even the lowly wheelbarrow and the match were used centuries earlier in China.[1]

But Confucian culture perceived innovation and technology as a threat rather than an opportunity. Western cultural values, rather than a Confucian worldview, shaped the industrial revolution and its amazing creation of wealth. Some of the results have been good, some evil. But they are all related to underlying Western cultural values which are a strange mixture of historic Christianity and Enlightenment naturalism.

Disasters

Whether caused by nature or humanity, disasters cause poverty.

A raging hurricane brings widespread devastation, throwing hundreds of thousands of people into instant poverty. Floods, earthquakes, and drought also produce hunger and starvation. Sometimes environmental decay caused by human foolishness is partly to blame. But often it is merely the mysterious work of the wind and water. No one is to blame. No one needs to repent. We simply need to activate our relief networks as quickly as possible to prevent starvation.

Human disasters are different. Ethnic conflicts, religious wars, and tribal hostility today produce tens of millions of refugees abruptly snatched from their homes and livelihood. Bread for the World's *Hunger 96* estimates that civil strife causes hunger for 100 million people. Immediate relief assistance must go hand in hand with patient efforts to overcome ancient hostilities in our response to human disasters and the poverty they bring.

Lack of Technology

Some people are eager to work but lack the proper tools and knowledge. Because they do not have the seeds or implements, their agricultural production is too low to provide enough food. Without the knowledge and skill to produce other things to exchange for food, they suffer, and sometimes die, of malnutrition.

Here the primary need is long-term community development[2]—helping to drill wells for irrigation, showing how to grow more productive strains of grain, or enabling people to fashion a better plow or storage bin.

Economists rightly insist that economics is not a zero-sum game, meaning that it is wrong to think of available wealth as a limited pie which must be recut into smaller portions if everyone is to have a piece. If that were the case, any gain on the part of the poor would mean a loss for the rich.

To the contrary, wealth can be created. Though ultimately the world is finite, there are vast possibilities, as the twentieth century has demonstrated, for producing much more of the things people need to enjoy material abundance. Applying knowledge to nature produces astonishing new products. The black goo we know as crude oil was useless until someone figured out how to use it to propel cars, airplanes, and electrical generators. The result was vast new wealth (also, alas, environmental destruction). Helping the poor acquire appropriate, sustainable technology is one central way to reduce poverty.

Great Inequalities of Power

Make no mistake. There is plenty of food in the world today. Powerlessness, not famine, causes much of today's poverty. "Fundamentally," Bread for the

World says, "hunger is a political question: hungry people lack the power to end their hunger."[3] Many people today are poor and hungry largely because a few people with enormous power neglect and/or mistreat the powerless. Using their unequal power, they create structures that benefit themselves and oppress others.

A large landowner in a poor village in Bangladesh, one of the poorest countries in the world, illustrates the problem. (In Bangladesh, 65 percent of all children are malnourished, 87 percent of the people live in the countryside, and 86 percent of that rural population lives below the poverty level.) In an attempt to increase agricultural output and reduce poverty, the World Bank financed an irrigation project in the rural village. The largest landowner in the area, however, was also active in the ruling political party, and he managed to gain control of the new irrigation project and get a monopoly on the new water supply. Naturally, the benefits of the new technology flowed to this powerful landowner, not to the poor. His agricultural output did expand, but this did not help the most needy.[4]

The examples of abused power are everywhere. Europeans were the first to apply gunpowder to warfare, using this enormous new power to colonize everybody else. They largely annihilated the native peoples of the Americas and forced millions of Africans into slavery.

Power itself is not evil. But as the famous British thinker Lord Acton said, "Power tends to corrupt and absolute power corrupts absolutely." Because of the Fall, sinful people regularly use great inequalities of power to oppress the weak. Again and again, the result is unfair social, economic, and political systems that produce poverty. If we are to understand one of the root causes of poverty, we must understand how unequal power nurtures social sin or structural injustice.

Inequalities of power come in all sizes and exist everywhere.

Local

The story of the Bangladeshi landowner is repeated—with local variation— almost everywhere. As Russia moves toward private ownership, local, formerly Communist, officials with inside knowledge and connections gain personal ownership of vast wealth. In many nations, a few people own vast amounts of land. Even when the poor do own land, they often do not have access to the resources needed to make it productive.

According to the United Nations' Food and Agriculture Organization (FAO), 1.3 percent of all landowners in Latin America own 71.6 percent of the land.[5] Poor farmers who do not have land often have to borrow money to purchase seed and fertilizer. Frequently, unscrupulous moneylenders are the only source of credit. But they often charge outrageous interest rates—sometimes even 20 percent per day, according to development specialist Michael Todaro.[6] Frequently the poor farmer defaults and loses his land—which was probably the moneylender's original goal.[7]

National

Wealthy elites—sometimes allied to corrupt, authoritarian rulers—dominate many poor nations.

The Philippines is a very poor nation where most people try to earn a living from the land. But most people don't have any land—10 percent of the people own 90 percent of the land. Large landowners and multinational companies own huge plantations. So 70 percent of the rural population cannot even afford enough food for a healthy diet.

For years President Marcos ruled the Philippines with a dictatorial fist, squelching efforts for land reform. Even when Mrs. Aquino won the hearts of the world with her brave non-violent victory over the brutal Marcos, little changed. Mrs. Aquino herself owns vast estates. And large landowners dominate the Congress. So even though most Filipinos support land reform, poor peasants have acquired almost no land.[8]

Or consider the case of President Mobutu, the fabulously wealthy ruler of Zaire from 1965–1997. During the 1960s and 70s, Belgium, France, and the U.S. sent cash and military forces to support Zaire's dictator, Mobutu Sese Seko, because he was a valuable opponent of communism in a strategic location. The people of Zaire are desperately poor, 70 percent living in poverty. It also has the world's highest infant mortality rate and child malnutrition rates of 42 to 65 percent.[9] During the 1980s, per capita income in Zaire declined by an annual average of 1.3 percent.

Meanwhile, there is good reason to believe that Mobutu stole $5 billion from the economy. Responsible government largely disappeared. Looting and riots became common. Mobutu fought every effort to move the country toward democracy. And 20,000 soldiers protected this powerful dictator.[10]

Looting from government coffers happens in many countries. In November 1995, the Swiss found over $80 million held by or for Raul Salinas, the brother of the former president of Mexico, Carlos Salinas. A further search later turned up other accounts in London and some off-shore havens.[11]

Or consider the U.S. Even though the purchasing power of the minimum wage dropped by 25 percent between 1978 and 1989, Congress refused to raise it. People who worked full time at the minimum wage in 1991 earned far less ($8,840) than the official poverty level for a family of three ($10,723). During that same period, Congress cut corporate taxes, capital gains taxes, and tax rates on the richest Americans. The richest 1 percent (2.5 million) got much richer while the poor lost ground. Between 1980 and 1990, this tiny rich 1 percent gained as much *additional* after-tax income as the poorest 20 percent (50 million) received in total income.[12] Surely the actions of Congress are connected to the fact that most political donations also come from the richest 1 percent of U.S. citizens.

Table 13 on the following page shows how income is divided in a wide variety of nations. In Brazil, the richest 20 percent received over 32 times as much income as the poorest 20 percent. In the U.S., it is about 9 times and in Japan it is 4.3 times. There is no obvious correlation between a country's total wealth and the gap between its rich and poor. In some rich countries, like the U.S. and Australia, the gap is quite large. In others, like Japan and the Netherlands, it is much less. Behind this simple table, however, lie enormous differences of power that profoundly shape the life of each nation.

Global

The five permanent members of the U.N. Security Council (U.S., Russia, Britain, France, and China) have veto power, and they regularly use that power for national advantage. With only 5 percent of the world's people, the U.S. controls 17 percent of the votes in the World Bank and 18 percent in the International Monetary Fund—two powerful global institutions whose decisions regularly impact poorer nations. Seven nations (U.S., Japan, Great Britain, France, Germany, Canada, and Italy) have only 12 percent of the world's people, but their annual summit is widely regarded as the most influential global economic institution.

Table 13—Income Distribution in various countries[13]
(listed in order of the ratio of the richest 20% / poorest 20%)

Country	Income of Poorest 20%	Income of Richest 20%	Ratio of Richest 20% / Poorest 20%
Brazil	2.1	67.5	32.1
Guatemala	2.1	46.6	30.0
Panama	2.0	59.8	29.9
South Africa	3.3	63.3	19.2
Kenya	3.4	62.1	18.3
Chile	3.5	61.0	17.4
Zimbabwe	4.0	62.3	15.6
Russia	3.7	53.8	14.5
Mexico	4.1	55.3	13.5
Australia	4.4	42.2	9.6
United Kingdom	4.6	44.3	9.6
United States	4.7	41.9	8.9
Hong Kong	5.4	47.0	8.7
France	5.6	41.9	7.5
Philippines	6.5	47.8	7.4
China	6.2	43.9	7.1
Uganda	6.8	48.1	7.1
Germany	7.0	40.3	5.8
India	8.5	42.6	5.0
Egypt	8.7	41.1	4.7
Indonesia	8.7	40.7	4.7
Sweden	8.0	36.9	4.6
Netherlands	8.2	36.9	4.5
Sri Lanka	8.9	39.3	4.4
Spain	8.3	36.6	4.4
Japan	8.7	37.5	4.3
Rwanda	9.7	39.1	4.0
Bangladesh	9.4	37.9	4.0
Hungary	9.5	36.6	3.9
Romania	9.2	34.8	3.8
Czech Republic	10.5	37.4	3.6
Slovak Republic	11.9	31.4	2.6

Source: World Bank[14]

The story of the long process to draw up an international treaty to tap the wealth at the bottom of the ocean illustrates the problem. Under the sea lies a wealth of unclaimed resources. Because no nation can justly claim property rights to the oceans, the untapped wealth of the ocean floor seemed to offer a chance for the Third World to gain without sacrifice from the wealthy nations. The seabed is a "common heritage" of humankind whose riches should benefit all. However, the developing nations do not possess the sophisticated technology needed to mine the resources.

This set of circumstances opened the door to the possibility of the transfer of technology from rich to poor. Negotiations began in 1973 and continued steadily until 1981. Then, at the last minute in 1981, when the final details were to be worked out and the treaty signed by all participating nations, the United States, under the direction of President Ronald Reagan, backed out. The reason? The administration feared the transfer of technology would jeopardize the economic advantage of U.S.-based mining companies.[15] It was only in 1995 that the U.S. finally signed the treaty.

Western Colonialism

The history of European colonialism is one of the most vivid historical examples of how great inequalities of power foster injustice.

From the sixteenth century on, white Europeans have had more power—military power—than anyone else. They knew how to make guns. Asians, Africans and Native-Americans did not.[16] The result is history. We wiped out most of the native peoples in North America; killed millions and decimated the rest in Latin America; enslaved millions of Africans; and divided up Asia, Africa, and the Americas as we pleased.

Economic historians still argue about the economic impact on colonized nations. But there is little doubt that colonialism is one reason for some poverty, even today. Respected development economist Mahbub ul Haq, for years a senior economist at the World Bank, writes that "the basic reasons for inequality between the presently developed and developing nations lie fairly deep in their history. In most parts of the Third World, centuries of colonial rule have left their legacy of dependency."[17]

It is now generally recognized by historians that many of the civilizations Europe "discovered" were highly developed in many ways; their most obvious "deficiency" was their lack of modern military technology. True, the civilizations of Asia, Africa, and the Americas were different in that they were not "Christian," but how Christian were the European colonizers?

In *Asian Drama*, a classic of development literature, Gunnar Myrdal places much of the blame for decades of economic stagnation in Southeast Asia at the feet of European colonizers:

> In general, the colonial regimes in South Asia were inimical to the development of manufacturing industry in the colonies. This was even more true when they gradually gave up, after the 1850s and 1870s, the crudely exploitative policies of early colonialism and began to encourage investment and production. It was predominantly or exclusively the production of raw materials for export that was encouraged.[18]

Most "Mother" countries used their colonies to enhance their own national status in the world community. Strong nation-states became the ultimate objective, and control over land and wealth around the world was the key to power.[19] The creation of colonies was extremely useful. Preoccupied with the status of the mother country, colonizers seldom exhibited much regard for the economic, social, and cultural conditions of the indigenous peoples.

In his book *Bread and Justice*, James B. McGinnis cites the example of the town of Potosi, Bolivia. Potosi was a thriving urban area in the seventeenth century when the Spaniards came to mine the area's gold and silver. At first the Spanish miners produced booming economic growth. But,

> when the silver ran out, Potosi's boom ended and the area was left to "underdevelop" . . .
>
> The underdevelopment of Potosi, then, began with the abuse of its people and resources through the European colonial system. The Latin American economy was geared by the Europeans to meet their own needs, not those of the local people. The underdevelopment has its roots in the history of military conquests. Underdeveloped countries are full of "ghost" towns like Potosi, and nearly all were European colonies at one time.[20]

A writer for the *Wall Street Journal* provides another example. June Kronholz wrote an article examining the modern attempt of Gabon (a small country in Africa) to build a transnational railroad. Why, she asked, was one not built in colonial days?

> The French built only what they needed to find and export Gabon's raw materials. In fact, colonials' habit of building only those roads and ports and power plants that served their purposes, while ignoring the rest of the country, still stifles Third World economies. "They inherited a legacy that condemned them to underdevelopment," complains the U.N.'s Mr. Doo Kingue, whose own country, Cameroon, was colonized by Germans, English and French.[21]

It would be simplistic, of course, to suggest that the impact of colonialism and subsequent economic and political relations with industrialized nations was entirely negative. It was not. Among other things, literacy rates rose and health care improved.

I also thank God that opportunities to spread the gospel around the world increased during the colonial period. But think of how different colonial history would be if missionaries had challenged imperial injustice more often. Christian values sometimes undercut ancient social evils, such as the caste system in India, but what a tragedy that so much of the impact of the "Christian" North on the developing political and economic structures of the colonies was shaped by economic self-interest rather than the biblical principles of justice. If the whole biblical message had been shared and lived in social and economic life, developing nations would know less misery today. If Christian attitudes toward property and wealth had ruled the colonizers' actions, if the principles of jubilee, the sabbatical year, and empowerment of the poor had been an integral part of the colonial venture and international economic activity, there would be less need for this book today.

Unfortunately, they were not. So the colonial legacy lingers. Not surprisingly, some of the injustices perpetuated in the early days of colonialism have become cemented in the institutions that govern contemporary economic activity.[22]

It would be silly, of course, to depict colonialism as the sole cause of present poverty. Wrong personal choices, misguided cultural values, disasters and inadequate technology all play a part. So do gross inequalities of power. At every level—whether local, national or global—people with great power use it for selfish purposes, enriching themselves and oppressing others. Widespread poverty is the result.

Study Questions

1. What causes of poverty do you and your friends emphasize? Why?
2. Do you agree or disagree with the explanation of poverty in this chapter? Why?
3. What parts of this chapter would be most widely challenged? What arguments would you develop to respond to those challenges?

8

Structural Injustice Today

Come now, you rich, weep and howl for the miseries that are coming upon you. Your riches have rotted and your garments are moth-eaten. Your gold and silver have rusted, and their rust will be evidence against you and will eat your flesh like fire. You have laid up treasure for the last days. Behold, the wages of the laborers who moved your fields, which you kept back by fraud, cry out; and the cries of the harvesters have reached the ears of the Lord of hosts. You have lived on the earth in luxury and in pleasure: you have fattened your hearts in a day of slaughter. (James 5:1–5)

I read some time ago that Upton Sinclair, the author, read this passage to a group of ministers. Then he attributed the passage to Emma Goldman, who at the time was an anarchist agitator. The ministers were indignant, and their response was, "This woman ought to be deported at once!" (unpublished sermon [1 June 1975] by Dr. Paul E. Toms, former president of the National Association of Evangelicals).

SHORTLY after the first edition of this book was published, I was lecturing at an evangelical college about God's concern for the poor and the existence of unjust structures that help create poverty. In my chapel talk, I suggested that some starvation results from economic structures that wealthy nations like the U.S. erect for their own advantage.

The college chaplain did not see things that way. He invited me to his class. But before I spoke he made his position very clear when he said, as I recall his words, "I can hardly believe that my country could do anything wrong."

Years of global experience as president of World Vision led another evangelical leader to a starkly different conclusion. Stanley Mooneyham condemned "the stranglehold which the developed West has kept on the economic throats of the Third World." That, I believe, is to overstate the problem. But Mooneyham makes an important point in saying that "the heart of the problems of poverty and hunger are human systems which ignore, mistreat and exploit man. . . . If the hungry are to be fed, . . . some of the systems will require drastic adjustments while others will have to be scrapped altogether."[1] This chapter explores evidence for this claim.

To do so, we must examine some complex economic ideas. I will try to use ordinary language rather than technical jargon. (After all, I am a theologian, not an economist.) However, the reader who has no interest in economics may want to skip to chapters 9 and 10, which deal with practical steps that individuals and churches can take to empower the poor.

Some critics of this chapter (and chapter 11) have suggested that I should have stayed with theology. Meddling theologians, they claim, never get their economics right. I have two responses. First, I have tried hard to listen to and learn from good economists. In fact, first-rate economists have provided extensive advice. Their careful review of these sections and their advice have greatly improved chapters 8 and 11. Second, even brilliant economists disagree and make mistakes. Since economics is central to our world, non-economists like you and me will have to do our best to understand without being intimidated by the fact that our understanding is only partial.

In citing the disturbing data that follows, I do so with neither sadistic enjoyment of an opportunity to flagellate the affluent, nor with a desire to create feelings of irresolvable guilt. God has no interest in groundless "guilt trips." But I do believe the God of the poor wants us all to feel deep pain over the agony and anguish that torment the poor. I also believe we must call sin by its biblical name.

As discussed in the previous chapter, the affluent North is not responsible for all the poverty in the world. There are many causes. But even if the rich did not cause any part of global poverty, we still would be responsible to help those in need. The story of the rich man and Lazarus (Luke 16:19–31) does not suggest that Lazarus's poverty resulted from oppression by his rich neighbor. The rich man merely neglected to help. His sin was one of omission. And it sent him to hell.

I do believe, however, that affluent nations have played a part in establishing economic structures that contribute to some of today's hunger and starvation. Surely our first responsibility is to understand and change what we are doing wrong.

How then are we a part of unjust structures that contribute to world hunger? A discussion of seven issues will reveal our involvement: (1) market economies; (2) international trade; (3) the debt of very poor nations; (4) natural resources and the environment; (5) food consumption and food imports; (6) multinational corporations in the Third World; and (7) discrimination and war.

Evaluating Market Economies

Do market economies help or hurt the poor? Our exploration of the structural causes of poverty must begin with this question. Democratic capitalism has won the most dramatic economic/political debate of the twentieth century. Almost every country in the world praises the ideal of democracy. Virtually every nation is taking steps toward "a market economy." Anybody concerned about the poor must struggle with how this momentous global embrace of market economies impacts the poorest.

But what is a market economy? Definition is crucial. There are a wide variety of actual market economies today. The "ideal type" of a pure laissez-faire economy (where the government never intervenes in economic life) does not exist in today's world. Whether in North America, Western Europe, or the successful Asian Tigers (Taiwan, South Korea, Singapore, and Hong Kong), the government plays a substantial role in what everyone nevertheless calls market economies.[2]

A market economy then is an economic arrangement in which the bulk of the wealth and means of production are privately owned and most wages and prices are set by supply and demand. This does not mean that government never intervenes in the economy. It does today in all existing market economies—although in the U.S., for example, the government intervenes less than in Germany.

Communist economies were fundamentally different. The state owned the means of production. State central planners determined wages, prices, and production. (There used to be a central office in Moscow that set 25 million prices every year!)[3]

At the end of the twentieth century, the modern world has rejected centrally planned economies in favor of market economies. Is that good news for the poor?

Yes, on balance, it is, although there are serious problems with the way present market economies are working.

Communism's state ownership and central planning do not work. They are inefficient and totalitarian. Market economies, on the other hand, have produced enormous wealth. And not only in Western nations. Many Asian countries have adopted market economies. The result has been a dramatic drop in poverty in the world's most populous continent. In 1970, chronic undernourishment plagued 35 percent of the people in all developing countries. Twenty-one years later—in spite of rapid population growth—only 20 percent were chronically undernourished.[4]

All around the globe, countries are seeking to copy the success of the "Asian Tigers," which have successfully combined a basic market framework with substantial government activity. The result? Stunning success.

A recent United Nations report indicated that "about 80 countries were in the process of economic liberalization and privatization."[5] Whether in former communist countries, in Sub-Saharan Africa, or Latin America, countries are adopting economic policies that place far greater emphasis on markets. Countries are privatizing government-owned corporations, reducing barriers to international trade, and welcoming foreign investments.[6]

The evidence is overwhelming. Market economies are more successful than centrally owned and planned economies at creating economic growth. China's phenomenal growth rate over the last decade is clearly the result of its substantial adoption of free-market measures in both agriculture and substantial parts of industrial production. Throughout most of East Asia—not just in the much-discussed "Tigers," but also in Malaysia, Indonesia, Thailand—market economies are producing explosive economic growth.

Central to this growth is the expansion of exports and international trade. The rapid growth of the Asian Tigers was directly related to their decision to reduce trade barriers and emphasize exports—along with substantial government activity. Scores of careful studies show that greater concentration on goods for export almost always produces economic growth.[7]

International trade also tends to increase real wages in developing countries.[8] Wages in export-oriented firms in developing countries are, of course, very low in comparison to wages in developed nations. (That, after all, is a major part of a poor nation's comparative advantage.) But those "low wages" are usually substantially higher—especially when trade unions have basic freedom—than the average wages in the country. Thus when international trading patterns use the comparative advantage of low wages in poor nations, two beneficial things can result: poor people receive higher wages and all of us pay lower prices for the products.[9]

International trade creates forces that tend to cause wages for labor with the same skills to equalize among trading partners.[10] Obviously, that hurts high-paid workers in industrialized nations who must compete with much lower-paid workers in Indonesia, Mexico, or China. But surely those most concerned with the poorest should support measures to improve wages in developing countries and then seek other ways (generous unemployment insurance and job training, for example) to help workers in rich nations who are hurt by global trade. In this way, developed nations focus more on areas where they have a comparative advantage.

Substantial evidence indicates that moving toward free markets often promotes economic growth. *World Development Report 1995* reports a study of 29 Sub-Saharan African countries. Between 1981 and 1986 and 1987 and 1991, the six countries that adopted the most market reforms experienced the strongest economic growth. Their economies expanded by 2 percent per year. Gross Domestic Product (GDP) in those countries that did not adopt market reforms fell by 2 percent per year.[11]

The first conclusion to draw therefore is that market economies are better at producing economic growth than present alternatives. Furthermore, since poor nations need economic growth in order to provide a modestly decent standard of living for the world's poorest people, those who care about the poorest should accept markets as an important, useful tool for empowering the poor.

Unfortunately today's market economies also have fundamental weaknesses. When measured by biblical standards, glaring injustices exist. Precisely as we adopt a market framework as better than known alternatives, we must examine and correct problems that exist in today's market economies.

The most glaring problem is that at least a quarter of the world's people lack the capital to participate in any major way in the global market economy. Land is still the basic capital in many agricultural societies.

Money and education are far more crucial in modern capital-intensive, knowledge-intensive economies. About one of four people in our world have almost no land, very little money, and virtually no education.

The market's mechanism of supply and demand is blind to the distinction between basic necessities (even minimal food needed to avoid starvation) and luxuries desired by the wealthy. Today, 20 percent of the world's people receive 83 percent of the world's income (see Table 14). Left to itself, a market-driven economy will simply supply what the wealthy can pay for—even if millions of poor folk starve.

Table 14—Distribution of Global Income
% of total quintiles of population ranked by income

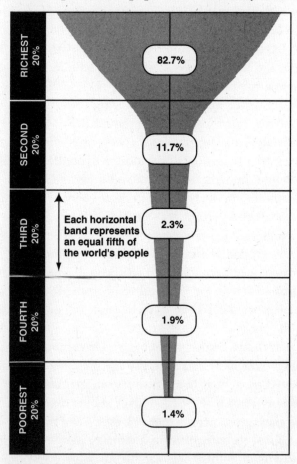

RICHEST 20% — 82.7%

SECOND 20% — 11.7%

THIRD 20% — Each horizontal band represents an equal fifth of the world's people — 2.3%

FOURTH 20% — 1.9%

POOREST 20% — 1.4%

Source: United Nations [12]

If we start with the present division of wealth, the outcome of the market will be ghastly injustice. Only if redistribution occurs—through both private and public measures—will the poorest obtain the capital to earn a decent living in the global market.

Second, at least in the short run, the poorest seem to suffer (or at least fail to gain in proportion to the rest of society) when countries move toward a market economy—unless government takes vigorous and wise corrective measures. The data is not conclusive. Economists still debate the issue. But there is increasing agreement that as economic growth lifts per capita income, the initial result is growing inequality between rich and poor.[13] Then as per capita income continues to rise, the inequality declines.

This basic analysis raises crucial questions. In the early stages of economic growth, do the poorest actually lose real income? Or do they gain, though not as fast as the middle and upper classes? There are no widely accepted answers to these questions. The outcome depends in part on whether government takes appropriate steps to provide capital and other things to the poorest at the same time that market reforms occur.

The situation in the past decade, however, has been that market reforms have been accompanied by a short-term increase in poverty in many places. Many of the people in Eastern Europe and the former Soviet Union are worse off than under communism. A number of studies indicate that the poor in Africa and Latin America have also become poorer as market reforms were introduced.[14] Was that outcome an inevitable part of market reforms? Or was it because of choices by governments to cut things like education and health care rather than military budgets? The answer is not yet clear.

What is indisputable is that over time the poor usually benefit. The poor in South Korea, Taiwan, Singapore, and Hong Kong are vastly better off economically than they were twenty-five years ago—because of a combination of market reforms and government activities. The same is true of vast numbers of formerly extremely poor people in China, Indonesia, Malaysia, and Thailand.

Very disturbing, however, is more recent data showing that the gap between rich and poor is increasing again in very wealthy countries, especially the U.S. and U.K.—the two wealthy market economies with the greatest reliance on the market. In the U.S., the gap between the rich and poor has grown enormously in the last twenty plus years. From 1973 to 1992, the richest 10 percent gained 18 percent while the real income of the poorest 10 percent fell by 11 percent.[15] On the other hand, wealthy European countries with more active governments have not experienced the same growing gap between rich and poor. The right kind of government intervention to help the poorest seems to be a significant factor.

Without corrective action, today's global markets appear to create unjust, dangerous extremes between rich and poor. Robert Frank, a Cornell University economist, argues in his book *Winner Take All* that complex developments (modern technology, the globalized economy, mass marketing, economies of scale, etc.) enable increasingly smaller numbers of people to acquire an ever larger share of the wealth. So, Bill Gates of Microsoft makes $15 billion before he's forty and becomes the richest American.[16] "The $20 million Michael Jordan reportedly received in 1992 for promoting Nike shoes exceeded the entire annual payroll of the Indonesian factories that made them."[17] Today, Michael Jordan earns as much for promoting Nike shoes as approximately 18,000 Indonesian workers who make these shoes (even after a doubling of wages since 1993!)[18] In response, Nike claims their workers earn 50 cents an hour (twice the country's minimum wage) as well as free meals and health care.[19]

Centralized wealth equals concentrated power. And that—as the conservative critics of communism rightly used to point out—is dangerous. It is not surprising that the relatively small numbers of wealthy people who control the largest corporations, which in turn own the media, also have vast political power. In the U.S., most of the private money for political campaigns comes from the richest 1 percent of the people. Not surprisingly, most politicians care more about the self-interest of their wealthy donors than about justice for the poor. Democracy is threatened and the poor suffer.

Third, pervasive cultural decline seems to follow the expansion of the market.[20] The most obvious perhaps is the sweeping materialism and consumerism that floods the world as country after country joins the global market. Material possessions and the money that buys them become all important to more and more people. The size of one's salary (and house) become more important than God, neighbor, and the creation. In fact, more and more people value making money more than marriage, parenting, or even honesty.

It is easy to see how materialistic consumerism develops. The competitive drive to increase market share encourages ever-more seductive advertising. American historian William Leach's book *Land of Desire: Merchants and the Rise of a New American Culture* tells how this happened. The Puritan and other Christian traditions had shaped early nineteenth century American culture to value thrift, frugality, and modest lifestyles. But that did not sell enough products. So large corporations developed advertising techniques to persuade us that joy and happiness come through fancy new clothes, the latest car models, and ever-more sophisticated gadgets.

The director of research labs of General Motors, Charles Kettering, decided that business needed to create a "dissatisfied consumer." Annual model changes—planned obsolescence—was his solution. Success, according to advertising historian Roland Marchard, came to depend on "the virtue of qualities like wastefulness, self-indulgence, and artificial obsolescence."[21]

Diabolically clever advertising agencies use the most sophisticated combinations of beautiful women, gorgeous color, and splendid sound tracks to guarantee that self-indulgence and instant gratification replace frugality and simplicity. The great economist John Maynard Keynes put it simply: "Consumption is the sole end and object of all economic activity."[22]

Television is the most powerful medium. The average five-year-old watches three and one-half hours of television a day. The average adult, five hours—that means watching 21,000 commercials a year. And the message is the same: "Buy something—do it now." It is hardly surprising that the largest 100 U.S. corporations pay for about 75 percent of all commercial television. And the producers and writers develop what the advertisers will support.[23]

What started in the U.S. has spread around the world. Even the poorest kid in India knows that Coca-Cola™ refreshes. And Avon's slick advertising persuades desperately poor Brazilian women to buy expensive skin cream. Television ads showing sensuous, light-skinned women suggest that older women can shed their aging skin, tanned and wrinkled by years of hard labor in the sun. "Renew" costs forty dollars a jar. And it works by burning off the top layer of skin. But Avon's communications director in Brazil says it works: "Women do everything to buy it. They stop buying other things like clothes, like shoes. If they feel good with their skin, they prefer to stop buying clothes and buy something that is on television."[24]

Global corporations own the global communications networks whose programs and advertising create a global lust for ever-more consumption.

Growing materialism creates growing markets and expanding profits. Tragically, this same materialism destroys social relationships and the creation. Increasingly, some people think the heart of parenting is supplying one's children with more and more material pleasures. And the consumptive overload pollutes the environment.

The market also corrupts culture by rewarding immoral actions. If there is a demand for pornography and dishonest advertisements, the market generously rewards the producers—even if the process corrupts the character of both the producers and the recipients.

Cultural decay also flows from the imperialistic tendency of the market to dominate all of life. The efficiency that follows from making some relationships mere interactions of economic exchange based on supply and demand is frequently good. It is often fine to choose a television salesperson based on market prices. But should the same concern determine the choice of a spouse? Or the decision whether or not to have one parent stay at home with young children? It may be economically advantageous to pay a full-time nanny rather than have skilled professionals "waste" precious time on parenting. But something terribly precious has been lost. There should never be a market in body parts, or sex, or infants for adoption. "If sexuality is made a commodity of exchange, it becomes prostitution."[25] The market's imperialistic tendency to become the sole way to organize all of life corrupts and destroys character and culture.

The environmental crisis reveals a fourth problem with our global market economy. Our rivers and lakes are polluted, the ozone layer is depleted, and global warming has already begun (see pp. 157–166). Unfortunately, markets pay little attention to the needs of future generations.[26] The market fails to account for environmental costs—both because national accounting systems fail to notice the loss of natural capital and because companies seldom count pollution costs in their profit-and-loss statements. Costa Rica experienced significant economic growth between 1970 and 1990. But environmental decay in its soils and forests produced lost natural capital totalling 6 percent of the GDP of that period. In Indonesia, the loss was 9 percent from 1971 to 1984.[27]

The market rewards polluters who pass their costs to neighbors—those who live downstream from where they dump polluted water into the river; those who live thousands of miles downwind from smokestacks that spew pollution into the air, which then quickly circles the globe; or all our grand-children who will suffer the consequences of today's arrogant neglect. Unless governments compel all companies to pay the real costs of environmental destruction, the market will reward those who choose pollution and the quick profits it offers, not those who opt for the slower profits that result from environmental responsibility.

It is idolatrous nonsense to equate justice with the outcome of a pure laissez-faire economy. It is false to think that a market economy, if freed from all government interference, would create what the Bible means by jus-tice. Masses of poor folk lacking capital are unable to afford even basic necessities. Concentrated wealth threatens democracy. Materialistic mes-sages and practices corrode moral values, family life, and God's creation.

To do these things in the name of efficiency is idolatrous. Christians know that Keynes was wrong. Consumption is *not* the sole end of economic life. The economy is made for people, not people for an autonomous, effi-cient, ever-expanding economy. Wholesome family life and wise steward-ship of God's garden matter more than economic efficiency. Yahweh is Lord even of economics.

International Trade

The industrialized nations have shaped the patterns of international trade for their own economic benefit. In colonial days, as we have seen, mother countries regularly made sure that economic affairs were organized to their own advantage.[28] Such advantage was largely achieved through manipulation of commodity trade. Western colonial nations adopted policies that increased the quantity of goods they wanted from their colonies and at the same time discouraged efforts in the colonies to develop or improve manufacturing capacities. As a result, many colonies became unnecessarily dependent on shipping primary products to and purchasing expensive manufactured prod-ucts from their "mother" countries.

Although colonialism ended decades ago, industrialized nations have continued, over the past several decades, to manipulate international trade by imposing restrictive tariffs and import quotas to keep out many of the goods (especially processed and manufactured goods) produced in the less-developed countries. Tariff structures and import quotas affecting the poor nations are in fact one fundamental aspect of systemic injustice today.

Major European countries (members of the EEC) charge four times as high a tariff on cloth imported from poor nations as from developed countries.[29] During the 1980s, 20 of the 24 industrialized countries increased their protection against manufactured or processed products from the developing countries. The United Nations reports that "the effective rate of protection against exports from developing countries is considerably higher than the rate against exports from industrial countries."[30]

This costs poor nations dearly—in fact, more than they receive in foreign aid. Estimates vary somewhat, but the overall picture is clear. The World Bank estimates that trade barriers imposed by rich nations on goods from poor nations cost poor nations $50 to $100 billion a year.[31] The United Nation's figure is that trade barriers cost the developing countries $75 billion a year.[32] Bread for the World's 1995 estimate is $80 billion.[33]

Typically, developed countries have allowed many agricultural and other primary products (minerals, cocoa, rubber, sisal, and so on) to enter relatively duty free. But they have been less generous with manufactured goods. The more manufacturing and processing done by the poor country, the higher the tariff rich nations charged.[34] At one point, for example, the tariff on candy bars was five times higher than on raw cocoa beans.[35] Similarly, while the tariff on raw sugar was 2 percent, the tariff on processed sugar was 20 percent.[36]

The reasons for such trade restrictions are obvious. In colonial times they were imposed in order to limit the competition with the mother country's own developing industrial enterprises and to facilitate the transfer of needed primary products. Today restrictions are maintained largely because their removal would threaten the interest of certain well-organized and politically entrenched groups. Both labor and management in the developed countries want to be able to buy cheap raw materials in order to profit from processing and manufacturing them here. They also want to hinder other countries' efforts at processing and manufacturing because those products, when imported, would directly compete with the domestic industry.

Trade barriers come in three basic forms: (1) tariffs—a fee charged for certain imports from other nations calculated as a percent of the value of the import, but an unlimited number of that product may be imported; (2) quotas—governments allow only a certain number of a particular product to enter the country; some quotas are "voluntary" (our government works out an agreement with another nation so that that country "voluntarily" agrees to export a limited quantity of some product to us); (3) other non-tariff barriers (e.g., safety standards).

Fortunately, recent trade negotiations (the "Uruguay Round" and the new World Trade Organization) have made progress in reducing tariffs that for decades penalized poor nations. Unfortunately, they have not reduced non-tariff barriers, which are growing.

A brief review of history shows how much things needed to be changed. The U.S. used its economic muscle in 1955, threatening to withdraw from GATT if it did not receive a special "temporary" exemption so it could use import quotas on agriculture imports to protect U.S. farmers. That exemption remains in effect forty years later.[37]

In the early 1960s, for instance, the Kennedy round of tariff negotiations lowered the tariffs on goods traded among the rich industrial nations by 50 percent. But it did little to lower tariffs on goods from poorer countries. The relative situation of the poor countries actually grew worse.[38] U.S. pressure helped develop the Multi-Fibre Agreement (now being slowly phased out) which for years protected the U.S. and other rich nations' manufactures from cheaper imports of textiles and garments from developing countries.[39]

The Uruguay Round, however, signed in 1994, is better. According to the World Bank, it is the "widest-ranging and most ambitious multilateral trade agreement ever negotiated." It brought down tariffs to an average of 3.9 percent, down from 6.3 percent in recent years and from 40 percent in 1947. Global gains from the accord are estimated to be between $100 and $200 billion, and roughly one-third of that will go to developing countries.[40] Unfortunately, many of these gains will be delayed, because much of the protection is being phased out over a number of years. For example, the Multi-Fibre Agreement (which affects clothing) will be phased out over ten years.[41] As trade barriers fall, most countries will benefit, although some observers think that many countries in Sub-Saharan Africa, as well as some of the countries in Latin America and Asia, may not have the economic dynamism necessary to take advantage of the new opportunities. Africa could fall further behind.[42] On balance, however, we can be grateful for the progress made in reducing tariffs on manufactured goods from poorer nations.

Unfortunately, the same is not true in the case of "voluntary" quotas and other non-tariff barriers to manufactured goods from less developed countries (LDCs). These have become more common. The World Bank's 1987 *World Development Report* showed that these non-tariff barriers were increasing and also that all the industrial nations had higher non-tariff barriers for developing nations than for industrial nations.[43] From 1987 to 1990, non-tariff barriers increased another 20 percent. They now are the main obstacle to developing countries' exports. Recently, the United Nations estimated that these barriers affect one-third of all developing country exports to industrialized countries. And new ones continue to be introduced.[44]

Non-tariff barriers include safety and health regulations, labeling requirements, and technical standards. Some of these are necessary and good, but many are only "thinly veiled disguises for restricting imports."[45] One example: in 1981, the French were importing 64,000 VCRs per month, mostly from Japan. Then the French government declared that all imported VCRs must clear customs in the tiny town of Poitiers, hundreds of miles from the ports. There, a tiny customs crew strictly enforced numerous time-consuming customs regulations. The result was that less than 10,000 VCRs cleared customs each month.[46] This example comes from two developed countries. But wealthy nations use the same kind of non-tariff barriers against poor nations. The result is fewer jobs in hungry lands and lower export earnings.

"Voluntary" quotas can also have a devastating impact. Industrialized countries simply threaten new tariff barriers on certain manufactures exported by poor countries unless they "voluntarily" limit the volume exported to them. An example from Brazil shows how it works.

Coffee used to provide Brazil with approximately one-half its total export earnings. Brazil's coffee exports increased 90 percent between 1953 and 1961. But the total revenue earned from coffee dropped by 35 percent. So in 1966 Brazil decided to process its own coffee in order to supply more jobs and earn more income for its people. But when it seized 14 percent of the U.S. market, the U.S. coffee manufacturers charged the Brazilians with unfair competition. What did the U.S. government do? It threatened to cut off aid to Brazil, warning that it might not renew the International Coffee Agreement (which until recently kept coffee prices somewhat stable). Brazil eventually was forced to tax its instant coffee exports, and its infant industry was seriously damaged.[47]

In spite of reduced tariffs, voluntary quotas and other non-tariff barriers erected by developed nations continue to hurt the poor. They deprive poor countries of millions of jobs and billions of dollars from increased exports.

One other aspect of international trade is important here. By and large the developing countries have been historically restricted to produce primary commodities for export. In many cases colonial governments coercively discouraged manufacturing industries and actively encouraged the production and export of certain agricultural products and other raw materials. More recently, tariff and non-tariff barriers to manufactured products from poorer nations discouraged such exports. For these and other reasons LDCs have specialized in primary products and have tended to import manufactured products from the industrialized nations.

Table 15 shows that the exports of developing nations tend to be primary products. Whereas 98 percent of Japan's exports are manufactured goods, only 7 percent of Zaire's and 11 percent of Kenya's exports are manufactured goods.

Table 15—Exports: Primary and Manufactured			
Country	Exports (% of GDP)	Primary Products' share of exports	Manufactured products' share of exports
Hong Kong	48.6	4	96
Togo	43.2	91	9
Venezuela	35.7	89	11
South Korea	27.4	7	93
Kenya	13.7	89	11
Zaire	13.2	93	7
Brazil	7.5	47	53
India	7.0	27	73
France	17.5	23	77
Japan	9.7	2	98
U.S.	9.5	22	78

Source: World Bank[48]

Many economists from developing nations have charged that this reliance on primary products has destined them to suffer continually declining relative terms of trade. They cite examples such as Brazil's ability in 1954 to buy one U.S. jeep for fourteen bags of coffee, while in 1968 the same U.S. jeep cost Brazil forty-five bags of coffee.[49] Tanzania could buy a tractor in 1963 for five tons of sisal; in 1970, by contrast, the same tractor cost ten tons of sisal.[50] Tanzania had to export four times the amount of cotton or ten times the amount of tobacco to buy a tractor in 1981 as was needed a mere five years earlier.[51]

Economists agree that prices for primary products are falling relative to prices for manufactured goods.[52] That means a loss of billions of dollars. The World Bank's *World Development Report 1991* said that between 1900 and 1986, non-fuel commodity terms of trade declined an average of .6 percent per year.[53] Between 1980 and 1992, the terms of trade was 20 to 30 percent below the 1975 level and 30 to 40 percent below the 1960 level.[54]

"One estimate has placed the extra costs of deteriorating terms of trade for the LDCs at over $2.5 billion per year during the past decade. As a result, developing nations' merchandise trade balances have steadily worsened during the 1980s—falling, for example, from plus $55.8 billion in 1981 to minus $1.2 billion in 1985."[55]

All of this, of course, is not due to some global plot. History of course plays a part. But so do factors like the creation of cheaper synthetic products that replace things like natural rubber and cotton.[56] It would be foolish and misguided to seek to reverse such trends. But the dramatic decline in the prices of primary products, which poorer nations have historically produced, underlines the importance of ending the trade barriers to the processed and manufactured products these nations want to export to rich nations. Those barriers help create poverty. Ending them could do the opposite.

Abstract analysis of unjust trading patterns may seem dull for comfortable North Americans. But experiencing the effects can be agony. A former President of World Vision tells the story of Juan Diaz, a coffee worker in El Salvador, a country which used to depend on coffee exports for a major share of its earnings.

> He and three of his five daughters spend long, hard days in the coffee fields of Montenango. On a good day, Juan picks enough coffee to earn $1.44; his daughters make a total of $3.35. With $1.24 of these wages, Juan and his wife Paula are able to feed their family for one day. In bad

times, Juan and his daughters make as little as 56 cents a day—less than half the money they need just to eat.

At the end of the six-week coffee season, Juan does odd jobs around the hacienda—provided there is work to be done. He can earn about 90 cents there for an eight-hour day. Paula Diaz supplements her husband's earnings by working in the market. When people have enough money to purchase the tomatoes, cabbages and other home-grown vegetables she sells, Paula can make about 40 cents a day.

The hacienda provides a simple dwelling for the Diaz family, but no modern facilities. Candles are used for light, water has to be hauled from a well, and furnishings consist of little more than a table and some chairs. Aside from a dress and shoes for each of the girls during the coffee season, the family has not been able to buy much else in the last five years. Whatever money doesn't go for food is spent for visits to the health clinic (40 cents each time), the high interest on bills at the company store, expenses for the children in school, and for the burial of Juan's father, who died last year.

"You know, I look forward to a better life for my children," Juan says. "I dream that if it is possible—if I can possibly afford it—my children will not follow in my footsteps, that they will break out of this terrible way of life. But the money problems we face every day blot out those dreams. I feel bad, nervous, I don't sleep nights worrying about how I'll get something for them to eat. I think and think, but don't find any answers. I work hard; my wife and daughters do, too. We all do. But still we suffer. Why?"[57]

The International Debt Crisis

Some poor nations, especially in Africa, cannot repay their international debts without increasing poverty and starvation.

Uganda is one of the poorest countries in the world. It is also one of the most highly indebted. When a country's debt repayments cost more than 20 percent of exports, bankers consider it to be in financial crisis.[58] In 1993, if Uganda had met all its repayment obligations, the ratio would have been 144 percent.[59] Those repayments take money that could be used for health care. Life expectancy in Uganda is only 45 years.[60] One in five children die before the age of five. One in two children is stunted from malnutrition. Nearly 1 percent of women giving birth will die because of limited access to health care facilities. The average Ugandan lives eight miles from a primary health clinic, and hospitals are even farther away. Today, the government spends $3 per person for health care, but it spends $16.70 per person on debt repayments. The World Bank estimates a comprehensive primary health care system for Uganda would cost about $12 per person.[61]

But surely not all debts are bad, someone will point out. And of course that is true. Home owners and businesses regularly borrow money, pay it back on schedule, and everybody profits. Loans from Europe helped Canada and the U.S. develop quickly in the nineteenth century.

So what's bad about debt in developing nations? Nothing, in principle. It's the way it developed and its current effects in some countries that are so problematic.

How did the debt crisis develop? And who is to blame? The truth is, almost everyone must share responsibility except, of course, the poor who suffer the most.

The fourfold leap in oil prices in 1973–1974 triggered a rapid increase in borrowing by developing countries who were eager to continue their growth. Commercial banks overflowing with petro dollars deposited by oil-producing nations made huge loans to Third World governments without asking proper questions about the use of the loans or the possibility of repayment. In the late seventies, Citicorp chairman Walter Wriston defended these loans with the optimistic credo, "countries never go bankrupt."

But mistaken government policies in poor debtor nations were also helping to prepare the way for disaster. Too much of what was loaned was spent on armaments, ill-planned projects, or wasted because of official corruption. (The Bura Irrigation project in Kenya cost over $100 million to complete, displaced over 20,000 people, and was never used![62]) Faced with budget deficits, governments chose to cut education and health programs rather than their military budgets. They also printed money, which produced surging inflation. High inflation encouraged rich people in poor countries to move their money to safe places like Swiss bank accounts or U.S. real estate.[63]

By 1982, the debt crisis was so severe that global leaders feared the international banking system might collapse. Fortunately, that did not happen.

Many of the middle-income developing countries that were the largest debtors (mostly in Latin America) signed Brady deals and have undergone structural adjustment in cooperation with the International Monetary Fund.[64] They are now successfully paying back their debts. Many of these countries have also experienced healthy economic growth, and private financial institutions are investing large amounts of money. Unless another recession hits or the value of the U.S. dollar rises dramatically, these countries will manage.

Bankers in rich countries consider the crisis to be over—their problematic loans have dropped significantly.[65] Unfortunately, many of the lower- and middle-class people in these countries continue to suffer under the austerity measures necessary to make the debt repayments. International development economist Michael Todaro says that the IMF policies may have been good at reducing inflation and improving the developing countries' balance of payments' problems, but they have disproportionately hurt the lower and middle classes.[66] But the wealthy elites in middle-income nations and global bankers consider the debt crisis to be over.

The crisis, however, is definitely not over for the low-income countries, especially those in Africa. The amount of their debt is small compared to the middle income countries (10 percent of all developing country debt[67]). But their economies are also small, so their debt burden is proportionally higher. The World Bank has identified 32 severely indebted low-income countries (SILICs), 25 of which are in Sub-Saharan Africa.[68]

These countries simply cannot repay all their debt. In 1995, repayments of $16 billion came due, equal to almost 50 percent of their export earnings. (Remember, 20 percent is considered a financial crisis.) SILICs were able to repay less than half of what came due. From 1990 to 1993, Mozambique was able to repay less than 10 percent of its scheduled payments.[69] Many of these countries are functionally bankrupt, but since there is no international equivalent for bankruptcy, these governments continue to squeeze what debt repayment they can out of their meager export earnings. Until late 1996, very little had been done to ease the SILICs' desperate plight.

Developing nations undoubtedly made some bad choices and wasted some of the borrowed funds (for example, the dictators in Zaire and Nigeria). But poor nations are not at fault for all their problems. One study estimated that nearly 85 percent of the total increase in the foreign debt of the non-oil-producing developing nations between 1973 and 1982 resulted from four causes about which they could do almost nothing: OPEC oil price increases; the spurt in dollar interest rates in 1981–82; the reduction of Third World exports because of worldwide recession; and the precipitous drop in the world price of primary exports from developing nations.[70]

It is dishonest to put all the blame on poor countries for their debt problems. Tragically, the poor suffer the most—especially the children—because health care and education have been reduced.

In the Arusha area of Tanzania, women often have to walk more than one hour each day to collect water from the nearest (often unsafe) source. Even though 14 million Tanzanians lack access to safe water, the government spent $155 million in 1993–94 on debt repayments. This was more than the combined budget for clean water and health.[71]

Poor nations' debt payments have also deprived children of basic education. In Tanzania, educational spending has declined and enrollment in primary school has fallen from over 90 percent in 1980 to 70 percent today. Illiteracy rates have increased by 50 percent in less than a decade.[72] In Zambia, government spending per student is one-sixth of what it was a decade ago. The Zambian government spent $37 million on primary school education from 1990 to 1993, but its scheduled debt repayments for the same period were $1.3 billion, 35 times that amount.[73]

One Oxfam worker observed a school in the Shinyanga area of Tanzania:

> The school comprises two classes, each of about fifty children . . . There are two or three pencils per class, which are passed between the children. Books are almost entirely absent. There are no desks or chairs, the children sitting on small rocks, or on the ground.[74]

This story underscores a widespread pattern. In many African countries the debt crisis has contributed to lowering standards in child education. As in the case of health care, the heaviest burden of debt has fallen on those who are least able to bear it.

Over 15 percent of all children in Sierre Leone die before age one.[75] In Angola and Niger, about 30 percent of all children die before they reach their fifth birthday.[76] In Ethiopia and Nigeria, almost half the children under five are malnourished.[77]

Overall, African governments spend more on debt repayment than on basic education and health care. The lives of 21 million children would be saved by the year 2000, according to Oxfam, if Africa spent its annual debt payments on health and education.[78]

A few years ago an African president posed a hard question: "Must we starve our children to pay our debts?" In chapter 11 we will explore how the international community can help answer that question.

Destroying the Environment and the Poor

Our present behavior threatens the well-being of our grandchildren. Economic life today, especially in industrialized societies, is producing such severe environmental pollution and degradation that the future for everyone—rich and poor alike—is endangered. We are destroying our air, forests, lands, and water so rapidly that we face disastrous problems in the next century unless we make major changes.

A majority of all living recipients of the Nobel Prize in the sciences recently signed the "World Scientists' Warning to Humanity." Together 104 Nobel laureates plus more than 1,500 prominent scientists from more than seventy countries pleaded with us to reduce our pollution and end our over-consumption before the dangers become irreversible. "No more than one or a few decades remain," they warn, "before the chance to avert the threats we now confront will be lost and the prospects for humanity immeasurably diminished."[79]

What is causing these problems? We overfish our seas, pollute our atmosphere, exhaust our supplies of fresh water, and destroy precious topsoil, forests, and unique species lovingly shaped by the Creator. In many countries, chemicals, pesticides, oil spills, and industrial emissions degrade air, water, and soil. "Is it not enough for you to feed on the good pasture?" the Creator asks. "Must you also trample the rest of the pasture with your feet? Is it not enough for you to drink clear water? Must you also muddy the rest with your feet?" (Ezekiel 34:18).

Always, of course, the poor suffer the most. This is true in two ways. They already suffer from reduced food production, unproductive land, polluted rivers, and toxic wastes that the rich do not want in their backyards. Furthermore, unless we can redirect economic life in a way that dramatically reduces environmental decay, it will be impossible to expand economic growth enough in poor nations to enable them to enjoy a decent standard of living.

Carbon emissions from the use of fossil fuel is one of the biggest problems. The affluent, of course, produce much of the atmospheric pollution. The top five per capita emitters of carbon emissions are, in order, the United Arab Emirates, the United States, Canada, Australia, and Singapore.

Harvard economist Amartya Sen puts it bluntly: "One additional American typically has a larger negative impact on the ozone layer, global warmth, and other elements of the earth's environment than dozens of Indians or Zimbabweans put together."[80]

The poor also damage the environment. Developing nations often use less sophisticated technology and consequently consume fossil fuels less efficiently. For example, China's older steel mills use twice as much energy per ton of steel as more sophisticated mills in Italy and Spain.[81] Desperately poor people also try to farm marginal land and destroy tropical forests. Unless poverty is dramatically reduced around the world, we cannot win the war against environmental destruction.

How are we destroying our air, land, water, and forests?

Global warming produced by "greenhouse gases" has been making newspaper headlines since the late 1980s. (Greenhouse gases, such as carbon dioxide, methane, nitrous oxide, etc., hold heat in the lower atmosphere of the earth and then slowly cause the temperature of the earth to rise.) In 1988, a NASA study reported a gradual long-term atmospheric warming. The result has been furious debate about the accuracy of the scientific studies and the possibilities of catastrophic changes in the world's climate and sea levels. Industries, especially those connected with fossil fuels, (for example the petroleum, automotive, and utility industries), spent millions to convince a skeptical public that the issue was only so much hot air. By 1995, the verdict was in. An international body of scientists, the Intergovernmental Panel on Climate Change (IPCC), formed in 1988 and operating under the joint supervision of the United Nations Environment Programme and the World Meteorological Organization, issued their findings.

The scientific data, they announced, indicate that global warming has *already begun*. While acknowledging that the science involved in predicting climate conditions still needs refinement, the IPCC reported that certain

Table 16—Carbon Emissions from Burning Fossil Fuel Top Twenty Emitters, 1994			
(Note: Countries with population over one million[82])			
	Total Emissions (million tons)	Emissions Per Person (tons)	Emissions $GNP (tons per million $)	Emission Growth 1990–94 (percent)
United States	1,371	5.26	210	4.4
China	8935	0.71	330	13.0
Russia	455	3.08	590	−24.1
Japan	299	2.39	110	0.1
Germany	234	2.89	140	−9.9
India	222	0.24	160	23.5
United Kingdom	153	2.62	150	−0.3
Ukraine	125	2.43	600	−43.5
Canada	116	3.97	200	5.3
Italy	104	1.81	110	0.8
France	90	1.56	80	−3.2
Poland	89	2.31	460	−4.5
South Korea	88	1.98	200	43.7
Mexico	88	0.96	140	7.1
South Africa	85	2.07	680	9.1
Kazahkstan	81	4.71	1250	na
Australia	75	4.19	230	4.2
North Korea	67	2.90	960	na
Iran	62	1.09	270	na
Brazil	60	0.39	70	15.8

trends in the data lead to inescapable conclusions. They presented a range of potential future scenarios, from best case to worst case. The "mid-range" scenario called for an increase in global mean surface temperature relative to 1990 of about 2 degrees C. by the year 2100. That may sound like a small amount. But in this scenario, the "average rate of warming would probably be greater than any seen in the last 10,000 years."[83]

The result would be serious. Rising global temperature will cause dislocations in agriculture and also melt more of the polar ice sheets. According to the IPCC, this could produce a rise of 50 centimeters (over 18 inches) in global ocean levels. Estimates are that this would put 46 million people at risk of flooding due to storm surges. If the rise was as much as 40 inches, up to 118 million people would be at risk. Island nations, coastal nations, and areas with large delta populations could suffer loss of territory and see massive movements of refugees. Both droughts and floods will become more severe, and tropical diseases may spread into new areas.

The use of fossil fuels today releases about six billion tons of carbon into the air each year. This means we are adding three billion tons beyond what the environment can absorb to the 170 billion tons that have accumulated since the beginning of the Industrial Revolution. If the earth's climate is ever to reach equilibrium again, carbon emissions will have to be less than, not more than, what the natural environment can absorb.[84]

We are doing just the opposite. In the past six years, emissions in the U.S. went up 4.4 percent.[85] Other countries are doing the same. Between 1990 and 1994, China's emissions went up 13 percent, Brazil's 16 percent, and South Korea's 44 percent.[86] These trends will continue unless we make substantial changes.

Industrialized countries must accept a major part of the burden. Why? Because developing nations should expand their economies to reduce poverty. Their carbon emissions are expanding rapidly and will continue to do so for some time even with new, cleaner technologies. Therefore the wealthy nations who are better able to afford it must cut carbon emissions significantly so that developing economies can expand to feed the poor without destroying the global ecological system.

At the Rio Earth Summit in 1992, developed nations agreed to do just that. Under the Rio treaty, they agreed to introduce action plans to hold greenhouse gases at or below the 1990 level by the year 2000. The industrial nations are not on schedule to meet this goal. The task of reducing U.S. emissions is less difficult than in some other nations because the U.S. is currently so wasteful. (The U.S. produces twice as much carbon emissions per person as Germany.) But the U.S. is behind schedule. It simply will not happen without active, organized citizens vigorously working to demand change.

I have emphasized carbon emissions and global warming. But these have not been the only problems in the atmosphere.

The Ozone Layer. By the late 1980s, it was obvious that we were depleting the protective ozone layer in the upper atmosphere at an alarming rate. Since ozone blocks the ultraviolet radiation that causes skin cancer and eye cataracts, this was a serious problem.

Fortunately, there is some good news here. The chief culprit behind ozone depletion is chlorofluorocarbons (CFCs) which are used primarily in refrigeration and air conditioning. In 1992, the nations of the world signed the Montreal Protocol and agreed to radically limit the emission of ozone depleting chemicals. By January 1996, the U.S. and the wealthiest nations (the OECD nations) had stopped producing CFCs.

Unfortunately, many poor nations (including Russia) find it very difficult to switch to more costly substitutes. In the Montreal Protocol, the rich nations agreed to bear all costs of the transition. But we have not provided adequate funding. In spite of good progress, this problem is not fully resolved.

Unfortunately, too, the replacement refrigerants, called HFCs, also have problems. These new chemicals, though ozone friendly, may contribute to global warming. In fact, certain of these HFC molecules have more than 1,000 times the potential to trap heat that a molecule of carbon dioxide has. More work by scientists and governments is essential. But, since leaky automobile air conditioners are a major source of HFCs in the atmosphere, we could all help by simply rolling down our car windows.

Deforestation. Rapid deforestation represents another serious problem. It increases flooding, deprives us of potential new medicines, and contributes to increasing levels of atmospheric carbon. Estimates suggest that an area larger than Poland is being deforested each year, and the rate of deforestation is increasing.[87] In the Third World, forests are cleared to provide for cropland, fuelwood, cattle ranching, and tropical hardwood for industrial countries. It is estimated that in the 1980s, we lost more than 10 percent of our tropical forests.[88]

Many poor people clear and farm forest land because inequitable land distribution, population growth, and expansion by large, export-cropping corporations have left them little land on which to grow food for their families. In 1996, four affiliates of the United Nations issued a report warning that poor farmers in the developing world could destroy half the remaining tropical forests. Each year, they reported, "poor farmers practicing slash and burn agriculture are major contributors to the loss of some 38 million acres of tropical forest."[89] Another study in 1993 found that during the eighties, 61 percent of deforestation resulted from a gradual nibbling away of forests by poor farmers seeking a little land for survival.[90]

Unfortunately, 97 percent of the nutrients needed for plant growth in the tropics are locked up in the vegetation that deforestation destroys. Consequently, deforested land in the tropics often quickly loses its productive capability. After a few growing seasons, this poor agricultural land is abandoned for more recently cleared forest land, continuing a cycle of poverty, displacement, and environmental abuse.

In 1984, Jose Lutzenberger, a Brazilian agronomist and engineer, testified before the U.S. Congress about one such example:

> He told how thousands of poor peasants from agriculturally rich southern Brazil were pouring into Amazonian Rondonia because they had been dispossessed of their land, either by large landowners or by government plantations covering thousands of hectares, all bent on growing soybeans and other cash crops. The Rondonia Rush was needed precisely because the government refused to undertake real land reform and confront the plantation owners. . . . Thus the Polonoreste project— financed by the World Bank—has become an infertile dumping ground for peasants who will never be able to earn a livelihood from poor land, leached of all nutrients, from which the tree cover has been removed. "It is quite common to see settlers give up their clearing after their first meager harvest. They have to make new clearings every year. Then, when the whole plot is cleared, they move on again."[91]

Using live trees for fuelwood is sometimes a last resort for the poor in areas where dead wood and branches have disappeared. It has been estimated that by the early nineties, 10,000 square kilometers per year of forest were disappearing due to the search for fuelwood.[92] For the very poor, boiling water sometimes becomes an unaffordable luxury. Where fuelwood is critically scarce, people often have no choice but to divert dried dung and crop residues from fields to cookstoves. Doing so diminishes soil fertility and depresses crop yields.

The demand for cheap beef by wealthy North Americans and Europeans also contributes to tropical deforestation. In Brazil and Central America alone, 15,000 square kilometers per year of forest are cleared for cattle ranching.[93] Much of this cleared land is used to grow exports for the developed world. Tragically, this is the least effective use of rainforests. One study found that using cleared tropical forest land for cattle ranching yields a value of $148 per hectare. If we just left the forest intact and harvested its fruits, rubber, and timber, the potential yield is estimated to be $6,280 per year![94] Even that is not the whole story. After several years of cattle grazing, nutrient leaching, and soil erosion, the tropical soil often turns into brick. The land becomes unable to support "even the most aggressive pasture grasses."[95]

Another significant drain on forests comes from the industrialized countries' demand for tropical hardwoods. In logging for commercially valuable trees (which sometimes account for less than 5 percent of any given hectare) loggers often destroy between 30 and 60 percent of unwanted trees.[96]

Deforestation produces floods, contributes to increased levels of atmospheric carbon, and also deprives us of important new medicines. When forests disappear, rainfall runs off much faster, causing soil erosion, immediate floods, and subsequent drought (because water quickly disappears rather than soaking into the soil). In India, a growing number of scientists now blame deforestation for the worsening of droughts and floods.[97]

Forests, especially tropical forests, are natural biochemical factories. Loss of these forests would be catastrophic. One-half of U.S. medicines come from genetic material from wild plants found mostly in tropical forests. The top twenty pharmaceutical products sold in the U.S. in 1988 were all derived from natural products. We have scientifically examined only 1 percent of the world's plant species regarding their potential beneficial use.[98] As Gordon Cragg, chief of the Natural Products Branch of the National Cancer Institute, says: "No chemists can dream up the complex bioactive molecules produced by nature."[99]

Scientists estimate that 80 to 90 percent of tropical rainforests will be destroyed by 2020 if deforestation continues at current rates.[100] The time available to safeguard our forest resources is quickly running out.

Misuse of the Land

Erosion of topsoil, desertification, overgrazing on rangelands, overcultivation of croplands, waterlogging and salinization of irrigated lands are exacting a terrible toll. Topsoil is eroding more quickly than it forms on about 35 percent of the world's croplands.[101] Since 1945, an area of land covered by vegetation larger than India and China has been degraded. The U.S. has 400 million acres of cropland. Every year, we pave over, build on, or somehow convert to urban use 3 million acres of this precious soil. Over much of what was formerly prairie land, we lose two bushels of topsoil for every bushel of corn grown.[102] Salinization—the process in which irrigated land becomes too salty to grow crops—increased in the 1980s. Egypt lost up to 40 percent of its irrigated land to it, Australia up to 20 percent, and the U.S. up to 25 percent.[103]

Our abuse of the soil may be partially responsible for a disturbing reversal of a long pattern of expanding grain production. Between 1950 and 1984 world grain harvests expanded 260 percent.[104] Since then, there has been no significant increase. In fact, world per capita grain production dropped from 336 kilograms in 1990 to 294 kilograms in 1995. Also troubling is the statistic reported by the U.S. Department of Agriculture: worldwide carryover stocks of grain (the amount of grain in storehouses) has reached an all-time low. At the end of 1996, there was only about 48 days worth of carryover stock available.[105]

Is this decline in per capita grain production a serious problem? Different experts respond in fundamentally different ways.

Many specialists (especially economists at the World Bank and elsewhere) believe that there is no long-term problem. Harvard economist Amartya Sen notes that food prices are declining relative to manufactured goods. In fact, he insists that lack of demand today actually holds back further expansion of available food production. (Sen does not mean that there are no hungry people; he means that if the poor had purchasing power, the farmers could easily expand food production.)[106] As soon as demand increases, the economists believe, new techniques will produce sufficient food and solve any resulting side effects of the technological innovations.

Others, especially environmentalists, are less optimistic. Some writers, like Lester Brown of the WorldWatch Institute, are very worried.[107] These people underline the fact that increased food production has resulted from new technologies that have had negative side effects.

Prior to 1950, most increased food output resulted from expanding the area cultivated. Since 1950, however, the emphasis has been on increasing land productivity with new technology.[108] The use of chemical fertilizers reduced the practice of crop rotation, which both fertilizes the soil and protects the soil from erosion. A study in Missouri in the 1930s showed soil erosion increased from 2.7 tons per acre annually when the land was in a corn-wheat-clover rotation to 19.7 tons per acre when the same land was continuously planted with corn. As the topsoil decreases, so does its productivity.

In the short run, the pessimists argue, reduced fertility of the land is masked by advances in technology. Heavy machinery, irrigation, and large doses of fertilizer and pesticides produce quick jumps in productivity. But they may not be sustainable. "Often the very practices that cause excessive erosion in the long run, such as the intensification of cropping patterns and the plowing of marginal land, lead to short term production gains, creating an illusion of progress and a false sense of security."[109]

The final verdict? Non-specialists like you and me cannot be sure. As we search for better information, we should avoid both superficial optimism and apocalyptic despair—and also a naive belief that technological fixes will always arrive just in time. Nor dare we forget that the amount of arable land per person is declining. In 1989, we had .28 hectares of fertile, arable land per person in the world. By 2030, it will only be .19.[110] That means one-third less land per person in less than forty years! Taking good care of our soil is a matter of life and death.

The poor, as always, suffer the most from environmental decay. They are most exposed to the vast array of environmental problems. They are the most likely to drink contaminated water, and the most likely to farm marginal land. They certainly will bear the brunt of whatever convulsive changes global warming forces upon everyone.

One striking symbol of this vulnerability is the fact that they are most likely to live near—and therefore suffer more from—toxic wastes. It is not coincidental that the environmental disaster in Bhopal, India, especially affected the poor. Everywhere around the world, poverty forces many people to live dangerously close to smoke-belching factories and toxic wastes. "The rich get richer and the poor get poisoned."[111]

One of the most astonishing examples of the connection between poverty and environmental destruction comes from anthropologist Sheldon Annis, who describes a scene in Guatemala:

> I recall watching in horrified fascination as an Indian farmer and his
> son planted their plot of corn on a forested slope. The land was so steep

that the son had to be held in place with a rope looped around his waist. As he hopped from furrow to furrow, his father let out the slack from around a tree stump. When I returned to the spot recently, I was not surprised to find that the farmer and his son were no longer there. And neither was the hillside. What remained was a reddish eroded nub— which looked like the next and the next and the next former hillside.[112]

We face a painful choice. To maintain and expand our material abundance, we are polluting our air and water, and destroying our lands and forests. We simply cannot continue these present economic patterns, *and* reduce global poverty, *and* preserve a livable planet all at the same time. We could choose both justice for the poor and a livable planet—but only if we give up rampant materialism and make hard choices to reverse environmental destruction.

Eating Food from Hungry Nations

Why do countries ravaged by famine export food? Why do poor nations today sell vast quantities of food to rich nations while many of their own people are malnourished or starving?

History provides numerous examples of private traders exporting food in the middle of a famine. It happened in Ireland in the 1840s. In the midst of the devastating Irish famine, Ireland exported substantial amounts of food to England because England was more wealthy and could pay higher prices than the starving Irish.[113]

The same thing happened in India in the 1870s. India was caught in famine, but large grain exports nevertheless went to England. Behind the cold, objective description of the Famine Commission Report of 1880, the devastating effects of powerlessness remain obvious:

> Unluckily for the Indian consumer, there have been several bad harvests in England, and this and the exchange have stimulated a great export of grain for the last few years. This gain of the producing class and its adjunct, the bunyah [trader], has been so far the loss of the consuming class. This seems inevitable.[114]

The same thing has happened recently in Africa.[15]

Less stark but also striking is the fact (see table 17) that in recent decades developing nations with large numbers of malnourished and even starving people nevertheless have exported substantial amounts of food to wealthy nations. In 1992, poor nations sent rich nations 16.4 billion dollars more food than they received.

Year	Food Exports from Developed World to Developing World	Food imports by Developed World from Developing World	Net Loss of Food by Poor Countries
1970	4,912	10,974	6,062
1975	16,058	20,807	4,749
1980	38,069	38,844	4,775
1985	28,823	36,450	7,627
1986	27,367	42,282	14,915
1990	41,710	54,416	12,706
1992	43,948	60,396	16,448

Table 17—Food Exports and Imports (in millions of U.S. dollars)

Source: United Nations Handbook of International Trade and Development Statistics, 1989, A8; 1994, A8.

The reason that countries with many hungry people willingly export food to wealthy nations is that the poor people in those nations do not have the money to pay for the food, and we do. And the powerful people in poor nations pay for their imports of high technology, oil, and luxury goods with the revenue from their exports.

Hungry people prefer food to feed their families. But they have no power, almost no money, little employment, and no land to grow food for themselves. Wealthy elites in poor nations have more in common with the rich in high-income nations than the poor in their own. So they sell the food that the poor need but cannot afford.

Sometimes, the origins of this problem go back to the colonial era[116] when colonial rulers encouraged plantations to grow export crops even to the detriment of food production for local consumption. Local people frequently lost their land and became slaves or poorly paid agricultural workers. Those who managed to keep some land were "encouraged" to produce foodstuffs desired in the mother countries. Growing food for the "mother" country was seen as the colony's highest priority. John Stuart Mill, the respected nineteenth-century British economist, "reasoned that colonies should not be thought of as civilizations or countries at all but as 'agricultural establishments' whose sole purpose was to supply the 'larger community to which they belong.'"[117]

Colonial days have ended, but some of the effects remain. The plantations have not been returned to the descendants of their original owners. New owners (whether local elites or multinational corporations) of the same large holdings still look to the industrialized countries as their trading partners—the poor, after all, have little purchasing power.

Owners of large landholdings could, of course, choose to grow beans, corn, or rice for the local population, but the local people cannot pay much because they have very little capital to produce anything marketable. Landholders can make *more* money by growing crops for export. So the owners look to rich countries for their markets. They send us cotton, beef, coffee, bananas, or other agricultural products, and we send them the goods they desire in return. The system favors the wealthy, and the poor suffer.

None of the above information leads to the conclusion that we ought to scrap international trade in food products or reject market economies in favor of Marxism. What it does mean is that the jubilee principle discussed in chapter 4 is enormously important.

God wants society's pool of productive assets to be distributed so that everyone has the resources to earn his or her own way. When members of a society lose their assets, by whatever means, it is difficult for them to participate in economic activity. People with no assets simply starve.

In most of today's poor nations the displacement of people from the land began many years ago and still continues. Seldom has anything like the jubilee occurred. So the problems persist. That is why rich people eat food from nations where poor people starve.

Consider the example of export agriculture in Central America. The bulk of the staple foods (beans, corn, rice) eaten by the poor in Central America are grown by small farmers on marginal lands. At the same time "virtually all the fertile, flat agricultural lands in the region [are] used for export oriented crops."[118]

The story of beef provides a striking example.[119] In the 1950s, almost all beef slaughtered in Central America was eaten locally. Then in 1957 the first beef packing plant approved by the U.S. Department of Agriculture (USDA) was built. By the late 1970s, three-fourths of Central America's beef was exported.[120] By 1978, Central America provided the U.S. with 250 million pounds of beef a year. U.S.-backed development programs built roads and provided credit to facilitate the expansion of beef exports. From 1960 to 1980, over one-half of all the loans made by the World Bank and the Inter-American Development Bank for agriculture and rural development in Central America went to promote the production of beef for export.[121]

Wealthy elites made great profits. But large numbers of poor farmers growing basic foodstuffs were pushed off the land as the ranchers demanded more and more grazing land to grow beef for export. In El Salvador, before the first USDA-approved beef packing plant was opened, 29 percent of rural households were landless. By 1980, one-half of all El Salvador's beef was going to the U.S.—and 65 percent of the rural households were landless.[122] It would be silly, of course, to suggest that the growing beef exports caused all the landlessness. Peasants lacked land for many reasons. But the beef industry was one of the factors. The poor protested, but the ranchers painted the peasant activists as communists. The national security forces trained by the U.S. often used repressive tactics, including torture and murder, to repress peasant protesters.[123] "Local ranchers in this way got free eviction forces, armed and trained at U.S. taxpayers' expense."[124]

Let me be very clear. I am not arguing that Central America should not export beef. It does have a competitive advantage over many areas in producing grass-fed beef. With different policies it would probably be possible to expand beef exports in a way that did not oppress the poor or destroy the environment. (Unfortunately, vast tropical forests were burned to provide the new pasture lands.) But it was not done that way.

Instead, the poor suffered to produce cheap hamburgers for American consumers. Since the 1960s, beef consumption within Central America has declined 20 percent. The poor cannot compete with us. A study by the Pan American Health Organization showed that between 1969 and 1975 malnutrition rose by 67 percent among children five years and under. According to a report in 1980, 50 percent of the children in Central America were dying before the age of six—largely because of malnutrition and related diseases.[125] Poor people don't need communists to tell them that is a bad deal.

Not all the examples come from Latin America. In the Philippines there is also widespread poverty, which we examined in chapter 7. Most Filipinos live in rural areas, but most of the land is owned by large landowners. So 70 percent of rural people are malnourished.

There too the tragic story goes back to colonial days. Before the Spanish conquerors arrived in the Philippines in the early 1600s, local villages owned land cooperatively. But the Spanish demand for surplus crops for taxes allowed the better-off Filipinos who collected the taxes for the Spanish colonialists to amass larger and larger holdings. After the United States replaced Spain in 1898, export cropping (and land concentration) increased still further. After 1960, export cropping grew even faster, as American pineapple producers moved from Hawaii to the Philippines to take advantage of cheaper wages. (They saved 47 percent in production costs.) From 1960 to 1980 the amount of land devoted to export crops increased from 15 percent to 30 percent.

Part of President Ferdinand Marcos's national development policy based on export crops included ruthlessly suppressing movements of workers who pressed for higher wages or land reform. (The average wage for a sugar-cane laborer working thirteen to fourteen hours a day was $7.00 a week.) Both Amnesty International and the International Commission of Jurists documented the existence of thousands of political prisoners. Electric-shock torture, water torture, extended solitary confinement, and beatings were widespread. Meanwhile, American military aid to Marcos continued.[126]

In February 1986, a nonviolent revolution overthrew Marcos.[127] Hope surged through the Philippines. President Cory Aquino promised both democracy and justice for the poor. Unfortunately, there has been very little land reform, as we saw in chapter 7, because the same powerful landowners still control the country. Not surprisingly, the majority of the people continue to live in poverty.

Who is responsible for the children dying in Central America or the Philippines? Wealthy national elites who want to increase their affluence? U.S. companies that work closely with the local elites? U.S. citizens who eat the beef unavailable to malnourished children in Central America?

Once again, it would be silly to make the simplistic assumption that if we stop eating food imported from poor nations, hungry children there will promptly enjoy it. Ending food imports is not the answer. What is needed is the economic empowerment of the poor so they can be productive and earn a decent living. Chapter 11 examines some of the ways we can promote such changes. My purpose here is simply to show that our eating patterns are interlocked with social and economic structures that leave millions hungry and starving.

Multinational Corporations in Developing Countries

Multinational corporations (MNCs) are children of the affluent North. Most of them began years ago as small, local firms. Slowly they expanded into sprawling corporations. For the most part their growth has been gradual and they have evolved alongside the economy as a whole. Consequently, the developed world, although at times exasperated at the frequent indifference of large corporations to wider social goals, has learned, at least to a degree, to work constructively with them.

After World War II these big corporations moved in droves to set up overseas operations. Most of their activity went to other developed countries, but increasingly they moved into less developed countries as well. Development economist Michael Todaro notes that in 1962 private investment in these countries was $2.4 billion. By the mid-seventies it was about $9 billion,[128] and by 1985 over $13 billion.[129] After slower growth during the 1980s, it increased to over $40 billion by 1992.[130]

Today, most developing countries welcome MNCs. The frequent nationalization of MNCs' assets that occurred in earlier decades has almost completely stopped. From 1970 to 1974, there were 40 nationalizations per year. By 1992, that figure had dropped to zero. The powerful local elites that govern developing nations have largely concluded that MNCs are more blessing than bane.[131]

Proponents of MNCs view them as a major engine of economic development and growth in developing nations. They argue that MNCs help in a number of ways:[132] (1) by providing access to scarce capital resources; (2) by increasing the flow of foreign exchange; (3) by providing developing governments with healthy businesses from which to generate the tax revenues needed for development projects; and (4) by creating jobs (MNCs employ 12 million people in LDCs, and the figure would double if we counted jobs with subcontractors)[133]; (5) by introducing technology and training local workers in technical and managerial skills; (6) by providing goods and services that otherwise would be unavailable.

The possibilities look promising. If the developing nations were equally powerful bargaining partners, and if the poor in developing countries shared equitably in the benefits, this might work well. Unfortunately, however, evidence shows that MNCs also have some negative effects on poor nations.

This should not surprise people with a biblical view of sin. Powerful agents regularly dominate and take advantage of weaker ones. MNCs, obviously, are interested primarily if not exclusively in profits for themselves.

We often overlook the extent of their power. The largest MNC in 1990, General Motors, had gross sales that were greater than the GNP of all but the five largest developing nations.[134] The five largest MNCs, in 1990, had combined sales greater than the GNP of countries like Switzerland, Australia, Spain, Sweden, and Belgium.[135] In 1990, 171 MNCs had gross sales of more than $5 billion. That is more than the total annual GNP of 22 of Africa's 37 countries.[136]

As development economist Professor Todaro points out, this kind of power results from and increases oligopolistic,[137] (non-competitive) market positions. By manipulating prices and profits, dominating new technologies, and restricting potential competition, they avoid the qualification of their power that a freer market would impose.[138] Anyone concerned with the dangers of centralized power should be concerned with the way huge MNCs have concentrated economic and political power.[139]

What is the case against MNCs? What are their economic, political, and cultural effects?

Economic Effects

Oxford economist Donald Hay has pointed to three problems.

First, MNCs do not really contribute the amount of capital they usually profess to.[140] Instead they borrow heavily from the banks in host countries, thereby reducing the funds available to local entrepreneurs and diminishing the level of indigenous business involvement.

Second, MNCs are naturally more concerned about their own profit than the welfare of the host countries. This sometimes results, for example, in the shutting down of an entire subsidiary operation—an action which devastates a small, poor nation while only marginally affecting the MNC. MNCs may also artificially vary their profit picture to avoid local taxes by selling their finished product to the parent company at below-market prices. This is particularly significant because approximately one-third of all the $3.3 trillion in world trade in goods and services in 1990 were transactions within individual firms.[141]

A third problem Hay finds is that MNCs frequently promote "the wrong sort of development" in developing nations. He argues that MNCs usually produce highly differentiated products for the wealthy instead of necessities for the poor. They also bring along capital-intensive, labor-saving technology inappropriate for poor countries with vast numbers of unemployed. By so doing, MNCs reinforce the dualistic structures that keep the majority in poverty and a minority in the mainstream of developed world economics.[142]

Political Effects

On the political side, MNCs sometimes work with local oppressive regimes in ways that benefit both the MNC and powerful national interests but not the poor.

Unions are one way workers can organize to increase wages and improve working conditions. However, many governments in developing nations prevent union organizing so that wages will remain low and MNCs will remain happy.

The *New York Times* reported a glaring example in 1996: "Nike and thousands of other manufacturers have been lured to set up business in Indonesia by the low wages—and the assurance that the Government will tolerate no strikes or independent unions."[143] When Tongris Situmorang, a twenty-two-year-old worker in the Nike factory in Serang, tried to organize a union, he was fired. The military locked him in a room at the plant for seven days and questioned him about his labor activities.[144]

On the U.S.-Mexico border, we find similar problems in the *maquiladora* assembly plants. (Maquiladoras are factories that produce goods for export to the U.S. market. They are located in Mexico very near the U.S. border to take advantage of cheap Mexican labor.) In 1987, "Ford Motor Company tore up its union contract, fired 3,400 workers, and cut wages by 45 percent. When the workers rallied around dissident labor leaders, gunmen hired by the official, government-dominated union shot workers at random in the factory."[145]

In addition, MNCs have built up a strong bargaining position both because of their size and the fact that over the years developing countries have become increasingly more dependent on their presence. By threatening to leave and thereby throwing a dependent economy into chaos, MNCs can sometimes extort one-sided agreements on such issues as tax concessions, profit-repatriation limits, indigenous training requirements, and so on. Once MNCs are established, they become pressure groups "lobbying" for preferred treatment for foreign firms. They can divert government spending away from development projects for the poor and toward expenditures on roads, harbors, and subsidies for high technology, to develop the infrastructure to support profitable private investment.[146] One example of this is an advertisement the Philippine government placed in *Fortune* in 1975:

> To attract companies like yours . . . we have leveled mountains, razed jungles, filled swamps, moved rivers, relocated towns . . . all to make it easier for you and your business to do business here.[147]

Cultural Effects

MNCs are on the cutting edge of industrialized nations' contact with the people of developing nations. MNCs thus communicate to a poverty-stricken world what life is like in affluent nations. But not only do they impress on the poor how affluent Northerners live; they also encourage them, through lavish advertising campaigns, to try and live the same way.

The result is that materialistic attitudes are spread everywhere, and many poor people are enticed into spending a disproportionate share of their incomes on goods of little value—whether Avon products or soft drinks.[148] Even more outrageous are the aggressive advertising campaigns of U.S. tobacco companies in poor nations. They seduce the poor into destroying their lungs with U.S. cigarettes.

Perhaps the most well-known and pernicious case involves the Nestle Corporation and its persistence in marketing infant formula to Third World women who were better off nursing their children. Company representatives were dressed to look like nurses and recommend to mothers that they feed their infants formula. Nestle routinely handed out free samples of formula, frequently by donating supplies to hospital maternity wards. The use of formula soon causes a mother's milk to dry up, rendering her incapable of nursing even if she wants to. Parents then must buy formula. Tragically, they are often unable to read the instructions, lack access to sanitary water with which to mix it, or overdilute it in order to make it last longer.

Prepared improperly, formula milk lacks the nutrition babies require. Even under the best of circumstances, formula milk lacks immunological protection that breast milk provides.[149] Frequently the result is "Bottle Baby Disease," severe malnutrition, and diarrhea. In 1990, UNICEF reported that bottle-fed infants are much more likely to get sick and are as much as twenty-five times more likely to die in childhood than infants exclusively breast-fed for the first six months of life.[150] UNICEF reports that in 1990, one million infants died who would not have died if they had been exclusively breast-fed for the first six months of their lives. In some cases, there undoubtedly was good reason for the mothers to be absent, and therefore the baby needed infant formula. But many of those mothers were available to breast feed their children, but fell prey to powerful advertising.[151]

Promotion like that of Nestle has drastically reduced the number of breast-fed babies in the developing nations. In its 1982–83 report, UNICEF noted that the percentage of breast-fed infants in Brazil declined from 96 percent in 1940 to 40 percent in 1974. In Chile it fell from 95 percent in 1955 to 20 percent in 1982–83.[152] In 1990, UNICEF reported that breast-feeding has continued to decline. The World Health Organization has estimated that the promotion of breast-feeding alone could reduce diarrhea mortality in the first six months of life by 10 percent.[153]

An international boycott of Nestle ended in 1984 after Nestle agreed to abide by the World Health Organization's Code of Marketing for Breast Milk Substitutes. But the boycott was renewed in October 1989 after it was discovered that Nestle continued to donate formula to hospitals and maternity clinics for distribution to new mothers.[154] In spite of pledges from companies selling infant formula to stop donating free samples of babymilk to hospitals by the end of 1992, Action for Corporate Accountability found in July 1994 that the practice was still occurring in forty-one developing countries. In March 1996, Nestle's advertising broke another part of WHO's Code.[155]

Too many big companies share the cynical attitude of H. W. Walter, chairman of the board of International Flavors and Fragrances:

> How often we see in developing countries that the poorer the economic
> outlook, the more important the small luxury of a flavored soft drink or

smoke. . . . To the dismay of many would-be benefactors, the poorer the malnourished are, the more likely they are to spend a disproportionate amount of whatever they have on some luxury rather than on what they need. . . . Observe, study, learn. . . . We try to do it at IFF. It seems to pay off for us. Perhaps it will for you.[156]

Development economist Todaro concludes that "MNCs typically produce *inappropriate products* (those demanded by a small minority of the population), stimulate *inappropriate consumption patterns* through advertising and their monopolistic market power, and do this all with *inappropriate* (capital intensive) *technologies of production.*"[157]

Are MNCs, on balance, good or bad for poor nations?[158] They are certainly good for the wealthy elites who usually run poor nations. They even help the poor in some situations. In other cases, they do the opposite. For the purposes of this book, however, we do not have to know the answer to the question of their overall impact. It is enough to know that some specific MNCs do inflict significant damage on the poor in developing nations.

Once again we must ask, Who is at fault? Is it the host governments and local governing elites who gladly cooperate with MNCs for their mutual benefit? Is it the MNCs for not taking a more charitable stance toward the poor? Is it the people in the developed world for unknowingly supporting MNCs by purchasing their products or owning their stock? The answer is, all three. All three share some responsibility for the negative impact of MNCs on developing countries.

Discrimination and War

Women. In most countries today, women suffer from discrimination. Linda Tripp, Vice-President of World Vision, Canada, has estimated that women work 67 percent of the world's work hours, earn 10 percent of the world's income, and own less than 1 percent of the world's property.[159] Most women simply do not have equal opportunities—whether legal, educational, economic, or social. And the result is poverty. In its 1995 report, the United Nations estimates that out of the 1.3 billion people in poverty, 70 percent of them are women.[160] Development economist Michael Todaro says: "Women and children are more likely to be poor and malnourished and less likely to receive medical services, clean water, sanitation or other benefits."[161]

Tragically, discrimination sometimes starts in the family. In Latin America, 31 percent of female children are underweight, while only 17 percent of male children are. In rural India in the state of Punjab, 21 percent of girls in low-income families suffer severe malnutrition—but only 3 percent of boys in the same families do.[162] Many cultures value boys more than girls, so parents feed them better.

The same prejudice limits women's educational opportunities. The U.N. estimates that of the 900 million people that cannot read on the earth, two-thirds are women.[163]

Table 18—Adult Illiteracy Rate, 1980 and 1995
(Percent of total population)

| | 1980 | | 1995 | |
	Female	Male	Female	Male
Developed regions	5	2	2	2
Sub-Saharan Africa	71	48	53	33
Latin America & Caribbean	23	18	15	12
North Africa & Western Asia	74	45	56	32
Eastern, Southern Asia & Oceania	42	20	24	9
Southern Asia	76	47	63	37

Source: United Nations[164]

Legal and administrative barriers also exist. "In much of Africa," according to the United Nations 1995 *Human Development Report*, "women are responsible for food production. . . . But in many parts of the developing world, women do not have legal control over the land they farm, even in female headed households." In Kenya, a woman has access to land only if she has a living husband or son.[165] In India, 48 percent of self-employed cultivators were women in 1983. But most Indian States do not provide agricultural extension services to women.

Especially tragic is the story of the "missing" women. China, South Asia, and West Asia have only 94 women for every 100 men. Harvard economist Amartya Sen has estimated that in Asia there are 100 million women "missing"—49 million in China alone.[166] Since these societies value boys more than girls, female babies are aborted or abandoned. China's ghastly "one-child per family" policy has caused particularly discriminatory results against women in a culture that values men more than women.

Finally, there is the horror of prostitution. In many countries, poor parents sell female daughters as prostitutes. Millions of poor women suffer this vile denial of their humanity.

Linda Tripp tells about a young girl (I'll call her Rojana) who managed to get to World Vision's Distressed Women's Center in Bangkok, Thailand. When Rojana was eleven, her parents sold her into prostitution. From age eleven to thirteen, Rojana worked in a brothel serving as many as thirty different men a night. Then she ran away. The police found Rojana sleeping on a garbage dump. They brought her to the center, but Rojana was beyond help. Her body was too full of disease.[167] Rojana is a ghastly symbol of how discrimination against women contributes to poverty and death.

Racism and ethnic hostility. Whether we think of Bosnia, South Africa, Rwanda and Burundi, or the United States, the connections between racism, poverty, hunger, and even starvation are painfully clear.

Thank God for the end of apartheid. But its deadly affects are still present in South Africa.

If we treated white South Africa as a separate country, it would rank 24th in the Human Development Index—right after Spain. Black South Africa would be 123rd—just above Congo.[168]

What if we made the same comparison in the United States? U.S. whites would be number one in the world. U.S. blacks would be down at the 31st spot, next to Trinidad and Tobago. And U.S. Latinos would be 35th, next to Estonia.[169]

Sudan's three-decade civil war is rooted in ethnic and religious discrimination. Those in northern Sudan are predominantly Arab Muslims. Those in the South are black and Christian (or adherents of traditional African religions). The north, which controls the government, has confiscated fertile agricultural land in the south. Both sides have blocked food aid deliveries. Farmers' fields are full of land mines. Nearly three million people have been displaced by the fighting, and 1.3 million have died due to war-related famine and disease. In the so-called "starvation triangle" in the south, malnutrition rates are above 80 percent. That is the highest ever documented in the world.[171]

Table 19—Differences between whites and blacks	Human Development Index	Average Income per capita (PPP$)	Life Expectancy
United States			
Whites	.986	$22,000	76.5
Blacks	.881	$17,100	70.8
Difference (Wh–Bl)	.105	$4,900	5.7
South Africa			
Whites	.878	$14,920	75
Blacks	.462	$1,710	60
Difference (Wh–Bl)	.416	$13,210	15

Source: United Nations (1994)[170]

Racial and ethnic bias, just like prejudice against women, becomes embedded in the legal, social, economic, and political systems in a way that produces poverty. And ghastly fighting—especially since the end of the Cold War.

War. War may not quite fit the category of structural injustice, but it results from a complex web of structural evils and certainly produces poverty and death.

In 1994, 164 armed conflicts raged. In over 22 of them, more than 1000 people died.[172] Wars destroy agricultural productivity, hospitals, schools, transportation systems, and the environment. They produce instant death or refugee status for millions and long-term poverty and hunger for tens of millions. Bread for the World estimates that today there are 100 million people around the world caught in a web of civil strife and hunger. Natural disasters used to be a primary cause of famine and starvation. Today, "human-made famines have become the primary cause of starvation."[173]

Sometimes the fighting is a lingering result of the Cold War. To counter the Soviet Union's invasion of Afghanistan, the U.S. invested up to $3 billion supplying arms to the Afghan rebels. The result? One million Afghans have died, two million have been displaced within Afghanistan, and seven million live in refugee camps outside their homeland. And warring factions continue to fight and spread chaos. Cultivated land has dropped by 40 percent. Child mortality is the fifth highest in the world. With the Cold War over, the U.S. has no major geopolitical interests so American humanitarian aid has ended.[174]

Often the conflicts result from a complex web of ethnic, tribal, racial, and religious factors plus economic and political motivations. Ancient ethnic and religious hostilities explode in rape and massacre in Yugoslavia. Rival political factions battle for control of Liberia. Tribal groups murder each other in Rwanda and Burundi. On and on the agonizing list goes . . .

Meanwhile developing countries spend $125 billion each year on their armed forces. One-quarter of that would cut adult illiteracy by 50 percent and provide primary health care for all their people. And the developed nations—with the U.S. in the lead—continue to sell billions of dollars of weapons.[175]

Women and children suffer the most. The words of Amer Kuay, an African mother and refugee from the Southern Sudan, captures a little of their agony:

> We were attacked by cattle raiders working for the government. They took all of our cattle. They burned our houses. They took all our belongings. . . . We were left with no tools and hardly any seed, so we harvested very little. By February we started to starve. There were still attacks. . . . So we decided to cross the Nile to . . . where it was safer. We had to wait in the marshes for some time to get a fishing boat to take us across. We had no money to pay, so I had to give my daughter's clothes to the fisherman. Some of the people in our group were dying of hunger even as we started to walk from our village. Young children and old people died. I lost my youngest girl. She was just two years old.[176]

In numerous complicated ways, you and I are involved in one way or another with unjust global structures. The mechanism of the market is a useful tool for organizing a great deal of economic life, but today's market economies also produce serious injustices that we must correct. International trade patterns contain injustice. Current patterns of economic life severely threaten the global environment and the long-term development opportunities of the Third World. Multinational corporations sometimes hinder rather than promote meaningful development in less developed nations. And discrimination adds its own sometimes blatant, sometimes subtle, oppression. The life of every person in developed countries is touched in some way by these structural injustices. Unless you have retreated to some isolated valley and grow or make everything you use, you participate in unjust structures that contribute directly to the desperate poverty of some of our billion suffering neighbors.

We should not, of course, conclude that international trade or investment by multinational corporations in poor countries is necessarily immoral. Nor would the economies of the developed world be destroyed if present injustices in today's global economic system were corrected. The proper conclusion is that injustice has become deeply embedded in some of our fundamental economic institutions. Biblical Christians—precisely to the extent that they are faithful to Scripture—will dare to call such structures sinful.

Most of us wish that international economics were less complex and that faithful discipleship in our time had less to do with such a complicated subject. But former U.N. Secretary General Dag Hammarskjold was right: "In our era, the road to holiness necessarily passes through the world of action."[177] To give the cup of cold water effectively in our Age of Affluence and Poverty requires some understanding of international economic and political structures.

In March 1974, several Central American banana-producing countries agreed to demand a one-dollar tax on every case of bananas exported. Banana prices for producers had not increased in the previous twenty inflation-ridden years, but the costs for manufactured goods had constantly escalated. As a result, the purchasing power of the banana exporters had declined by 60 percent. This was a significant factor in the economy of Honduras and Panama because at least half of their export income came from bananas.

When the exporting countries demanded this one-dollar tax on bananas, the North American banana companies adamantly refused to pay. Since three large companies (United Brands, Castle and Cooke, and Del Monte) controlled 90 percent of the marketing and distribution of bananas, they had powerful leverage. In Panama, the fruit company abruptly stopped cutting bananas, and in Honduras, the banana company allowed 145,000 crates of fruit to rot at the docks.

One after another the poor countries gave in. Costa Rica finally settled for twenty-five cents a crate, Panama for thirty-five cents, and Honduras agreed to a thirty-cent tax.[178]

In April 1975, North Americans learned that United Brands, one of three huge U.S. companies that grow and import bananas, had arranged to pay $2.5 million[179] in bribes to top government officials in Honduras to persuade them to tax bananas at a rate less than half what they had requested.[180] The Honduran government accepted the bribe and lowered the export tax, even though the money was desperately needed in Honduras.

A U.N. fact-finding commission concluded later that year that "The banana-producing countries with very much less income are subsidizing the consumption of the fruit, and consequently the development of the more industrialized countries."[181]

Why don't the poor demand change? They do. But too often they have little power. Until recently, dictators representing tiny, wealthy elites working closely with American business interests ruled many Latin American countries.

The history of Guatemala, also a producer of bananas for United Brands, shows why change is difficult. In 1954 the CIA helped overthrow a democratically elected government in Guatemala because it had initiated a modest program of agricultural reform that seemed to threaten unused land owned by the United Fruit Company (the former name of United Brands). The U.S. secretary of state in 1954 was John Foster Dulles. His law firm had written the company's agreements with Guatemala in 1930 and 1936. The CIA director was Allen Dulles, brother of the secretary of state and previous president of United Fruit Company. The assistant secretary of state was a major shareholder in United Fruit Company.[182] In Guatemala and elsewhere change is difficult when U.S. companies work closely with wealthy, local elites to protect their mutual economic interests.

In the past, most North Americans knew little about the injustice in Central America. This began to change in the early 1980s. With radical guerrilla movements gaining ground in El Salvador and Guatemala, President Reagan launched a vigorous military response. Front page headlines on Central America became a regular feature of U.S. newspapers.

The civil wars that raged in Central America in the eighties undoubtedly had many roots.[183] Certainly the fact that some of the guerrilla movements had Marxist elements and received support and supplies from Marxist countries complicated the problems. Soviet shipments of arms was rightly condemned. One of the last things we needed was another ghastly Marxist-

Leninist experiment in the world. But the U.S. attempt in the eighties to solve the problems primarily via a military response was both immoral and foolish. The root causes of the violence and war were the long-standing economic injustice and desperate poverty of the poor majority in the region. When parents cannot protect their children from malnutrition and starvation, they do not need Marxist-Leninists to tell them something needs to change.

Tragically there will always be those eager to provide plausible rationalizations. Andrew M. Greeley, a prominent sociologist at the University of Chicago, has mocked those who condemn aspects of the United States' economic relationships with developing nations:

> Well, let us suppose that our guilt finally becomes too much to bear and we decide to reform. . . . We inform the fruit orchards in Central America that we can dispense with bananas in our diets. . . . Their joy will hardly be noticed as massive unemployment and depression sweep those countries.[184]

One wonders if Greeley is naive or perverse. The point is not—and Greeley surely knows this—that we should stop importing bananas. Rather, it is that (1) multinational firms and huge agribusinesses, in complicity with all the buyers of bananas in the developed world, benefit from complex systems that make it more difficult for the poor to escape their poverty; and that (2) we should encourage the reorganization of economic structures and promote programs here and in Central America that will help poor people share more equitably in the benefits of agricultural production and trade.

The story of the bananas shows how all of us are involved in unjust international economic structures. The words of the apostle James speak directly to our situation.

> Come now, you rich, weep and howl for the miseries that are coming upon you. . . . Your gold and silver have rusted, and their rust will be evidence against you. . . . Behold, the wages of the laborers who mowed your fields, which you kept back by fraud, cry out; and the cries of the harvesters have reached the ears of the Lord of hosts. You have lived on the earth in luxury and in pleasure; you have fattened your hearts in a day of slaughter. (James 5:1-5)

Repentance

What should be our response? For biblical Christians the only correct response to sin is repentance. We have become entangled, to some degree unconsciously, in a complex web of institutionalized sin. Thank God we can repent. God is merciful. God forgives. But only if we repent. And biblical repentance involves more than a hasty tear and a weekly prayer of confession. Biblical repentance involves conversion. It involves a whole new lifestyle. The One who stands ready to forgive us for our sinful involvement in economic injustice offers us his grace to begin living a generous new lifestyle that empowers the poor and oppressed.

Sin is not just an inconvenience or a tragedy for our neighbors. It is a damnable outrage against the Almighty Lord of the universe. If God's Word is true, then all of us who dwell in affluent nations are trapped in sin. We have profited from systematic injustice—sometimes only half-knowing, sometimes only half-caring, and always half-hoping not to know. We are guilty of sin against God and neighbor.

But that is not God's last word to us. If it were, honest acknowledgment of our involvement would be almost impossible. If there were no hope of forgiveness, admission of our sinful complicity in evil of this magnitude would be an act of despair.[185] But there is hope. The One who writes our indictment is the One who died for us sinners.

John Newton was captain of a slave ship in the eighteenth century. A brutal, callous man, he played a central role in a system that fed thousands to the sharks and delivered millions to a living death. But eventually, after he gave up his career as captain, he saw his sin and repented. His familiar hymn overflows with joy and gratitude for God's acceptance and forgiveness.

> *Amazing grace! How sweet the sound,*
> *that saved a wretch like me;*
> *I once was lost, but now am found,*
> *was blind but now I see.*
> *'Twas grace that taught my heart to fear,*
> *and grace my fears relieved;*
> *How precious did that grace appear*
> *the hour I first believed.*

John Newton became a founding member of a society for the abolition of slavery. The church he pastored, St. Mary Woolnoth in the City of London, was a meeting place for abolitionists. William Wilberforce frequently went to him for spiritual counsel. Newton delivered impassioned sermons against the slave trade, convincing many of its evil. He campaigned against the slave trade until he died in the year of its abolition, 1807.

We are participants in structures that also contribute to the suffering and death of millions of people. If we have eyes to see, God's grace will also teach our hearts to fear and tremble, and then also to rest and trust.

But only if we repent. Repentance is not just coming forward at the close of a service. It is not just repeating a spiritual law. It is not just mumbling a liturgical confession. All of these things may help. But they are no substitute for the kind of deep inner anguish that leads to a new way of living.

Biblical repentance entails conversion, which means "turning around." The Greek word *metanoia* means a total change of mind. The New Testament links repentance to a transformed style of living. Sensing the hypocrisy of the Pharisees who came seeking baptism, John the Baptist denounced them as a brood of vipers. "Bear fruit that befits repentance," he demanded (Matthew 3:8). Paul told King Agrippa that wherever he preached, he called on people to "repent and turn to God and perform deeds worthy of . . . repentance" (Acts 26:20).

Zacchaeus should be our model. As a greedy Roman tax collector, Zacchaeus was enmeshed in sinful economic structures. But he never supposed that he could come to Jesus and continue to enjoy the economic benefits of that evil system. Coming to Jesus meant repenting of his complicity in social injustice. It meant publicly giving reparations. And it meant a whole new lifestyle.

What might genuine, biblical repentance mean for affluent Christians entangled in sinful structures? And would not deep joy flow from obedient sharing that empowered others?

Study Questions

1. Are you convinced that present international economic structures involve us all in structural evil? How, specifically, does that happen?
2. What are the good and bad features of today's market economies?
3. How do tariffs and import quotas of industrialized countries hurt the poor? How are they related to the debt crisis?
4. What are the connections between environmental pollution and poverty?
5. What are the advantages and disadvantages of multinational corporations in reducing poverty?
6. How do discrimination and war contribute to poverty?
7. How does the original setting of "Amazing Grace" parallel the problems described here?
8. What were your strongest emotions as you read this chapter? Why?

Part Four

Implementation

A prominent Washington think tank once assembled a large cross-section of distinguished religious leaders to discuss the problems of world hunger. The conferees expressed deep concern. They called for significant structural change. But their words rang hollow. They were meeting at an exclusive resort in Colorado!

Simpler personal lifestyles are essential. But personal change is insufficient. A friend of mine has forsaken the city for a rural community. He grows almost all his own food, lives simply, and places few demands on the poor of the earth. This person has considerable speaking and writing talents that could promote change in church and society, but he uses them less than he might because of the time absorbed by his "simple" lifestyle.

We need to change at three levels. Appropriate personal lifestyles are crucial to symbolize, validate, and facilitate our concern for the hungry. The church must change so that its common life presents a new model for a divided world. Finally, both here and abroad, we must make the structures of society more fair.

Implementation demands specific proposals. But offering concrete suggestions is risky. We seldom know enough to be certain about the exact consequences of suggested changes. Broad generalizations, however, are not enough if we want to change our personal lifestyles, our churches, and our societies. So I have dared to be specific—even though I know I may be wrong.

If you question my suggestions, ask two questions: Are the suggestions grounded in biblical principles? Is the underlying social analysis valid? If the answers are yes, try the proposal. If no, develop a better way to solve the problem. Furthermore, let me know about your better proposal. Precisely because I want to empower God's poor, I am eager to abandon poor ideas— even my own!—as quickly as possible, and exchange them for effective ones.

9

Toward a Simpler Lifestyle:
The Graduated Tithe and Other Modest Proposals

Before God and a billion hungry neighbors, we must rethink our values regarding our present standard of living and promote more just acquisition and distribution of the world's resources.[1]
—The Chicago Declaration of Evangelical Social Concern, 1973

Those of us who live in affluent circumstances accept our duty to develop a simple life style in order to contribute more generously to both relief and evangelism.[2]
—Lausanne Covenant, 1974

The rich must live more simply that the poor may simply live.[3]
—Dr. Charles Birch, 1974

A STATE SENATOR from Pennsylvania once argued that his constituents were so poor that they simply could not afford to pay another cent in taxes. He cited a letter from an irate voter as proof. This good person had written him announcing that her family could not possibly pay any more taxes. Why, she said, they already paid the government income taxes and sales taxes—and besides that they bought licenses for their two cars, summer camper, houseboat, and motorboat!

Many of us actually believe that we can barely get along on the thirty-five, forty-five, or sixty thousand dollars that we make each year. We are in an incredible rat race. When our income goes up by another $2,000, we convince ourselves that we *need* that much more to live—comfortably.

How can we escape this delusion? Perhaps it will help to be reminded again that thousands of children starve every day. That over one billion people live in desperate poverty. And that another two billion are very poor. The problem, we know, is that the world's resources are not fairly distributed. North Americans, Western Europeans, and rich elites around the world are an affluent minority in a world where half the people are poor.

How will we respond to this inequity? Former President Richard Nixon enunciated one response in a June 13, 1973, speech to the nation: "I have made this basic decision: In allocating the products of America's farms between markets abroad and those in the United States, we must put the American consumer first."[4]

Such a statement may be good politics, but it certainly is not good theology.

But how much should we give? John Wesley gave a startling answer. One of his frequently repeated sermons was on Matthew 6:19–23 ("Lay not up for yourselves treasures upon earth . . ." KJV).[5] Christians, Wesley said, should give away all but "the plain necessaries of life"—that is, plain, wholesome food, clean clothes, and enough to carry on one's business. One should earn what one can, justly and honestly. Capital need not be given away. But Wesley wanted all income given to the poor after bare necessities were met. Unfortunately, Wesley discovered, not one person in five hundred in any "Christian city" obeys Jesus' command. But that simply demonstrates that most professed believers are "living men but dead Christians." "Any 'Christian' who takes for himself anything more than the plain necessaries of life," Wesley insisted, "lives in an open, habitual denial of the Lord." He has "gained riches and hell-fire!"[6]

Wesley lived what he preached. Sales of his books often earned him fourteen hundred pounds annually, but he spent only thirty pounds on himself. The rest he gave away. He always wore inexpensive clothes and dined on simple food. "If I leave behind me ten pounds," he once wrote, "you and all mankind bear witness against me that I lived and died a thief and a robber."[7]

We need not agree with Wesley's every word to see that he was struggling to follow the biblical summons to share with the needy. How much should we give? Knowing that God wants every person to have the resources to earn a decent living, we should give until our lives truly reflect the principles of Leviticus 25 and 2 Corinthians 8. Surely Paul's advice to the Corinthians applies even more forcefully to rich Christians today: "I do not mean that others should be eased and you burdened, but that as a matter of equality your abundance at the present time should supply their want . . . that there may be equality" (2 Corinthians 8:13–14). Will we be that generous?

The God of North America

Why are we so unconcerned, so slow to care? We learn one reason from the story of the rich young ruler. When he asked Jesus how to obtain eternal life, Jesus told him to sell his goods and give to the poor. The man went away sad because he had great possessions. The point of the story, as we are usually told, is that Christ alone must be at the center of the affections and plans of his followers. Whatever our idol—whether it be riches, fame, status, academic distinction, or membership in some "in" group— we must be willing to abandon it for Christ's sake. Riches just happened to be this young man's idol. Jesus then is not commanding us to sell all our possessions. He is only demanding total submission to himself.

This interpretation is both unquestionably true and unquestionably inadequate. To say no more is to miss the fact that possessions are the most common idol for rich Christians today. Jesus must have meant it when he added, "Truly, I tell you, it will be hard for a rich person to enter the kingdom of heaven. Again I tell you, it is easier for a camel to go through the eye of a needle than for someone who is rich to enter the kingdom of God" (Matthew 19:23–24 NRSV).

We have become ensnared by unprecedented material luxury. Advertising constantly convinces us that we need one unnecessary luxury after another. Affluence is the god of twentieth-century North Americans, and the adman is his prophet.

We all know how subtle the materialistic temptations are and how convincing the rationalizations. Only by God's grace and with great effort can we "Just say no!" to the shower of luxuries that has almost suffocated our Christian compassion.

All of us face this problem. Some years ago I spent about fifty dollars on an extra suit after persuading myself that it was a wise investment (thanks to the 75 percent discount). But that money would have fed a starving child in India for about a year. In all honesty we have to ask ourselves: Dare we care at all about current fashions if that means reducing our ability to help hungry neighbors? How many more luxuries should we buy for ourselves and our children when others are dying for lack of bread?

I do not pretend that giving an honest answer to some questions is easy. Our responsibility is not always clear. One Saturday morning as I was beginning to prepare a lecture (on poverty!), a poor man came into my office and asked for five dollars. He was drinking. He had no food, no job, no home. The Christ of the poor confronted me in this man. But I didn't have the time, I said. I had to prepare a lecture on the Christian view of poverty. I did give him a couple of dollars, but that was not what he needed. He needed somebody to talk to, somebody to love him. He needed my time. He needed me. But I was too busy. "Inasmuch as you did it not to the least of these, you did it not. . . ."

We need to make some dramatic, concrete moves to escape the materialism that seeps into our minds via diabolically clever and incessant advertising. We have been brainwashed to believe that bigger houses, more prosperous businesses, and more sophisticated gadgets are the way to joy and fulfillment. As a result, we are caught in an absurd, materialistic spiral. The more we make, the more we think we need in order to live decently and respectably. Somehow we have to break this cycle because it makes us sin against our needy brothers and sisters and, therefore, against our Lord. And it also destroys us. Sharing with others is the way to real joy.

Some Examples

In the mid-1970s Graham Kerr was the Galloping Gourmet for two hundred million TV viewers each week. He was rich and successful, but his personal life was falling apart. In 1975 he came to Christ, and since then his family life has been miraculously restored. He abandoned his gourmet TV series and gave away most of his money.

For more than a decade Graham devoted his time and used his knowledge of nutrition to develop a new kind of agricultural missionary who both shares the gospel and helps poor Third World people develop a better diet with locally available products.

In 1990 Graham returned to international television. He and his wife, Treena, still live with what they call "relative simplicity"—but not because they are ascetics. They live simply because they want to share their lives and influence wherever possible. They care deeply about those who do not enjoy the Gospel, good food, and good health. So they use their influence to encourage others to share out of abundance with those who are left out.[8]

Are Graham and Treena happy? They are immeasurably happier than before. Every time I see them I see joy and contentment flooding their lives. While living more simply, they are having the time of their lives.

Robert Bainum was a successful Christian businessman—in fact, a millionaire, but when he read the first edition of this book, God called him to share more with the poor of the earth. He gave away half of his wealth and then devoted a major portion of his creative energy and organizational abilities to relief and development programs among the poor, both at home and abroad.[9]

In her delightful book *Living More with Less*, Doris Longacre gives us glimpses of several hundred Christians who are learning the joy of sharing more.[10] Some still live in what I consider substantial affluence. Others live far more simply than I do. But everyone is trying to spend less on themselves in order to share more with others.

Biblical Christians are experimenting with a variety of simpler lifestyles. Three billion poor neighbors demand drastic change. But we must be careful to avoid legalism and self-righteousness. "We have to beware of the reverse snobbery of spiritual one-up-manship."[11]

The Graduated Tithe

The graduated tithe is one of many models that can help break the materialistic stranglehold. It is not the only useful model, but it has proved helpful in our family. Certainly it is not a biblical norm to be prescribed legalistically for others. It is just one family's story.

I tell it partly to show how the concept has evolved in our family. When we hit the high school and college years in the family life cycle, we were astounded by how much more seemed right to spend on our family. We didn't always get it right, but we tried to be more concerned with persons (specifically our children's changing needs) than with some arbitrary "rule" or abstract theory.

When my wife, Arbutus, and I decided to adopt a graduated scale for our giving in 1969, we sat down and tried to calculate honestly what we would need to live for a year. We wanted a figure that would permit reasonable comfort but not all the luxuries. We decided that we would give a tithe (10 percent) on our base figure and then give a graduated tithe (15 percent or more) on income above that. For each thousand dollars above our base, we decided to increase our giving by another 5 percent on that thousand.

In 1969 our base figure was $7,000. By 1973 we had increased it to $8,000. And in 1982 we increased it again—to $10,000. (This time we decided to use an approximation of the 1982 federal poverty level: $9,862 for a family of four.)

Then came high school and college years. We decided that in our situation a Christian high school was important. That added major costs. So did college expenses. Soon we could no longer continue our original scheme, so we added costs for Christian education and college to our base.

What about taxes? At first we did not include taxes in our base figure. Obviously one would have to do that beyond a certain income or the graduated tithe and taxes would eat up all income. So in 1979 we added taxes to our base.

Eventually we stumbled into the following pattern. We give 10 percent on a base figure that includes: (a) the current U.S. poverty level ($16,029 in 1996 for a family of four)[12]; (b) Christian education and college/university expenses; (c) taxes; (d) genuine emergencies. On our income above this base, we apply the graduated tithe (see Table 20).

We don't always make it! But this is what we aim for.

Every family is unique. Housing costs vary enormously in different parts of the country and city. Probably the single most important decision on family expenses is where you decide to live. Our choice to live in a lower-income, interracial city neighborhood where housing and related expenses are vastly less than in the suburbs has helped us immensely. (It also lowered the children's sense of what they "needed.")

There are a near limitless set of variations. Some families need emergency counseling. Some children need special dental work. Some people with special entrepreneurial skills require large sums of capital for investment and may choose to count that as part of their base. What do you do about untaxed employer contributions to a pension fund? (We don't count it at all—but will when it appears as income during retirement.) What about employer-paid medical insurance?

Every family must work out its own answers to these questions. Our story is not a law for everyone—not even for one other person! Each person or family will need to develop an individualized plan, but the basic pattern is easy to follow. Through prayer, study, and conversation with sympathetic friends, decide what you should consider the base on which you will give 10 percent. Then for every $1,000 of income above the base, give an additional 5 percent. Table 20 shows how to do the calculations.

Table 20—Graduated Tithe		
Total Income	Percent Given Away	Dollars Given Away
Base	10% of Base	10% of Base
Base + $1,000	15% of last $1,000	10% of Base + 150
Base + 2,000	20% of last 1,000	10% of Base + 350
Base + 3,000	25% of last 1,000	10% of Base + 600
Base + 4,000	30% of last 1,000	10% of Base + 900
Base + 5,000	35% of last 1,000	10% of Base + 1,250
Base + 6,000	40% of last 1,000	10% of Base + 1,650
Base + 7,000	45% of last 1,000	10% of Base + 2,100
Base + 8,000	50% of last 1,000	10% of Base + 2,600
Base + 9,000	55% of last 1,000	10% of Base + 3,150
Base + 10,000	60% of last 1,000	10% of Base + 3,750
Base + 11,000	65% of last 1,000	10% of Base + 4,400
Base + 12,000	70% of last 1,000	10% of Base + 5,100
Base + 13,000	75% of last 1,000	10% of Base + 5,850
Base + 14,000	80% of last 1,000	10% of Base + 6,650
Base + 15,000	85% of last 1,000	10% of Base + 7,500
Base + 16,000	90% of last 1,000	10% of Base + 8,400
Base + 17,000	95% of last 1,000	10% of Base + 9,350
Base + 18,000	100% of last 1,000	10% of Base + 10,350

If you believe God is leading you to adopt the graduated tithe, here are a few suggestions.

First, discuss the idea with the whole family. Everyone needs to understand the reasons so that the family can come to a common decision. Second, put your plan in writing at the beginning of the year. It is relatively painless, sometimes even exciting, to work it out theoretically. After you have committed yourself to the abstract figures, it hurts less to dole out the cash each month. Third, discuss your proposal with a committed Christian friend or couple who share your concern for justice. Fourth, discuss major expenditures with the same people. It is easier for others to spot rationalizations than it is for you. They may also have helpful hints on simple living. Fifth, each year see if it is possible to reduce your basic figure and total expenditures. (This does not mean that you ignore the need for capital investment to increase productivity, either in your own company or via Christian organizations making loans to the poor.)

This proposal for a graduated tithe is a modest one, so modest in fact that it verges on unfaithfulness to the apostle Paul. But at the same time it is sufficiently radical that its implementation would revolutionize the ministry and life of the church.

Some Christians are experimenting with far more radical attempts to win the war on affluence.

Communal Living

The model that permits the simplest standard of living is probably the commune. Housing, furniture, appliances, tools, and cars that would normally serve one nuclear family can accommodate ten or twenty people. Communal living releases vast amounts of money and time for alternative activities.

Some Christian communes have been initiated as conscious attempts to develop a more ecologically responsible, sharing standard of living. Others emerged as a spontaneous response to human need. Jerry Barker, a member of a Christian community in Texas, put it this way:

> It soon became obvious that the needs we were faced with would . . . take lots of resources and so we began to cut expenses for things we had been accustomed to. We stopped buying new cars and new televisions and things of that sort. We didn't even think of them. We started driving our cars until they literally fell apart, and then we'd buy a used car or something like that to replace it. We began to turn in some of our insurance policies so that they would not be such a financial drain on us. We found such a security in our relationship with the Lord that it was no longer important to have security for the future. . . . We never have had any rule about it, or felt this was a necessary part of the Christian life. It was just a matter of using the money we had available most effectively, particularly in supporting so many extra people. We learned to live very economically. We quit eating steaks and expensive roasts and

things like that and we began to eat simple fare. . . . We'd often eat things that people would bring us—a box of groceries or a sack of rice.[13]

The standard of living in Christian communities varies. But almost all live far more simply than the average North American family. For many years at Chicago's Reba Place, for example, eating patterns were based on the welfare level of the city (see chapter 10). In the last few decades, Christian communes have had a symbolic importance out of all proportion to their numbers. They quietly question society's affluence. And they offer a striking alternative.

Communal living, of course, is not for everyone. In fact, I personally believe that it is the right setting for only a small percentage of Christians. We need many more diverse models.

No one model is God's will for everyone. God loves variety and diversity. Does that mean, however, that we ought to settle for typical Western individualism, with each person or family doing what is good in its own eyes? By no means.

Two things can help. First, we need the help of other brothers and sisters—in our local congregation, in our town or city, and around the world. We need a process for discussing our economic lifestyles with close Christian friends. We also need new ways to dialog about the shape of a faithful lifestyle with poor Christians.[14]

Second, certain criteria can help us determine what is right for us.

Guidelines for Giving

I offer eight guidelines—as suggestions, *not* as norms or laws.

1. Move toward a personal lifestyle that could be sustained over a long period of time if it were shared by everyone in the world.

2. Distinguish between necessities and luxuries; withstand the desire to indulge regularly in luxuries and resist the inclination to blur the distinction.[15]

3. Distinguish between legitimate and non-legitimate reasons for spending/buying. (For example, expenditures to elevate or maintain our social status, feed our pride, stay in fashion, or "keep up with the Joneses" are wrong.)

4. Distinguish talents and hobbies from a curious interest in current

fads. Allow expenditures that will develop talents and hobbies, but don't indulge in all the latest recreational equipment simply because it is popular with those who seem "successful." Each person has unique interests and gifts. We should be able to express our creativity in those areas. But if we begin justifying lots of things in many areas, we should become suspicious.

5. Distinguish between occasional celebration and normal day-to-day indulgence. A turkey feast with all the trimmings at Thanksgiving to celebrate the good gift of creation is biblical (Deuteronomy 14:22–27). Unfortunately, many of us overeat every day, and that is sin.

6. Resist buying things just because we can afford them. The amount we earn has nothing to do with what we need.

7. Seek a balance between supporting emergency relief, development, and broad structural change. Emergency food is important when people are starving. But more money needs to go for long-term community development so folk can feed themselves. It is especially crucial to give to organizations that increase understanding and promote just public policy and structural change (especially since so few Christians understand this last area). Part of a family's graduated tithe might very appropriately go to political campaigns to support candidates who will work for justice for the poor.

8. Do not neglect other areas of Christian work. Evangelism and Christian education are extremely important and deserve continuing support. Give approximately as much to support evangelism as you do for social justice activities. (Wholistic programs that combine both are ideal.)[16]

Some Practical Suggestions

The following are hints, not rules, for living more simply. Freedom, joy, and laughter are essential elements of responsible living. (See the Appendix for addresses and information about books, groups, and organizations named.)

1. Question your own lifestyle, not your neighbor's.

2. Reduce your food budget by:
   • Gardening: try hoeing instead of mowing.
   • Substituting vegetable protein for animal protein. Cookbooks like *Recipes for a Small Planet* and *More with Less Cookbook* tell how to

prepare delicious, meatless meals. Our daily requirement of protein costs more than five times as much via veal cutlets as it does via peanut butter.[17]

- Joining a food co-op (if there's none in your area, write to The Cooperative League of the U.S.A. for materials on how to start one).
- Fasting regularly.
- Opposing (by speech and example) the flagrant misuse of grain for making beer and other alcoholic beverages (the United States annually uses enough grain—5.2 million tons—in the production of alcoholic beverages, enough to feed 26 million people in a country like India).[18]
- Setting a monthly budget and sticking to it.

3. Lower energy consumption by:
- Keeping your thermostat (at the home and office) at 68 degrees F. or lower during winter months.
- Supporting public transportation with your feet and your vote.
- Using bicycles, carpools, and, for short trips, your feet.
- Making dish washing a family time instead of buying a dish washer.
- Buying a fan instead of an air conditioner.

4. Resist consumerism by:
- Laughing regularly at TV commercials.
- Developing family slogans like: "Who Are You Kidding?" and "You Can't Take It with You!"
- Making a list of dishonest ads and boycotting those products.
- Using the postage-paid envelopes of direct-mail advertisers to object to unscrupulous advertising.

5. Buy and renovate an old house in the inner city. (Persuade a few friends to do the same so you can enjoy Christian community.)

6. Reduce your consumption of nonrenewable natural resources by:
- Resisting obsolescence (buy quality products when you buy).
- Sharing appliances, tools, lawnmowers, sports equipment, books, even a car (this is easier if you live close to other Christians committed to living more simply).
- Organizing a "things closet" in your church for items used only occasionally such as edger, clippers, cots for unexpected guests, lawnmowers, camping equipment, big ladder.

7. Determine how much of what you spend is for status and eliminate such spending.
8. Refuse to keep up with clothing fashions. (Very few readers of this book need to buy clothes—except maybe shoes—for two or three years.)
9. Enjoy what is free.
10. Live on a welfare budget for a month.
11. Examine *Shopping for a Better World* from the Council on Economic Priorities and *Alternatives Celebrations Catalog* published by Alternatives. It provides exciting, inexpensive, ecologically sound alternative ideas for celebrating Christmas, Valentine's Day, Thanksgiving, and other holidays.
12. Give your children more love and time rather than more things.

That's enough for a beginning.

Evaluating Organizations

If ten percent of all North American Christians adopted the graduated tithe, huge sums of money would become available to empower the poor. Where would that money do the most good? Which relief and development agencies are doing the best job? This issue is important, but you must decide for yourself. Here are some general questions to ask :

1. Do the funds support wholistic projects in the Third World, working simultaneously at an integrated program of evangelism, social change, education, agricultural development?
2. Do the funds support truly indigenous projects? In other words: (a) Are the leaders and most of the staff of the projects in the developing nations indigenous persons? (They should be.) (b) Do the projects use materials suited to the culture or have the leaders unthinkingly adopted Western ideas, materials, and technology? (c) Did the project arise from the needs of the people rather than from an outside "expert"?
3. Are the projects primarily engaged in long-range development (including people development), or in emergency aid only?
4. Are the programs designed to help the poor understand that God wants sinful social structures changed and that they can help effect that change?

5. Do the programs work through and foster the growth of local churches?

6. Are the programs potentially self-supporting after an initial injection of seed capital? And do the programs from the beginning require commitment and a significant contribution of capital or time (or both) from the people themselves?

7. Do the programs aid the poorest people in the poorest developing countries?

8. Is agricultural development involved? (It need not always be, but in many cases it should be.)

9. Is justice rather than continual charity the result?[19]

10. Is the international agency through which you channel funds run efficiently and wisely? Ask these questions as you pick an organization: (a) Does the organization spend more than 10 or 15 percent of total funds on fund-raising and administration? (b) Are Third World persons, minority people, and women represented among the board and top staff? (c) Is the organization audited annually by an independent CPA firm? (d) Are the board members and staff persons of known integrity? Is the board paid? (It should not be.) (e) Are staff salaries consistent with the biblical call for jubilee among all God's people? (f) Does the organization object to answering these questions?[20]

The following example will help clarify the kind of wholistic program that meets most of the above criteria.

> Elizabeth Native Interior Mission [is] in southern Liberia. ENI is headed by Augustus Marwieh who became a Christian under Mother George, one of the first black American missionaries to Africa. Ten years ago Gus went to work at the struggling mission where he had been saved. The young people were leaving the villages to go to the capital city of Monrovia; there, most found only unemployment, alcohol, and prostitution. Local skills like log sawing, blacksmithing, and making pottery were dying out as the people became dependent on outside traders (usually foreigners) and became poorer and poorer. At least 90 percent of the people were illiterate, and many suffered from protein deficiency.
>
> Today 160 churches have been started, and 10,000 people have become Christians. Eleven primary schools are operating, and they

stress locally usable skills instead of the usual Liberian fare of Spot and Jane in English. A vocational school is forming that will help revive local trades and encourage new skills; and steps are being taken to form co-operatives which will avoid middlemen, replace foreign merchants, provide capital, etc.

One crucial element, especially in view of their protein shortage, is agriculture, and in the last ten years the people have made great strides. But they are so poor that often the only farming tool they have is a machete (a heavy knife). So Gus is burdened to start a revolving loan fund from which people can borrow to buy a hoe, a shovel, a water can, spraying equipment, a pick, or an ax. You and I buy tools like that on a whim for the garden in our backyards, but for these people such purchases are completely out of reach even though they need them to fight malnutrition. So next time you start feeling poor, remember Gus's people.[21]

When those words were written in 1976, there were not too many indigenous organizations of that kind. Today there are scores of similar wholistic programs operated by biblical Christians in developing countries. They can use additional funds wisely and effectively. Organizations that channel assistance to such ministries in developing nations offer you and me a contemporary way to live the jubilee.

Opportunity International is one such organization. David Bussau, whom I mentioned in the Preface, is one of the leaders. In my book, *Cup of Water, Bread of Life* I tell the amazing story of David's life. Twenty-two years ago, David was a highly successful evangelical businessman in Australia.[22] Today he is one of the world's important bankers for the poor. For several years David and his family lived among the desperately poor in Indonesia. Slowly, they discovered that one of the best ways to help is to make tiny loans at fair interest rates to poor people whom the banks ignore.

In 1995, Opportunity International, which David helps lead, loaned $14.8 million to 36,674 small entrepreneurs. Those loans created or sustained 75,000 jobs. Between 1996 and 2001, Opportunity International expects to help one million families. Because Opportunity also receives government grants, each dollar you or I donate means $5.75 loaned to poor people. And the money is paid back and reloaned every year. So over ten years, a $1 gift enables Opportunity to loan $46 to poor people. That is a great investment.

On average, David tells me, every new job created for poor folk costs $500 (that includes the loan itself plus training seminars and consulting services). On average, every new job raises the standard of living of a family of five by 50 percent—within one year. The next year the money is reloaned and impacts another family of five. As I said in the Preface, if the Christians of the world used just one percent of their income ($10 trillion) for micro loans, we could raise the standard of living of the poorest 1 billion people by 50 percent in just one year.[23]

We have the money. Will we be generous? Almost every reader of this book could give $500 and start a new job among the poor. Most readers of this book could sign the Agra Covenant and promise to give 1 percent of their income for micro loans.[24]

Donating money is not the only way to make loans and create jobs among the poor. Using one's bank accounts and investment fund is another.

A growing number of people are depositing some of their liquid cash in banks and Community Development Loan Funds (CDLF) which focus on making loans to poor persons whom ordinary banks ignore. Money deposited with these institutions is not given away. You get it back on demand and earn interest—although often less than the current market rate. Robert Lavelle is a devoutly Christian, African-American banker in Pittsburgh. His bank, Dwelling House Savings and Loan (see organizations in the Appendix), focuses on housing loans to poor black inner city residents. The WCC's Ecumenical Bank makes loans to poor people in developing nations. The National Association of Community Development Loan Funds supports numerous local CDLFs which make loans to small businesses and non-profits serving the poor. Their loan funds come from individuals, churches, corporations, and governments which deposit funds at interest. (See Appendix B for addresses.)

Wise use of stocks can also help. Using some money (funds for retirement, for example) to purchase shares of companies that have solid track records concerning the poor, the environment, and workers' rights is a good way to promote the wholeness God desires. The Interfaith Center on Corporate Responsibility and the Council on Economic Priorities (see Appendix B) offer detailed information. The return on investment may not match the fastest-growing mutual funds, but by using the same funds to promote justice *and* prepare for retirement we can accomplish two things with the same amount of dollars. God's Word and the world's needs call us to greater generosity both with how much money we give away and how we invest what we keep.

How Generous Are We?

Do you know how much the average person in the U.S. gives to *all* charitable causes? Just 2.1 percent according to the 1995 *Statistical Abstract of the U.S.* Church members do better—at least a little better. A recent study traced how much church members in the U.S. give to their local churches. In 1992, the figure was 2.52 percent of total income. Even if these church members gave another 2 percent to charities beyond their congregation, the total figure is not even close to the biblical standard of the 10 percent tithe.

Even more disturbing is that the percentage keeps falling even though our income keeps climbing. A careful study recently completed by John and Sylvia Ronsvalle provides the details. U.S. per capita income has increased almost every year from 1968 to 1994. (They take inflation into account and use constant 1987 dollars.) The percent given to the church declined almost every year. If present patterns of church giving continue, church members will not be giving anything in 210 years! Table 21[25] on the facing page shows how we give less as we get richer.

What does God think of rich Christians whose church giving has fallen from 3.14 percent to 2.48 percent during exactly the same years that their incomes have increased from $9,831 to $15,148? Tragically, these statistics on church giving provide an accurate picture of total Christian giving. In fact, about 90 percent of all religious giving goes through local congregations.[26]

I think God pleads with you and me to be far more generous. Start with a tithe if your current giving is less than that. Then ask God and a few Christian friends to help you develop your own version of the graduated tithe. But don't try to get there in one big jump. You may want to increase your giving (beyond the tithe) by 5 percent a year until you reach the level of generous sharing that you believe God wants you to enjoy.

That will not mean poverty. But it will mean giving up some luxuries. At the same time, if Jesus knew what he was talking about, it will lead to a new joy that will surprise you. And the additional resources your generosity offers to others will spread the Gospel and empower the poor.

Table 21—The State of Church Giving through 1994 by John and Sylvia Ronsvalle (Champaign, IL: Empty tomb, Inc., forthcoming)

Per member Giving as a percentage of U.S. Per Capita Income, 29 Denominations, 1968–1994				U.S. Per Capita Income In Constant 1987 Dollars, 1968–1994	
Year	Total Contributions Per Member	Congregational Finances	Benevolences	Year	U.S. Per Capita Income
1968	3.14%	2.48%	0.66%	1968	$9,831
1969	3.07%	2.41%	0.66%	1969	9,951
1970	2.95%	2.35%	0.60%	1970	$10,147
1971	2.90%	2.30%	0.60%	1971	$10,325
1972	2.89%	2.30%	0.60%	1972	$10,526
1973	2.81%	2.25%	0.56%	1973	$11,054
1974	2.84%	2.26%	0.57%	1974	$11,045
1975	2.81%	2.22%	0.60%	1975	$10,965
1976	2.81%	2.22%	0.58%	1976	$11,211
1977	2.78%	2.21%	0.56%	1977	$11,401
1978	2.73%	2.19%	0.54%	1978	$11,756
1979	2.71%	2.17%	0.54%	1979	$11,943
1980	2.70%	2.16%	0.54%	1980	$12,079
1981	2.70%	2.16%	0.54%	1981	$12,200
1982	2.76%	2.23%	0.53%	1982	$12,123
1983	2.75%	2.22%	0.53%	1983	$12,346
1984	2.70%	2.20%	0.51%	1984	$12,927
1985	2.72%	2.21%	0.51%	1985	$13,155
1986	2.71%	2.21%	0.50%	1986	$13,468
1987	2.71%	2.22%	0.49%	1987	$13,545
1988	2.64%	2.16%	0.48%	1988	$13,920
1989	2.63%	2.16%	0.48%	1989	$14,082
1990	2.59%	2.13%	0.46%	1990	$14,278
1991	2.59%	2.14%	0.45%	1991	$14,257
1992	2.52%	2.08%	0.44%	1992	$14,515
1993	2.52%	2.09%	0.43%	1993	$14,569
1994	2.48%	2.06%	0.42%	1994	$15,148

Details in the above table may not compute to the numbers shown due to rounding.

This chapter has focused on monetary giving, but giving of ourselves is equally important. Some Christians choose low-paying jobs because the opportunity for service is great. Others decline opportunities to work overtime to be involved in more volunteer activity. Tens of thousands have volunteered a few days each year to help Habitat for Humanity build houses for the poor. Thousands of Christian doctors, teachers, farmers, and carpenters have given a few years to serve in developing countries or needy inner cities.

There is a great need for sensitive persons who will live with people in rural villages, showing the poor that God wants them to have both the tools to earn a decent living and the knowledge and power to change the unjust structures which oppress them. Agricultural workers who can share intermediate technological skills are in high demand. "One person with practical skills who's prepared to work and live in a remote village is generally worth a dozen visiting university professors and business tycoons."[27] Time is money. Sharing time is just as important as sharing financial resources.

We should be more generous with our money and our time. But that does not mean we should run ever more frantically at a dizzying pace so we can help the poor. Living a faithful lifestyle includes remembering the fourth Commandment:

> Observe the Sabbath by keeping it holy, as the LORD your God has commanded you. . . . Remember that you were slaves in Egypt and that the LORD your God brought you out of there with a mighty hand and an outstretched arm. Therefore the LORD your God has commanded you to observe the Sabbath day. (Deuteronomy 5:12–15 NIV)

The Sabbath and Our Lifestyles

Genuine recovery of the Sabbath is just what both materialistic consumers and workaholic social activists need. One day out of seven, we should just stop. Stop feverish production of more gadgets. Stop even passionate pursuit of social justice. Just stop, pray, and enjoy.

God's provision of the Sabbath is not some harsh legalism but a divine reminder of our finitude and limitations. We are not God. And we are not made to find our ultimate fulfillment in an ever greater abundance of material things—or even an unlimited pursuit of justice for the poor.

Modern people have lost the biblical sense of human limitation. We want more and more faster and faster. And we destroy ourselves, our marriages, our families and the environment to get it. God's Word is strikingly different: "Do not wear yourself out to get rich; have the wisdom to show restraint" (Proverbs 23:4). The Sabbath is a divine mechanism to nurture restraint and moderation. It puts a halt to our frantic striving to produce more and more things—or even to work desperately to change the world for the sake of the poor!

Make no mistake. The material world is good and so is our work in creating wealth—not to mention empowering the needy. But God never intended us to forget our finitude and dependence on the Creator in our proper concern for shaping culture and doing mission. That's what the Sabbath is all about.

Once a week we are to stop, be quiet, and worship. It does not matter that for a whole day we fail to produce good things or even do good kingdom work. We are finite. Arrogantly thinking we must do it all is blasphemy. Just resting our bodies, enjoying our families, and praising our God is enough for one day out of seven.

If Christians could recover the practice of the Sabbath, it would help us turn away from the mad consumerism that is destroying people and the environment. Almost everything in our culture undermines what the fourth Commandment wisely insists on preserving. If the spirit of the Sabbath would truly penetrate our minds and values, we would long to rest our tired psyches, enjoy our families and neighbors, and take quiet delight in the presence of our God—just "wasting" the whole day on worship and leisure! We would treasure this holy leisure more than the opportunity to use Sunday to accomplish still one more important task, or build one more balcony in our Tower of Babel. And in those quiet times in the divine presence, the God of the poor would transform our materialistic hearts and make us more generous.

A Call for Loyalty

I am convinced that simpler living is a biblical imperative for contemporary Christians in affluent lands. But we must remain clear about our reasons. We are not committed to a simple lifestyle. We have only one absolute loyalty, and that is to Jesus and his kingdom. But the head of this kingdom is the God of the poor! And hundreds of millions of his poor are starving.

An age of hunger and poverty summons affluent people to a lower standard of living. But vague assent to this truth will not protect us from the daily seductions of Madison Avenue. Each of us needs a specific plan. The examples of Robert Bainum, David Bussau, and Graham and Treena Kerr provide suggestions. The graduated tithe and communal living are two other possibilities. There are many more.

By all means avoid legalism and self-righteousness. But have the courage to commit yourself to some specific method for moving toward a just personal lifestyle.

Will we dare to measure our living standards by the needs of the poor rather than by the lifestyles of our neighbors? Will we have the faith to believe Jesus' word that joy and happiness flow from sharing? Will rich Christians also be generous?

Study Questions

1. How does the graduated tithe work? How would you want to adapt it if you chose to use it in your life?
2. What other specific mechanisms could help Christians avoid materialism? Which ones do you think are: (a) most biblical; (b) most workable?
3. Which practical suggestions for consuming less did you find most helpful? Can you add others?
4. In the light of the criteria for giving, how do you evaluate your own giving? Your church's giving?
5. In what ways are you being challenged to change your spending patterns?
6. How did this chapter make you feel?

10

Watching Over One Another in Love

Extra ecclesiam, nulla salus.[1]

Somehow the pressures of modern society were making it increasingly difficult for us to live by the values we had been taught. We thought our church should constitute a community of believers capable of withstanding these pressures, yet it seemed to go along with things as they were instead of encouraging an alternative. The "pillars" of the church seemed as severely trapped by material concerns and alienation as most non-Christians we knew.[2]

—Dave and Neta Jackson

ONE DAY a man with a serious drinking problem dropped in to talk with Virgil Vogt, one of the elders of Reba Place Fellowship in Evanston, Illinois. When Virgil invited him to accept Christ and join the community of believers, the man insisted that he simply wanted money for a bus ticket to Cleveland.

"Okay," Virgil agreed, "we can give you that kind of help too, if that's all you really want." He was quiet a moment, then he shook his head. "You know something?" he said, looking straight at the man. "You've just really let me off the hook. Because if you had chosen a new way of life in the kingdom of God, then as your brother I would have had to lay down my whole life for you. This house, my time, all my money, whatever you needed to meet your needs would have been totally at your disposal for the rest of your life. But all you want is some money for a bus ticket. . . ."[3]

The man was so startled he stood up and left, forgetting to take the money. But on Sunday he was back, this time sitting next to Virgil in the worship service.

The church should consist of communities of loving defiance. Instead it consists largely of comfortable clubs of conformity. A far-reaching reformation is necessary if the church is going to resist the materialism of our day and share God's concern for the poor.

If the analysis in the preceding chapters is even approximately correct, then the God of the Bible is calling Christians today to live in fundamental nonconformity to contemporary society, to confess and turn away from our obsession with materialism, sex, and economic success. Things have become more important to us than persons. Job security and salary increases matter more than starving children and poor peasants. Paul's warning to the Romans is especially pertinent: "Don't let the world around you squeeze you into its own mould" (Romans 12:2 Phillips). Biblical revelation summons us to defy many of the basic values of our materialistic, adulterous society.

But that is impossible! As individuals, that is. It is hardly possible for isolated believers to resist the anti-Christian values pouring from our radios, TVs, and billboards. The values of our affluent society seep slowly and subtly into our hearts and minds. The only way to defy them is to immerse ourselves in Christian fellowship so that God can remold our thinking as we find our primary identity with brothers and sisters who also are unconditionally committed to biblical values.

We should not be surprised that faithful obedience is possible only in the context of powerful Christian fellowship. The early church was able to defy the decadent values of Roman civilization precisely because it experienced Christian fellowship in a mighty way. For the early Christians, *koinonia* was not the "frilly fellowship" of church-sponsored, biweekly bowling parties. It was not tea, cookies, and sophisticated small talk in the Fellowship Hall after the sermon. It was an almost unconditional sharing of their lives with other members of Christ's body.

When one member suffered, they all suffered. When one rejoiced, they all rejoiced (1 Corinthians 12:26). When a person or church experienced economic trouble, the others shared generously. And when a brother or sister fell into sin, the others gently restored the straying person (Matthew 18:15–17; 1 Corinthians 5; 2 Corinthians 2:5–11; Galatians 6:1–3).[4] The sisters and brothers were available to each other, liable for each other, and accountable to each other—emotionally, financially, and spiritually.

The early church, of course, did not always live out the New Testament vision of the body of Christ. There were tragic lapses. But the network of tiny house churches scattered throughout the Roman Empire did experience oneness in Christ so vividly that they were able to defy and eventually conquer a powerful, pagan civilization.

John Wesley's early Methodist class meetings captured something of the spirit alive in the early church. Every week they gathered together in houses, "united in order to pray together, to receive the word of exhortation, and to watch over one another in love, that they may help each other to work out their salvation."[5] The overwhelming majority of churches today, however, do not provide a context in which brothers and sisters can encourage, admonish, and disciple each other. We desperately need new structures for watching over one another in love, new settings that will help us live like Jesus rather than like our broken culture.

A Sociological Perspective

Sociologists of knowledge have studied the relationship between ideas and the social conditions in which they arise and have discovered that the plausibility of ideas depends on the social support they have.

> We obtain our notions about the world originally from other human beings, and these notions continue to be plausible to us in a very large measure because others continue to affirm them.[6]

This underlines the importance of Christian community for those who long to conform to Jesus rather than to the world. An Amish youth who migrates to New York City will soon begin to question earlier values. The sociological reason for this change is that the "significant others" who previously supported his ideas and values are no longer present.

The complicated network of social interactions in which people develop and maintain their view of reality is called a plausibility structure. It consists of ongoing conversation with "significant others" as well as specific practices, rituals, and legitimations designed to support the validity of certain ideas. As long as these continue, people tend to accept the corresponding beliefs as true or plausible. But if the supportive structures disappear, doubt and uncertainty arise.

Hence the difficulty of small groups of people who hold a set of beliefs that differ sharply from the majority view in their society. (Sociologists call such people a cognitive minority.) Because they constantly meet people who challenge their fundamental ideas, members have difficulty maintaining their distinctive beliefs. According to well-known sociologist Peter Berger, these groups maintain their unpopular ideas only if they have a strong community structure:

> Unless our theologian has the inner fortitude of a desert saint, he has only one effective remedy against the threat of cognitive collapse in the face of these pressures. He must huddle together with like-minded fellow deviants—and huddle very closely indeed. Only in a countercommunity of considerable strength does cognitive deviance have a chance to maintain itself. The countercommunity provides continuing therapy against the creeping doubt as to whether, after all, one may not be wrong and the majority right. To fulfill its function of providing social support for the deviant body of "knowledge," the countercommunity must provide a strong sense of solidarity among its members.[7]

Berger's analysis relates directly to contemporary Christians determined to follow biblical teaching on the poor and possessions. Berger analyzed the problem of orthodox Christians who defy the dominant "scientific" ideas of contemporary secularism and maintain a biblical belief in the supernatural. But his analysis pertains just as clearly to the problem of living the ethics of Jesus' kingdom in a world that follows different standards. Most of our contemporaries—both inside and outside the churches—accept the dominant values of our consumption-oriented, materialistic culture. Genuine Christians, on the other hand, are committed to the very different norms revealed in Scripture. It should not surprise us that only a faithful remnant clings to these values. And the fact that genuine Christians are a minority upholding unpopular beliefs alerts us to the need for strong Christian community.

This does not mean that all Christians should imitate the Amish and retreat to isolated rural solitude. We must remain at the center of contemporary society in order to challenge, witness against, and, hopefully, even change it. But precisely as we are in the world but not of it, the pressure to abandon biblical norms in favor of contemporary values will be intense. Hence the need for new forms of Christian community.

The ancient Catholic dictum *extra ecclesiam, nulla salus* ("outside the church there is no salvation") contains a significant sociological truth. Certainly it is not impossible for individual Christians to maintain biblical beliefs even if a hostile majority disagrees. But if the church is to consist of communities of loving defiance in a sinful world, it must pay more attention to the quality of its fellowship and find new models of Christian community.

New Patterns of Christian Community

At the mere mention of Christian community, some people instantly think of Christian communes. This is unfortunate. Communes are only one of many forms for genuine Christian fellowship today. Discipleship and mission groups within larger congregations, individual house churches, and small traditional churches all offer excellent contexts for living out the biblical vision of the church.

I am convinced, however, that the overwhelming majority of Western churches no longer understand or experience biblical *koinonia* to any significant degree. As mentioned earlier, the essence of Christian community is far-reaching accountability to and liability for sisters and brothers in the body of Christ. That means that our time, our money, and our very selves are available to one another.

Such fellowship rarely happens in groups of one hundred or more persons. It requires small communities of believers like the early Christian house churches. The movement that conquered the Roman Empire was a network of small house churches. The apostle Paul frequently mentioned "the church that meets in the house of . . ." (Romans 16:5, 23; 1 Corinthians 16:19; Colossians 4:15; Philemon 2; see also Acts 2:46; 12:12; 20:7–12). The structure of the early church fostered close interaction and fellowship.[8] Only in the latter part of the third century did the church start to construct church buildings.

When God grants the gift of genuine Christian fellowship, deep, joyful sharing replaces the polite prattle typically exchanged by Christians on

Sunday morning. Sisters and brothers begin to discuss the things that really matter to them. They disclose their inner fears, their areas of peculiar temptation, their deepest joys. And they begin to challenge and disciple each other according to Matthew 18:15–17 and Galatians 6:1–3.

In that kind of setting—and perhaps only in that kind of setting—the church today will be able to forge a faithful, generous lifestyle for rich Christians in a time of hunger and wealth. In small house-church settings, brothers and sisters can challenge each other's affluent lifestyles. They can discuss each other's finances and annual budgets. Larger expenditures (like those for houses, cars, and long vacations) can be evaluated honestly in terms of the needs of both the individuals involved and God's poor around the world. They can exchange tips for simple living, discuss voting patterns that liberate the poor, support jobs that are ecologically responsible, and encourage charitable donations that build self-reliance among the needy. These and many other issues can be wrestled with openly and honestly by persons who have pledged themselves to each other as brothers and sisters in Christ.

A Congregation of House Churches

Congregations composed of clusters of house churches make up, in my opinion, a viable alternative to the typical congregation. Here are two examples.

Koinonia Fellowship[9]

Thirty years ago Koinonia Fellowship was a typical, successful Pentecostal church with a large, growing congregation of several hundred people. The church had a young dynamic pastor, a packed schedule of meetings, a full repertoire of church committees, and, according to the pastor, little real Christian fellowship.

In 1970 the church decided to change drastically. It dropped all existing activities except the Sunday morning worship service and urged everyone to attend "home meetings," where twelve to twenty people met weekly for study, prayer, worship, and discipling.

For a couple of years they wondered if they had made a gigantic mistake. "To move from a pew to a living room chair and look at people face to face was terrifying," one of the pastors told me. But a breakthrough occurred when the leaders of the home meetings realized that most people did not know how to meet each other's needs. The leaders started making suggestions: "Would you two please go to Jane Brown's house and make dinner for her because she is sick?" "Would you three people paint Jerry's apartment on Saturday?"

Oneness and caring began to develop. The weekly gatherings became the center of spiritual activity. Counseling, discipling, even evangelistic outreach, began to happen primarily in the home meetings. One result was rapid growth. As soon as a home meeting reached twenty-five persons, it was divided into two home meetings. By the mid-seventies, thirteen to fourteen hundred people were attending weekend services. There were fifty home meetings and four Sunday services.

Several new congregations evolved. One met on Sunday morning in the original downtown sanctuary. Another rented space from another church and held a service on Sunday afternoon. As a result they avoided costly building programs and kept financial resources available for more important matters.

Genuine Christian community emerged from this drastic restructuring, and leaders could confidently assert that all their members received personal, pastoral care because every home meeting knew and dealt with each person's individual troubles.

Financial sharing was not part of the original vision, but it began to happen in a significant way. Members of home meetings dug into savings and stocks to provide interest-free loans for two families who purchased house trailers for homes. When members went to sign the papers for an interest-free mortgage for another family's house, the unusual agreement left secular folk present for the transfer totally perplexed! If a member of a home meeting needed a small amount of financial assistance, the other members helped out. A congregational fund met larger needs. A food co-op and a store for used clothing and furniture supplied some basic needs inexpensively. Eventually, a sizable portion of total congregational giving went to economic sharing in the church.

Koinonia Fellowship also began to develop a deeper concern for the poor. The leaders preached about social justice. The church began to work in a major way with refugees from Southeast Asia and to contribute thousands of dollars each year to relieve world poverty.

An interracial subcongregation of 150 persons also developed. It started with an evangelistic outreach in the poorest Hispanic section of the city. Drug rehabilitation, job counseling, emergency food distribution, and ministry to battered women were all part of this wholistic outreach. Some church members then relocated to this needy area to continue with evangelism and discipling. Eventually they developed a large wholistic health center, ministering to one of the poorest inner-city neighborhoods.

Koinonia Fellowship has demonstrated that a traditional congregation can be transformed into a cluster of house churches. And the result can be growth—in discipleship, community, and numbers.

Church of the Savior

At the end of World War II, the Church of the Savior in Washington, D.C., pioneered the small-group model.[10] All members had to be in one of its many mission groups. Prospective members took five classes over a period of about two years. The membership covenant, renewed annually, committed every member to four disciplines: daily prayer, daily Bible study, weekly worship, and proportionate giving, beginning with a tithe of total gross income.

Consisting of five to twelve persons, the mission groups were the heart of the Church of the Savior. They were not merely prayer cells, Bible studies, encounter groups, or social action committees (although they were all of these). Gordon Cosby, founder and long-time pastor of Church of the Savior, insisted that it was in the mission groups that the members experienced the reality of the body of Christ.

> The mission group embodies the varied dimensions of church. It is total in scope. It is both inward and outward. It requires that we be accountable to Christ and to one another for the totality of our lives. It assumes that we share unlimited liability for one another.[11]

Via verbal or written reports, each member of a mission group reported weekly on failure or success in following the covenanted disciplines, on new scriptural insight, and on the problems and joys of the week.

Economics figured prominently in the membership commitment. Part of the membership covenant read,

I believe that God is the total owner of my life and resources. I give God the throne in relation to the material aspect of my life. God is the owner. I am the ower. Because God is a lavish giver, I too shall be lavish and cheerful in my regular gifts.[12]

The church has held out the goal of accountability to each other in the use of personal finances. Some mission groups shared personal income tax returns as a basis for discussing family budgets and finances. Concern for simpler lifestyles has been a part of their life together.

The goal of many of the mission groups has been empowerment of the poor. One group, Jubilee Housing, has renovated deteriorating housing in inner-city Washington. Along with other mission groups (Jubilee Jobs, Columbia Road Health Service, Family Place), they have brought hope of genuine change to hundreds of people in the inner city. For Love of Children has fought for the rights of neglected children through court action, legislation, and monitoring of local and federal governmental activity. Several of the church's mission groups have dedicated themselves to peace and justice in the international arena. The Church of the Savior International Good Neighbors has made it possible for several hundred Americans to serve in Thailand refugee camps. They also provided direct relief to Central American refugees driven by violence from their homes into neighboring countries and the United States. At the same time, several mission groups worked to change U.S. foreign policy, which was contributing to the Central American refugee problem.

Increasing size, however, threatened genuine community at Church of the Savior. In 1995, the church divided into nine faith communities. Each is legally and formally separate and has a distinct name, but all are informally linked together. Each community has approximately 130 members and 40 to 50 intern members. In the future, the original Church of the Savior will no longer exist as a church body or as a directing board for the faith communities. Instead, the principles started by Gordon Cosby and implemented so successfully in the Church of the Savior over the past forty years will live on in the life of the separate faith communities. Like Koinonia Fellowship, Church of the Savior preferred to subdivide into small congregations than risk diluting Christian community.

Thousands of churches today have small groups—encounter groups, biweekly fellowship groups, serendipity groups, prayer cells, and an almost infinite variety of action groups. They all claim to promote fellowship. Do these small groups fulfill the same function as Koinonia Fellowship's home meetings and Church of the Savior's mission groups? Hardly ever.

Though the numerous small groups flourishing in churches today are useful and valuable, they seldom go far enough.[13] Participants may agree to share deeply in one or two areas of life, but they do not assume responsibility for the other brothers' and sisters' growth toward Christian maturity in every area of life. Hardly ever do they dream that truly being sisters and brothers in Christ means costly, sweeping economic liability for each other or responsibility for the economic lifestyles of the other members. The crucial question is, have the participants committed themselves to be brothers and sisters to each other so unreservedly that they enjoy far-reaching liability for and accountability to each other?

Almost everyone expects small groups to dissolve in six months or two years and that life will then continue as before. These short-term, "limited liability" groups serve a purpose, but people today desperately need a church that functions as the church—a body of believers who accept liability for one another, are available to one another, and make themselves accountable to one another.

The Individual House Church

Another structure where true Christian community can happen, and which involves virtually no expense, is the individual house church. When it is impossible to find genuine Christian community in any other way, small groups of Christians should begin meeting in their own homes. (But they should promptly seek a relationship with other bodies of Christians. Lone rangers are not God's will for his church!)

An ideal house church arrangement is to have several families or single persons purchase houses within a block or two of each other. In many inner-city locations, especially in changing neighborhoods, inexpensive houses change hands rapidly. Living across the street or down the block from each other makes it convenient to share such things as cars, washers and dryers, freezers, and lawnmowers (or gardening equipment). Living close also encourages Christian community, by creating open relationships that foster honest, mutual searching for a responsible standard of living.

In his book on church structures, Howard A. Snyder proposed that denominations adopt the house church model for church planting, especially in the city. This structure is flexible, mobile, inclusive, and personal. It can grow by division, is an effective means of evangelism, and needs little professional leadership.[14]

"All Things in Common"

Reba Place Fellowship in Evanston, Illinois, began in 1957 with three people.[15] By 1996, there were about one hundred persons living with a common treasury. A small percentage of these live in large households, but most have their own apartments. They live close to one another in two neighborhoods.

In addition to the one hundred who share a common treasury, another 400 persons are part of Reba Place Church. These have their own private budgets but share a calling to faithfully embrace the astonishing teachings of Jesus about how we should handle our money and how much we are to love one another. An emphasis on community pervades the entire fellowship.

Those who share a common treasury place their earnings in a central fund. The central fund pays directly for large expenditures like housing, utilities, transportation, medical and educational expenses. Each month, every family and single person receives an allowance for food, clothing, and incidentals. This allowance is based on family size and is adjusted for special needs. It has nothing to do with how much the individual contributed to the common treasury. The sharing of equipment such as cars, lawnmowers, and washing machines makes it possible for people to function effectively and efficiently at substantial savings.

The community forgoes most insurance policies, except those required by law. And generally they choose to disperse extra funds rather than to accumulate them. Trusting God for future needs while living simply results in having remarkable amounts of money available to respond to the needs of others in the immediate neighborhood and around the world.

Although not for everyone, Reba Place and other Christian communes offer one setting in which widespread liability for and accountability to other brothers and sisters can become a reality.[16] They are one means of living biblically in our increasingly materialistic society.

Thousands of communal experiments have occurred in the last decades.

Many have been explicitly Christian. The fact that many have not survived indicates that this model is not easy to follow. Although communal living is certainly not a requirement for faithful discipleship, it does represent an alternative way of life for Christians dissatisfied with today's individualistic, materialistic society.

Glass Cathedrals in an Age of Hunger?

In early 1976, Eastminster Presbyterian Church in suburban Wichita, Kansas, had an ambitious church construction program in the works. Their architect had prepared a $525,000 church building program. Then a devastating earthquake struck in Guatemala on February 4, destroying thousands of homes and buildings. Many evangelical congregations lost their churches.

When Eastminster's board of elders met shortly after the Guatemalan tragedy, a layman posed a simple question: "How can we set out to buy an ecclesiastical Cadillac when our brothers and sisters in Guatemala have just lost their little Volkswagen?"

The elders courageously opted for a dramatic change of plans. They slashed their building program by nearly two-thirds and settled instead for church construction costing $180,000. Then they sent their pastor and two elders to Guatemala to see how they could help. When the three returned and reported tremendous need, the church borrowed $120,000 from a local bank and rebuilt twenty-six Guatemalan churches and twenty-eight Guatemalan pastors' houses.

I talked with Eastminster's pastor, Dr. Frank Kirk. He told me that Eastminster stayed in close touch with the church in Central America and later pledged $40,000 to an evangelical seminary there. In the years after their unusual decision, Eastminster Presbyterian experienced tremendous growth—in spiritual vitality, concern for missions, and even in attendance and budget. Dr. Kirk believes that cutting their building program to share with needy sisters and brothers in Guatemala "meant far more to Eastminster Presbyterian than to Guatemala."

The Eastminster Presbyterian congregation asked the right questions. They asked whether their building program was justified at this moment in history given the particular needs of the body of Christ worldwide and the mission of the church in the world. The question is not, Are gothic (or glass) cathedrals ever legitimate? Of course they are. The right question is: Is God calling our congregation to spend millions on church construction when more than a billion people have not yet heard of Jesus Christ and over one billion people are starving or malnourished?

The Triple Five Plan

If a congregation wants to increase their giving, how can they begin? Denominational offices, Christian relief and development organizations, Bread for the World, Evangelicals for Social Action, and many other groups (see the Appendix) all have helpful materials.

One simple approach is the Triple Five Plan.[17] After careful study of biblical teaching and world poverty, a congregation could decide to expand their giving and volunteer time to empower the poor by five percent each year for three successive years. They could also urge each member to do the same. *After* they have completed the first three-year cycle, the congregation could then write to political leaders asking government to expand effective programs for the poor by five percent each year for three years. To add authority to their appeal to government, the congregation could report their three years of growing church commitment to the poor and promise that as a congregation they will expand their church giving in the same way in the next three years. Politicians might listen to that kind of appeal.

The Bible and the daily newspaper issue the same summons. Faithful, generous people in an age of hunger and poverty must adopt simpler lifestyles and change unjust economic structures. But that is not a popular path to tread in an affluent society. Unless Christians anchor themselves in genuine Christian community, they will be unable to live the radical nonconformity commanded by Scripture and essential in our time. Our only hope is a return to the New Testament vision of the body of Christ. If that happens, the Lord of the church may again create communities of loving defiance able to withstand and conquer today's powerful, pagan civilizations worshipping at the shrine of Mammon.

Study Questions

1. What is Christian community? Why is it so important for helping the poor?

2. What specific structures encourage closer Christian community? Which ones are most biblical? Which are most workable?

3. How close is your local church to the ideal of Christian community? What do you think God is leading you to do about that?

11

Making the World More Fair

Let justice roll down like waters, and righteousness
like an everflowing stream.
(Amos 5:24)

A GROUP of devout Christians once lived in a small village at the foot of a mountain. A winding, slippery road with hairpin curves and steep precipices wound its way up one side of the mountain and down the other. There were no guardrails, and fatal accidents were frequent. The Christians in the village's three churches decided to act. They pooled their resources and purchased an ambulance so they could rush the injured to the hospital in the next town. Week after week, church volunteers gave faithfully, even sacrificially, of their time to operate the ambulance twenty-four hours a day. They saved many lives, although some victims remained crippled for life.

One day a visitor came to town. Puzzled, he asked why they did not close the road over the mountain and build a tunnel instead. Startled, the ambulance volunteers quickly pointed out that this approach, though technically possible, was not realistic or advisable. After all, the narrow mountain road had been there for a long time. Besides, the mayor would bitterly oppose the idea. (He owned a large restaurant and service station halfway up the mountain.)

The visitor was shocked that the mayor's economic interests mattered more to these Christians than the many human casualties. Somewhat hesitantly, he suggested that perhaps the churches ought to speak to the mayor.

After all, he was an elder in the oldest church in town. Perhaps they should even elect a different mayor if he proved stubborn and unconcerned.

Now the Christians were shocked. With rising indignation and righteous conviction they informed the young radical that the church dare not become involved in politics. The church is called to preach the gospel and give a cup of cold water, they said. Its mission is not to dabble in worldly things like changing social and political structures.

Perplexed and bitter, the visitor left. As he wandered out of the village, one question churned in his muddled mind. Is it really more spiritual, he wondered, to operate ambulances that pick up the bloody victims of destructive social structures than to try to change the structures themselves?

Ambulance Drivers or Tunnel Builders?

An age of affluence and poverty demands compassionate action and simplicity in personal lifestyles. But compassion and simple living apart from structural change may be little more than a gloriously irrelevant ego trip or proud pursuit of personal purity.

By itself, living on less will not feed a single starving child. If millions of North Americans and Europeans reduce their consumption but do not act politically to change public policy, the result will not necessarily be less starvation in the developing world. To be sure, if people give the money saved to private agencies promoting economic development in poor nations, the result may be less hunger. But if local elites and the patterns of international trade trample and destroy the new found hope of the poor, our simple personal lifestyles and model churches will help very little. Changes in public policy are also essential. If justice is to roll down like an everflowing stream, structural change is necessary.

Many questions promptly arise. What specific structural changes are consistent with biblical principles and economic facts? Indeed, are biblical principles pertinent to secular society? Israel, after all, was a theocracy. Can we really expect unbelievers to live according to biblical ethics?

The Bible does not directly answer all these questions. Although biblical revelation tells us that God and his faithful people are always at work liberating the oppressed, Scripture gives us no comprehensive blueprint for a new economic order. We do find, however, important principles about justice in society.

Certainly the first application of biblical truth concerning just relationships should be to the church. As the new people of God, the church should be a new society incarnating in its common life the biblical principles on justice (Galatians 3:6–9; 6:16; 1 Peter 2:9–10). Indeed, only as the church itself is a visible model of transformed socioeconomic relationships will any appeal to government possess integrity. Too much Christian social action is ineffective because Christian leaders call on the government to legislate what they cannot persuade their church members to live.

Biblical principles, however, are also relevant to secular societies as well as to the church. We must be careful, of course, to remember that church and state are two distinct institutions with different tasks and roles. The state should not make every item of Christian ethics a law. But biblical principles of justice are not arbitrary rules relevant only for believers. Therefore, a carefully developed political philosophy is essential.[1] The Creator revealed basic principles about social justice because he knew what would lead to lasting peace, social harmony, and happiness for his creatures.

The Bible is full of material that suggests the kind of social order God wills. And the church is supposed to be a model (imperfect, to be sure) of what the final kingdom of perfect justice and peace will be like. Thus, as the church models the coming kingdom, it exercises a powerful leavening influence in society (Luke 13:20–21).

Furthermore, the more faithfully and appropriately any secular society applies the biblical norms on justice in society, the more peace, happiness, and harmony that society will enjoy. Obviously, sinful persons and societies will never get beyond a dreadfully imperfect approximation. But social structures do exert a powerful influence on saint and sinner alike. Christians, therefore, should exercise political influence to make societal systems more fair.

That the biblical authors did not hesitate to apply revealed standards to persons and societies outside the people of God supports this point. Amos announced divine punishment on the surrounding nations for their evil and injustice (Amos 1–2). Isaiah denounced Assyria for its pride and injustice (Isaiah 10:12–19). The book of Daniel shows that God removed pagan kings like Nebuchadnezzar in the same way he destroyed Israel's rulers when they failed to show mercy to the oppressed (Daniel 4:27). God obliterated Sodom and Gomorrah no less than Israel and Judah because they neglected to aid the poor and feed the hungry (Ezekiel 16:49). The Lord of the universe applies the same standards of social justice to all nations.

This last principle bears directly on the issues of this chapter. Some countries, like the United States, Russia, Canada, and Australia, have a bountiful supply of natural resources within their national boundaries. Do they therefore have an absolute right to use these resources solely for the advantage of their own citizens? Not according to the Bible. If we believe Scripture, we must conclude that the human right of all persons to have the opportunity to earn a just living clearly supersedes the right of the rich nations to use resources exclusively for themselves. We are only stewards, not absolute owners. God is the only absolute owner, and he insists that the earth's resources be shared.

Before sketching specific steps for applying these principles to today's economic structures, I must register one disclaimer and one clarification.

We must constantly remember the large gulf between revealed principles and contemporary application. There are many valid ways to apply biblical principles. The application of biblical norms to socioeconomic questions today leaves room for creativity and honest disagreement among biblical Christians. Objecting to my application of biblical ethics to contemporary society is not at all the same as rejecting biblical principles. Of course, not all applications are equally valid. But humility and tolerance of each other's views are imperative.[2] We can and must help each other see where we are unfaithful to biblical revelation and inadequately grounded in social analysis. We must combine biblical norms and solid study of society.

One clarification is also necessary. To argue that Christians should work politically to change aspects of our economic structures that are unjust is not to call for a violent revolution that would forcibly impose a centralized, statist society. I believe that the way of Jesus is the way of nonviolent love, even for enemies. I therefore reject the use of lethal violence.[3] The exercise of political influence in a democratic society, of course, involves the use of nonlethal pressure (or force). When we legislate penalties for drunken driving or speeding, we use an appropriate kind of nonlethal "force." The same is true when we pass legislation that changes a nation's foreign policy toward poor nations, makes trade patterns more just, restricts the unfair practices of multinational corporations, or increases foreign economic aid. In a democratic society, of course, such changes can occur only if a majority agrees.

As we work to correct unjust economic structures, it is important constantly to promote decentralized, democratic decision-making and control.[4] Marxist totalitarianism clearly, and multinational corporations to a lesser but dangerous degree, centralize power in the hands of a tiny group of individuals. Often, the choices of these powerful elites reflect their own self-interest, not what is good for the majority. Biblical people will work both for a decentralization of economic power and a more just economy built on the basic biblical affirmation that God is on the side of justice for all and therefore has a special concern for the poor and oppressed.

That can be done! Change is possible. Just think of what has happened since this book first appeared twenty years ago. Communism has fallen. Apartheid collapsed. Democratically elected governments have replaced dictators in many nations. A smaller percentage of the world's people suffer from chronic malnutrition.

Societies can change. We can correct unjust structures. Our challenge today is to take the next practical, concrete steps to empower the poor.

This chapter explores measures that could make economic structures more fair: corrections in today's market economies; changes in international trade; reducing the debt of the poorest nations; restoring our global environment; and improving economic foreign aid.

Who Will Be Helped?

Before we examine those issues, however, we must face a complex question. Given the great imbalance of power in many poor nations today, who would benefit from increased foreign aid, expanded exports to rich nations, or a growing economy?

Would a growing economy automatically help the poor? The most obvious structural solution to hunger is rapid economic development in poorer nations. These countries could then either produce all their own food and basic necessities or trade for them on the world market.

Throughout the fifties and sixties and into the seventies, this was the main focus of people concerned about poor nations. Many economists advocated, and many Third World governments implemented, economic programs designed to produce economic growth, which at that time was thought to be synonymous with economic development. As the GNP of a country grew, people expected the forthcoming benefits eventually to "trickle down" to the poor so that the entire society would benefit. The poor would obtain jobs in a growing economy, and poverty would vanish.

Over the years, however, it became evident that even when the GNP increased the conditions of the poor did not automatically improve.[5] In light of the experience of the last several decades, it is now widely recognized that this trickle-down approach to development benefits the middle and upper classes but does much less to help the poor.[6] Mahbub ul Haq, an economist with the World Bank, speaks for the growing consensus: "Growth in the GNP often does not filter down. What is needed is a direct attack on mass poverty."[7]

Wealthy nations should provide more foreign aid and reduce trade barriers against poorer countries. But that will not necessarily benefit the poorest half of the developing countries one iota. As we saw in chapter 7, North Americans and Europeans are not to blame for all the poverty in the world today. Sin is not just a White European phenomenon. Wealthy elites, largely unconcerned about the suffering of the poor masses in their lands, rule many developing countries. They often own a large percentage of the best land, on which they grow cash crops for export to earn the foreign exchange they need to buy luxury goods from the developed world. Meanwhile, the poorest 30 to 70 percent of the people face grinding poverty. More foreign aid and expanding exports might simply enable these wealthy elites to strengthen their repressive regimes.

Does that mean that North Americans and Europeans can wash their hands of the whole problem? Not at all. In many cases over the past few decades, the wealthy elites continued in power partly because they received massive military aid and diplomatic support from the United States and other industrial nations.[8] The United States actually trained large numbers of military officers and police who then tortured thousands of people working for social justice in many countries in Latin America.[9] In 1996, the Pentagon finally released a manual that had been used for many years at the U.S. Army's School of the Americas, which trained about 60,000 Latin American police and military officers. The manual recommended "interrogation techniques like torture, execution, blackmail and arresting relatives."[10]

Western-based multinational corporations have worked closely with repressive governments. The histories of Brazil, Chile, El Salvador, and the Philippines demonstrate that the United States supported dictatorships that used torture and did little for the poorest one-half as long as these regimes were friendly to U.S. investments and foreign policy objectives.[11]

A Change in Foreign Policy

What can be done? Citizens of industrialized countries could demand a major reorientation of foreign policy. We could insist that our nations unequivocally focus on justice for the poor.

If we truly believe that all people are created equal, then our foreign policy must be redesigned to promote the interests of all people and not just the wealthy elites in developing countries or our own multinational corporations. We should use our economic and diplomatic power to promote justice for all, especially the poorest. That would mean placing greater weight in U.S. foreign policy on democracy and human rights; free, effective trade unions; correcting abuses of MNCs; and foreign aid that reaches the poorest.

Poor majorities in many countries eagerly seek to end repressive regimes that benefit primarily wealthy elites in their nation. The U.S. and other developed nations could use their vast diplomatic and economic power far more than they do to promote human rights, encourage democracy, and nurture a civil society in which thousands of private voluntary organizations can flourish. Vast numbers of popular peoples' organizations have sprung up in Africa, Asia, Latin America, and the former Soviet Union as more democratic, pluralistic governments have replaced repressive regimes.[12] This should be encouraged so the poor can demand new opportunity and power.

Trade unions in poor countries are one crucial piece of the puzzle. Developed nations should work hard to strengthen workers' rights and trade unions in negotiations over international trade. Unfortunately, precisely the opposite has happened. A working paper for the U.S. Congress Joint Economic Committee pointed out that labor is the only significant factor "which did not receive special protection in the Uruguay Round of trade negotiations."[13]

U.S. law mandates that workers' rights be an integral part of U.S. trade policy. In practice, however, "U.S. trade policy has virtually ignored workers' rights."[14] The North American Free Trade Agreement devotes whole chapters to things like intellectual property rights. But NAFTA simply "does not address the vast difference" in workers' rights between Mexico on the one hand and the U.S. and Canada on the other.[15] What is the result? Because NAFTA enables companies to produce in Mexico rather than the U.S. or Canada, NAFTA tends to weaken workers' rights and working conditions and unions in the U.S. and Canada rather than strengthen them in Mexico. That benefits the rich and hurts the poor in all three countries. Fortunately, a different emphasis in U.S. foreign policy could change that.

Insisting on ethical norms for multinational corporations would also help. This is difficult, of course, precisely because MNCs are large and international. But the United States and Britain are the countries of origin for 50 of the 100 largest multinational corporations and, with West Germany and France, control over 60 percent of all MNCs. Citizens in those nations have a particular responsibility to see that the impact of MNCs on poor nations is positive rather than negative.[16]

Unfortunately, U.S. foreign policy has usually supported the economic interests of U.S. MNCs rather than the poor in the developing nations. In May 1981, for instance, the United States was the only nation in the world to vote in the World Health Organization against a code to control the advertising and marketing of infant formula by MNCs in the Third World (the vote was 119–1). In spite of worldwide documentation of the evil effects of the marketing activities of Nestle and other MNCs,[17] the Reagan administration voted no because it said the code might damage "free enterprise."[18]

A foreign policy that seeks biblical justice for the poor will have to be willing to place ethical controls on the operations of MNCs, even if that is not in the short-term economic interest of the MNC and its U.S. shareholders. Both by political activity and by well-designed citizen protests like the Nestle boycott, Christian citizens can help reduce the negative impact of MNCs on the poor of the earth.[19]

We should also insist that our foreign aid benefit primarily the poorest in the most needy nations, and that those nations work for "growth with equity." Aid to countries whose governments care little about improving the condition of the poor will likely end up in the pockets of the rich.

Our nation's foreign policy ought to have a special focus on the poorest. Only then will proposed structural changes in areas like international trade and foreign aid programs actually improve the lot of the poorest billion people.

Social Change and Conversion

A fundamental change in our policy toward developing nations is imperative. But it is not enough. In addition, the poor in those nations must somehow find the courage to demand sweeping structural changes in their own lands.

Such changes, however, can happen only if a fundamental transformation of values occurs. In a scholarly book on land tenure in India, Robert Frykenberg of the University of Wisconsin lamented the growing gulf between rich and poor. "No amount of aid, science, and/or technology," he concluded, "can alter the direction of current processes without the occurrence of a more fundamental 'awakening' or 'conversion' among significantly larger numbers of people. . . . Changes of a revolutionary character are required, changes which can only begin in the hearts and minds of individuals."[20]

At precisely this point the Christian church—and evangelistic activities in particular—can play a crucial role. Two things are important: first, evangelism; and second, the whole message of Scripture. Evangelism is central to social change. Nothing so transforms the self-identity, self-worth, and initiative of a poor, oppressed person as a personal, living relationship with God in Christ. Discovering that the Creator of the world lives in each of them gives new worth and energy to people psychologically crippled by centuries of oppression.[21]

The second important component is sharing the whole biblical vision. Some religious worldviews tend, as we saw in chapter 7, to create a fatalistic attitude toward poverty. Hinduism, for instance, teaches that those in the lower castes (usually also the poorest) are there because of sinful choices in prior incarnations. Only by patiently enduring their present lot can they hope for a better life in future incarnations. In addition, Eastern religions de-emphasize the importance of history and material reality, considering them illusions to be escaped.

Biblical faith, on the other hand, affirms the goodness of the created, material world and teaches that the Creator and Lord of history demands justice now for the poor of the earth. As missionaries and others share this total biblical message, they can make a profound contribution to the battle against hunger, poverty, and injustice.[22] To be sure, missionaries cannot engage directly in political activity in foreign countries. But they can and must teach the whole Word for the whole person. Why have missionaries so often taught Romans but not Amos to new converts in poor lands? If it is true, as we argued in Part 2, that Scripture constantly asserts that God is on the side of the poor, then missionaries should make this biblical theme a central part of their teaching. If we accept our Lord's Great Commission to teach "all that I have commanded you," then we dare not omit or de-emphasize the biblical message of justice for the oppressed, even if it offends ruling elites.

Cross-cultural missionaries need not engage directly in politics. But they must carefully and fully expound for new converts the explosive biblical message that God has a special concern for the poor and oppressed. The poor will quickly learn how to apply these biblical principles to their own oppressive societies. The result will be changed social structures in developing countries.

Thus far we have looked at two things: a fundamental change in the foreign policy of rich nations and a mass movement of social change rooted in new religious values in the poorer countries. Christians should promote both.

What else needs to happen?

First, we need to correct problems in market economies. Second, we should make international trade more fair. Third, we must reduce the international debt of the poorest nations. Fourth, we need to care for God's creation so our grandchildren can enjoy a sustainable environment. And finally, we must be willing to help with economic foreign aid, which will help prevent starvation during emergencies and empower the poor to earn their own way.

Correcting Weaknesses of Market Economies

Market economies have been far more successful than existing alternatives in creating wealth. Those who care about the poor should endorse market-oriented economies—rather than state-owned, centrally planned ones—as the best basic framework currently known for economic life. This does not mean that we uncritically embrace everything done in the name of market reform. Nor does it mean that we endorse a libertarian view that condemns virtually all government intervention in the market. But it does mean that we support a decentralized economic system in which the bulk of productive resources are privately owned, and in which supply and demand rather than a centralized government bureaucracy determines most prices and wages.

There are, however, glaring weaknesses in present market economies, as we saw in chapter 8. Here I outline four specific corrective measures: providing the poor with basic capital so they can participate in economic life; insisting on the right amount and right kind of government intervention; finding new measures for economic life; and redefining the good life.

Capital for the Poor

We must end the outrage of Christians celebrating the market economy and then failing to provide the poorest with access to the capital they need to earn a decent living in the global market. The mechanism of supply and demand pays no attention whatsoever to whether the purchaser wants basic food to keep her children from starving or luxury items to parade social status. The market only rewards purchasing power.

We do know of course what to do to strengthen the purchasing power of the poorest. They need capital. The poorest billion have hardly any capital, so they and their children waste away in malnutrition and starvation. To endorse market economies without redistributing resources so the poorest have the capital to earn a decent living is damnable defiance of the biblical God of justice.

Today's wealth is divided in a way that flatly contradicts the Bible. God wants every family to have the basic capital—land, money, knowledge—to earn their own way and be dignified, participating members of society.[23] (See discussion in chapter 4.) If we want to implement this biblical teaching on economic justice—and enable market economies to operate justly—we must fundamentally change the terrible injustice of allowing many of the world's people to exist with little or no capital.

The poorest billion plus have virtually no capital. Another three billion have very little. The poorest 20 percent of the world's people (just over one billion people) own 1 percent of the world's wealth. In fact, the poorest 60 percent (about 3.5 billion people) own only 6 percent of the world's wealth. The richest 20 percent own 81 percent.[24]

Christians must insist on redistribution—both private voluntary efforts and effective government programs. The word "redistribution" is a red flag for some. Redistribution does not mean state ownership. Not every redistribution scheme is wise, but the right kind are essential and successful.

What kind of capital do people need? It varies with the situation. In a largely agricultural society, land reform is essential. In an information society, equality of educational opportunity is the most basic way to empower the poor. Wise schemes to enable the poor to acquire the money needed to buy a house, start a small business, or prepare for retirement are also important.[25]

Providing capital so the poor have economic opportunity to earn their own way can happen through both private voluntary programs and the activities of democratic governments.

In the last few decades, pioneers in micro-enterprise development (MED) have demonstrated the great success of tiny loans to poor people. Both the preface and chapter 9 show the stunning results of the work of David Bussau and Opportunity International in this area. Many other Christian development agencies, such as World Vision and Mennonite Economic Development Associates, are also engaged in MED. So are secular organizations like the World Bank and the U.S. government (USAID).

Mohammed Yunus, a Bangladeshi economist, pioneered one of the earliest and most successful MED programs. He founded the Grameen Bank to make tiny loans to the rural poor—$50, $75, or $120 to buy a cow, a plow, or a small irrigation pump. He soon discovered that women were more likely than men to use the profits to care for their children's health and education and to expand their businesses. So the Grameen Bank concentrated on women. Today it has about 2 million borrowers in Bangladesh—and most of them are women.

Having that many women with new opportunities, new wealth, and new power is a threatening situation to the Muslim religious leaders and politicians, which is resulting in a vigorous backlash. Muslim clerics have confined some women to their homes or declared them outcasts. Dozens of elementary schools for girls have been burned.[26] Women empowered by micro-loans are challenging traditional established centers of power.

I believe that Christians today should greatly expand Christian micro-loan programs like those done by David Bussau. The Agra Covenant on

Christian Capital calls on Christians around the world to devote 1 percent of their income to micro-loans:

> The God of Israel gave every Israelite family enough land to earn their own way. The same God now summons Christians to struggle for justice and to offer similar opportunity to the one billion persons almost totally excluded from today's growing economies. For some, the necessary capital will be land; for others, education, a small loan or a decent job opportunity. The God who summons all those created in His image to responsible work demands that they have the opportunity. There are many ways to provide the basic capital. Governments, churches, businesses and voluntary organizations all have important responsibilities.
>
> We believe that small loans to poor people for micro-enterprise development is one of the very promising ways to empower the poor to help themselves. In the last decade private Christian organizations making such loans have enabled the poor to create hundreds of thousands of jobs.
>
> Now is the time to expand this successful model a hundredfold. The Christians of the world enjoy an income of at least $10 trillion a year. It takes only about $500 to create a new job among the poor and improve the living standard of a family of five by 50 percent within a year. At $500 per job, 1 percent of Christian income for just one year could create new small loans producing 200 million new jobs. In one year, that many new jobs could improve the well-being of one billion people![27]

By themselves, of course, private (and public) micro-loans are inadequate. Gifted, tiny entrepreneurs cannot flourish if they lack fair legal systems, reliable infrastructures (such as roads and communication systems), wise macro-economic policies, and appropriate public services.[28] But certainly one thing Christians today should do is increase on a massive scale the resources devoted to providing the poorest with needed capital through voluntary organizations.

The right kinds of government programs of redistribution are also essential. Every tax-based system of education, health care, and social security involves taxing those with resources to guarantee basic resources of knowledge and health care to everyone, especially the poorest members of society.

Some government programs, of course, are disastrously ineffective. We should promptly abolish them! We must avoid both libertarian views that reject almost all government intervention in the economy and statist approaches that seek to abandon a basic market framework.

Measures such as the Pell Grants and the Earned Income Tax Credit (EITC) in the U.S. illustrate the *kind* of government redistributive program that works well. Pell Grants to college students from poor families do not encourage long-term welfare dependency. They end in a semester or two if the student fails to study and flunks out. And they create capital for a lifetime. The EITC subsidizes the income of low-income workers who faithfully carry out their responsibility to work but can find only low-paying jobs that do not provide a living wage. Republican President Ronald Reagan called the EITC "the best anti-poverty, the best pro-family, the best job creation measure to come out of Congress"—precisely because it rewarded work and responsibility and worked within the market framework.

Both private and public programs to provide capital so that the poor have genuine opportunity to earn their own way are absolutely indispensable if today's market economies are to work with even minimal justice. Failure to do that would be like freeing illiterate slaves and then providing no land, money, or education.[29]

Government Activity

What works and what doesn't? The history of communist societies clearly demonstrates that consolidating economic and political power in the same hands brings totalitarianism. We must avoid that kind of centralized power. But it is also clear today that the largest corporations and the elites who control them also wield vast political power. Highly centralized power inevitably threatens democratic life. We need intensive study of how much and what kind of government activity promotes both political freedom and economic justice. Through painstaking analysis and careful experimentation, we must discover how government can work within a basic market framework to empower the poor and restrain those aspects of today's markets that are destructive.

Libertarian views that condemn all government intervention make nonsense of twentieth-century economic history. In the U.S., most elderly folk are no longer in poverty precisely because of government-sponsored social security and medicare. A number of anti-poverty measures have failed and need drastic reform. But others—such as Pell Grants—have been very successful.

The lesson of the Asian Tigers is *not* that the market will produce magic if governments will just get out of the way. Governments played a major role in the "economic miracles" of South Korea, Taiwan, and many other Asian countries. Professor Michael Todaro, author of one of the most widely used texts on economic development, insists that "public-private cooperation, and not the triumph of free market and laissez-faire economics, is the real lesson of the success stories of South Korea, Taiwan, and Singapore."[30]

The South Korean miracle started with government organized land reform. From 1952 to 1954 the percentage of farmers who owned their own land (rather than working as tenants) jumped from 50 to 94 percent.[31] Something similar happened in Taiwan. The governments of both countries invested heavily in health, education, and job training. The result? Their people were ready to use the most recent technologies. The productivity of labor has been growing by 10 percent a year—and half of that growth results from the state's investment in education and technical skills.[32] An activist government was central to the economic growth of South Korea and Taiwan.

Equally important was the way these governments intervened in the economy. They worked with the market rather than against it. They encouraged private enterprise and the growth of exports and refused—over the long haul—to protect the nations' companies from international competition. The right kind of market-friendly government activity is essential.[33]

The contrast between South Korea and Brazil is striking. Both countries have experienced rapid economic growth since 1960. The South Korean government invested heavily in health care and education for the poor, but the Brazilian government did not. The result? In Brazil, tens of millions of poor folk remained stuck in poverty, benefitting very little from the country's growing economy. In South Korea, by contrast, the poorest gained ground significantly (and the economy also grew faster!). The richest fifth of the Korean population has about seven times as much income as the poorest fifth. In Brazil, the ratio is 30 to 1.[34] Harvard economist Amartya Sen calls Brazil's pattern "unaimed opulence" and South Korea's "participatory growth." The Korean government's far greater investment in public health and education is a key to this strikingly different outcome.

Even the World Bank insists that "markets in developing countries cannot generally be relied upon to provide people—especially the poorest—with adequate education (especially primary education), health care, nutrition, and family-planning services."[35] Governments, the World Bank says, should do less where markets work and more where they don't:

> Above all this means [government] investing in education, health, nutrition, family planning, and poverty alleviation: building social, physical, administrative, regulatory, and legal infrastructure of better quality; mobilizing the resources to finance public expenditures; and providing a stable macroeconomic foundation, without which little can be achieved. Government intervention to protect the environment is necessary for sustainable development.[36]

Growing market economies do not automatically help the poor. The right kind and amount of government activity is also essential if the poor are to benefit from an expanding GNP. Recent history demonstrates that government is an essential partner along with private business if we want just, participatory growth that empowers the poorest.

New Measures of Social and Economic Well-Being

Is society better off when a huge oil spill costs a billion dollars to clean up? Or when a wealthy person hires expensive lawyers to arrange a complicated divorce? Obviously not. And yet the common (mis)understanding of the GDP would tell us that it is! In the minds of many, the GDP is our basic measure of economic progress. They assume that if the economy is growing, society is improving. This widespread notion is absurd.

Even though politicians often use it as such, the Gross Domestic Product (GDP) is a poor measure of economic or social well-being (as discussed in chapter 8). To begin with, the GDP measures only economic transactions—i.e., activity where money changes hands. It does not count unpaid work in the family or the community at all! If one parent leaves paid employment to stay home to parent children, the GDP actually goes down. If Mom and

Dad get a divorce—and in doing so pay lawyers, pay realtors to sell one house and buy two others, pay for "professional" childcare, etc.—GDP goes up! Volunteering to improve one's local community does not count at all.

The GDP also counts many negatives as positive growth. Crime adds to the GDP. More lawyers, police, judges, prisons, plus all kinds of crime-prevention devices all raise the GDP. When TV and home videos replace storytelling by parents and grandparents, the GDP goes up. When cigarette advertising creates addictive smoking, the GDP goes up. Gambling, alcoholism, and pornography all have the same wonderful result.

Environmental pollution raises the GDP twice! Once when a factory creates products with byproducts that pollute, and again when the nation spends billions to clean up the toxic site.

Obviously we need a better measure of social and economic well-being. The Genuine Progress Indicator (GPI) produced by people in an organization called Redefining Progress offers a good start.[37] Their GPI measures more than twenty things the GDP ignores.

Parents at home to care for children or grandparents get counted. So do volunteer workers in the community. These things raise the GPI.

Destructive things lower the GPI, including expenses that result from crime and any environmental pollution that damages health, agriculture, beaches, or buildings. If people work longer hours for the same pay, that also lowers the GPI. The GPI counts a nation's use of non-renewable resources in the same way a private business does, not the way government does. When a private company uses up its non-renewable resources, it counts as a cost. But when a nation does the same thing to its oil and other minerals, the GDP counts it as a gain.

This new, more accurate measure of economic well-being tells an astonishingly different story from the GDP. The GDP indicates that things have gotten better and better in the U.S. since the early 1950s. But the GPI shows that after some growth through about 1970, things have gotten progressively worse—roughly by 45 percent! What we call progress is, to a large extent, correcting mistakes, borrowing from the future, or shifting activity away from the home and community to the marketplace.

The folk at Redefining Progress may or may not have all the details right.[38] We need not accept their detailed findings to recognize that they have raised a very basic issue. Indeed, in recent years, many people, including the

World Bank and most European nations, have been working on better ways to measure social and economic growth.[39]

One potentially far-reaching result of this kind of new analysis is that it is beginning to bring environmentalists and social conservatives together. Environmentalists deplore the way an unrestricted market economy destroys the environment. Social conservatives denounce the way that a preoccupation with economic growth (which demands ever-more consumption) destroys the family and communal life.

Both groups, for example, rightly see problems with currently popular "takings" legislation. ("Takings" bills would force taxpayers to reimburse property owners when laws reduce potential income from the unrestricted use of their property.) The conservative preacher and anti-smut crusader Rev. Donald Wildmon recently denounced "takings" legislation as the "porn owners' relief measure." Why? Because the taxpayers would, for example, have to compensate the owners of topless bars if government passed any restrictive laws.[40]

The folk at Redefining Progress have raised some fundamental issues about the nature of "economic growth." But the problem really lies deeper than they indicate. During the eighteenth-century Enlightenment, a human-centered, pseudo-scientific view of reality replaced the historic God-centered view. The autonomous individual replaced God as the source of ethics. The scientific method became the only avenue to truth. Nature, according to naturalistic scientist Carl Sagan, is all that exists.

Tragically, this new view abandons the limits of economic growth imposed by historic Christian faith. In a God-centered, biblical worldview, persons, family, and God's good creation matter more than money and unlimited material consumption. The scientific method, however, cannot measure love or joy in the family. But it can measure a growing bank account, larger cars, and increasingly sophisticated gadgets. Modern folk cast aside the limits imposed on economic life by the biblical truth that Yahweh is Lord even of economics. The result has been preoccupation with economic growth that is now devastating the family, community life, and the environment.

Jesus' question is still relevant: Do we want to worship God and there-fore accept God's perspective on everything, including the relative impor-tance of economic "growth," more gadgets, and family time? Or do we prefer to absolutize the material world and the things that scientific technology can produce?

Getting a more accurate measure of social and economic well-being via some new Genuine Progress Indicator will not answer that fundamental question. But it will make it easier for us to think about it more carefully if we really want to choose God rather than Mammon.

Redefining the Good Life

It is idolatrous nonsense to suggest that human fulfillment comes from an ever-increasing supply of material things. Genuine, lasting joy comes from a right relationship with God, neighbor, self, and the earth. As body-soul beings created for community, we do need significant material resources. But looking for happiness in ever-expanding material wealth is both theologically heretical and environmentally destructive. It also hardens our hearts to the cry of the poor.

We must redefine the good life. We must develop a theology of enough. We must meditate on Proverbs 23:4 until it seeps deep into our psyches: "Do not wear yourself out to get rich; have the wisdom to show restraint." We must develop models of simpler lifestyles; corporate policies that permit people to choose parenting, leisure, and community service over maximizing income and profits; and macro-economic policies and advertising practices that discourage overconsumption. Unlimited economic growth is an economic Tower of Babel, not a biblical goal.

The developed world should consume less and pollute less. But there are complications. As MIT economist Lester Thurow points out, given today's economic structures, environmental crusades that reduce growth and advocate greater pollution control may well benefit the middle and upper classes at the expense of the poor. Under current structures, reducing growth may lead to a rise in unemployment which hits the poor (both here and abroad) harder than the rich. Increased pollution control equipment may raise the prices of goods needed by the poor. Furthermore, a cleaner environment may well raise the standard of living of the wealthier classes who retain their jobs and have enough money to get out and enjoy the enhanced environment.[41]

Few economists doubt the validity of this analysis. But that does not mean that we should ignore environmental pollution as we seek to help the poor. Rather, Thurow's warning illuminates the size and complexity of the obstacles that we must overcome.

The pervasive notion that increased consumption leads to greater happiness is at the heart of our dilemma. In fact, even some economists understand that economic growth and rising affluence do not guarantee greater happiness. Economist Richard Easterlin argues that people tend to measure their happiness by how much they consume relative to their neighbors. As all try to get ahead, most tend to rise together so everyone is frustrated by their unsuccessful efforts to achieve happiness by getting ahead of the others! Easterlin concludes:

> To the outside observer, economic growth appears to be producing an ever-more affluent society, but to those involved in the process, affluence will always remain a distant, urgently sought, but never attained goal.[42]

Growth occurs, the earth is used and abused—but happiness is still beyond one's grasp.

To Christians this should be no surprise. We should be the first to reject this rat race in which everyone is trying to surpass the other guy. Knowing that material goods are not what brings ultimate happiness, we should be the first to experiment with simpler lifestyles. As we reduce our demand for dwindling resources that pollute the environment, we witness to others that happiness is not found primarily in material possessions.

As we move in this direction, however, we need to be alert to Thurow's warning. If, in our advanced state of technology, significant numbers of people consume less, there will be less need for production. Declining demand will signal a decline in the need for workers. Therefore, we need long-term structural changes if displaced workers are to find other jobs. Due to the monumental proportions of the changes needed, they must be made slowly and gradually. The suggestions I offer, therefore, are for both the immediate and the more distant future.

In the short run, a simpler lifestyle lived by Christians will mean more money not being spent on consumption goods. If large numbers of people save rather than spend this income, severe unemployment might ensue. If, however, we donate the income we have saved to Christian agencies promoting development in poor nations, a major reduction in employment is unlikely. Aid recipients will spend the money on goods they need to create wealth and attain an adequate level of material well-being. As they do, the dollars spent on these goods will eventually return to buy things from businesses in industrialized nations. As the developed nations consume less and share more, we will also spur indigenous development in the developing nations, thus fostering a more just distribution of goods and assets.

As we adopt this short-run approach, Christians all over the world ought to re-examine priorities at a still deeper level. Suppose that by a miracle of God's grace we succeeded in ending the scandal of a world where a billion plus people live in grinding poverty while the affluent live like kings. Even if we reached the biblical norm of distributional justice, we would have to ask ourselves the next question: Should we again pursue the same sort of economic growth we formerly did? The obvious answer is no. The earth's resources are limited, and we dare not destroy the environment.

Christians must strive to redirect the demand for goods and services away from heavy resource usage and environment-damaging goods toward goods and services that make less demand on the earth's carrying capacity. Christians could spend more of their time and money creating vibrant, active Christian churches. Everyone could spend more money on the arts (drama, music, and other creative expressions), thus creating an incentive for more people to engage in these activities instead of in the production of more material goods. People could work fewer hours at their jobs, and in their new leisure they could do volunteer work in their community or spend more time with their families or in constructive hobbies.

In the long run, sweeping changes will eventually come. Hopefully, Christians will lead the way in redefining the good life by returning to a biblical understanding of what produces joy and happiness.[43]

I am not a pessimist. Continued, wise use of modern technology and market economies can offer new hope to those who are still poor. It is possible, within the framework of market economies, to empower most of the world's people to enjoy a generously adequate level of material well-being without creating environmental catastrophe. But to accomplish that we must make sure that the poor have access to capital, that government plays its proper role, and that society rediscovers the ancient faith that persons do not live by bread alone.

Making International Trade More Fair

Unfairness in international trade hurts poor countries (as shown in chapter 8). Various kinds of trade barriers cost poor nations $50-$100 billion a year. Unfortunately, a long history starting with colonialism has resulted in a situation where some developing countries' exports consist largely of a few primary commodities. The prices of most of these commodities experience periods of wide fluctuation, and some of them have undergone a long-term decline relative to the prices of manufactured goods coming from the developed countries.

Two things need to be done in the short run. First, developed nations should drastically reduce or eliminate trade barriers on imports from the developing countries. Second, we must deal with the problem that some commodities exported by Third World nations have experienced a long-term decline of relative prices.

Trade Barriers

Trade barriers hurt not only poor nations but also the average person in rich nations. Without trade barriers, we could buy many imported goods more cheaply than before. In 1971, the *Columbia Journal of World Business* estimated that trade restrictions annually cost U.S. consumers an extra $10 to $15 billion—$200 to $300 for every U.S. family.[44] The World Bank's *World Development Report 1987* indicates that barriers to clothing imports alone cost U.S. consumers $18 billion in 1984.[45] Without those barriers, of course, the developing nations would be better off because they would increase both their production and income via increased exports.

Recent news is both good and bad. The recently completed "Uruguay Round" (see above, pp. 149-153) reduces tariffs significantly. But non-tariff barriers remain. In fact they are getting worse. In the U.S., there are strong protectionist sentiments in both the Democratic and Republican parties.

It is politically difficult to remove such trade restrictions because the people employed in the businesses protected by them will suffer. Although the numbers would be relatively small, considering the size of our total economy, some people will lose their jobs. But there is a remedy for this problem. It is called adjustment assistance.[46] Adjustment assistance is a government program designed to facilitate the movement of unemployed workers into new areas of employment. It compensates workers for the period during which they are unemployed, and it helps them to relocate and find jobs with comparable pay.

All this talk about free trade and adjustment may seem abstract and boring. But statistics on how many jobs in poor nations result from just one job lost in the rich nations underline how important it is. Careful studies have shown that if Northern countries reduced trade barriers on manufactured goods from the South, they would directly create 4.6 jobs in low-income countries for every one lost in the European Economic Community, and 6.5 jobs in poor nations for every one lost in the U.S. And indirectly, through multiplier effects, the impact would be two to five times greater! Oxford economist Donald Hay concludes: "Thus in a very poor country, the effect could be as high as twenty additional jobs for one worker displaced in Europe or the U.S.A."[47]

A relatively modest sacrifice by rich Northerners would produce major benefits in the South. And in the long run, economists expect, the North would not even lose jobs. As developing nations returned to industrialized countries to spend their new income, the businesses they patronized would need to hire the displaced workers to meet the new demand. In the short run, however, there will be a cost to removing trade barriers. Will Christian voters be more concerned about hungry people abroad or economic convenience at home?

Merely removing restrictions on imports, however, does not guarantee that the poor in developing nations will enjoy the benefits. If local governing elites seize the land of peasants so that they and multinational corporations can grow crops for export, only the rich benefit. If local governing elites suppress labor unions so that the workers who manufacture the goods for export receive very low wages, only the rich benefit. How then can we remove our trade barriers in such a way that the poorest people will benefit?

The law on the Generalized System of Preferences (GSP) governs U.S. trade incentives with poor nations. Its alleged purpose is to increase imports of manufactured goods from developing nations. But the law needs reform. Almost none of its benefits go to African nations who need it the most. Most go to the better off developing nations and to subsidiaries of U.S. firms that moved their operations to take advantage of cheap labor. Only one-tenth of

1 percent (.1 percent) of GSP imports come from the least developed countries.[48] We ought to reform the GSP so that it largely benefits the poorest nations, especially the poorest people in those countries.

We could write two important provisions into the GSP that would help. The law could require that countries exporting agricultural products under the GSP have a Stable Food Production Plan. Such a plan would be designed to make sure that production of food for export does not undercut the need to grow food for domestic consumption. A second set of provisions could demand that countries exporting goods to us under the GSP have fair labor practices and respect for human rights. These stipulations would encourage labor unions and other movements, which would enable the workers to benefit from the economic growth stimulated by our trade preferences.

In fact, the issue of fair labor practices is a crucial aspect of international trade that goes far beyond just the GSP. Earlier, we saw how the NAFTA has more likely damaged working conditions in the U.S. and Canada rather than improving them in Mexico. Unless corrective action happens, that might occur everywhere. If workers' rights are not protected in developing nations, workers there will not be the only ones who will suffer. Global competition will erode working conditions in developed nations as well.

We can work at decent standards for workers at four levels: international, national, corporations, and individual consumers.[49]

International standards are especially important. Otherwise, individual nations with despicable working conditions have a comparative advantage.[50]

The International Labor Organization's conventions provide a good starting point internationally. These standards include: (1) the right and freedom of association; (2) the right to organize and bargain collectively; (3) prohibitions against forced labor; (4) standards for wages and worker safety; (5) and a minimum age for child labor.[51] Most nations have endorsed these standards. But they are often ignored because there is no global enforcement mechanism. That is needed.[52]

Developed nations can also do far more. Above, (pp. 229–230) we saw that the U.S. has largely ignored the rights of workers in its global trade negotiations. That should change. A concern for unions and working conditions should become a central focus of concern and aggressive action in the trade policy of all developed nations. That will help workers in both poor and rich nations.

Corporations can also play a significant role—and you and I can encourage them! Some large corporations (e.g., Levi Strauss, Sears, and Starbucks Coffee) have already adopted codes of conduct to improve workers' rights and environmental protection in   their global operations. Christian executives can encourage that from inside. Consumers can do the same from outside—with letters and conscientious decisions about where to buy things.[53]

Fair labor practices around the globe are essential if the poor are to receive their fair share of the benefits of growing international trade.

Declining Prices

The problem of long-term decline of relative prices of some commodities must also be faced squarely. We saw in chapter 8 how costly this problem is for poor nations. When the manufactured imports they buy from us cost more and more relative to the primary products they sell us, they have a big problem. Unfortunately, the suggestion that developed nations pay higher prices will probably not do much good—especially when cheap synthetic substitutes are available. The only lasting solution is to assist poor nations severely affected by declining prices to move into the production of other goods.

But poor countries cannot do this by themselves. They need economic aid from the developed world to foster the development of their economies and to move their people, land, and other resources into the production of other goods. Ending our trade barriers in manufactured goods from poor nations, of course, is one of the best ways to help. Trade—fair trade—could reduce hunger and starvation abroad.

Reducing Unmanageable Debt

The debt burden of the poorest nations (mostly in Sub-Saharan Africa) is unmanageably high. (See chapter 8.) Most of these very poor countries are repaying only a fraction of what they owe. That debt, according to the United Nations, "is a major constraint on economic growth and on investment in human development."[54]

The following principles will help:

1. One central goal must be to foster sustainable, healthy economies in which poor people can participate and improve their quality of life.

2. Both creditor and debtor countries contributed to the problem and therefore both should share the cost of solving it.

3. The poor, who had virtually nothing to do with obtaining the loans, should not be asked to bear a major part of the burden of repayment.

4. When debt is adjusted (i.e., canceled or reduced) the debtor countries' record on human rights, democratic process, capital flight, and military expenditures should be taken into account.[55]

Different groups around the world, including Oxfam (a widely respected international development agency), have offered possible solutions.[56]

The increasing calls for debt relief for the poorest countries has finally reached the ears of the World Bank and the IMF. In September 1996, both organizations agreed to the broad outlines of a new debt-reduction plan for twenty very poor countries. Seven rich nations (the G-7 countries) also promised to help. These steps represent progress, but it will cost $6 to $8 billion and the funding is still uncertain.[57]

In 1995, both organizations began working on a Multilateral Debt Facility (MDF). It is still in its preliminary stages, and details are scarce, but its goal is to reduce the poorest countries' debt burden by cancelling some debt.

Cancelling debt will definitely cost money and will be fraught with difficulty. Where does the money come from? How much debt do we reduce? How do we make sure the money freed up by debt relief helps the poor instead of being spent on arms or ending up in the pockets of developing country leaders? How can debt relief encourage democracy in poor nations? How do we make sure the structural adjustment policies of the IMF do not disproportionately hurt the poor? Which countries deserve debt relief and which do not?

In its proposals, Oxfam has tried to develop flexible measures to determine what level of debt is sustainable by very poor countries. They include social need in the country, balance of payments criteria, and debt-to-export ratios.[58]

To make sure the relief helps the poor, Oxfam says that debt relief must depend on a country agreeing to use the money freed up to meet basic human needs. "Targets for improving access to primary health, basic education, and water and sanitation could be established along with the costs of meeting them."[59]

Most economists agree that many heavily indebted nations need what they call structural adjustment programs (SAPs). Why? To make their economies more market-oriented in order to increase economic growth. Unfortunately, in the words of development economist Michael Todaro, the IMF's "early-1980s policies of severe financial repression of debtor countries tended to inflict a harsh and often unnecessary economic burden on nations that in many cases [could] ill afford it." Often the poor suffered the most. Fortunately, the IMF has become more flexible in administering its structural adjustment policies.[60] Protection of the poor must become even more central in future SAPs.

Which countries merit debt relief? Dictators need not apply. Countries like Zaire and Nigeria, as long as dictators administer corrupt, repressive regimes, should not be considered. Countries receiving debt relief should also agree to shift substantial sums from the military to health and education for the poor.

Debt cancellation will be a complicated and difficult task. Not attempting it at all, however, will be even worse. "The price of failure will also be high, with the toll of wasted lives and frustrated potential continuing into the next century."[61] We certainly can afford it. The total foreign debt of the poorest 35 countries is $226 billion. No one is suggesting that all that debt be cancelled. To forgive it all, however, would only take the money that people in the U.S. spend every year on food and drink when they go out to restaurants to eat.[62] Citizens in developed nations must insist that rich countries and the international financial institutions they control offer far more debt relief for the poorest nations.

Preserving the Earth and Empowering the Poor

We have polluted the environment so severely that everyone, especially the poor, face grave dangers in the next century. (See chapter 8.) What can be done?

Restoring environmental integrity is a task for individuals and governments, children and adults, churches and businesses. It can be worked on at every level. Each family can make a difference by deciding to recycle garbage formerly dispatched to the growing mountains of urban waste sites. Churches can teach biblical principles—like temperance, patience, justice, and self-restraint—which are essential if we are to develop a sustainable society. Businesses must prepare to shoulder more costs, and politicians must dare to adopt more courageous public policies.

The basic direction we need to travel is fairly clear. We want to make decisions now that will allow our grandchildren and their grandchildren to have a decent, sustainable life. We want their future to be one where they can continue to rejoice in the earth's goodness and splendor. Therefore we must end the degradation of the environment by making changes in the way we think, believe, and act. Some changes, such as recycling and buying energy-efficient appliances, are a matter of individual choice. Others involve forces and institutions that no individual or family can change by themselves. Yet all these changes are necessary, and they will all be difficult.

Government action is essential. Without rules that apply to all, businesses that invest in pollution controls and environmental sanity are at a competitive disadvantage with callous competitors who continue dumping on everyone. In the short run, the market ignores environmental costs. Therefore, legislation that justly compels all businesses to end pollution places all competitors on an even playing field.

If this is true for businesses, it is also true for nations. Pollution does not respect international boundaries. Table 22 on the facing page demonstrates that for many countries, a great deal of the pollution degrading their nation comes from abroad. And they in turn export much of the pollution they produce. So if one country decides to spend the money to reduce pollution, and surrounding nations refuse, the investment largely improves the life of ornery, selfish neighbors.

International standards are essential. Fortunately, several key international treaties and protocols have recently been developed and adopted. On January 1, 1989, the Montreal Protocol on Substances that Deplete the Ozone Layer, which was adopted by 155 countries, came into force. Three years later, in June 1992, the world's nations gathered in Brazil for what came to be known as the Rio "Earth Summit" on the Environment. One hundred and fifty states signed the United Nations Framework Convention on Climate Change. In doing so, they recognized that climate change is a "common concern of humankind." As part of the convention, all parties agreed to seek to achieve the ultimate objective of stabilizing "greenhouse gas concentrations in the atmosphere at a level that would prevent dangerous anthropocentric [human made] interference with the climate system."[63]

Country	Total Emissions	Total Deposition	Share of Emissions Exported	Share of Deposition Imported
	(thousand tons)		(percent)	
Norway	37	210	76	96
Austria	62	181	74	91
Sweden	110	302	69	89
Switzerland	37	65	81	89
Netherlands	145	104	80	72
France	760	622	67	59
West Germany	750	628	63	56
Czechoslovakia	1,400	659	75	47
Poland	2,090	1,248	68	46
Soviet Union	5,150	3,201	61	38
Italy	1,185	510	72	36
East Germany	2,425	787	75	22
Spain	1,625	590	72	22
United Kingdom	1,890	636	71	15

Table 22—Sulfur Pollution in Selected European Countries (1988)

Used with permission from Brown, State of the World 1990, p. 115

The nations of the world have made a good start. In fact, by 1995, the World Bank had invested $10 billion in loans to help developing nations improve their environmental management.[64] But the 1995 Berlin Conference (the first major follow up to the Rio Summit), highlighted the fact that many nations were falling short of the Rio goal of holding emissions of greenhouse gases by industrialized nations to 1990 levels by the year 2000. In some of these countries, levels of carbon dioxide, the most important greenhouse gas, were as much as 5 percent *above* 1990 levels. Even more disturbing were the increases of 10, 20, 30, and even 40 percent reported by some developing nations. Much remains to be done on a global level.

Some things can be done only by strengthened global institutions like the United Nations. Obviously, it would be unwise to centralize vast power in any one global agency. (Centralized power in a fallen world is always dangerous.) But that does not mean we can ignore the need for a strengthened United Nations to deal with our inextricably interrelated countries on planet Earth.

While we do that, however, we must be careful both to do all we can on a local level and also to make sure there are careful checks and balances for the centralized global institutions that the environmental crisis requires.

If we want to pass on a sustainable world to our grandchildren, what concrete things should we do?

Renewable Energy

If we are to use less fossil fuels, there are two alternative energy possibilities: nuclear energy or renewable energy sources such as sun, water, and wind. Unfortunately, nuclear power plants present us with a danger that lasts for tens of thousands of years—as yet, no one has found a safe way to dispose of nuclear wastes. Renewable energy from sun, wind, and water is the better alternative.

Hydroelectric power can be developed further, although we must beware of related problems. Today, hydroelectric facilities supply 10 to 12 percent of the electricity generated in the United States.[65] (U.S. nuclear power plants produce twice that much electricity.) In the developing world, there are still major untapped sources of hydropower. But the large dams associated with hydropower often harm the environment. In South Asia, the Ganges no longer reaches the Bay of Bengal during the dry season because of upstream diversions. The result? The destruction of essential fisheries and mangrove forests in Bangladesh, the disruption of the local economy, and devastation of one of the last refuges of the Bengal tiger. In Egypt, the High Aswan dam has proved a crucial hedge against drought in the Nile Valley. But it has also caused the near destruction of 30 out of 47 commercial fish species in the Nile River. Commercial sardine fisheries in the eastern Mediterranean, dependent on annual infusions of silt from the Nile, have dropped to 17 percent of their former capacity.[66] The costs of dams and hydropower projects are often not seen for many years after construction, and are usually irreversible.

Far more encouraging are the developing technologies for wind and solar power. Rates for wind power are becoming increasingly competitive with rates for power generated by fossil fuels. In some regions, wind power costs only five to seven cents per kilowatt-hour. Europe has taken the lead, especially in Germany. European wind power capacity is up nearly threefold from 1992. India leads the way in the developing world, now having the world's most active market for wind power.[67] In fact, global wind power generating capacity leapt 22 percent in 1994 alone.[68]

Solar energy is also becoming increasingly competitive. World shipments of photovoltaic chips, the core technology of solar energy, jumped 50 percent between 1990 and 1994. Solar cells register double-digit growth in any typical year. Because of new technology coming on line, the cost of a solar kilowatt-hour is one-third of the 1993 cost.[69] Government policies that cooperate with the market and encourage wise investment in the necessary research can foster greater reliance on solar energy.

One attractive side benefit of solar technology is that the tiny units can be installed in every farm and house. The result is a democratization of economic power that breaks the monopoly of vast utility companies. Several recent examples of this decentralization are encouraging. In one recent period, 20,000 Kenyan homes received solar cells, while only 17,000 were hooked up to the central power grid. In South Africa, there are plans to electrify 10,000 homes, 600 clinics, and 1,000 schools with solar panels made in a local factory.[70] Precisely because of this success, however, we can expect monopolies to fight decentralized solar power. Here too a change in government policy would help. Today, 80 percent of all research and development money spent on non-fossil fuels goes to nuclear energy. Research and development to improve solar and wind energy receive only 10 percent. As Andrew Steer, Director of the Environment Department of the World Bank, says, "This should be reversed."[71]

Public Transportation and Cycling

Public policy that fosters greater use of public transportation and bicycling reduces consumption of fossil fuels. The cost of our daily commute by car is staggering. Out of the 17 million barrels of oil consumed daily in the United States, cars use 43 percent. Commuters stuck in traffic jams waste almost $25 billion annually in just 29 major U.S. cities.[72]

Citizens need to insist that government policy switches more resources from road construction for private cars to safer, more accessible public transportation systems. Using high taxes on private cars and very expensive drivers' licenses, the Japanese encourage large numbers of people to travel by train rather than personal automobile. Los Angeles' ghastly air pollution has prompted the region to undertake a bold plan to discourage automobile use and improve public transportation. They even plan to limit the number of cars per family!

Even bicycles make a difference! The energy that a bicycle rider expends to travel 33 kilometers on a bicycle will power an automobile only 1.5 km. Approximately 54 percent of Americans live within 5 miles of their job. Only 1.67 percent of Americans commute to work by bicycle.[73] In a fascinating essay, "Cycling in the Future," Marcia Lowe shows how public policy even in rich nations can encourage widespread use of bicycles. China leads the world in using bicycles—in 1987, more bicycles were purchased in China than cars in the whole world.[74] However, the other three leaders in bicycle transportation are wealthy nations—the Netherlands, Denmark, and Japan.

Public policy decisions in both Japan and the Netherlands were crucial in achieving greater dependence upon bicycling by the public. Government decided that using bicycles for short distances and rail transportation for longer trips would be the basic pattern for Japan. Legislation enabled localities to require railways and businesses to install facilities for parking bicycles. The Netherlands cut highway funds and invested more in direct, uninterrupted cycling roads.

Bicycles are obviously a more realistic mode of transportation for larger numbers of people in small, densely populated places like Japan than for the vast distances of the United States. But China is hardly small. And large North American cities could encourage much more cycling by installing interconnected networks of safe cycle ways and bike lanes on streets.

Cycling is good for health as well. It is also easier on creation than the private automobile. So is public transportation. Government should provide economic incentives for switching to both of these by insisting that car owners pay the real costs (including the hidden costs) of cars. Some estimate that the hidden costs of cars is $300 billion a year in the U.S. Even those who cannot afford to own cars help subsidize car owners through public taxes that build and maintain highways and cover costs for accident-produced illnesses and air pollution. The U.S. has the lowest gasoline tax of the industrial world, averaging nine cents per liter (34 cents per gallon). Other rich countries tax gasoline at rates from 20 to 85 cents per liter (75 cents to $3.22 per gallon).[75]

We should tax the ownership and use of automobiles at a much higher rate and invest the money in mass transit systems and bicycle routes. Studies clearly show that driving decreases when car owners have to pay more of the real costs. And think of the opportunity for extra reading while commuting by train to work, or the exhilaration of a healthy body able to pedal to work!

Energy efficiency is also crucial. Using currently available technology, we could double the gas mileage of cars, triple the output of electric lights, and cut typical heating requirements by 75 percent. Superinsulated houses in Canada require only one-tenth the U.S. average to heat them.[76]

Obviously we do not want government to legislate every new cost-saving device. The market provides the basic incentive. But there is a place for appropriate legislation that provides parameters, incentives, and research to increase energy efficiency. In 1993, the White House launched a climate action plan. Part of the plan involved enhancing previous legislative measures, including the appliance standards passed by Congress in 1986. These standards had, by 1990, saved the U.S. $28 billion in electrical and gas bills, while sparing the atmosphere 340 million tons of carbon. Congress passed more stringent standards in 1992. Unfortunately, the 1994 Congress cut the funding for the enforcement of these standards. The 1995 Congress cut enforcement funds even more drastically, and simultaneously weakened existing lighting and appliance standards. According to Worldwatch, these and other rollbacks in research and funding could result in U.S. carbon emissions exceeding 1990 levels by as much as 10 percent by 2000.[77]

Recycling Waste

The entire U.S. commercial air fleet could be rebuilt from the aluminum Americans throw away every three months. About 40 percent of this aluminum is being used solely for packaging.[78] At a time when city governments despair of finding adequate waste disposal sites, it is astonishing that the U.S. Congress cannot pass even a simple national bottle recycling bill. The statistics on waste are dumbfounding. The average American family produces about 100 pounds of trash each week. Americans annually produce the equivalent of 10 pounds of plastic for every person on earth. At the rate we are generating garbage, we will need 500 new landfills every year.

Fortunately, there are also hopeful signs in American industry. In 1996, the Chicago Board of Trade launched its Recyclables Exchange. What was formerly trash is now traded on the open market as an asset. Glass, plastics, and paper now have their own market. It is expected that the large price fluctuations that have plagued the recycling industry in past years will end.[79]

We can all work at recycling: at home as we teach our children by separating tin, glass, and paper for recycling; at work as we push our employers to recycle; at the polls as we elect politicians who will resist special interests and vote for public policy that fosters recycling; and at church as we rediscover a recycling ethic for a sustainable world.

Reversing Deforestation

According to the panel of distinguished scientists on the Intergovernmental Panel on Climate Control (IPCC) who are working on global warming, reducing deforestation is crucial. Trees transform carbon dioxide into oxygen, which replenishes the air, and carbon, which stays in the tree. The vast forests in temperate climates are already gone. The tropical rainforests are fast disappearing.

Obviously it is the height of hypocrisy for industrialized nations who long ago cut down vast sections of their own forests and now produce most of the world's carbon emissions to ask poor nations to bear the cost of saving the world from global warming. We cause the problem and we need to pay for it.

The task is vast, and we can all work at it—by planting a few trees in our backyards, by voting for politicians who will work legislatively to protect and enhance intact forest ecosystems, and by making informed consumer choices about the source and environmental cost of the wood fiber products we purchase. As we do that, we can reflect on the fresh air our grandchildren will enjoy.

A Carbon Tax

There are a lot of promising steps for improving our environment. But they all cost money! In the short run, therefore, the temptation is to continue old patterns even though they pollute cities, destroy our forests and lakes, and lead to likely disaster in the next century.

A rigorous carbon tax is an urgent necessity. There are other ways to reduce carbon emissions. A steep carbon tax, however, is probably most efficient and most market-friendly. The calculations would not be exact, but scientists and economists could attempt to estimate the real costs of fossil fuels—including all the negative environmental results of the present pollution and the future costs of global warming. Since coal produces the most carbon, the tax on coal would be the highest—then oil, then gas. Renewable energies, such as that from sun and wind, produce no carbon emissions and therefore would suffer no tax. A carbon tax would mean the market would then work to apply the real costs of pollution. A major part of the additional revenues should be offset by lowering other taxes, especially for the poor. Another substantial portion of the new revenues should go to encourage global energy efficiency and increase economic foreign aid to poor nations.

A serious carbon tax that would truly make a difference must be steep. Many economists suggest that gasoline prices in the U.S. should double.[80] That kind of change would be politically difficult. But it would help correct the absurd situation that emerged in 1996, when the sports utility vehicle—a gas-guzzling, emission-spewing environmental nightmare—became one of the most popular choices for American drivers.

A global agreement on a carbon tax is desirable. Otherwise, countries that impose the tax suffer a competitive disadvantage with countries that do not. But an international agreement is by no means essential. Energy prices today in Japan and Germany are double those in the U.S., yet they compete quite successfully. U.S. energy taxes are the lowest of all developed (OECD) nations. It is time for the U.S. to enact a steep carbon tax. We owe it to our grandchildren—and the poor of the earth.

We cannot preserve the earth without empowering the poor because poverty contributes to environmental degradation (see chapter 8). Poor desperate people chop down rainforests and damage marginal lands unsuited for farming. Rich nations must understand that to preserve a decent global environment, they must do more than recycle garbage or collect expensive carbon taxes. They must also use some of their abundance to reduce the poverty of desperate people driven to environmentally destructive behavior because they have no other way to feed their children. We cannot have environmental integrity without justice.

Does Foreign Aid Help?

Many critics want to reduce or eliminate foreign aid. Conservatives argue that it has failed to reduce anti-American hostility or to promote U.S. foreign policy and that it has often been wasted by corrupt, inefficient governments. Radicals have argued that the purpose was never the reduction of hunger, but rather the promotion of U.S. foreign policy objectives; that it never gets to the real problem, which is the powerlessness of the poor; and that in fact aid strengthens the power of oppressive elites in poor nations.[81]

Sometimes these problems and the news stories about waste and corruption tempt us to abandon foreign aid. But that would be a hasty response. Fundamental changes are imperative. But wisely targeted economic foreign aid can make a difference. In 1967 smallpox killed two million people in the world. By 1981 smallpox had totally disappeared. The reason? A massive program to eradicate this killer. Millions of dollars in U.S. foreign aid helped defeat this annual destroyer of two million people.[82]

Foreign aid can help if we change the way we give it. Here are ten suggestions for improving governmental foreign aid.

1. *Focus on the poorest of the poor.* The purpose of economic foreign aid should be to enable the poorest people in the poorest nations to meet their own basic needs. Since most poor people live in rural areas, the focus must be on integrated rural development. This usually means land reform; agricultural extension services including credit, improved seeds, and fertilizer; rural public works programs such as irrigation projects; agricultural research; introduction of appropriate technology; and the development of light industry located in rural areas to complement the agricultural development.

It is particularly important that basic, minimal health care, education, and a secure food supply be available to the rural masses.[84] Only then will the population explosion slow down. A study by the World Bank concluded,

> In all developing countries, policies which succeed in improving the conditions of life for the poor, and in providing education and employment opportunities for women, are likely to reduce fertility. An improvement in the welfare of the poor appears to be essential before fertility can fall to developed country levels.[85]

Such a conclusion should not surprise the Christian. If, as the Bible teaches, God is at work in history liberating the poor and oppressed, then we should expect that an effective development strategy would be one that brings justice to the poor masses. At the same time this approach to development focused on the poorest of the poor provides a decisive answer to "lifeboat" theorists. Foreign aid to promote rural development is not a foolish gesture that sustains millions now only to doom even more later. Rather, foreign aid that encourages agricultural production as well as (at the least) minimal education and health care among the rural masses, especially women, is probably the best way to slow down population growth. Justice and effectiveness coincide.

Tragically, the bulk of U.S. economic assistance has not gone to the truly poor. There have been various efforts like the "New Direction" reforms in 1973 and legislation in 1982 directing 40 percent of U.S. development assistance to the poorest. A careful study, however, concluded that the bulk of U.S. foreign aid has gone to "Third World institutions that have no links to the poor." Instead, we have channeled "billions of dollars through unresponsive, ineffective bureaucracies of often corrupt and repressive governments or through private structures controlled by these countries' wealthy elites." The result? Further concentration of wealth and power.[86]

Political concerns rather than humanitarian compassion for the poorest has determined where a lot of foreign aid has gone. Bread for the World (BFW) is the most prominent U.S. Christian political movement focused on reducing hunger and poverty. BFW points out that U.S. foreign aid has been heavily concentrated in countries where the United States has strong political or security interests.[87] For example, 47 percent of the entire U.S. foreign aid budget for 1994 went to Egypt and Israel.[88] In addition, 69 percent of the world's malnourished people live in Asia, but in 1994, the U.S. allocated only 6 percent of its foreign aid budget to the region.[89]

2. Channel more aid through private voluntary organizations (PVOs). In the last four decades, a large number of effective, grass-roots organizations empowering the poor have sprung up in developing countries. During the same years, many effective international private voluntary organizations, both Christian and secular, have developed highly successful programs working with the poorest. These PVOs do a far better job than central government bureaucracies controlled by wealthy elites in getting aid to the poorest in the most cost-effective way. The U.S. government's aid agency (USAID) realizes that relying on these local and international PVOs makes sense. In fact, in 1995 Vice President Albert Gore promised that USAID funding channelled through PVOs would increase from 29 to 40 percent. Tragically, the recent dramatic cuts in U.S. foreign aid will reduce the money available to these highly effective voluntary organizations.[90]

PVOs channeled about $2.5 billion of Official Development Assistance (from governments and multinational institutions) to developing countries in 1992, as well as $6 billion of privately donated money (for a total of $8.5 billion).[91] More than 2,200 PVOs today touch the lives of about 250 million people in developing countries.[92] During the 1980s their assistance was equivalent to 8 percent of Official Development Assistance, but it probably had a greater impact, since they are more effective at reaching the poor.[93]

3. *Focus on empowerment.* Development assistance should empower the powerless. Empowerment of the poor will often mean land reform and an end to the political corruption by which the powerful maintain oppressive systems. It will also mean an end to the violation of human rights and the promotion of unions and other organizations that enable the poor to exercise influence in shaping their societies. Obviously, empowering the poor will threaten some oppressive corrupt elites currently in power—in the local village, the state, the nation, and the globe. But only if development assistance empowers the poor so that they can shape their own destiny will it foster justice rather than dependence.

When we do give government-to-government assistance, it ought to go primarily to countries that agree to an overall development strategy to empower the absolutely poor by means of land reform, secure human rights, and an open democratic process. We could offer such countries trade preferences on their exports to us. We could also forgive a portion of their crippling foreign debts.

4. *De-emphasize the donor's political and economic interests.* Short-term economic and political considerations have hindered the effectiveness of foreign aid. Too much aid continues to go to nations because they are currently of geopolitical interest to the donor.[94] The long-range goal of a global society free of widespread hunger and poverty, rather than immediate political or economic concerns, should govern the granting of aid.

We should give more aid through multilateral channels such as effective

United Nations programs like UNICEF and the International Fund for Agricultural Development.[95] Multilateral aid rather than bilateral agreements between the United States and individual developing countries tends to reduce the influence of short-term political considerations.

Also problematic is the fact that the United States has "tied" a good portion of its aid, demanding that the money be used to purchase U.S. goods and services. Since U.S. prices are often higher than global market prices, the aid provides fewer goods and services than it could otherwise. For example, in Egypt, in a child survival program funded by USAID, the children receive amoxicillin made in the U.S. even though the same drug is produced far more cheaply in Egypt. Buying this medicine there would also stimulate the local pharmaceutical industry.[96]

Aid is also too closely tied to our desire to increase exports. One-third of U.S. food aid is provided as loans used to promote U.S. exports.[97] Unfortunately, BFW also says, efforts to use the foreign aid program to promote U.S. exports have become more agressive in recent years. This is tragic because tying U.S. exports to foreign aid "is often not cost effective or the best way to achieve sustainable development."[98] Denis Goulet is right: "'Aid' cannot be successful—that is cannot contribute to genuine development—if it is given primarily as an instrument of a rich country's economic or trade policy, a carrot-and-stick device to purchase ideological or political loyalties or a bribe to fend off politically violent revolutions of poor masses."[99]

5. *Nurture economic sustainability.* We dare not continue destroying the world's soil, water, and forests. Northern capital-intensive farming, for instance, is not a model to promote in developing nations. Our aid should promote appropriate technology and a labor-intensive approach that is sensitive to preserving a sound global ecosystem.[100] Bread for the World estimated that in 1994, only 17 percent of U.S. foreign aid went to sustainable development.[101] That percentage should increase.

6. *Create wealth through tiny loans.* A wide variety of organizations have discovered that tiny, interest-bearing loans to very poor entrepreneurs is one of the most effective ways to reduce poverty (see pages 203, 234–235). Starting in the late 1980s, some U.S. foreign aid began to flow to groups offering tiny loans to the poor. More government funds should go to what we now know is a highly successful strategy.

7. *Separate development aid from military aid.* U.S. citizens are sometimes

confused because military aid and economic assistance both appear in the annual U.S. foreign aid bill authorizing money for developing countries. Military aid should be authorized separately from development aid.

8. *Help countries committed to "growth with equity."* There are several variants of the growth-with-equity approach to development, but the one most popular and perhaps most consistent with Christian principles is referred to as Basic Needs Development. Basic Needs Development focuses on the situation of the poor. It holds that all people have in common certain basic needs and that the highest priority of any economic program is to meet those needs for all people. Denis Goulet, Christian author of many books on development and development ethics, outlines these three basic needs: (1) life sustenance, (2) self-esteem, and (3) freedom to choose one's own course of action.[102]

It is really no surprise that basic needs go beyond the purely physical items of food, clothing, shelter, and health care needed to sustain life. Physical goods, for instance, could be generously supplied by some foreign agent in a paternalistic fashion. But while short-term aid is necessary and appreciated in some situations of desperate need, long-term reliance on handouts reduces self-esteem and motivation. Similarly, a totalitarian society that meets all physical needs is not God's will for us. Persons should be free to shape their lives and societies.

According to Paul Streeten, editor of the prestigious journal *World Development*, basic needs include not just the need for material goods but also "the need for self-determination, self-reliance, political freedom and security, participation in making the decisions that affect workers and citizens, national and cultural identity, and a sense of purpose in life and work."[103] Goulet's categories of self-esteem and freedom move in the same direction.

Foreign aid that encourages developing nations to emphasize a development strategy of Basic Needs Development can truly help the poor.

9. *Emphasize better education and health care for women.* Poverty affects more women than men. Futhermore, the data clearly shows that improving the lot of women is the best way to slow population growth. "Educating girls is three times more likely to lower family size than educating boys."[104] Educated women often delay marriage or delay childbearing to finish school, reducing the number of births. For every additional year of schooling for

women in poor countries, infant mortality rates decline by 5 to 10 percent.[105] Table 23 makes the point vividly. High infant mortality rates and high fertility go along with low levels of education for women. High educational levels go hand in hand with low rates of infant mortality and population growth. Women are generally the ones who take care of the children, so when they learn about hygiene and family planning, the results are greater.

	Table 23—Female Education Index, Infant Mortality Rate and Total Fertility Rate[104] (in percentages)		
Country	Female Education Index	Infant Mortality Rate	Total Fertility Rate
Canada	99.4	7	1.7
United States	97.7	9	1.9
U.K.	96.1	8	1.8
Australia	95.8	8	1.9
Germany	95.7	7	1.5
Japan	95.7	5	1.6
Former USSR	90.0	23	2.3
Poland	88.2	16	2.1
Chile	86.8	17	2.5
Venezuela	78.3	34	3.6
Mexico	77.9	39	3.3
Brazil	74.7	57	3.2
Indonesia	68.8	61	3.1
China	67.0	29	2.5
Egypt	66.9	66	4.0
Turkey	63.0	60	3.5
Kenya	57.0	67	6.5
India	50.4	92	4.0
Tanzania	50.0	115	6.6
Mozambique	38.0	137	6.4
Sierra Leone	36.5	147	6.5
Mali	24.2	166	7.1

Source: Population Action International [106]

10. *Reduce military aid.* In 1994, 34 percent of all U.S. foreign assistance went for military and security aid. Most of those funds should be spent on long-term development. Poor nations don't need more tanks and bullets. They need more help to win an effective war on poverty.

If we improve the way we give foreign aid, it can help reduce hunger, poverty, and injustice. But how much aid is needed?

Bombs, Bread, and Illusions

The world faces a crucial choice. Substantial steps to help the poor and hungry on the scale needed require major sums of money.

Many U.S. citizens think the U.S. is already doing that. In a November 1995 poll, the *Washington Post* discovered that the average respondent thought the United States spends 26 percent of the federal budget on foreign aid. They suggested that 13 percent would be more reasonable. The actual figure for official development assistance is 0.5 percent—i.e., only 1/52 of what the people thought.[108]

After the Second World War, the U.S. was generous. Between 1947 and 1952, the United States poured $23 billion (approximately $125 billion in terms of 1994 dollars) into Western Europe under the Marshall Plan.[109] One has only to look at the material prosperity of Western Europe today to realize that it was one of the most successful aid programs the world has ever seen.

The plight of over a billion poor people today is more desperate than that of the people of war-ravaged Europe in the late 1940s. And yet, we give a vastly smaller percentage of our wealth to today's needy even though our wealth has grown enormously.[110] In fact, U.S. government aid for economic development is at a fifty-year year low, and many politicians want to cut it still more. Committed Christians could lead the fight to change that.

Fortunately, we stand at a moment in history when the world could safely increase development aid by cutting military expenditures. In fact, when Soviet Communism collapsed and the Cold War ended, many people expected that to happen. In early 1990, Senator Mark Hatfield and others introduced the Harvest of Peace Resolution into the U.S. Senate. Supported by Evangelicals for Social Action and a broad range of other organizations, this resolution called on the U.S. to negotiate a 50 percent reduction of military spending with the U.S.S.R. and other nations world-wide to take effect by the year 2000. Global military expenditures, in fact, have fallen somewhat—by 3.6 percent annually from 1987 to 1994.[111] But we have not spent the resulting peace dividend ($935 billion) on the poor. Foreign aid for the poor keeps dropping.

And we still spend too much on military budgets. Global military expenditures today amount to four times as much as the total annual income of the poorest one billion people in the world.[112] President Eisenhower's ringing words, spoken many years ago, are still relevant:

> Every gun that is made, every warship launched, every rocket fired signifies, in the final sense, a theft from those who hunger and are not fed, those who are cold and are not clothed.[113]

Government budgets reflect fundamental values and priorities in the same way that church and family budgets do. What kind of national values do we want reflected in our foreign aid and military budgets? Will Christians act to persuade fellow citizens that budgets should reflect wise generosity toward the poor?

Organizations that Make a Difference

The tasks outlined in this chapter seem vast and overwhelming. Only as individuals join with other concerned citizens can they effectively promote the necessary structural changes. Here are a few organizations working to change public policy.

Bread for the World (BFW) is a nationwide Christian citizens' movement that seeks justice for the world's hungry people by lobbying our nation's decision makers. BFW has members in every congressional district across the country and has organized local groups at the grassroots level in many of those. BFW's newsletter, published eight times a year—and various Action Alerts and Quicklines—keep members up-to-date on current issues and legislation affecting hungry people. Members influence legislation by calling, writing, or visiting government officials, especially their own congressional representatives.

Bread for the World is an explicitly Christian organization. Local groups are encouraged to open their meetings with prayer and Bible study, and the national staff gathers for worship every Friday morning. Both BFW's founder, Arthur Simon, and its current president, David Beckmann, are Lutheran pastors. BFW makes a conscious effort to involve Catholics, Orthodox, evangelicals, and mainline Protestants at every level, including staff and board. BFW's local activities are carried out by volunteer activists, of whom there are some 2,500 across the nation. Founded in 1974, BFW has grown to 44,000 members, whose membership fees and additional contributions supply the bulk of the support required to keep the organization going.

Because BFW has 44,000 "lobbyists" working at the local level, it has been very successful in affecting public policy on behalf of hungry people. Over the years, BFW staff and members have developed, helped introduce, and greatly facilitated passage of numerous pieces of legislation that have benefitted poor and hungry people both in the U.S. and in the developing world. Examples of successful international efforts include the Child Survival Fund, several initiatives aimed at reforming foreign aid to assure more support for development assistance that benefits poor farmers, and special African initiatives.

BFW's Christian activists make a difference. In 1995, they sent Congress 70,000 letters in a campaign to protect aid to Africa. Those letters probably saved $100 million for poor people. BFW's president, David Beckman, thinks each letter was worth $1,000! In 1991, BFW's dedicated members sent even more letters to Washington urging the U.S. to mediate a peace agreement in Ethiopia. Five hundred thousand lives were saved. Beckman thinks each letter in that effort saved at least one person's life.

Evangelicals for Social Action (ESA) is a biblical movement helping Christians combine social transformation with evangelism and spiritual formation. ESA believes that prayer and radical dependence on the Holy Spirit must be central to any successful movement to bring structural change in society.

ESA's *Generous Christians Campaign* is especially helpful for readers of this book. Everyone who has read this far wants to make a difference in the lives of poor people! But you also know that ending poverty is not simple. It requires many different things. And no one of us can know about, support, or work in all the different ways that are needed to overcome poverty. Just a short list of these things can be overwhelming: community development, micro-loans, better social systems, affordable housing, converted individuals, transformed churches, less materialistic lifestyles and cultural institutions. We can't do everything, and we shouldn't feel guilty for our finitude.

That is where ESA's *Generous Christians Campaign* can help you. This campaign enables you to link arms with other Christians who are struggling to demonstrate God's love to the poor. This campaign puts you in touch with a wide range of other Christian ministries doing many of the things this book has shown to be crucial in reducing poverty—from child sponsorship to micro-loans to relief and development to affordable home ownership to wholistic inner-city ministry to good public policy. We can work together, learn from each other, challenge each other to greater faithfulness, and together be more effective servants of the kingdom of God. Nobody can do everything, but everybody can do something. Together we can empower millions.

ESA's *Generous Christians Campaign* also brings you *PRISM*, ESA's national bi-monthly magazine that challenges and inspires believers to follow Jesus with the entirety of their lives. (For more information, see the appendix and back page of this book.)

In addition to the *Generous Christians Campaign*, ESA publishes popular magazines, produces careful studies on public policy, and sponsors conferences and local chapters.

ESA's *PRISM* magazine is an alternative evangelical voice calling the church to costly discipleship and critiquing contemporary culture and politics from a biblical perspective. *PRISM*'s regular Washington Update helps keep readers informed on key political developments.

ESA's Crossroads program publishes careful studies on specific current issues of public policy. Each monograph outlines relevant biblical principles and provides rigorous social analysis in order to reach concrete recommendations on today's toughest political issues.

ESA's *Green Cross* magazine is the only biblical environmental quarterly. *Green Cross* also sponsors local chapters and makes available a variety of educational tools on the care of creation.

ESA's rapidly growing membership is a network of biblical Christians who seek to change the world and empower the poor because they know and love the God of the poor.

Numerous other organizations attempt to change public policy. Here, I can mention only a few.

The Interfaith Centre on Corporate Responsibility (ICCR) provides information to help people understand the impact of multinational corporations on the poor, the environment, and society. For twenty-five years, the ICCR has used shareholder resolutions, careful research, and public pressure to make corporations more responsible.[114]

Other citizen lobbies include *Network*, an organization staffed by Catholic sisters who publish a monthly newsletter, a quarterly, and a hunger packet; and *Friends Committee on National Legislation*, which also issues a monthly newsletter. The United States Catholic Conference's *Department of Social Development and World Peace* works extensively and produces helpful materials on questions of poverty and justice.

In this chapter I have called for the reform of present economic structures. At a time when Marxism has collapsed and democratic capitalism is in danger of an overconfident neglect of its own failures, we must continue to re-examine economics from a thoroughly biblical perspective. We need economists immersed in biblical faith who will rethink economics as if poor people mattered. As a theologian and ethicist, I have only a very incomplete idea of what a modern version of the year of jubilee might look like. But at the heart of God's call for jubilee is a divine demand for socioeconomic structures that provide all people with the opportunity to acquire the capital so they can earn their own way. We must discover new, concrete models for applying this biblical principle in our interdependent world. I hope and pray for a new generation of economists and political scientists who will devote their lives to formulating, developing, and implementing a contemporary model of jubilee.

The Liberty Bell hanging in historic Philadelphia could become a powerful symbol for citizens working to share resources with the poor of the world. The inscription on the Liberty Bell, "Proclaim liberty throughout the land," comes from the biblical passage about the jubilee (Leviticus 25:10). To Hebrews enslaved in debt, these words promised the freedom and the land necessary to earn a living. Billions today long for the same opportunity. The God of the Bible still demands institutionalized mechanisms that will offer everyone the opportunity to earn a just living. The jubilee inscription on the Liberty Bell issues a ringing call for international economic justice.

Do Christians today have the generosity and courage to demand and implement the structural changes needed to make that ancient inscription a contemporary reality?

Study Questions

1. Chapter 11 starts with a parable. Which character in the parable do most Christians you know most identify with and imitate?

2. Chapters 9 and 10 discuss how we can respond as individuals and churches. Are these two responses enough? If not, why not?

3. Do biblical norms apply to modern secular societies? If so, how?

4. What are the strengths and weaknesses of the structural changes suggested in this chapter?

5. How much difference would it make if we ended trade barriers to goods from poor nations? Why don't we?

6. How can we reduce the debt crisis? And environmental pollution?

7. How does this chapter underline chapter 9's call for living more simply?

8. Should foreign aid be given to poor nations? If so, how could it be more effective?

9. Should we redirect money from military expenditures to reducing poverty? What typical objections do people raise to this suggestion? How would you respond?

10. How do you sense God calling you to work for structural change in our world?

Epilogue

We live at one of the great turning points in history. The present division of the world's resources must not continue. And it cannot. Either generous Christians will persuade their affluent neighbors to transform today's market economies so that everyone can share the good earth's bounty, or growing divisions between rich and poor will lead not only to more starvation and death but also to increasing civil strife and war.

Christians should be in the vanguard. The world will change if Christians obey the One we worship. But to obey will mean to follow. And He lives among the poor and oppressed, seeking justice for those in agony. In our time, following in His steps will mean more simple personal lifestyles. It will mean transformed churches with a corporate lifestyle consistent with worship of the God of the poor. It will mean costly commitment to building societal systems that work fairly for all.

Do Christians today have that kind of generosity and courage? Will we pioneer new models of sharing in our interdependent world? Will we dare to become the pioneers in the struggle for more just societies?

I am not pessimistic, in spite of widespread materialism. God regularly accomplishes his will through faithful remnants.[1] Even in affluent nations, there are millions of Christians who love their Lord Jesus more than houses and lands.

I can, however, hear people saying: "I want to do my part, but the task is so complex and my time and resources are so small. How can I make a real difference? That is where Evangelicals for Social Action's Generous Christians Campaign can help.

Each of us can do something. But none of us can know about and support all the things that are needed to overcome poverty: effective community development, micro loans, personal conversion, cultural renewal, better social systems, affordable housing, transformed churches, less materialistic lifestyles and TV programs. All these things and more are crucial. But you should not feel guilty because you can do only one or two! God made you and me finite.

What we can do, however, is link arms with other Christians who also want to be effective partners with the poor. The Generous Christians Campaign helps you do that by putting you in touch with a wide range of Christian ministries doing many of the different kinds of things this book has shown to be so important to reduce poverty (see the Appendix or call 1-800-650-6600).

If at this moment in history a few million generous Christians blessed with material abundance dare to join hands with the poor around the world, we will decisively influence the course of world history. Together we must strive to be a biblical people ready to follow wherever Scripture leads. We must pray for the courage to bear any cross, suffer any loss, and joyfully embrace any sacrifice that biblical faith requires in an age of affluence and poverty.

If you want to be a member of God's generous minority, I invite you to do one simple thing each day. It will only take a minute, but it might change your life. Daily, stop for a moment, look into the face of Jesus Christ, and whisper softly, "Lord Jesus, teach my heart to share your love for the poor."

We know that our Lord Jesus is alive! We know that the decisive victory over sin and death has occurred. We know that the Sovereign of the universe wills an end to hunger, injustice, and oppression. The resurrection of Jesus is our guarantee that, in spite of the massive evil that sometimes almost overwhelms us, the final victory will surely come.[2] Secure on that solid rock, we will plunge into this unjust world, changing now all we can and knowing that the Risen King will complete the victory at his glorious return.

Appendix A

General Works

Bauer, P. T. *Equality, the Third World, and Economic Delusion.* Cambridge, MA: Harvard Univ. Press, 1981.

Beisner, Calvin E. *Prospects for Growth: A Biblical View of Population, Resources, and the Future.* Westchester: Crossway Books, 1990.

Bello, Walden. *Dark Victory: The United States, Structural Adjustment, and Global Poverty.* Oakland, CA: Pluto Press, 1994.

Benne, Robert. *The Ethic of Democratic Capitalism: A Moral Reassesment.* Philadelphia: Fortress Press, 1981.

Berger, Peter. *Pyramids of Sacrifice.* New York: Basic Books, 1975. A sociological analysis.

Birch, Bruce C., and Larry L. Rasmussen. *The Predicament of the Prosperous.* Philadelphia: Westminster Press, 1978.

Brandt, Willy, et al. *North-South: A Program for Survival.* Cambridge, MA: MIT Press, 1980.

Bread for the World Institute. *Hunger 1997: What Governments Can Do.* Silver Spring: Bread for the World Institute, 1996. (A superb annual publication.)

Brown, J. Larry, and H. F. Pizer. *Living Hungry in America.* New York: Macmillan Publishing Co., 1987.

Brown, Lester R., et al. *State of the World 1996.* New York: Norton, 1996.

Brown, Peter. *Restoring the Public Trust: A Fresh Vision for Progressive Government in America.* Boston: Beacon Press, 1994.

Brown, Robert M., *Unexpected News: Reading the Bible with Third World Eyes.* Philadelphia: Westminster Press. 1984.

Byron, William, ed. *The Causes of World Hunger.* New York: Paulist Press, 1982.

Cahill, Kevin M., ed. *Famine.* Maryknoll, NY: Orbis Books, 1982.

Carlson-Thies, Stanley W., et al. *Welfare in America: Christian Perspectives on a Policy in Crisis.* Grand Rapids, MI: Eerdmans, 1996.

Camara, Dom Helder. *Revolution through Peace.* New York: Harper & Row, 1971.

Chinweizu. *The West and the Rest of Us.* New York: Random House, 1975.

Christian Aid, *Banking on the Poor: The Ethics of Third World Debt.* London: Christian Aid, 1988.

Cobb, John. *For the Common Good: Redirecting the Economy Toward Community, the Environment and a Sustainable Future.* Boston: Beacon Press, 1989.

Cromartie, Michael, ed. *The Nine Lives of Population Control.* Washington, DC: Ethics and Public Policy Center, 1995.

Davis, Shelton H. *Victims of the Miracle: Development and the Indians of Brazil.* Cambridge: At the University Press, 1977.

De Jesús, Carolina María. *Child of the Dark.* Trans. David St. Clair. New York: Signet Books, 1962. An explosive personal account of urban Brazilian poverty.

Dreze, Jean, and Amartya Sen. *Hunger and Public Action.* New York: Oxford Univ. Press, 1989.

Duchrow, Ulrich. *Alternatives to Global Capitalism.* Utrecht: International Books, 1995.

Duchrow, Ulrich. *Global Economy: A Confessional Issue for the Churches?* Geneva: WCC Publications, 1987.

Fenton, Thomas P., and Mary J. Heffron, comps. & eds. *Food, Hunger, Agribusiness: A Directory of Resources.* New York: Orbis Books, 1987.

Freudenberger, C. Dean, and Paul M. Minus, Jr. *Christian Responsibility in a Hungry World.* Nashville: Abingdon Press, 1976.

Gay, Craig M. *With Liberty and Justice for Whom? The Recent Evangelical Debate Over Capitalism.* Grand Rapids, MI: Eerdmans, 1991

George, Susan. *Debt and Hunger.* Minneapolis: American Lutheran Church Hunger Program, 1987.

George, Susan and Nigel Paige. *Food for Beginners.* NY: Norton, 1983.

Gheddo, Piero. *Why is the Third World Poor?* Maryknoll, NY: Orbis Books, 1973.

Gilder, George. *Wealth and Poverty.* NY: Basic Books, 1981.

Goudzwaard, Bob. *Aid for the Overdeveloped West.* Toronto: Wedge, 1975.

——————. *Capitalism and Progress: A Diagnosis of Western Society.* Trans. Josina Van Nuis Zylstra. Grand Rapids, MI: Eerdmans, 1979.

Goudzwaard, Bob, and Harry de Lange. *Beyond Poverty and Affluence: Toward an Economy of Care.* Grand Rapids, MI: Eerdmans, 1995.

Griffiths, Brian. *Morality and the Market Place: Christian Alternatives to Capitalism and Socialism.* London: Hodder and Stoughton, 1982.

——————. *The Creation of Wealth: A Christian's Case for Capitalism.* Downers Grove, IL: InterVarsity, 1984.

Halteman, James. *The Clashing Worlds of Economics and Faith.* Scottdale: Herald Press, 1995.

Halteman, Jim. *Market Capitalism & Christianity.* Grand Rapids, MI: Baker Book House, 1988.

Hawken, Paul. *The Ecology of Commerce: A Declaration of Sustainability.* New York: Harper Business, 1993.

Hay, Donald. *Economics Today: A Christian Critique.* Grand Rapids, MI: Eerdmans, 1989.

Jegen, Mary Evelyn, and Charles K. Wilbur, eds. *Growth with Equity.* New York: Paulist Press, 1979.

Korten, David C. *When Corporations Rule the World.* West Hartford: Kumarian Press Inc., 1996.

Lappé, Frances Moore, and Joseph Collins and David Kinley. *Aid as Obstacle: Twenty Questions about Our Foreign Aid and the Hungry.* San Francisco: Institute for Food and Development Policy, 1980.

Lutz, Charles P., ed. *Farming the Lord's Land: Christian Perspectives on American Agriculture.* Minneapolis: Augsburg, 1980.

Kutzner, Patricia. *Who's Involved with Hunger: An Organization Guide for Education and Advocacy.* Washington, DC: World Hunger Education Service/BFWI, 1995.

McGinnis, James B. *Bread and Justice: Toward a New International Economic Order.* New York: Paulist Press, 1979.

Miller, G. Tyler, Jr. *Living in the Environment.* Belmont, Calif.: Wadsworth, 1988.

Millett, Richard. *Guardians of the Dynasty: A History of the U.S. Created Guardia Nacional de Nicaragua and the Somoza Family.* Maryknoll, NY: Orbis Books, 1977.

Morgan, Elizabeth, Van Weigel and Eric DeBaufre. *Global Poverty and Personal Responsibility.* New York: Paulist, 1989.

Myrdal, Gunnar. *The Challenge of World Poverty.* New York: Random House, 1971. A classic.

Nelson, Jack A. *Hunger for Justice: The Politics of Food and Faith.* Maryknoll, NY: Orbis Books, 1981.

Physicians' Task Force on Hunger in America. *Hunger in America: The Growing Epidemic.* Boston: Harvard University School of Public Health, 1985.

Rau, Bill. *Feast to Famine: The Course of Africa's Underdevelopment.* Washington, DC: Africa Faith and Justice Network, 1985.

Rich, William. *Smaller Families through Social and Economic Progress.* Washington, DC: Overseas Development Council, 1973.

Rodney, Walter. *How Europe Underdeveloped Africa.* London: Bogle-L'Ouverture, 1972.

Sachs, Jeffrey, D., ed. *Developing Country Debt and the World Economy.* Chicago: University of Chicago Press, 1989.

Schlossberg, Herbert, Vinay Samuel, and Ronald J. Sider, eds., *Christianity and Economics in the Post-Cold War Era: The Oxford Declaration and Beyond.* Grand Rapids, MI: Eerdmans, 1994.

Schor, Juliet B. *The Overworked American: The Unexpected Decline of Leisure.* New York: BasicBooks, 1992.

Schumacher, E.F. *Small is Beautiful: Economics As If People Mattered.* New York: Harper & Row, 1973.

Simon, Arthur. *Bread for the World.* Grand Rapids, MI: Eerdmans; New York: Paulist Press, 1975. Superb overview of public policy issues. Rev. ed. 1984.

Simon, Julian L. *Population and Development in Poor Countries.* Princeton: Princeton University Press, 1992.

Sivard, Ruth Leger. *World Military and Social Expenditures 1990.* Leesburg, VA: World Priorities. 1989. An annual collection of useful data.

Skillen, James W. *International Politics and the Demand for Global Justice.* Sioux Center, IA: Dordt College Press, 1981.

Spykman, Gordon, et al. *Let My People Live: Faith and Struggle in Central America.* Grand Rapids, MI: Eerdmans, 1988.

Stackhouse, Marx L., et al. *On Moral Business: Classical and Contemporary Resources for Ethics in Economic Life.* Grand Rapids, MI: Eerdmans, 1995.

State of America's Children 1996. Washington, DC: Children's Defense Fund, 1996.

State of the World's Children 1996. New York: UNICEF/Oxford, 1996.

Tamari, Meir. *With All Your Possessions: Jewish Ethics and Economic Life.* New York: The Free Press, 1987.

Taylor, John V. *Enough Is Enough.* London: SCM Press, 1975.

Thurow, Lester C. *The Future of Capitalism: How Today's Economic Forces Shape Tomorrow's World.* New York: William Morrow and Company, 1996.

Todaro, Michael P. *Economic Development.* Fifth Edition. New York: Longman, 1994.

United Nations Children's Fund. *The State of the World's Children 1995.* Oxford: Oxford University Press. (Annual)

Wilkinson, Loren, ed. *Earthkeeping: Christian Stewardship of Natural Resources.* Grand Rapids, MI: Eerdmans, 1980.

Williams, Robert G. *Export Agriculture and the Crisis in Central America.* Chapel Hill: University of North Carolina Press, 1986.

Wilson, Francis, and Mamphela Ramphele. *Uprooting Poverty: The South African Challenge.* New York: W.W. Norton, 1989.

Withers, Leslie, and Tom Peterson, eds. *Hunger and Action Handbook.* Decatur, GA: Seeds Magazine, 1987.

World Bank. *World Development Report 1996.* New York: Oxford Univ. Press, 1996. Annual.

World Bank. *Mainstreaming the Environment.* Washington, DC: World Bank, 1995.

World Hunger Program, Brown University. *Hunger in History: Food Shortage, Poverty, and Deprivation.* New York: Basil Blackwell, 1990.

Lifestyle

Alexander, John. *Your Money or Your Life: A New Look at Jesus' View of Wealth and Power.* San Fransisco: Harper and Row, 1986.

Bascom, Tim. *The Comfort Trap: Spiritual Dangers of the Convenience Culture.* Downers Grove, IL: InterVarsity Press, 1993.

Beckmann, David M. and Elizabeth A. Donnelly, *The Overseas List: Opportunities for Living and Working in Developing Countries.* Minneapolis: Augsburg, 1979.

Conn, Harvie M. *Bible Studies on World Evangelization and the Simple Lifestyle.* Phillipsburg, NJ: Presbyterian and Reformed Publishing, 1981.

Eller, Vernard. *The Simple Life: The Christian Stance Toward Possessions.* Grand Rapids, MI: Eerdmans, 1973. It is important to read Eller's warning against legalism, but the overall effect is to give aid and comfort to our carnal inclination to rationalize our sinful affluence.

Ewald, Ellen Buchman. *Recipes for a Small Planet.* New York: Ballantine Books, 1973. Recipes for delicious, meatless dishes.

Foster, Richard J. *Freedom of Simplicity.* New York: Harper & Row, 1981.

Fuller, Millard. *The Theology of the Hammer.* Macon, GA: Smyth & Helwys, 1994.

Greenway, Roger S., ed. *Discipling the City: A Comprehensive Approach to Urban Mission.* 2d ed. Grand Rapids, MI: Baker Book House, 1992.

Irwin, Kevin W., et al. *Preserving the Creation: Environmental Theology and Ethics.* Washington, DC: Georgetown University Press, 1994.

Kerr, Graham. *The Graham Kerr Step-by-Step Cookbook.* Elgin, IL: David C. Cook, 1982.

Lappé, Frances Moore. *Diet for a Small Planet.* Rev. ed. New York: Ballantine, 1975.

Longacre, Doris Janzen. *More-with-Less Cookbook.* Scottdale, PA: Herald Press, 1976. Commissioned by the Mennonite Central Committee; simple lifestyle recipes of Pennsylvania Dutch quality!

——————————. *Living More with Less.* Scottdale, PA: Herald Press, 1980.

Macmanus, Sheila. *Community Action Sourcebook: Empowerment of People.* New York: Paulist Press, 1982.

McGinnis, James, and Kathleen McGinnis. *Parenting for Peace and Justice.* Maryknoll, NY: Orbis Books, 1981.

Ronsvalle, John L., and Sylvia Ronsvalle. *The State of Church Giving Through 1993.* Champaign: Empty Tomb Inc., 1995.

Schneider, John. *Godly Materialism: Rethinking Money & Possessions.* Downers Grove, IL: InterVarsity Press, 1994.

Shannon-Thornberry, Milo. *Alternate Celebrations Catalogue.* Washington, DC: Alternatives, 1982.

Shopping for a Better World. Available from CEP, 30 Irving Pl., New York, NY 10003; 1-800-729-4CEP.

Sider, Ronald J., ed. *Lifestyle in the Eighties: An Evangelical Commitment to Simple Lifestyle.* Philadelphia: Westminster, 1982.

——————————. *Living More Simply: Biblical Principles and Practical Models.* Downers Grove, IL: InterVarsity Press, 1980.

Sine, Tom. *Why Settle for More and Miss the Best?* Waco, TX: Word, 1987.

Wuthnow, Robert. *God and Mammon in America.* New York: The Free Press, 1994.

Theology, Biblical Studies, and the Church

Armerding, Carl E., ed. *Evangelicals and Liberation.* Nutley, NJ: Presbyterian and Reformed, 1977.

Banks, Robert J. *Paul's Idea of Community*. Grand Rapids, MI: Eerdmans, 1980.

Batey, Richard. *Jesus and the Poor: The Poverty Program of the First Christians*. New York: Harper & Row, 1972.

Baum, Gregory. *The Priority of Labor: A Commentary on Laborem Exercens; Encyclical Letter of Pope John Paul II*. New York: Paulist, 1982.

Beisner, E. Calvin. *Prosperity and Poverty: The Compassionate Use of Resources in a World of Scarcity*. Westchester, IL: Crossway, 1988.

Boerma, Conrad. *The Rich, the Poor—and the Bible*. Philadelphia: Westminster, 1979.

Brueggemann, Walter. *The Land*. Philadelphia: Fortress Press, 1977.

Byron, William J. *Toward Stewardship: An Interim Ethic of Poverty, Pollution and Power*. New York: Paulist Press, 1975.

Cassidy, Richard J. *Jesus, Politics and Society: A Study of Luke's Gospel*. Maryknoll, NY: Orbis Books, 1978.

Catherwood, Sir Frederick. *The Christian in Industrial Society*. London: Tyndale Press, 1964.

Cesaretti, C.A., and Stephen Cummins, eds. *Let the Earth Bless the Lord: A Christian Perspective on Land Use*. New York: Seabury Press, 1981.

Cosby, Gordon. *Handbook for Mission Groups*. Waco, TX: Word Books, 1975.

Cone, James H. *God of the Oppressed*. New York: Seabury Press, 1975.

Dayton, Donald W. *Discovering an Evangelical Heritage*. NY: Harper & Row, 1976.

De Santa Ana, Julio. *Good News to the Poor: The Challenge of the Poor in the History of the Church*. Geneva: WCC Publications, 1977.

Economic Justice for All: Pastoral Letter on Catholic Social Teaching and the U.S. Economy. Washington, DC: National Conference of Catholic Bishops, 1986.

Escobar, Samuel, and John Driver. *Christian Mission and Social Justice*. Scottdale, PA: Herald Press, 1978.

Finn, Daniel R., and Pemberton L. Prentiss. *Toward a Christian Economic Ethic: Stewardship and Social Power*. Minneapolis: Winston, 1985.

Gill, Athol. *Life on the Road: The Gospel Basis for a Messianic Lifestyle*. Homebush West (Australia): Anzea Publishers, 1989.

Gollwitzer, Helmut. *The Rich Christians and Poor Lazarus*. Trans. David Cairns. New York: Macmillan, 1970.

Gremillion, John, ed. *The Gospel of Peace and Justice: Catholic Social Teaching since Pope John*. Maryknoll, NY: Orbis Books, 1976.

Grigg, Viv. *Cry of the Urban Poor*. Monrovia, Calif: Mission Advanced Research and Communication Center, 1992.

Hengel, Martin. *Poverty and Riches in the Early Church: Aspects of a Social History of Early Christianity.* Philadelphia: Fortress Press, 1974.

Johnson, Luke T. *Sharing Possessions.* Philadelphia: Fortress Press, 1981.

Keith-Lucas, Alan. *The Poor You Have Always With You: Concepts of Aid to the Poor in the Western World From Biblical Times to the Present.* St. Davids, PA: North American Association of Christians in Social Work, 1989. (Box S-90, St. Davids, PA 19087)

Kerans, Patrick. *Sinful Social Structures.* New York: Paulist Press, 1974.

Kirk, Andrew. *Liberation Theology: An Evangelical View from the Third World.* Atlanta: John Knox Press, 1979.

Kraybill, Donald B. *The Upside Down Kingdom.* Scottdale, PA: Herald Press, 1978.

Kreider, Carl. *The Rich and the Poor: A Christian Perspective on Global Economics.* Scottdale, PA: Herald Press, 1987.

Lernoux, Penny. *Cry of the People.* Garden City, NY: Doubleday, 1980.

Ludwig, Thomas E. et al. *Inflation, Poortalk and the Gospel.* Valley Forge, PA: Judson Press, 1981.

Meeks, M. Douglas. *God the Economist: The Doctrine of God and Political Economy.* Minneapolis: Fortress, 1989.

Mott, Stephen C. *Biblical Ethics and Social Change.* New York: Oxford, 1982.

Novak, Michael. *Will It Liberate? Questions About Liberation Theology.* New York: Paulist, 1986.

Owensby, Walter L. *Economics for Prophets: A Primer on Concepts, Realities, and Values in Our Economic System.* Grand Rapids, MI: Eerdmans, 1988.

Padilla, C. Rene. *Mission Between the Times.* Grand Rapids, MI: Eerdmans, 1985.

Perkins, John. *With Justice for All.* Glendale, CA: Regal, 1982.

Pilgrim, Walter E. *Good News to the Poor: Wealth and Poverty in Luke-Acts.* Minneapolis: Augsburg, 1981.

Presbyterian Eco-Justice Task Force. *Keeping and Healing the Creation.* Louisville: Committee on Social Witness, Presbyterian Church (USA), 1989.

Preston, Ronald H. *Religion and the Ambiguities of Capitalism.* London: SCM Press, 1991.

Ronsvalle, John and Sylvia. *Behind the Stained Glass Window: Money Dynamics in the Church.* Grand Rapids, MI: Baker, 1996.

Samuel, Vinay. *The Meaning and Cost of Discipleship.* Bombay: Bombay Urban Industrial League for Development, 1981.

Samuel, Vinay and Albrecht Hauser, eds. *Proclaiming Christ in Christ's Way: Studies in Integral Evangelism.* Oxford: Regnum Books, 1989.

Scott, Waldron. *Bring Forth Justice.* Grand Rapids, MI: Eerdmans, 1980.

Seccombe, David Peter. *Possessions and the Poor in Luke-Acts.* Studien zum Neuen Testament und seiner Umwelt, 1982.

Sider, Ronald J., ed. *Cry Justice: The Bible Speaks on Hunger and Poverty.* Downers Grove, IL: InterVarsity Press; New York: Paulist Press, 1980. (1997 edition: *For They Shall Be Fed.* Dallas: Word.)

Sider, Ronald J. *One Sided Christianity: Uniting the Church to Heal a Lost and Broken World.* Grand Rapids, MI: Zondervan, 1993.

Sider, Ronald J. *Cup of Water, Bread of Life.* Grand Rapids, MI: Zondervan, 1994.

Sider, Ronald J. *Genuine Christianity.* Grand Rapids, MI: Zondervan, 1996.

Sine, Tom. *The Mustard Seed Conspiracy.* Waco, TX: Word, 1981.

Speiser, Stuart M. *Ethical Economics and the Faith Community.* Bloomington, IN: Meyer-Stove, 1989.

Taylor, Richard K. *Economics and the Gospel.* Philadelphia: United Church Press, 1973.

Villafane, Eldin. *The Liberating Spirit: Toward an Hispanic American Pentecostal Social Ethic.* Grand Rapids, MI: Eerdmans, 1993.

Wallis, James. *Agenda for Biblical People.* New York: Harper & Row, 1976.

_____. *The Call to Conversion: Recovering the Gospel for These Times.* New York: Harper & Row, 1981.

Westphal, Carol. "Covenant Parenting for Peace and Justice." Office of Family Life, Reformed Church of America. (Write RCA Distribution Center, 18525 Torrence Avenue, Lansing, IL 60438.)

White, John. *The Golden Cow: Materialism in the Twentieth-Century Church.* Downers Grove, IL: InterVarsity Press, 1979.

Wright, Christopher J.H. *An Eye for An Eye: The Place of Old Testament Ethics Today.* Downers Grove, IL: InterVarsity, 1983.

_____. *God's People in God's Land: Family, Land and Property in the Old Testament.* Grand Rapids, MI: Eerdmans, 1990.

Ziesler, J.A. *Christian Asceticism.* Grand Rapids, MI: Eerdmans, 1973.

Development

Batchelor, Peter. *People in Rural Development.* Exeter: Paternoster, 1981.

Freire, Paulo. *Pedagogy of the Oppressed.* Trans. Myra B. Ramos. New York: Herder and Herder, 1970.

Elliston, Edgar J., ed. *Christian Relief and Development: Developing Workers for Effective Ministry.* Dallas: Word, 1989.

Goulet, Denis. *A New Moral Order.* Maryknoll, NY: Orbis Books, 1974.

Myers, Bryant L. *The Changing Shape of World Mission.* Monrovia, CA: Mission Advanced Research and Communication Center, 1993.

Perkins, John M. *Beyond Charity: The Call to Christian Community Development.* Grand Rapids, MI: Baker Book House, 1993.

Perkins, John M., ed. *Restoring At-Risk Communities.* Grand Rapids, MI: Baker, 1995.

Samuel, Vinay and Chris Sugden. *The Church in Response to Human Need.* Monrovia, CA: Missions Advanced Research Communication Center, 1983.

Sider, Ronald J., ed. *Evangelicals and Development: Toward a Theology of Social Change.* Philadelphia: Westminster, 1982.

Sinclair, Maurice. *The Green Finger of God.* Exeter: Paternoster, 1980.

Yamamori, Tetsunao, et al. *Serving with the Poor in Asia.* Monrovia: MARC, 1995.

Periodicals

Boycott Quarterly. Center for Economic Democracy. P.O. Box 30727, Seattle, WA 98103-0720. News and list of boycotted products.

Green Cross. 6 Lancaster Ave., Wynnewood, PA 19096. 1-800-650-6600. The only biblical environmental magazine.

Multinational Monitor. 1530 P St., N.W., Washington, DC 20005. Founded by Ralph Nader, it reports on large corporations.

The New Internationalist. 113 Atlantic Ave., Brooklyn, NY 11201. An influential development periodical.

The Other Side. 300 W. Apsley St., Philadelphia, PA 19144.

PRISM. 6 Lancaster Ave, Wynnewood, PA 19096. 1-800-650-6600. Regular articles on justice and the poor.

Seeds. P.O. Box 6170, Waco, TX 76706.

Sojourners. 2401 15th St. NW, Washington, DC 20009. A biblical magazine with regular articles on economic justice, discipleship, and community (202-328-8842).

Together. 121 E. Huntington Drive, Monrovia, CA 91016. Regular discussion of development issues.

Transformation: An International Evangelical Dialogue on Mission and Ethics. 6 Lancaster Ave., Wynnewood, PA 19096. One of the best places to listen to all parts of the worldwide evangelical community. esa@esa.mhs.compuserve.com.

U.N. Development Forum. A monthly tabloid free from Center for Economic and

Social Information, United Nations, New York, NY 10017.

World Watch. 1776 Massachusetts Ave., N.W., Washington, DC 20036. Bimonthly.

Numerous other religious journals regularly carry related items: *Christian Century, Christianity and Crisis, Christianity Today, Commonweal, Engage/Social Action, Worldview.*

Audiovisuals

A vast array of excellent audiovisuals are available. For lists, write to almost any of the organizations listed in Appendix B.

Appendix B

Organizations

Alternatives, P.O. Box 429, 5263 Bouldercrest Rd., Ellenwood, CA 30049. 404-961-0102. Publishers of a newsletter on simple living, an *Alternative Celebrations Catalog*, and so on.

American Enterprise Institute for Policy Research, 1150 17th St., N.W., Washington, DC 20036. An influential conservative think tank on a wide range of public policy issues, including hunger.

American Friends Service Committee, 1501 Cherry St., Philadelphia, PA 19102. 215-241-7060. An established Quaker relief, development and justice agency.

Amnesty International, 304 W. 58th St., New York, NY 10023. 800-266-3789. Amnesty's focus is human rights.

Bread for the World, 1100 Wayne Ave., Suite 1000, Silver Spring, MD 20910. 301-608-2400. An effective Christian citizens' lobby (see description in chapter 11).

Canadian Hunger Foundation, 323 Chapel St., Ottawa, Ontario KIN7Z2, Canada.

Catholic Relief Services, 209 W. Fayette St., Baltimore, MD 21201. The major Catholic relief and development agency. 410-625-2220, 800-235-2772.

Christian Community Development Association. 3848 W. Ogden Ave. Chicago, IL 60623. 312-762-0994.

Church World Service—The CROP WALK People, 28606 Phillips St., P.O. Box 968, Elkhart, IN 46515. 219-264-3102, 800-456-1310. CWS is the relief, development, refugee assistance and global education arm of the 33 Protestant, Orthodox, and Anglican denominations of the NCCC. Educational resources and free-loan videos.

Compassion International, Box 7000, Colorado Springs, CO 80933. 800-336-7676.

Cooperative League of the U.S.A., 59 E. Van Buren St., Chicago, IL 60605.

Council on Economic Priorities (CEP), 30 Irving Place, New York, NY 10003. 800-729-4CEP. http://www.accesspt.com/cep/. Social and environmental research on corporations for consumers, investors, managers, employees and activists.

Dwelling House Savings and Loan, 501 Herron Ave. Pittsburgh, PA 15219. 412-683-5116.

Ecumenical Bank: see World Council of Churches.

Educational Concerns for Hunger Organizations (ECHO), 17430 Durrance Rd., North Ft. Meyers, FL 33917-2200. 941-543-3246. Echo@xc.org. Provides technical information, seeds, and training to agricultural missionaries and development workers in tropical countries.

Environmental Defense Fund, 162 Old Town Road, East Setauket, NY 11733. 800-225-5333.

Evangelicals for Social Action, 10 East Lancaster Ave., Wynnewood, PA 19096. 610-645-9391. esa@esa.mhs.compuserve.com.

Food and Agricultural Organization (FAO), 1001 22nd St. N.W., Suite 300, Washington, DC 20437. A United Nations agency.

Friends Committee on National Legislation, 245 Second St., N.E., Washington, DC 20002. 202-547-6000. Issues a monthly newsletter and weekly legislative update.

Generous Christians Campaign. 10 Lancaster Ave., Wynnewood, PA 19096. 1-800-650-6600.

Green Cross, 10 Lancaster Ave., Wynnewood, PA 19096. 1-800-650-6600.

Habitat for Humanity, 121 Habitat St., Americus, GA 31709. 1-800-HABITAT.

Heart Institute. 5301 U.S. Hwy. 27 South, Lake Wales, FL 33853. 813-638-1188.

Institute for Consumer Responsibility. 3618 Wallingford Ave. N., Seattle, WA 98103. 206-632-5230.

Interfaith Centre on Corporate Responsibility, 475 Riverside Dr. Suite 566, New York, NY 10027. See chapter 11 for description.

Mennonite Central Committee, 21 S. 12th St., Akron, PA 17501. A large Mennonite relief and development agency heavily involved in long-range development. The Washington office publishes an excellent newsletter, *Washington Memo*.

Mennonite Economic Development Associates (MEDA), Domestic Division Office 302-280 Smith St., Winnepeg, Manitoba MB R3C 1K2. 204-944-1995.

National Association of Community Development Loan Funds, 924 Cherry St., Second Floor, Philadelphia, PA 19107. 215-923-4754.

Network, 224 D St., S.E., Washington, D.C. 20005. A citizen lobby staffed by Catholic sisters who publish a monthly newsletter, a quarterly, and a hunger packet.

OPPORTUNITY Foundation (formerly Maranatha Trust), P.O. Box 886, Bondi Junction 2022 NSW, Australia. 011-612-9233-7133.

OPPORTUNITY International, Box 3695, Oakbrook, IL 60522. 708-279-9300, 800-793-9455. An excellent microenterprise development organization (see description in chapter 9).

World Concern, 19303 Fremont Avenue, N., Seattle, WA 98133.

World Council of Churches, U.S. Office: 475 Riverside Dr., New York, NY 10027. 212-870-3193. Main Office: 150 route de Ferney, CH-1211, Geneva, Switzerland. 41-0-22-791-6111. Books, pamphlets, and newsletters on a wide range of hunger and development issues.

World Relief Corporation, P.O. Box WRC, Wheaton, IL 60187. 708-665-0235, 800-535-5433. WorldRelief@xc.org. The international assistance arm of the National Association of Evangelicals.

World Vision Inc., P.O. Box 9716, Federal Way, WA 98063-9716. 800-423-4200.

Worldwatch Institute, 1776 Massachusette Ave., N.W., Washington, D.C. 20036. 202-452-1999.

Endnotes

Preface

1. For his story, see my *Cup of Water, Bread of Life* (Grand Rapids: Zondervan, 1994), chapter 7.

Chapter 1

1. "Iracema's Story," *Christian Century,* 12 November 1975, p. 1030.
2. Robert L. Heilbroner, *The Great Ascent: The Struggle for Economic Development in Our Time* (New York: Harper & Row, 1963), pp. 33–36.
3. A. Cecilia Snyder, *Hunger Facts* (BFW Background Paper No. 124, February, 1994). The United Nations Development Programme claims that there are 1.3 billion people in poverty, although they do not call it desperate nor absolute poverty (*Human Development Report 1995,* p. 16). A World Bank report, released June 1996, said that 1.31 billion people live on less than one dollar a day (*New York Times,* June 15, 1996, p. A3.).
4. *New York Times,* June 24, 1996, p. A3.
5. Bread for the World Institute (hereafter BFWI), *Hunger 1997* (Silver Spring: BFWI, 1996), p. 19.
6. BFWI, *Hunger 1997: What Governments Can Do* (Silver Spring: BFWI, 1996).
7. United Nations Development Programme (hereafter UNDP), *Human Development Report* (New York: UNDP, 1995), p. 16.
8. BFWI, *Hunger 1997,* p. 15.
9. BFWI, *Hunger 1995: Causes of Hunger* (Silver Spring: BFWI, 1994), pp. 10–15.

10. World Bank, *World Development Report 1995* (New York: Oxford University Press, 1995), p. 162.

11. World Bank, *World Development Report 1990*, p. 1.

12. BFWI, *Hunger 1995*, pp. 10–15; BFWI, *Hunger 1997*, p. 15.

13. World Bank, *World Development Report 1995*, pp. 162–3. The term *Third World* was created during the cold war. At that time, the countries belonging to the democratic capitalist world were called the *First World*. The countries belonging to the communist world were called the *Second World*. The remaining countries were grouped into the *Third World*. In an effort to sound less demeaning, most observers have begun using the terms "less-developed countries" or "developing countries" to refer to the Third World and "developed" or "industrialized countries" to refer to the First World. In this book, developing countries will refer to the low-income, lower-middle-income, and upper-middle-income countries. The developed countries will refer to the high-income countries.

14. Ibid.

15. Ibid., pp. 214–215.

16. Ibid., pp. 162–163.

17. These population and income statistics come from the World Bank's *World Development Report 1995*, pp. 162–3. Per capita GNP is in 1987 dollars.

18. World Bank, *World Development Report 1990*, p. 8, table 1.1.

19. World Bank, *World Development Report 1990*, p. 10. The 1980–93 numbers are from World Development Report 1995, pp. 162–163.

20. The 1980–93 numbers are from *World Development Report 1995*, pp. 162–163. The rest come from *World Development Report 1990*, p. 11, table 1.2.

21. Ibid., p. 166.

22. World Bank, *World Development Report 1995*, p. 163.

23. James Brooke, "Brazilians Vote Today for President in a Free and Unpredictable Election," *New York Times*, 15 Nov. 1989, A10.

24. "Trade with Justice," BFW Background Paper, no. 67 (August 1983):4.

25. BFWI, *Hunger 1996: Countries in Crisis*, p. 90.

26. BFWI, *Hunger 1995*, p. 76.

27. World Bank, *World Development Report 1995*, p. 221.

28. World Bank, *World Development Report 1983*, pp. 200–201 and *World Development Report 1991*, pp. 262–263.

29. W. Stanley Mooneyham, *What Do You Say to a Hungry World?* (Waco, TX: Word, 1975), pp. 38–39.

30. Lester R. Brown, *In the Human Interest* (New York: Norton, 1974), pp. 55–56.

31. United Nations Children's Fund, *The State of the World's Children 1994* (New York: Oxford University Press, 1994, p. 16.

32. World Bank, *World Development Report 1993*, p. 1. To clarify: *Child* mortality rates refer to children under age five. *Infant* mortality rates refer to babies under age one.

33. *Child of the Dark: The Diary of Carolina Maria de Jesus* (New York: Dutton, 1962), p. 42.

34. Mooneyham, *Hungry World*, p. 191.

35. Donald Hay, *Economics Today* (Leicester: InterVarsity, 1989), p. 257.

36. UNICEF, *The State of the World's Children 1994*, p. 64.

37. Michael Todaro, *Economic Development*, 5th ed. (New York: Longman, 1994), p. 368.

38. World Bank, *World Development Report 1993*, p. 23.

39. UNDP, *Human Development Report* (New York: Oxford University Press, 1992), pp. 132–133.

40. Todaro, *Economic Development*, p. 348.

41. World Bank, *World Development Report 1993*, p. 1.

42. UNICEF, *The State of the World's Children 1995*, (New York: Oxford University Press, 1995), pp. 66–67.

43. *Tufts University Diet and Nutrition Letter*, Oct. 94, p. 3.

44. UNICEF, *The State of the World's Children 1994*, p. 16.

45. Mooneyham, *Hungry World*, p. 191.

46. UNICEF, *The State of the World's Children 1995*, p. 17.

47. World Health Organization, *Health Conditions in the Americas* (Pan-American Health Organization, Scientific Publications Series, no. 427, 1982), p. 102.

48. UNDP, *Human Development Report 1994*, p. 50, figure 3.2.

49. UNICEF, *The State of the World's Children 1995*, p. 45.

50. Ibid., p. 21.

51. UNICEF, *The State of the World's Children 1994*, p. 7.

52. UNICEF, *The State of the World's Children 1989*, pp. 2–3 and *The State of the World's Children 1990*, pp. 16–17.

53. Ruth L. Sivard, *World Military and Social Expenditures 1993* (Washington, D.C., World Priorities Inc., 1993) p. 27.

54. World Bank, *World Development Report 1993*, p. 19.

55. UNICEF, *The State of the World's Children 1995*, p. 14.

56. Sivard, *World Military and Social Expenditures* 1993, p. 28.

57. The 1980 figure comes from UNICEF, *The State of the World's Children 1990*, pp. 16–17. The 1993 figure comes from *The State of the World's Children 1994*, p. 6.

58. UNICEF, *The State of the World's Children 1990*, pp. 16–17.

59. UNICEF, *The State of the World's Children 1994*, p. 12.

60. Samuel L. Katz, "Polio Vaccine—Time for a Change," *Abstracts of the IDSA, 1996 (34th Annual Meeting)*, p. 109.

61. UNICEF, *The State of the World's Children 1995*, pp. 10, 13.

62. Ibid., p. 59.

63. *The Economist*, "In the bunker," 8 Jan. 1994, p. 63.

64. Population Reference Bureau, *1995 World Population Data Sheet* (Washington, DC: Population Reference Bureau, Inc.).

65. *Population Bulletin*, Mar 95, p. 4.

66. Population Reference Bureau, *1995 World Population Data Sheet*.

67. UNICEF, *The State of the World's Children 1995*, p. 9. The low prediction for 2050 is 7.8 billion, and the high prediction is 12.5 billion.

68. *Population Bulletin*, Mar 95, pp. 4–5.

69. Lester Brown, *The Twenty-Ninth Day* (New York: Norton, 1978), p. 74. The 1999 figure came from extrapolating the 1995 world population growth rate (1.5 percent) on the 1995 world population (5.7 billion). Both figures come from the Population Reference Bureau, *1995 World Population Data Sheet*.

70. Population Reference Bureau, *1995 World Population Data Sheet*.

71. Quoted in BFW *Newsletter*, July 1976. This issue has an excellent refutation of Hardin and Paddock's call for triage and lifeboat ethics.

72. Amartya Sen, "Population, Delusion and Reality," *New York Review of Books*, Sept. 22, 1994; reprinted in Mike Cromartie, ed., *The Nine Lives of Population Control* (Grand Rapids, MI: Eerdmans, 1995), pp. 101ff.

73. Population Reference Bureau, *1995 World Population Data Sheet*.

74. Lester R. Brown, *State of the World 1993* (New York: Norton, 1993), p. 3.

75. "The academies believe that ultimate success in dealing with global social, economic and environmental problems cannot be achieved without a stable world population. The goal should be to reach zero population growth within the lifetime of our children." Quoted at the Population Summit of the World's Scientific Academies: Statement of 58 Scientific Academies, New Delhi, 24–27 October 1993 (Washington, DC, National Academy Press, 1994).

76. Todaro, *Economic Development*, p. 330.

77. UNICEF, *The State of the World's Children 1994*, p. 31.

78. Todaro, *Economic Development*, p. 330.

79. Mark Hatfield, "World Hunger," *World Vision 19* (February 1975):5.

80. Quoted in Stephen Coats, "Hunger, Security and U.S. Foreign Policy," BFW Background Paper, no. 53 (May 1981).

81. UNICEF, *The State of the World's Children 1994*, p. 34.

82. Supplement to *Radar News*, January 1975, pp. 3–4.

Chapter 2

1. Revolution through Peace (New York: Harper & Row, 1971), p. 142.

2. *New York Times*, 12 July 1949. Quoted in Jules Henry, *Culture Against Man* (New York: Random House, 1963), p. 19.

3. U.S. Bureau of the Census, *Statistical Abstract of the United States: 1995*, pp. 151, 858.

4. Ibid., p. 584.

5. Bob Coen, of McCann-Erickson, "the official source for much of the ad industry's statistics," made this prediction in *Advertising Age*, 12/11/95, p. 40.

6. Bob Coen made this prediction in *Advertising Age*, 6/19/95, p. 40.

7. Richard K. Taylor, "The Imperative of Economic De-Development," *The Other Side 10*, no. 4 (July-August 1974):17. For the figures on advertising and education, see U.S. Bureau of Commerce, *Statistical Abstract of the United States 1989*, pp. 126, 550.

8. Based on Korten, *When Corporations Rule the World*, p. 152.

9. Bellah, *The Broken Covenant*, p. 134.

10. *Newsweek*, 28 October, 1974, p. 69; my emphasis.

11. John V. Taylor, *Enough is Enough* (London: SCM Press, 1975), p. 71.

12. Patrick Kerans, *Sinful Social Structures* (New York: Paulist Press, 1974), pp. 80–81. See further, chapter 6.

13. See the helpful comments on this in Art Gish, *Beyond the Rat Race* (Scottdale, PA: Herald Press, 1973), pp. 122–126.

14. UNDP, *Human Development Report 1994* (New York, UNDP, 1994), p. 35.

15. UNDP, *Human Development Report 1992*, p. 3.

16. Bread for the World Institute (hereafter BFWI), *Hunger 1996: Countries in Crisis* (Baltimore: Communications Graphics, 1995) p. 4.

17. Minus the profit and interest payments that leave the country to pay foreign owners of capital, and plus similar payments that are made to local business-folk who own capital in foreign countries.

18. There are several serious problems with using GNP as a standard for comparison: (a) GNP and GNP per capita say nothing about the distribution of income. A country with a certain GNP per capita that is evenly distributed may be much better off than a country with a much higher GNP per capita in which a small proportion of the population controls a disproportionately high share of the GNP. (b) Less-developed economies are usually largely rural and may trade goods and services without using money. Although World Bank figures attempt to account for such contingencies, there is no doubt a wide margin of error in their statistics. (c) Since we are really interested in what each person can buy with his or her income, international comparisons can be quite difficult. Prices of similar goods and services are different in different counties. (d) GNP figures may not be all that closely correlated with measures of welfare. If, for example, the government of Iran decides to produce a great stock of military equipment, the GNP may rise significantly, but it would be hard to argue that the people in Iran are better off.

19. World Bank, *World Development Report 1995* (New York: Oxford University Press, 1995) pp. 162–163.

20. The $13 figure is based on the World Bank's figures. The GNP per capita figures come from *World Development Report 1995*, pp. 162–163, except for the figures for the Middle East, which come from the *World Development Report 1994*, p. 163. The growth rate projections come from the *World Development Report 1995*, p. 120. Using the more pessimistic projections for future income growth, for every $1 increase in the developing countries' GNP per capita, the World Bank projection would mean a $19.80 increase in GNP per capita in the industrialized countries.

21. World Bank, *World Development Report 1995*, pp. 162–163.

22. See the several criticisms in note 18.

23. Price of a haircut in Bangladesh is based on personal communication with Rosalind Hawlader, June 23, 1996.

24. BFWI, *Hunger 1996*, "Measuring Inequality," pp. 49–50.

25. GNP per capita and GDP per capita come from World Bank, *World Development Report 1995*, pp. 162–163, 220–221, except for Saudi Arabia, which is for 1992 and comes from World Bank, *World Development Report 1994*, p.

163, 221. HDI information comes from UNDP, *Human Development Report 1995*, pp. 156–157.

26. U.S. Bureau of the Census, *Statistical Abstract of the United States 1995*, 115th ed. (Washington, DC, 1995), pp. 868–869.

27. Todaro, *Economic Development 1994*, p. 213. Also, *Statistical Abstract of the United States 1995*, pp. 868–869.

28. World Agricultural Trends and Indicators (Economic Research Service, USDA, 1/94) http://www.econ.ag.gov.

29. Ibid. (1989 is the most current year available).

30. *Ardell Wellness Report*, Fall 94, Issue 36, p. 6.

31. Paul Hawken, *The Ecology of Commerce* (New York: Harper Business, 1993), p. 161.

32. UNICEF, *The State of the World's Children 1995* (New York: Oxford University Press, 1995), pp. 68–69.

33. BFWI, *Hunger 1995*, p. 64.

34. "Middle Class? Not on $15,000 a Year," *Philadelphia Inquirer*, 28 October 1974, p. 9a. I have updated Arnett's figures to account for inflation. He actually spoke of $15,000 and $18,000. But $15,000 in 1974 equals $40,898 in 1994, and $18,000 in 1974 equals $49,077 in 1994. According to the Department of Commerce, Bureau of Economic Analysis, setting 1974 prices equals 100, inflation (actually the implicit GDP deflator) raised prices to 272.65 (a 273 percent increase) by 1994. *Economic Report of the President* (Washington, DC: U.S. Government Printing Office, 1996), p. 286.

35. *Newsweek*, 21 September 1977, pp. 30–31. I have updated the figures as in footnote 34. *Newsweek's* original figures of $15,000, $18,000, and $25,000 are equal to $33,241, $39,890, and $55,403 in 1994. *Economic Report of the President*, p. 286.

36. Quoted in Juliet B. Schor, *The Overworked American* (New York: HarperCollins, 1992), p. 116.

37. National Public Radio, *Morning Edition*, 10/26/95.

38. World Bank, *World Development Report 1995*, p. 196.

39. BFW *Newsletter*, May 1976, p. 1; James W. Howe et. al., *Agenda for Action*, *1975*, (New York: Praeger, 1975), p. 258.

40. Paul A. Laudicina, *World Poverty and Development: A Survey of American Opinion* (Washington, DC: Overseas Development Council, 1973), p. 21.

41. World Bank, *World Development Report 1995*, pp. 163, 196.

42. Earlier percentages are from Lewis and Kallab, eds., *U.S. Foreign Policy and the*

Third World: Agenda 1983, p. 273. 1980–1993 percentages and 1993 foreign aid figures are from *World Development Report 1995*, pp. 163, 196.

43. UNDP, *Human Development Report 1994*, p. 48.

44. UNICEF, *The State of the World's Children 1995*, p. 60.

45. Sivard, *World Military and Social Expenditures 1993* (Washington, DC: World Priorities Inc., 1993), p. 7.

46. UNDP, *Human Development Report 1995*, p. 8.

47. Garrett Hardin, "Lifeboat Ethics: The Case against Helping the Poor," *Psychology Today 8*, no. 4 (September 1974):38ff. See also William and Paul Paddock, *Famine 1975!* (Boston: Little, Brown and Co., 1967), reprinted in 1976 under the title Time of *Famines: America and the World Food Crisis.*

48. Brown, *In the Human Interest*, pp. 113–14, my emphasis.

49. See Michael Cromartie, ed., *The Nine Lives of Population Control*, (Grand Rapids, MI: Eerdmans, 1995), pp. 101–127.

50. BFWI, *Hunger 95*, p. 63.

51. The right kind of aid often encourages labor-intensive development and intermediate technology. See E. F. Schumacher, *Small is Beautiful* (New York: Harper Torchbooks, 1973), esp. pp. 161–79.

52. UNDP, *Human Development Report 1994*, p. 27.

53. For short critiques of triage and lifeboat ethics, see Lester Brown, *The Politics and Responsibility of the North American Breadbasket*, Worldwatch Paper, no. 2 (October 1975), p. 36; and BFW *Newsletter*, July 1976.

54. Robert H. Schuller, *Your Church Has Real Possibilities!* (Glendale, CA: Regal Books, 1974). p. 117.

Part 2

1. Quoted in *Post-American*, 1, no. 4 (Summer 1972), p. 1.

2. Laudicina, *World Poverty and Development*, p. 21.

3. Ronald J. Sider, *For They Shall Be Fed* (Dallas: Word, 1997). An earlier edition was called *Cry Justice: The Bible Speaks on Hunger and Poverty* (New York: Paulist Press; Downers Grove, IL: InterVarsity, 1983).

Chapter 3

1. See, for instance, Enzo Gatti, *Rich Church—Poor Church* (Maryknoll, NY:

Orbis Books, 1974), p. 43. Liberation theology in general leans in this direction. For excellent evaluations of liberation theology, see J. Andrew Kirk, *Liberation Theology: An Evangelical View from the Third World* (Atlanta, GA: John Knox Press, 1980); and Harvie Conn's two excellent chapters (8 and 9) on liberation theology in Stanley N. Gundry and Alan F. Johnson, eds., *Tensions in Contemporary Theology* (Chicago: Moody Press, 1976).

2. Ernst Bammel, "prochos," in Gerhard Kittel and Gerhard Friedrich, eds., *Theological Dictionary of the New Testament*, trans. Geoffrey W. Bromiley, 10 vols. (Grand Rapids, MI: Eerdmans, 1968), 6:888. Hereafter called TDNT.

3. A. Gelin, *The Poor of Yahweh* (Collegeville, MN: Liturgical Press, 1964), pp. 19–20.

4. *TDNT*, VI, 885ff. *Penes* is used only once and means a humble workman with no property (*TDNT*, VI, 37ff).

5. See the helpful distinctions among those who are poor because of (1) sloth, (2) calamity, (3) exploitation, and (4) voluntary choice in R. C. Sproul, "Who Are the Poor?" *Tabletalk* 3, no. 6 (July 1979). See also the discussion of the "spiritual poor" below, note 12.

6. Unlike some liberation theologians who take the exodus merely as an inspirational device, I assert that in the exodus God was both liberating oppressed persons and also calling out a special people to be the recipients of his special revelation. Yahweh called forth a special people so that through them he could reveal his will and salvation for all people. But his will included, as he revealed even more clearly to his covenant people, that his people should follow him and be very concerned for justice for the poor and oppressed. The fact that Yahweh did not liberate all poor Egyptians at the exodus does not mean that God was not concerned for the poor everywhere any more than the fact that he did not give the Ten Commandments to everyone in the Near East means that God did not intend them to have universal application. Because God chose to reveal himself in history, he disclosed to particular people at particular points in time what he willed for all people everywhere.

7. John Bright, *A History of Israel* (Philadelphia: Westminster Press, 1959), pp. 240–41.

8. Ibid.

9. Roland de Vaux, *Ancient Israel* (New York: McGraw Hill, 1965), 2:72–73.

10. So also in the case of Judah; compare Ezekiel 20, Jeremiah 11:9–10.

11. Preaching the gospel and seeking justice for the poor are distinct, equally

important dimensions of the total mission of the church; see my "Evangelism, Salvation and Social Justice: Definitions and Interrelationships," *International Review of Mission*, July 1975, pp. 251ff. (esp. p. 258); my "Evangelism or Social Justice: Eliminating the Options," *Christianity Today*, 8 October 1976, pp. 26–29; and, more recently, *One-Sided Christianity?* (Grand Rapids, MI: Zondervan, 1993) and *Cup of Water, Bread of Life* (Grand Rapids, MI: Zondervan, 1994).

12. This is not to deny that a "spiritual" usage of the term "the poor" emerged in the intertestamental period. But even then, the material, economic foundation was never absent. See my "An Evangelical Theology of Liberation," in Kenneth S. Kantzer and Stanley N. Gundry, eds., *Perspectives on Evangelical Theology* (Grand Rapids, MI: Baker, 1979), pp. 122–24.

13. See also Revelation 7:16.

14. Richard Batey, *Jesus and the Poor* (New York: Harper & Row, 1972), p. 7.

15. This paragraph represents a change from earlier editions. I think John Schneider's critique at this point is partly correct. See his *Godly Materialism* (Downers Grove, IL: InterVarsity, 1994), pp. 103–121 (especially pp. 107–110).

16. Martin Hengel, *Property and Riches in the Early Church: Aspects of a Social History of Early Christianity* (Philadelphia: Fortress Press, 1974), p. 38.

17. Batey, *Jesus and the Poor*, p. 6. Again, however, I think Schneider is right (*Godly Materialism*, p. 110) that my earlier editions overstated the marginality of Nazareth.

18. See also Psalm 107:35–41. See chapter 5, p. 103–104, for a discussion of the different versions of the beatitudes in Matthew 5 and Luke 6.

19. I do not overlook, of course, the biblical teaching that obedience brings prosperity. See chapter 5, pp. 101–103, for a discussion of this theme.

20. Bright, *History of Israel*, p. 306. For a similar event, see Daniel 4 (esp. v. 27).

21. See also Micah 2:1–3.

22. Joachim Jeremias, *The Parables of Jesus* (London: SCM Press, 1954), pp. 128–30, and others have argued that Jesus' point was an entirely different one. But I am still inclined to follow the usual interpretation; see, for instance, *The Interpreter's Bible*, 8:288–92.

23. Ibid., p. 290.

24. Clark H. Pinnock, "An Evangelical Theology of Human Liberation," *Sojourners*, February 1976, p. 31.

25. "The Bible and the Other Side," *The Other Side 11*, no. 5 (September–October 1975):57.

26. See J. A. Motyer, *The Day of the Lion: The Message of Amos* (Downers Grove, IL: InterVarsity, 1974), pp. 129–37, for a good exegesis of these verses. See also Micah 6:6–8; James 2:14–17.

27. This is not to say that God is unconcerned with true worship. Nor does Amos 5:21–24 mean that God is saying, "I do not want you to defend my rights, real or imaginary; I want you to struggle and expend your energies in advancing the rights of the poor and oppressed" (Gatti, *Rich Church—Poor Church*, p. 17). Such a dichotomy ignores the central prophetic attack on idolatry. God wants both worship and justice. Tragically, some people today concentrate on one, some on the other. Few seek both simultaneously.

28. G. E. Ladd, *A Theology of the New Testament* (Grand Rapids, MI: Eerdmans, 1974), p. 133. For this whole topic of whether Matthew 25, 1 John 3, and so on must be limited in their application to Christians, see the superb discussion of Stephen C. Mott, *Biblical Ethics and Social Change* (New York: Oxford Univ. Press, 1982), pp. 34–36.

29. God does not desire the salvation of the poor more than the salvation of the rich. I disagree strongly with Gatti's assertion: "They [the poor and oppressed] are the ones that have the best right to that word [of salvation]; they are the privileged recipients of the Gospel" (*Rich Church—Poor Church?* p. 43). God desires all people—oppressors and oppressed alike—to be saved. No one has any "right" to hear God's Word. We all deserve death. It is only by contrast with the sinful perversity of Christians who prefer to minister in the suburbs rather than the slums that Jesus and Paul seem to be biased in favor of preaching to the poor.

30. For a more elaborate development of these points, see my "An Evangelical Theology of Liberation," pp. 117–20.

31. See chapter 6.

32. See my articles on the resurrection listed in note 2 of the epilogue.

Chapter 4

1. I adapt here some material from my article, "Toward a Biblical Perspective on Equality," *Interpretation*, April, 1989, pp. 156–169.

2. See Roland de Vaux, *Ancient Israel: Its Life and Institutions*, trans. John McHugh (London: Darton, Longman and Todd, 1961), I, 164.

3. H. Eberhard von Waldow, "Social Responsibility and Social Structure in Early Israel," CBQ 32 (1970), 195.

4. Albrecht Alt, "Micah 2. 1–5: Ges Anadasmos in Juda." *Kleine Schriften zur Geschichte des Volkes Israel* (Munich: C.H. Beck, 1959), III, 374.

5. In his study of early Israel, Norman Gottwald concluded that Israel was "an egalitarian, extended-family, segmentary tribal society with an agricultural-pastoral economic base . . . characterized by profound resistance and opposition to the forms of political domination and social stratification that had become normative in the chief cultural and political centers of the ancient Near East." *The Tribes of Yahweh: A Sociology of the Religion of Liberated Israel* 1250-1050 BCE (London: SCM Press, 1979), p. 10.

6. For a survey of the literature on Leviticus 25, see R. Gnuse, "Jubilee Legislation in Leviticus: Israel's Vision of Social Reform," *Biblical Theology Bulletin 15* (1983), pp. 43–48.

7. Also Ezekiel 47:14. See the discussion and the literature cited in Mott, *Biblical Ethics and Social Change*, pp. 65–66; and Stephen Charles Mott, "Egalitarian Aspects of the Biblical Theory of Justice," in the *American Society of Christian Ethics, Selected Papers* 1978, ed. Max Stackhouse (Newton, MA: American Society of Christian Ethics, 1978), pp. 8–26.

8. See the excellent book edited by Loren Wilkinson, *Earthkeeping: Christian Stewardship of Natural Resources*, 2nd ed. (Grand Rapids, MI: Eerdmans, 1980), esp. pp. 232–37.

9. See in this connection the fine article by Paul G. Schrotenboer, "The Return of Jubilee," *International Reformed Bulletin*, Fall 1973, pp. 19ff. (esp. pp. 23–24).

10. See also Ephesians 2:13–18. Marc H. Tanenbaum points out the significance of the day of atonement in "Holy Year 1975 and Its Origins in the Jewish Jubilee Year," *Jubilaeum* (1974), p. 64.

11. For the meaning of the word liberty in Leviticus 25:10, see Martin Noth, *Leviticus* (Philadelphia: Westminster, 1965), p. 187: "Deror, a 'liberation' . . . is a feudal word from the Accadian (an)duraru—'freeing from burdens.'"

12. Roland de Vaux reflects the scholarly consensus that Leviticus 25 "was a Utopian law and it remained a dead letter" (*Ancient Israel*, 1:177). Tanenbaum ("Holy Year 1975," pp. 75–76) on the other hand, thinks it was practiced. The only other certain references to it are in Leviticus 27:16–25, Numbers 36:4, and Ezekiel 46:17. It would be exceedingly significant if one could show that Isaiah 61:1–2 (which Jesus cited to outline his mission in Luke 4:18–19) also refers to the year of jubilee. De Vaux doubts that Isaiah 61:1 refers to the jubilee (*Ancient Israel*, 1:176). The same word, however, is used in Isaiah 61:1 and

Leviticus 25:10. See John H. Yoder's argument in *Politics of Jesus* (Grand Rapids, MI: Eerdmans, 1972), pp. 64–77; see also Robert Sloan, *The Acceptable Year of the Lord* (Austin, TX: Scholar Press, 1977); and Donald W. Blosser, "Jesus and the Jubilee" (Ph. D. diss., Univ. of St. Andrews, 1979).

13. My understanding of the centrality of the land in Israel's self-understanding owes a good deal to Christopher J. H. Wright, *An Eye for an Eye: The Place of Old Testament Ethics Today* (Downers Grove, IL: InterVarsity, 1983), esp. chapters 3 and 4. Walter Brueggemann's *The Land* (Philadelphia: Fortress Press, 1977), is also a particularly important work on this topic.

14. De Vaux, *Ancient Israel*, 1:173–75.

15. Leviticus 25 seems to provide for emancipation of slaves only every fiftieth year.

16. See Jeremiah 34 for a fascinating account of God's anger at Israel for their failure to obey this command.

17. Some modern commentators think that Deuteronomy 15:1–11 provides for a one-year suspension of repayment of loans rather than an outright remission of them. See, for example, C. J. H. Wright, *God's People in God's Land* (Grand Rapids, MI: Eerdmans, 1990), p. 148 and S. R. Driver, *Deuteronomy*, International Critical Commentary, 3d ed. (Edinburgh: T. and T. Clark, 1895), pp. 179–80. But Driver's argument is basically that remission would have been impractical. He admits that v. 9 seems to point toward remission of loans. So too Gerhard von Rad, *Deuteronomy* (Philadelphia: Westminster, 1966), p. 106.

18. See de Vaux, *Ancient Israel*, 1:174–75, for discussion of the law's implementation. In the Hellenistic period, there is clear evidence that it was put into effect.

19. See also de Vaux, *Ancient Israel*, 1:171.

20. John Mason has done some masterful work on the type of "welfare system" suggested by the Old Testament; see "Biblical Teaching and Assisting the Poor," *Transformation*, 4 (April–June, 1987), pp. 1–14, and his essay, "Biblical Teaching and the Objectives of Welfare Policy in the United States," in Stanley W. Carlson-Thies and James W. Skillen, eds., *Welfare in America: Christian Perspectives on a Policy in Crisis* (Grand Rapids, MI: Eerdmans, 1996), pp. 145–185.

21. This is an extremely complicated problem which has been debated throughout church history. The long dispute among Lutherans over the "third use of the law" is one example of the perennial debate.

22. De Vaux, *Ancient Israel*, 1:171.

23. See ibid., p. 170; and Taylor, *Enough Is Enough*, pp. 56–60.

24. Driver, *Deuteronomy*, p. 178.

25. For a highly fascinating, scholarly account of the entire history, see Benjamin Nelson, *The Idea of Usury: From Tribal Brotherhood to Universal Otherhood*, 2d ed. (Chicago: Univ. of Chicago Press, 1969).

26. See the excellent discussion by Bob Goudzwaard, *Capitalism and Progress: A Diagnosis of Western Society* (Grand Rapids, MI: Eerdmans, 1979).

27. See Matthew 4:23; 24:14; Mark 1:14–15; Luke 4:43; 16:16; and see the long discussion of the prophetic hope and the Gospel of the kingdom in my *One-Sided Christianity?* (Grand Rapids, MI: Zondervan, 1993), chapters 3–4.

28. For this common interpretation, see Batey, *Jesus and the Poor*, pp. 3, 9, 100, note 8; J. A. Ziesler, *Christian Asceticism* (Grand Rapids, MI: Eerdmans, 1973), p. 45; TDNT 3:796; *Interpreter's Bible*, 8:655, 690; Carl Henry, "Christian Perspective on Private Property," in *God and the Good*, ed. C. Oriebeke and L. Smedes (Grand Rapids, MI: Eerdmans, 1975), p. 98.

29. See also Batey, *Jesus and the Poor*, p. 8.

30. Taylor, *Economics and the Gospel*, p. 21.

31. See D. Guthrie et al., ed., *The New Bible Commentary Revised* (Grand Rapids, MI: Eerdmans, 1970), p. 980; Batey, *Jesus and the Poor*, p. 38.

32. *TDNT*, 3:796.

33. The key verbs are *epipraskon* and *diemerizon* (Acts 2:45) and *epheron* (Acts 4:34). See *Interpreter's Bible*, 9:52; Batey, *Jesus and the Poor*, pp. 33, 105, note 9.

34. Ziesler, *Christian Asceticism*, p. 110.

35. Batey, *Jesus and the Poor*, pp. 36, 96–97.

36. See Keith F. Nickle, *The Collection: A Study of Paul's Strategy*, Studies in Biblical Theology, no. 48 (Naperville, IL: Allenson, 1966), p. 29; and *Interpreter's Bible*, 9:153.

37. See Diane MacDonald, "The Shared Life of the Acts Community," *Post-American*, July 1975, p. 28.

38. See *Interpreter's Bible*, 9:150–52, for a summary of the reasons for accepting the reliability of this account.

39. See Nickle, *The Collection*, pp. 68–69.

40. See *TDNT*, 3:804ff.

41. In fact, Paul was probably at Jerusalem to deliver the gift mentioned in Acts 11:27–30. See *Interpreter's Bible*, 9:151.

42. See *TDNT*, 3:807–8.

43. See also the striking use of *koinonos* in Philemon 17–20. As fellow Christians, the slave Onesimus, his master Philemon, and Paul are all partners (*koinonoi*). This common fellowship means that Paul can ask Philemon to charge Onesimus' debt to his own account. But Paul and Philemon are also partners in Christ. Furthermore, Philemon owes Paul his very soul. Therefore, Paul suggests there is no need for anyone to reimburse Philemon. Their fellowship in Christ cancels any debt that Onesimus might otherwise owe. See *TDNT*, 3:807.

44. For example, Proverbs 6:6–11; 10:4–5. See my "Towards a Biblical Perspective on Equality," esp. p. 164.

45. Quoted in Hengel, *Property and Riches in the Early Church*, pp. 42–43.

46. Ibid., pp. 42–44.

47. Quoted in ibid., p. 45.

48. On December 5, 1975, the *Wall Street Journal* reported that since 1971 a professional archaeologist had been measuring the amount of food thrown away in Tucson, Arizona. He discovered that the average family discards $100 worth of food each year (and that does not count food given to pets or ground up in the garabage disposal). Assuming a family size of five, 236 million North Americans discard $4.7 billion worth of food each year. Using the figures on per capita GNP (1973) in Roger D. Hansen, *Agenda for Action*, 1976 (New York: Praeger, 1976), p. 146, I estimated (in 1976) that 120 million African Christians earned $25 billion annually. (I assumed 74 million at $150 per year; 45 million at $300; and 1 million at $1,000.)

49. C. H. Jacquet, Jr., ed., *Yearbook of American and Canadian Churches: 1991* (New York: National Council of Churches, 1991), p. 305.

50. See Helmut Gollwitzer, *The Rich Christians and Poor Lazarus*, trans. David Cairns (New York: Macmillan, 1970), p. 5, and Arthur C. Cochrane, *Eating and Drinking with Jesus* (Philadelphia: Westminster Press, 1974).

Chapter 5

1. Quoted in *Discernment*, Spring, 1995, p. 3.

2. Carl F. H. Henry, "Christian Perspective on Private Property," p. 97; Hengel, *Property and Riches in the Early Church*, p. 15.

3. See further Emil Brunner, *Justice and the Social Order*, trans. Mary Hottinger (London: Lutterworth Press, 1945), pp. 42ff., 133ff.; and E. Clinton Gardner, *Biblical Faith and Social Ethics* (New York: Harper & Row, 1960), pp. 285–91.

4. Adam Smith, *The Wealth of Nations* (1776; reprint ed., New York: Modern Library, 1937).

5. See, for example, Gary North, "Free Market Capitalism," *Wealth and Poverty: Four Christian Views of Economics*, ed. Robert G. Clouse (Downers Grove, IL: InterVarsity, 1984).

6. See Goudzwaard, *Capitalism and Progress*.

7. Henry, "Christian Perspective on Private Property," p. 97.

8. Hengel, *Property and Riches in the Early Church*, p. 12.

9. Walther Eichrodt, "The Question of Property in the Light of the Old Testament," *Biblical Authority for Today*, ed. Alan Richardson and W. Schweitzer (London: SCM Press, 1951), p. 261.

10. Ibid., p. 271.

11. Dom Helder Camara, *Revolution through Peace* (New York: Harper & Row, 1971), pp. 142–43.

12. *TDNT*, 6:271. Taylor (*Enough is Enough*, p. 45) suggests that the word connotes "excess" or "wanting more and more."

13. For a discussion of church discipline, see my "Watching Over One Another in Love," *The Other Side 11*, no. 3 (May–June, 1975): 13–20, 58–60 (esp. p. 59).

14. For a good discussion of this issue, see Ziesler, *Christian Asceticism*.

15. See the biblical texts in my *Cry Justice*, pp. 175–87 for the former and pp. 148–53 for the latter.

16. See Gordon D. Fee, "The New Testament View of Wealth and Possessions," *New Oxford Review* (May 1981):9: "It is only as one is righteous—i.e., walks in accordance with God's law—that one is promised the blessing of abundance and family. But to be righteous meant especially that one cared for or pleaded the cause of the poor and the oppressed."

17. Taylor, *Enough Is Enough*, chapter 3.

18. See further the twenty references in Batey, *Jesus and the Poor*, p. 92.

19. Ziesler, *Christian Asceticism*, p. 52. See further my "An Evangelical Theology of Liberation," pp. 122–25.

20. See further Gardner, *Biblical Faith and Social Ethics*, pp. 276–77. Also, see the "Oxford Declaration on Christian Faith and Economics" in Herbert Schlossberg, Vinay Samuel, and Ronald J. Sider, eds., *Christianity and Economics in the Post-Cold War Era* (Grand Rapids, MI: Eerdmans, 1994), pp. 11–32.

21. *Interpreter's Bible*, 7:320; see also 1 Timothy 6:17–19.

22. A. W. Argyle, Matthew, *The Cambridge Bible Commentary* (Cambridge: Cambridge Univ. Press, 1963), p. 53. So too *Interpreter's Bible*, 7:318.

Chapter 6

1. Quoted in Richard K. Taylor, *Economics and the Gospel* (Philadelphia: United Church Press, 1973), p. 45.

2. "Edison High School—A History of Benign and Malevolent Neglect," *Oakes Newsletter 5*, no. 4 (14 December 1973):1–4; and "Northeast High Took the Glory Away," *Sunday Bulletin*, 27 January 1974, sect. 1, p. 3.

3. Rodney Stark et al., "Sounds of Silence," *Psychology Today*, April 1970, pp. 38–41, 60–67.

4. Bright, *History of Israel*, p. 241, note 84.

5. Compare Isaiah 3:13–17.

6. Schneider, *Godly Materialism*, p. 113.

7. Ronald J. Sider, "Racism," *United Evangelical Action*, Spring, 1977, p. 11.

8. Schneider, p. 114.

9. Ibid., p. 115.

10. See my *One-Sided Christianity?* for a discussion of "Jesus and Politics" (pp. 154–56).

11. See further my *One-Sided Christianity?* pp. 154–56.

12. This section is taken from my *One-Sided Christianity?* pp. 151–153; see further, pp. 147–156.

13. See Mott, *Biblical Ethics and Social Change*, pp. 4–6. For an excellent, extended treatment of systemic evil (including a discussion of the Pauline concept of the "principalities and powers"), see Mott, *Biblical Ethics and Social Change*, chapter 1.

14. Ibid., p. 4; *TDNT*, III, 868.

15. Quoted in Mott, *Biblical Ethics*, p. 6. Sometimes, of course, cosmos simply means God's good creation (e.g., John 1:9–10a). See Richard Mouw's delightful distinction in *Called to Holy Worldliness* (Philadelphia: Fortress, 1980), p. 75.

16. Clinton E. Arnold, *Powers of Darkness: Principalities and Powers in Paul's Letters* (Downers Grove, IL: InterVarsity, 1992), p. 203.

17. See Mott, *Biblical Ethics*, pp. 6–10; Arnold, *Powers of Darkness*, esp. pp. 87–210; and the massive, three-volume work by Walter Wink published by Fortress Press: *Naming the Powers* (1984); *Unmasking the Powers* (1986); *Engaging the Powers* (1992).

18. John Paul II, *Sollicitudo Rei Socialis* (Dec. 30, 1987), sect. 36. John Paul insists that we cannot gain a "profound understanding of the reality that confronts us" in our complex world without the ethical category of *"structures of sin"* (my italics).

19. See my *One-Sided Christianity?* (Zondervan, 1993)

Part 3

1. See, for example, analysis of the many causes of long-term poverty in the U.S. that any welfare reform plan must deal with, in Ronald J. Sider and Heidi Rolland, "Correcting the Welfare Tragedy," in Stanley W. Carlson-Thies and James W. Skillen, eds., *Welfare in America* (Grand Rapids, MI: Eerdmans, 1996), pp. 456–63.

Chapter 7

1. Lester C. Thurow, *The Future of Capitalism*, (New York: Morrow, 1996), p. 15.
2. This is not to deny the universality of sin and therefore everyone's need to hear the Gospel. Nor is it to overlook the significance of cultural values in the adoption of technology.
3. BFWI, *Hunger 1995*, p. 22.
4. BFWI, *Hunger 1995*, p. 25.
5. Todaro, *Economic Development*, 1994, pp. 292–95.
6. Todaro, *Economic Development*, 1994, p. 608.
7. Todaro, *Economic Development*, 1994, pp. 296–297.
8. BFWI, *Hunger 1995*, p. 22.
9. BFWI, *Hunger 1995*, pp. 24–25.
10. UNDP, *Human Development Report 1994*, p. 43.
11. *Economist*, June 22, 1996, p. 45.
12. BFWI, *Hunger 1995*, p. 23.
13. The income of the poorest 20 percent means that is the percentage of the total income of the country which the poorest one-fifth of the population earned. It should also be noted that the data for each country comes from different years. Most are from the early 1990s and late 1980s, but the earliest is from 1979.
14. World Bank, *World Development Report 1996*, pp. 196–7.
15. For a summary of the details of the nearly finalized treaty, see S. P. Jagota, "Developments in the UN Conference on the Law of the Sea," *Third World*

Quarterly 3, no. 2 (April 1981):286–319. See also "Sea-Law Conference Begins Final Phase," *UN Chronicle 18* (May 1981); and *Newsweek*, March 23, 1981.

16. The Chinese apparently knew how, but chose not to.

17. Mahbub ul Haq, *The Poverty Curtain* (New York: Columbia Univ. Press, 1976), p. 162. For more on the impact of colonialism on the Third World, see Walter Rodney, *How Europe Undeveloped Africa* (London: Bogle-L'Ouverture Pub., 1972). Rodney explains how European nations found culturally sophisticated African nations and under colonial practices gradually stripped them of their cultural, social, and economic vitality. In a shorter but succinct case study, Cristobal Kay points out the injustices that prevailed during the first years of European contact in South America ("Comparative Development of the European Manorial System and the Latin American Hacienda System," *Journal of Peasant Studies 2*, no. 2 [January 1975]). It would be silly, of course, to accept uncritically Marxist scholars who explain all history in terms of class struggle, but there is equal danger in denying the importance of history as a crucial explanatory factor. P. T. Bauer, for example, in *Equality, the Third World, and Economic Delusion* (Cambridge, Mass.: Harvard Univ. Press, 1981), disregards history and argues instead that current economic inequalities are almost totally due to differences in ingenuity, effort, and resource distribution rather than to historical misuses of political and economic power. But Bauer's extremism on the one side is just as wrong as the Marxist extremism on the other. For a balanced criticism of Bauer from a rather traditional economist, see Amartya Sen, "Just Desserts," a review of Bauer's book in the *New York Review of Books*, 4 March 1982. David Beckmann, a Christian economist who formerly worked at the World Bank, attributes much of Third World poverty to colonial and other exploitative practices, *Where Faith and Economics Meet* (Minneapolis: Augsburg Press, 1981).

18. Gunnar Myrdal, *Asian Drama: An Inquiry into the Poverty of Nations*, 3 vols. (New York: Twentieth Century Fund, 1968), 1:455. See pp. 447–62 for a more extended analysis.

19. For two divergent views about the origin and validity of mercantilism, see William Cunningham, "Medieval and Modern Economic Ideas Contrasted," *Growth of English Industry and Commerce*, 3 vols. (London: John Murray, 1910), 1:457–72; and G. Schmoller, *The Mercantile System and Its Historical Significance* (New York: Macmillan, 1895).

20. James B. McGinnis, *Bread and Justice* (New York: Paulist Press, 1979), pp. 29–31.

21. June Kronholz, "Gabon's Been Working on Its New Railroad, but Pay Day is Far Off," *Wall Street Journal*, July 30, 1981, pp. 1ff.
22. Joan Robinson shows how trade structures and land and labor institutions in the Third World, as well as international financial structures, all developed substantially from the foundation that was laid in the colonial era. Robinson, *Aspects of Development and Underdevelopment* (Cambridge: At the University Press, 1979).

Chapter 8

1. Mooneyham, *Hungry World*, pp. 117, 128.
2. See the helpful distinction of different types of economies today in *Transformation*, July–September, 1995, p. 18.
3. Democratic socialism refers to a society where politically there is a democratic rather than a totalitarian political arrangement, but the economy is largely centrally planned and state-owned.
4. BFWI, *Hunger 1997*, p. 15.
5. UNDP, *Human Development Report 1993*, p. 44.
6. Of the 373 changes in investment rules in developing countries between 1991 and 1994, all but five encourage international investment, which comes largely from multinational corporations. (From a personal memo from Linwood T. Geiger.)
7. See the paper by economist Linwood T. Geiger, "Market Activity and the Poor," *Transformation* (July, 1995), p. 20. This paper was prepared for the Third Oxford Conference on Christian Faith and Economics (Agra, 1995).
8. World Bank, *World Development Report 1995*, p. 5. One study covering 1970–1990 compared 37 countries where the relative importance of the country's exports was falling with 32 countries where exports were rising. Real wages grew an average of 3 percent per year in countries where exports were rising and fell where exports were declining in importance. In the first set of countries, the ratio of exports to GNP was falling; in the latter, this ratio was rising. World Bank, *World Development Report 1995*, p. 5.
9. Other possible negative factors may also occur. Local elites that work with global corporations to prevent poor workers from developing unions reduces or prevents the benefit of increasing wages. And unnecessary shipping of materials around the world is environmentally foolish.

10. Paul Samuelson's "factor price equalization theorem," articulated decades ago, has been confirmed repeatedly.

11. World Bank, *World Development Report 1995*, p. 104. The data, however, is not entirely conclusive. And it is debated! The United Nations' Human Development Report 1993 says: "Three quarters of adjusting countries in Sub-Saharan Africa have suffered declining per capita incomes and in Latin America the declines were at least as bad" (p. 45). We must remain open to further, more extensive data. Obviously, not every kind of privatization is good. See the section on the "Seven Sins of Privatization," ibid., pp. 49–51.

12. UNDP, *Human Development Report 1992*, front page and inside front page. See also *Together*, January–March, 1995, p. 1.

13. Simon Kuznets first proposed the hypothesis of the "Inverted U." See Geiger, "Market Activity and Poverty," pp. 27–28.

14. Geiger, "Market Activity and Poverty," pp. 27–28.

15. Geiger, "Market Activity and Poverty," p. 28. See also Juliet B. Schor, *The Overworked American* (New York: Basic Books, 1992).

16. Lester C. Thurow, *The Failure of Capitalism* (New York: Morrow, 1996), p. 73.

17. Korten, *When Corporations Rule the World*, p. 111.

18. Personal communication with Jeff Ballinger of *Press for Change*, a corporate watchdog group, on 5/22/96. It is also true that the wages these 18,000 workers earn (around $2.50 per day), are higher than prevailing Indonesian wages.

19. *Time*, June 17, 1996, p. 30.

20. Not all cultural change is bad. A small, poor nation with twenty small tribes and twenty different languages and no modern sense of time will be unable to participate in the global economy. Certainly they are welcome to retain their traditional culture, but they should not then blame the rest of the world for their poverty.

21. Quoted in Juliet B. Schor, *The Overworked American* (New York: Harper Collins, 1992), p. 120.

22. Quoted in George F. Will, "The Politics of Soulcraft," *Newsweek*, May 13, 1996, p. 82.

23. Korten, *When Corporations Rule the World*, p. 152.

24. Quoted in David C. Korten, *When Corporations Rule the World* (West Hartford: Kumarian Press Inc., 1996), p. 158.

25. M. Douglas Meeks, *God the Economist* (Minneapolis: Fortress, 1989), p. 39.

26. This is not to say communist societies did better. In fact, the environmental destruction in the former Soviet bloc is much worse than in the West.

27. UNDP, *Human Development Report 1993*, p. 37.

28. For a summary, see Gheddo, *Why is the Third World Poor?* pp. 69–100.

29. Brown, *State of the World 1990*, p. 144.

30. Todaro, *Economic Development*, 1994, p. 490–91.

31. Brown, *State of the World 1990*, p. 144.

32. UNDP, *Human Development Report 1992*, pp. 5–6. If one includes lack of access to capital markets and labor markets (industrialized countries preventing workers in developing countries from migrating and sending back money to their families), the figure is $500 billion per year, ten times what they receive in foreign aid.

33. BFWI, *Hunger 95*, p. 23.

34. Theodore Morgan, *Economic Development: Concept and Strategy* (New York: Harper and Row, 1975), p. 316.

35. McGinnis, *Bread and Justice*, p. 72.

36. World Bank, *World Development Report 1992*, p. 63.

37. The Food and Agriculture Organization of the United Nations (FAO), *The State of Food and Agriculture 1995*, (Rome: 1995), p. 244.

38. James P. Grant, "Can the Churches Promote Development?" *Ecumenical Review 26* (January 1974):26.

39. BFWI, *Hunger 1995*, p. 24.

40. World Bank, *World Development Report 1995*, p. 57. The UNDP estimates that the global gains will be $275 billion by 2002, with less than one-third going to developing countries. UNDP, *Human Development Report 1994*, p. 63.

41. UNDP, *Human Development Report 1994*, p. 63.

42. World Bank, *World Development Report 1995*, p. 58.

43. World Bank, *World Development Report 1987* (Washington, D.C.: Oxford University Press, 1987), table 8.3, p. 142.

44. UNDP, *Human Development Report 1992*, p. 63.

45. Dominick Salvatore, International Economics (Prentice Hall: Englewood Cliffs, NJ, 1995), p. 263.

46. Militades Chacholiades, *International Economics* (McGraw Hill: NY, 1990), p. 209.

47. "Brazil vs. The U.S.," *New York Times*, January 7, 1968; "Brazil Agrees to Accept Terms," *Wall Street Journal*, February 20, 1968.

48. World Bank, *World Development Report 1992*, Tables 3, 14, and 16, quoted in Todaro, *Economic Development*, p. 416.

49. Gheddo, *Why is the Third World Poor?* p. 83.

50. *New Internationalist*, August 1975, p. 1.

51. Barbara Segal, "The Debt Crisis," BFW Background Paper, 1990.

52. See, for example, United Nations, *World Economic and Social Survey 1995*, p. 38.

53. World Bank, *World Development Report 1991*, p. 106.

54. Todaro, *Economic Development*, 1994, p. 418; estimated from figure 12.2.

55. Todaro, *Economic Development*, 1989, p. 376.

56. Between 1950 and 1980, the share of the natural rubber (from trees) in total world rubber consumption fell from 62 percent to 28 percent and cotton's share of total fiber use fell from 41 percent to 29 percent. Todaro, *Economic Development*, 1994, p. 431.

57. Stan Mooneyham, *Hungry World*, pp. 117–8.

58. UNDP, *Human Development Report 1992*, p. 46.

59. World Bank, *World Development Report 1995*, p. 206.

60. Ibid., p. 162.

61. Oxfam, *Multilateral Debt*, p. 12.

62. BFW, *Africa's Debt Burden: Briefing Paper*, February 8, 1995, pp. 1–2.

63. Kenneth Jameson and Peter Henriot, "International Debt, Austerity and the Poor," Lee Travis, ed., *Rekindling Development* (Notre Dame: University of Notre Dame Press, 1988), pp. 15–56.

64. In Brady deals, commercial banks agreed to write off or renegotiate some of a country's debt, and a multilateral institution, like the World Bank or the IMF, agreed to provide collateral for the remaining debt.

65. Todaro, *Economic Development*, 1994, p. 469.

66. Ibid., pp. 465–66.

67. Oxfam, *Multilateral Debt*, February, 1996, p. 3.

68. World Bank, *World Debt Tables 1994–95*, p. 37. Burundi, Central African Republic, Cote d'Ivore, Equatorial Guinea, Ethiopia, Ghana, Guinea, Guinea–Bissau, Guyana, Honduras, Kenya, Laos, Liberia, Madagascar, Mali, Mauritania, Mozambique, Myanmar, Nicaragua, Niger, Nigeria, Rwanda, Sao Tome and Principe, Sierra Leone, Somalia, Sudan, Tanzania, Uganda, Viet Nam, Yemen, Zaire and Zambia. Each country has either a ratio of the present value of debt service to GNP above 80 percent or a ratio the present value of debt service to exports above 220 percent.

69. Oxfam, *Multilateral Debt*, February, 1996, p. 3.

70. William R. Cline, *International Debt and the Stability of the World Economy* (1983: Institute for International Economics, Washington, D.C.); see also Todaro, *Economic Development*, 1989, p. 423).

71. Oxfam International Position Paper, *Multilateral Debt: The Human Costs*, February, 1996, p. 10.

72. Oxfam, *Multilateral Debt*, p. 10.

73. Ibid., p. 11.

74. Ibid., p. 10.

75. World Bank, *World Development Report 1996*, p. 198.

76. UNDP, *Human Development Report 1995*, p. 169.

77. Ethiopia (47 percent); Nigeria (43 percent); World Bank, *World Development Report 1996*, p. 198.

78. BFW Background Paper, No. 137 in BFW *Newsletter*, Nov/Dec, 1996.

79. Union of Concerned Scientists, *World Scientists' Warning to Humanity*, http://www-formal.stanford.edu/jmc/progress/ucs-statement.txt.

80. "Population: Delusion and Reality," Michael Cromartie, *Nine Lives of Population Control*, p. 118.

81. Brown, *State of the World 1996*, p. 158.

82. This table comes from Robert Engelman, *Stabilizing the Atmosphere: Population, Consumption and Greenhouse Gases* (Washington, D.C.: Population and Environment Program, 1994), n.p. (the chart was included with the book).

83. Union of Concerned Scientists, Frequently Asked Questions about Climate Change, #5, http://www.UCSUSA.org/global/climfaq.html (February, 1997).

84. Union of Concerned Scientists, The Science of Climate Change, #5, http://www.UCSUSA.org/global/climbacksci.html (February, 1997).

85. Brown, *State of the World 1996*, p. 30.

86. Ibid.

87. Rain Forest Action Network, *Rates of Rainforest Loss*, http://www.ran.org/ran/info-center/rates.html (February, 1997).

88. Food and Agriculture Organization of the United Nations, Monitoring the State of World's Forests, http://www.fao.org/unfao/FORES-E.HTM (October, 1996).

89. *New York Times*, August 4, 1996, p. 9.

90. Tropical Deforestation and Habitat Destruction, http://www.esd.ornl.gov/iab2-4.htm (February, 1997).

91. Quoted from Susan George, *A Fate Worse Than Debt* (New York: Grove Press, 1988), pp. 164–65.

92. Tropical Deforestation: Not Just a problem in Amazonia, http://cotf.edu/ETE/scen/rainforest/deforestation.html (February, 1997).

93. Ibid.

94. Rainforest Action Network, Rates of Rainforest Loss, http://www.ran.org/info_center/rates.html (February, 1997).

95. Robert C. Williams, *Export Agriculture and the Crisis in Central America* (Chapel Hill: University of North Carolina Press, 1986), pp. 116–17.

96. Brown, *State of the World 1988*, p. 86.

97. Brown, *State of the World 1989*, pp. 31–32.

98. *The Developing World: Danger Point for U.S. Security*, released on August 1, 1989, to the Arms Control and Foreign Policy Caucus in the U.S. Congress, p. 32.

99. Dr. Peter Raven, *Why It Matters*, http://www.gene.com/AE/AB/IWT/Why It Matters.html (February, 1997).

100. Rainforest Action Network, Rates of Rainforest Loss, http://www.ran.org/info_center/rates.html (February, 1997).

101. G. Tyler Miller, Jr., *Living in the Environment* (Belmont, CA: Wadsworth, 1988), p. 197.

102. Calvin B. DeWitt, *Earth-Wise*, (Grand Rapids, MI: CRC Publications, 1994), pp. 30–31.

103. Environmental Development Research Centre, *Environmental Insecurity*, http://runet.edu/CollegeDept/Geography/GEOG340/read 001.html (February 1997).

104. Brown, *State of the World 1990*, p. 3.

105. Worldwatch Institute, *Worldwatch Vital Signs Brief 96–1*, http://www.worldwatch.org/worldwatch/alerts/pr960125. html.

106. Sen, "Population, Delusion and Reality," Cromartie, *Nine Lives of Population Control*, pp. 114–16.

107. Lester Brown, Lester Brown Guru Lectures, http://globeint.org/html/guru-lectures/brown-toc.html (September, 1996).

108. Lester Brown, *State of the World 1989*, p. 46.

109. Charles H. Southwick, ed., *Global Ecology* (Sutherland, MA: Sinauer Associates Inc., 1983), pp. 166, 169.

110. Brown, *State of the World 1990*, p. 185.

111. Ibid., p. 148.

112. Quoted in BFWI, *Hunger 95*, p. 67.

113. Jean Dreze and Amartya Sen, *Hunger and Public Action* (New York: Oxford Univ. Press, 1989), p. 90.

114. Quoted in Dreze and Sen, *Hunger and Public Action*, p. 90.

115. Dreze and Sen, *Hunger and Public Action*, p. 91.

116. For a summary, see part 3 of Frances Moore Lappe and Joseph Collins, *Food First* (Boston: Houghton Mifflin, 1977).

117. Quoted in Lappe and Collins, *Food First*, p. 77.

118. J. Jeffrey Leonard, *Natural Resources and Economic Development in Central America: A Regional Environment Profile* (Washington, DC: International Institute for Environment and Development, 1987), pp. 179–80.

119. See the careful study by Robert G. Williams, *Export Agriculture and the Crisis in Central America* (Chapel Hill: University of North Carolina Press, 1986).

120. Ibid., p. 170.

121. Beverly Keene, "Export Cropping in Central America," *BFW Background Paper*, No. 43 (Jan. 1980).

122. Williams, *Export Agriculture*, p. 170.

123. See chapter 11, notes 8–10.

124. Williams, *Export Agriculture*, p. 160.

125. Keene, "Export Cropping."

126. Ricki Ross, "Land and Hunger: Philippines," *BFW Background Paper*, no. 55 (July 1981).

127. See chapter 3 in my *Non-violence: The Invincible Weapon?* (Dallas: Word, 1989).

128. Todaro, *Economic Development*, 1977, p. 326.

129. Todaro, *Economic Development*, 1989, p. 469.

130. UNDP, *Human Development Report 1994*, p. 62, figure 4.1.

131. Class lectures, Dr. Lin Geiger.

132. Todaro, *Economic Development*, 1977, pp. 328–29.

133. World Bank, *World Development Report 1995*, p. 62.

134. Todaro, *Economic Development*, 1994, pp. 529–530.

135. Todaro, *Economic Development*, 1994, p. 530.

136. Ibid.

137. An oligopoly is a situation in which a small number of companies control the market in a given commodity or service.

138. Todaro, *Economic Development*, 1989, p. 474.

139. See my "Towards a Political Philosophy," *ESA/Advocate*, Oct. 1988, pp. 1ff.

140. Streeten and Lall (as noted in Donald Hay, "The International Socio-Economic-Political Order and Our Lifestyle," in Ronald J. Sider, ed., *Lifestyles in the Eighties* [Philadelphia: Westminster, 1982], p. 113) found in their sampling of MNC investments in LDCs that only 12 percent of new capital investment represented an inflow of funds from outside the LDCs. See also Hay's more recent discussion of MNCs in *Economics Today* (1989), pp. 264–66.

141. Korten, *When Corporations Rule the World*, p. 79.

142. Hay, "International Socio-Economic Political Order," p. 84.

143. *New York Times*, "An Indonesian Asset is Also a Liability," 3/16/96, p. B1, B36.

144. Ibid.

145. Korten, *When Corporations Rule the World*, p. 129.

146. Barnet, "Multinationals and Development," p. 224; also mentioned by Hay, "International Socio-Economic Political Order," p. 113.

147. Korten, *When Corporations Rule the World*, p. 159.

148. Ivan Illich, author of "Outwitting the 'Developed' Countries," *The Political Economy of Development and Underdevelopment*, ed. Charles K. Wilber (New York: Random House, 1979), pp. 436–44, is a development ethicist who is particularly galled by the proliferation of soft drinks in the LDCs.

149. Danny Collum, "Nestle Boycott," *Sojourners* (October 1989), p. 8.

150. UNICEF, *The State of the World's Children 1990*, p. 26.

151. UNICEF, *The State of the World's Children 1995*, p. 20.

152. UNICEF, *The State of the World's Children 1982–83*, pp. 3–4.

153. Letter from James P. Grant, Executive Director of UNICEF, to Regional Directors, August 16, 1989.

154. Collum, "Nestle Boycott." For more information about the boycott, see above, p. 173.

155. Unpublished material from Action for Corporate Accountability, June 1996.

156. H. W. Walter, "Marketing in Developing Countries," *Columbia Journal of World Business* (Winter, 1974), quoted in Lappe and Collins, *Food First*, p. 309.

157. Todaro, *Economic Development*, 1977, p. 330; Todaro's emphasis.

158. See Todaro's overall assessment, *Economic Development*, 1994, pp. 535, 537.

159. "A Voice for Women," *Transformation*, January–March 1992, p. 21.

160. UNDP, *Human Development Report 1995*, p. 4.

161. Todaro, *Economic Development*, 1994, p. 151.

162. UNDP, *Human Development Report 1995*, p. 35.

163. Ibid., p. 35.

164. United Nations, *The World's Women 1995: Trends and Statistics*, chart 4.1.

165. UNDP, *Human Development Report 1995*, p. 38.

166. Ibid., p. 35.

167. Tripp, *Transformation*, January–March, 1992, p. 23.

168. UNDP, *Human Development Report 1994*, p. 98. (For the Human Development Index and PPP$, see chapter 2, pp. 27–28).

169. UNDP, *Human Development Report 1993*, p. 18.

170. UNDP, *Human Development Report 1994*, p. 98.

171. BFWI, *Hunger 1995: Causes of Hunger*, pp. 74–75.

172. BFWI, *Hunger 1996*, p. 11.

173. Ibid., p. 95.

174. Ibid., p. 17.

175. BFWI, *Hunger 1995*, p. 39.

176. BFWI, *Hunger 1996*, p. 11.

177. *Markings* (New York: Knopf, 1964), p. xxi.

178. See "Bananas," *New Internationalist*, August 1975, p. 32.

179. Only $1.25 million was actually paid.

180. *Philadelphia Inquirer*, April 10, 1975, pp. 1–2.

181. "Action," *New Internationalist*, August 1975, p. 32.

182. Carl Oglesby and Richard Schaull, *Containment and Change* (NY: Macmillan, 1967), p. 104; and Stephen Schlesinger and Stephen Kinzer, *Bitter Fruit: The Untold Story of the American Coup in Guatemala* (Garden City, NY: Doubleday, 1982).

183. See, for instance, Schlesinger and Kinzer, *Bitter Fruit*.

184. "America's World Role: Should We Feel Guilty?" *Philadelphia Inquirer*, July 18, 1974, p. 7a.

185. See the helpful comments on this in Patrick Kerans, *Sinful Social Structures* (New York: Paulist Press, 1974), pp. 47–51.

Chapter 9

1. Ronald J. Sider, ed., *The Chicago Declaration* (Carol Stream, IL: Creation House, 1974), p. 2.

2. J. D. Douglas, ed., *Let the Earth Hear His Voice: International Congress on World Evangelization*, Lausanne, Switzerland (Minneapolis: World Wide Publications, 1975), p. 6, sect. 9.

3. "Creation, Technology, and Human Survival," *Plenary Address*, WCC's Fifth Assembly, 1 December 1975. This is a recent rendition of Elizabeth Seton's statement, "Live simply that others may simply live."

4. *New York Times*, 14 June 1973.

5. This sermon was one of the series of sermons which constituted the standard doctrines of the early Methodists. See *The Works of John Wesley*, 14 vols. (1872; reprint ed., Grand Rapids, Mich.: Zondervan, n.d.), 5:361–77.

6. Ibid., pp. 365–68.

7. J. Wesley Bready, *England: Before and After Wesley* (London: Hodder and Stoughton, n.d.), p. 238.

8. See his moving testimony, "From Galloping Gourmet to Serving the Poor," in my *Lifestyles in the Eighties*, pp. 174–82; and more recently, "The Graham Kerr Story: From Galloping Gourmet to Kingdom Cook," *PRISM*, September–October, 1996, pp. 16–19.

9. See Gene M. Daffern, "One Man Can Make a Difference," *These Times*, September 1982, pp. 6–11.

10. Doris Longacre, *Living More with Less* (Scottdale, PA: Herald Press, 1980). See also the personal testimonies in Ronald J. Sider, ed., *Living More Simply: Biblical Principles and Practical Models* (Downers Grove, IL: InterVarsity, 1980), pp. 59–159.

11. Ginny Hearn and Walter Hearn, "The Price is Right," *Right On*, May 1973, pp. 1, 11.

12. You can get the current figure from the U.S. Bureau of the Census.

13. Michael Harper, *A New Way of Living* (Plainfield, NJ: Logos International, 1973), p. 93.

14. See my suggestions on this in "Living More Simply for Evangelism and Justice," in Sider, *Lifestyles in the Eighties*, pp. 32–35.

15. See my response to the critique of this distinction in John Schneider, *Godly Materialism* (Downers Grove, IL: InterVarsity, 1994), in "Rich Christians in an Age of Hunger—Revisited," *Christian Scholars' Review*, XXVI:3 (Spring, 1997), p. 328.

16. For great examples, see my *Cup of Water, Bread of Life* (Grand Rapids, MI: Zondervan, 1994) and *One-Sided Christianity?* (Grand Rapids, MI: Zondervan, 1993). In addition, *Transformation* and *PRISM* regularly publish wholistic models of evangelism and social concern.

17. Lester R. Brown with Erick P. Eckholm, *By Bread Alone* (New York: Praeger, 1974), p. 198.

18. The figure for grain used in making alcoholic beverages is from the U.S. Department of Agriculture. One ton of grain will feed five persons in India for a year.
19. I owe much to John F. Alexander in the development of these criteria.
20. Criteria a, c, d, and f are adapted from Edward R. Dayton, "Where to Go from Here," Fuller Seminary's *Theology News and Notes*, October 1975, p. 19.
21. Quoted from a fund-raising piece written by John F. Alexander. Much has changed in Liberia since John wrote these words in 1976, but they still illustrate the criteria I have listed.
22. See my *Cup of Water, Bread of Life* (Grand Rapids, MI: Zondervan, 1994), chapter 7.
23. This is a rough estimate. Efficiency ratios would change if we did MED on this scale. Not all poor folk would be good entrepreneurs. But the impact would still be enormous. For the address of Opportunity, see the Appendix—Organizations.
24. See chapter 11, p. 233. For a copy of the Agra Covenant and more information on micro loans, write to ESA, 10 Lancaster Avenue, Wynnewood, PA 19096, or call 1-800-650-6600.
25. John and Sylvia Ronsvalle, *The State of Church Giving through 1994* (Champaign, IL: Empty Tomb, Inc., 1997). This chart is used with their permission.
26. Personal conversation with Sylvia Ronsvalle, January 31, 1997. As the Ronsvalles indicate in their studies (see note 25), precise figures on non-church giving are not available.
27. Larry Minear, *New Hope for the Hungry* (New York: Friendship Press, 1975), p. 79.

Chapter 10
1. The Latin phrase means, "Beyond the church, there is no salvation."
2. Dave Jackson and Neta Jackson, *Living Together in a World Falling Apart* (Carol Stream, IL: Creation House, 1974), p. 15.
3. For a discussion of Reba Place, see Jackson and Jackson, *Living Together in a World Falling Apart*, esp. pp. 36–39, 230–33. I received more recent information through personal corrrespondence with Virgil Vogt, one of Reba Place's oldest leaders.
4. See my "Spare the Rod and Spoil the Church," *Eternity*, October, 1976.

5. From John Wesley's account (1748) of the origin of the class meetings (*The Works of John Wesley*, 8:269).

6. Peter Berger, *A Rumor of Angels* (Garden City, NY: Anchor Books, 1970), p. 34 (also pp. 6–37). See also Peter Berger and Thomas Luckman, *The Social Construction of Reality* (Garden City, NY: Doubleday, 1956).

7. Berger, *A Rumor of Angels*, p. 17. See further pp. 41ff for Berger's rejection of the common idea that the sociology of knowledge leads inexorably to thoroughgoing relativism.

8. See Floyd Filson, "The Significance of the Early House Churches," *Journal of Biblical Literature* 58 (1939):105–12.

9. This is not its real name. The congregation (which I have known for almost thirty years) has experienced some difficult struggles in the last ten years, but those problems are not the result of its exciting exploration of genuine Christian community.

10. I have relied largely on Gordon Cosby's Handbook for Mission Groups (Waco, TX: Word, 1975) for this discussion. See also Elizabeth O'Connor's several books, all of which are rooted in the experience of Church of the Savior, including: *Call to Commitment* (New York: Harper & Row, 1963), *Journey Inward, Journey Outward* (New York: Harper & Row, 1968). For further information, write to: Church of the Savior, 2025 Massachusetts Ave., N.W., Washington, D.C. 20036.

11. Cosby, *Handbook for Mission Groups*, p. 63.

12. Ibid., p. 140.

13. Ronald Klaus and I are currently at work on a book on how small groups can be effective instruments for far-reaching discipling.

14. Howard A. Snyder, *The Problem of Wineskins: Church Structure in a Technological Age* (Downers Grove, IL: InterVarsity, 1975), pp. 140–42. See also his *Liberating the Church: The Ecology of Church and Kingdom* (Downers Grove, IL: InterVarsity, 1983).

15. See Jackson and Jackson, *Living Together in a World Falling Apart*, esp. pp. 36–39, 230–33.

16. For a good historical perspective on Christian communes and an excellent bibliography, see Donald G. Bloesch, *Wellsprings of Renewal: Promise in Christian Communal Life* (Grand Rapids, MI: Eerdmans, 1974). For a handbook by a Catholic charismatic, see Stephen B. Clark, *Building Christian Communities* (Notre Dame, IN: Ave Maria Press, 1972). And very recently,

David Janzen, et al., *Fire, Salt and Peace: Intentional Christian Communities Alive in North America* (1996); write to David Janzen, 726 Seward, Evanston, IL 60602.

17. I owe this idea to a lively conversation with a good friend, Malcolm Street, who asked, after I was arrested in Washington, D.C. for protesting cuts in government programs for the poor, why I did not challenge the churches just as strongly!

Chapter 11

1. See my "Towards an Evangelical Political Philosophy," available from ESA, 10 Lancaster Ave., Wynnewood, PA 19096.

2. See my plea for tolerance and understanding of the specific reasons for disagreement in "A Plea for More Radical Conservatives and More Conserving Radicals," *Transformation*, January–March, 1987, pp. 11–16.

3. See my *Non-Violence: The Invincible Weapon?* (Dallas: Word, 1989); *Nuclear Holocaust and Christian Hope* (Downers Grove, IL: InterVarsity, 1982), co-authored with Richard K. Taylor; and earlier my *Christ and Violence* (Scottdale, PA: Herald Press, 1978).

4. See note 1.

5. See, for example, page 5–6 in chapter 1 and corresponding notes pages 25–27.

6. See, for example, Normal Faramelli, "Trade Barriers to Development in Poor Nations," *The Causes of World Hunger*, ed. William Byron (New York: Paulist Press, 1982), chapter 9.

7. Quoted in Ernest Levinsohn, "Getting Aid to the Poor," *BFW Background Paper*, no. 59 (April 1982):2.

8. See, for instance, Ogelsby and Shaull, *Containment and Change*, pp. 72–111.

9. Amnesty International, *Report on Torture* (New York: Farrar, Straus, and Giroux, 1975), especially the special report on Chile on pp. 243ff. See also Fred B. Morris, "Sustained by Faith under Brazilian Torture," *Christian Century*, January 22, 1975, pp. 56–60; *Latin America and Empire Report* 10, no. 1, January 1976; and BFWI, "Military Aid, the World's Poor and U.S. Security." The School of the Americas (SOA), in Georgia, trains military personnel from other countries. Among its graduates: Manuel Noriega, currently serving 40 years for drug trafficking. Also, a 1992 international human rights tribunal in Colombia cited 246 officers for human rights violations. 100 of them were SOA graduates. *At the Crossroads: The Future of Foreign Aid*, (Silver Spring, MD: BFWI, 1995), p. 15.

10. "School of the Dictators," *New York Times*, September 28, 1996, p. 22.

11. Penny Lernoux, *Cry of the People* (New York: Penguin, 1982).

12. BFWI, *Hunger 1995*, p. 30.

13. William E. Spriggs and Robert E. Scott, "Economists' Views of Workers' Rights and U.S. Trade Policy," A working paper for the U.S. Congress Joint Economic Committee, reprinted by the Center for International Business Education and Research (http://www.bmgt.umd.edu/Ciber/wp60.html), 1996, p. 14. I owe this reference to a former student, Fred Clark.

14. Ibid., p. 4.

15. Ibid., p. 4.

16. Todaro, *Economic Development*, 1994, p. 530. The United States is home to 44 of the largest 100 MNCs, while Japan is second with 18.

17. See UNICEF, *The State of the World's Children 1982–83*, pp. 3–4.

18. "The Breast vs. the Bottle," *Newsweek*, 1 June 1981, p. 54.

19. This is not to argue that the total impact of MNCs is negative. For information on the Nestle boycott and the analyses of its impact, write to the Interfaith Centre on Corporate Responsibility (475 Riverside Drive, New York, NY 10027) and Action for Corporate Accountability (3255 Hennepin Avenue South, Suite 230, Minneapolis, MN 55408).

20. Robert E. Frykenberg, ed., *Land Tenure and the Peasant in South Asia: An Anthology of Recent Research* (Madison, WI: Land Tenure Center, 1976), p. 14.

21. See the discussion in my *One Sided Christianity?* pp. 114–18 and all the stories in my *Cup of Water, Bread of Life*.

22. See the interesting Indian case study, Saral K. Chatterji, *Religious Values and Economic Development: A Case Study*, Social Research Series, no. 5 (Bangalore: Christian Institute for the Study of Religion and Society, 1967).

23. I am using the word capital in a broader sense than do most economists. I use it as a short hand for productive resources.

24. UNDP, *Human Development Report 1992*, p. 36. Wealth is defined as domestic savings. The actual figures are much worse than this. The reason? In making these calculations, the UNDP used only averages for each country. If we took the poorest people anywhere in the world, the figures would be worse. The United Nations estimates that the richest 20 percent of the world's persons are at least 150 times richer than the poorest 20 percent. UNDP, *Human Development Report 1992*, p. 3.

25. One interesting example is the Central Provident Fund in Singapore (see the *Economist*, January 13, 1996, p. 38).

26. "Mothers vs. Mullahs," *Newsweek*, April 17, 1995, p. 56. One cautionary note is important. It's not clear that the Grameen Bank has paid enough attention to strengthening both husbands and wives and therefore the family unit. It is not progress to empower women in ways that destroy family life.

27. Quoted from *Transformation*, July 1995, p. 8. It should be noted that the statement assumes that the efficiency ratio would remain the same when 200 million micro-loans were made. In practice it would change—and probably fall.

28. Bureaucratic regulations designed to favor special groups must also be abolished. See Hernando de Soto, *The Other Path: The Invisible Revolution in the Third World* (New York: Harper, 1989).

29. This is precisely what American society did in the 1860s.

30. Todaro, *Economic Development*, 1994, p. 590.

31. United Nations, *Human Development Report 1993*, p. 30.

32. Ibid., p. 38.

33. World Bank, *World Development Report 1991*, pp. 5–11. See its helpful summary of criteria for market-friendly government activity.

34. BFWI, *Hunger 1995*, p. 49. See also Jean Dreze and Amartya Sen, *Hunger and Public Action*, (New York: Oxford Univ. Press, 1989), p. 13.

35. World Bank, *World Development 1991*, p. 6.

36. World Bank, *World Development Report 1991*, p. 9. One of the committees from the Third Oxford Conference on Christian Faith and Economics offered an excellent summary of what the market does well and poorly; see sections 3 and 4 of "The Market Economy," *Transformation*, July 1995, p. 12.

37. See "If the GDP is Up Why is America Down?" *Atlantic Monthly*, October 1995, pp. 59–78. The organization's address is: Redefining Progress, 116 New Montgomery, Suite 209, San Francisco, CA 94105.

38. Professor Lin Geiger has shared with me some substantial reservations about some of their assumptions.

39. For example, the UNDP Human Development Index uses statistics on health and education as well as income to measure human development. See *Human Development Report 1992*, pp. 12–25.

40. This section is a revised version of my column in *PRISM*, January–February, 1996, p. 34.

41. Lester C. Thurow, *The Zero-Sum Society* (New York: Viking, 1981), pp. 103–107.

42. Richard A. Easterlin, "Does Money Buy Happiness?" *The Public Interest, no. 3*

(Winter 1973):10. See also Martin Bolt and David G. Myers, "Why Do the Rich Feel So Poor?" in *The Human Connection* (Downers Grove, IL: InterVarsity, 1984); and Paul L. Wachtel, *The Poverty of Affluence: A Psychological Portrait of the American Way of Life* (New York: Macmillan, 1983).

43. Christians ought to provide powerful counter-evidence to Francis Fukuyama's prediction that democratic consumer capitalism will prevail everywhere by offering happiness through material abundance and overwhelm all claims that persons do not live by bread alone. See Francis Fukuyama, "The End of History," *The National Interest* (Summer, 1989), pp. 3–18.

44. Guy F. Erb, "U.S. Trade Policies toward Developing Areas," *Columbia Journal of World Business*, no. 3 (Fall 1973):60.

45. World Bank, *World Development Report 1987*, p. 150.

46. Brandt, North-South, p. 186. For some alternatives to trade adjustment assistance, see chapter 11 by George R. Neumann in *International Trade and Finance: Readings*, eds. Robert E. Baldwin and David J. Richardson, 2d ed. (Boston, Mass.: Little, Brown, 1981).

47. Donald Hay, *Economics Today*, p. 262.

48. *The Reality of Aid 1996*, (Silver Spring, MD: BFWI, 1996) p. 197.

49. I want to thank Fred Clark for calling the following data to my attention.

50. I am not ignoring or rejecting the comparative advantage that poor nations have because all labor costs there are much lower than in rich nations. As I pointed out (p. 139), using this comparative advantage is one way greater global justice emerges. But it is important that just labor laws and active unions exist in poor nations so that workers receive a fair share of the benefits from global trade.

51. Spriggs and Scott, p. 2.

52. Perhaps via trade sanctions through the World Trade Organization.

53. See *Boycott Quarterly* (P.O. Box 30727, Seattle, WA 98103) and the Interfaith Center on Corporate Responsibility (see appendix).

54. UNDP, *Human Development Report 1994*, p. 63.

55. See "Relieving Third World Debt," published by the USCC (September 27, 1989), pp. 30–31.

56. Oxfam, *Multilateral Debt*, February, 1996, p. 2.

57. BFW Background Paper No. 137 in *BFW Newsletter*, Nov/Dec, 1996; *Economist*, October 5, 1996, p. 70, and November 9, 1996, p. 95.

58. Oxfam, *Multilateral Debt*, February, 1996, p. 2.

59. Ibid., p. 17.

60. Todaro, *Economic Development*, 1994, p. 467.

61. Oxfam, *Multilateral Debt*, February, 1996, p. 18.

62. BFW Background Paper No. 137, in *BFW Newsletter*, Nov/Dec, 1996.

63. The United Nations Environmental Programme, The United Nations Framework Convention on Climate Change: What Does It Mean? http://www.unep.ch/iucc/leaflet.html (October, 1996).

64. World Bank, *Mainstreaming the Environment* (Washington, D.C.: World Bank, 1995), p. 2.

65. Michael Brower, "The Renewable Alternative, Cool Energy," in Union of Concerned Scientists, ed., *World Scientists' Warning Briefing Book* (Cambridge: Union of Concerned Scientists, 1993), p. 73.

66. Sayed El-Sayed and Gert L. Van Dijken, *The Southeastern Meditteranean Ecosystem Revisited*, http://www.ocean.tamv.edu/Quarterdeck/QD3.1/Elsayed/elsayed.html (October, 1996).

67. Worldwatch, "Wind Power Fastest Growing Energy Source Ready to Displace Coal, Slow Climate Change" (Press release, August 14, 1996).

68. Brown, *State of the World 1996*, p. 154.

69. Ibid.

70. Ibid., p. 155.

71. Andrew Steer (in a personal letter to me, April 9, 1996).

72. Michael Totten and Nita Settina, Energy Wise Options for State and Local Governments, http://www.solstice.crest.org/efficiency/energywise_options/ch2-5html (October, 1996).

73. Ibid.

74. Ibid. Thus, in China, bicycles outnumber cars 250–1. Since it takes the same energy and resources needed to produce 100 bicycles that it takes to produce one car, this is a significant savings of natural resource use and reduction of pollution. (Unfortunately, the Chinese government has recently begun to move toward a more automobile-centered transportion system.)

75. Brown, *State of the World 1996*, p. 178.

76. Brown, *State of the World 1990*, p. 180.

77. Brown, *State of the World 1996*, p. 154.

78. Recycling Trivia, http:bapco.bellsouth.com/html/trivia.html (September, 1996).

79. PlanetENN, *Recycling the Future*, http://www.enn.com/planetenn/031896/index.html (Oct., 1996).

80. IPCC, *The Economics of Carbon Taxes*, http://www.evin.gov.au/portfolio/esd/climate/newsletter/ipcc_2.html (October, 1996).

81. See, for a good recent overview, *At the Crossroads: The Future of Foreign Aid*, (Silver Spring, Md.: BFWI, 1995) and *The Reality of Aid 1996*, (Silver Spring, MD: BFWI, 1996). See, also, Frances Moore Lappe, *Aid as Obstacle: Twenty Questions about Our Foreign Aid and the Hungry*, (San Francisco: Institute for Food and Development Policy, 1980). See also James A. Cogswell's excellent summary of pros and cons in his "Crisis of Confidence in U.S. Aid to Poor Nations," *The Causes of World Hunger*, ed. William Byron (New York: Paulist Press, 1982), pp. 141–45. Stephen Hellinger, Douglas Hellinger, and Fred M. O'Regan call for radical changes in *Aid for Just Development: Report on the Future of Foreign Assistance* (Boulder: Lynne Rienner, 1988). Very recently, the Heritage Foundation has been highly critical of foreign aid. See Bryan T. Johnson and Thomas P. Sheehy, *1996 Index of Economic Freedom* (Washington, D.C.: Heritage Foundation, 1996), and the refutation in BFWI, *Hunger 1997*, pp. 83–84.

82. Ernst Loevinsohn, "Making Foreign Aid More Effective," BFW Background Paper, no. 49 (March 1981).

83. BFWI, At the Crossroads: The Future of Foreign Aid, May, 1995, p. 47.

84. Loevinsohn, p. 34.

85. Timothy King, ed. *Population Policies and Economic Development*, published for the World Bank (Baltimore: Johns Hopkins Univ. Press, 1974), p. 54. See also William Rich, *Smaller Families Through Social and Economic Progress*, monograph, no. 7 (Washington, D.C.: Overseas Development Council, 1973), esp. p. 76.

86. Hellinger, et al., *Aid for Just Development*, pp. 162, 180.

87. BFWI, *The Future of Foreign Aid*, p. 18.

88. Ibid., p. 19.

89. Ibid., pp. 22–23.

90. BFWI, *Hunger 1997*, pp. 87–89.

91. World Bank, *World Debt Tables 94–95*, p. 23.

92. UNDP, *Human Development Report 1993*, p. 93.

93. UNDP, *Human Development Report 1991*, p. 75.

94. See Hellinger, et al., *Aid for Just Development*, p. 4.

95. See *At the Crossroads*, pp. 62–63, for a summary of the successes of UNICEF and IFAD.

96. Based on phone conversation with Marc Cohen of BFW on August 12, 1996.

97. BFWI, *The Future of Foreign Aid*, p. 18.

98. Ibid., p. 52.

99. Denis Goulet, *Development Ethics*, p. 158.

100. BFWI, *The Future of Foreign Aid*, pp. 25–33.

101. Ibid., p. 35.

102. See Denis Goulet, *The Cruel Choice* (New York: Atheneum, 1971), pp. 123–52.

103. Paul Streeten, "A Basic-Needs Approach to Economic Development," *Directions in Economic Development*, ed. Kenneth P. Jameson and Charles K. Wilber (Notre Dame, ID: University of Notre Dame Press, 1979), p. 74.

104. Population Action International, "Closing the Gender Gap: Educating Girls," 1993.

105. Ibid.

106. The Female Education Index is created from five different categories, each set on a scale from 0 to 100: educational attainment for women, primary female-male enrollment ratio, secondary female-male enrollment ratio, gross primary enrollment rate for girls, and gross secondary enrollment rate for girls. The index essentially measures how well women, compared with men in their own country and also with other women around the world, are being educated in each particular country. Infant Mortality Rate measures how many children die before the age of one, out of 1,000 live births. Total Fertility Rate is the average number of children per woman.

107. "Closing the Gender Gap: Educating Girls," 1993.

108. BFWI, Reality of Aid, p. 201. Other polls also include the same gross misunderstanding (e.g., At the Crossroads: The Future of Foreign Aid, p. 14.).

109. Simon, *Bread for the World*, p. 113. (The figure in Simon's text was in 1975 dollars; 1994 figure calculated based on Consumer Price Index factor of 5.48 (The actual figure is $126.04 billion).

110. See tables 11 and 12 in chapter 2.

111. See chapter 2, p. 33.

112. UNDP, *Human Development Report 1994*, p. 48.

113. Quoted in Simon, *Bread for the World*, p. 170.

114. See David M. Schilling, "Sneakers and Sweatshops: Holding Corporations Accountable," *Christian Century*, October 9, 1996, pp. 932–36.

Index of Persons and Topics

Index of Scripture References

photography: Jeff Wright / ADRA International ("education" photograph: Tereza Byrne / ADRA International)

FIS

TEACHING THE WORLD TO

H?!

At ADRA that's what we do. Teach the world to fish. After fifteen years in the business of improving lives we believe in the adage **"Give a man a fish and you feed him for a day. Teach a man to fish, and you feed him for a lifetime."** As a result of this philosophy, the majority of our resources are dedicated to programs that promote long term developmental goals. Our complete scope of work is summarized in five "core" portfolios.

1 FOOD SECURITY

ADRA strives to reduce starvation and hunger—not only by meeting immediate needs; but by developing programs to help reduce the food insecurity, which prevents needs from recurring again. Using a model of sustainable agriculture, ADRA promotes agricultural methods that are environmentally nondegrading, technically appropriate, economically viable, socially just, and culturally appropriate.

2 ECONOMIC DEVELOPMENT

To stimulate economic growth, ADRA's Micro-enterprise Development (MED) initiatives provide loans to groups or individuals in developing countries at affordable rates. ADRA's economic development portfolio includes financial services in credit and savings; in-kind credit such as grain or other goods; and non-financial services such as technical assistance and technology transfer. ADRA promotes gender equality and often targets MED programs to women responsible for supporting families.

3 PRIMARY HEALTH

ADRA works to provide prevention education and raise community awareness of local health problems such as AIDS and maternal mortality. Through ADRA's Child Survival and Mother/Child Health programs, it aims to protect infants and mothers from death and disease, and to enable children to achieve optimum development. In addition, ADRA operates programs and classes for mothers in family planning, breast-feeding, immunizations, oral rehydration therapy, and nutrition.

4 DISASTER RESPONSE & PREPAREDNESS

Whether the disaster is natural or human-made, in the U.S. and around the globe, ADRA is there in the immediate aftermath, providing concrete relief assistance through food, medical care, water and emergency supplies. And after the media frenzy has dissipated and when survivors begin the task of rebuilding their lives, ADRA remains to assist them through its rehabilitation and development programs.

5 BASIC EDUCATION

Education is key to breaking the poverty cycle. However, worldwide, many children are denied an education, particularly young girls. ADRA responds by building primary schools and initiating adult literacy and numeracy programs as well as agriculture and vocational training. This education teaches marketable skills which increase employment opportunities and personal economic independence.

For more information about ADRA, call toll free on 800-424-ADRA, or visit us online at www.adra.org

ADRA Adventist Development and Relief Agency International

12501 Old Columbia Pike / Silver Spring, MD 20904 / 800-424-ADRA(2372) / www.adra.org